W9-AIW-686

ALL
THE
GIRLS

ALL THE GIRLS

MARTIN O'BRIEN

St. Martin's Press/Marek
New York

Design by Manuela Paul

Library of Congress Cataloging in Publication Data

O'Brien, Martin.
  All the girls.

  "A St. Martin's Press/Marek book."
  1. Prostitutes. I. Title.
HQ117.027   306.7′42   82-5625
ISBN 0-312-02003-1   AACR2

First Edition
10 9 8 7 6 5 4 3 2 1

To all the girls who took my money
and who took me into their lives
for an hour or a day,
good and bad, young and old,
plain and pretty alike.

Contents

Acknowledgments

For their help and encouragement, and for their friendship, I would like to thank the following: In *London:* Ed Victor; Alan Maclean; A. J. "Sonny" Mehta; Andrew Osmond; Christopher, Marilyn, and Jamie Draper; Clare Williams; Grace Coddington; Emma Gibbs; Jane Rutherford; Peter and Sarah Saugman. In *Buenos Aires:* Maria Luz Gavina; Teresa Gowland; Teresa Fernandez; Maria della Facio. In *Caracas:* Anthony Northrop. In *Sydney:* Susie Westwood; Rae Francis. In *Tokyo:* Simon Heale. In *Moscow* and in *Leningrad:* Andrew Nurnberg. In *Los Angeles* and in *Los Altos:* Michael Hodgson; Richard and Judy Wenderlich. In *Chicago:* Bill Plummer and J.W. And in *New York:* Richard Marek; Joan Juliet Buck; A. K.; Alex Chatelain. And, of course, thanks to my parents.

Introduction

The Velvet Curtains

Like most fascinations, mine started early.

I was sixteen, I was in London, and it was summer. I had hitched two hundred miles from my home in the south for a jazz festival being held on a racecourse in the suburbs. It was the first I had been allowed to attend. Of course I had arranged to stay with friends from school. Of course! I was expected back after four days —the duration of the festival. In the meantime, I was a young public schoolboy, in the Sixties, closer to the capital than I had ever been before on my own.

On the second day (I spent the first night in one of the large communal tents provided by the organizers for those who had arrived only with sleeping bags) I gave up my place in the crowd, left the racecourse against a stream of people just arriving and caught a local commuter train into the city proper. The suburbs, I had discovered, were the poor substitute. I had a small duffel bag with a drawstring top that I wore over my shoulder and carried a curved briar pipe (one of my father's) that, unknown to my parents, I had recently taken up. I smoked a particularly sweet, aromatic blend of tobacco that at the festival, I imagined, might pass for marijuana— which of course I had heard of but never tried. I was an anxious, image-conscious teenager with hair cut painfully short from school. I think I wore a hat but can't remember it.

That whole morning I walked the streets of the West End with no specific destination in mind, rarely stopping to take in the sights except obliquely, pretending instead a certain familiarity and haste —as if I had an appointment, was meeting a friend, had seen it all

3

before anyway. In Soho I slowed my pace and some streets, cheeks glowing, I contrived to walk down twice. I spent my lunchtime with the tramps and tourists in Leicester Square, sitting on a bench and watching the pigeons, waiting for the start of an afternoon matinee I had decided to see at a cinema close by. I suppose, looking back, it wasn't the most inspired way to spend my first time alone in London, but it gave my visit some sense of purpose—a certain justification. Besides, I was tired of just walking about with no-where to go and nothing to do.

The cinema seemed, to my small eyes, enormous after the one at home. I took a seat in the middle, settled back in the near-darkness and lit my pipe. There were only a few other people there —way down at the front—on that hot summer's afternoon. I was quite content except for a niggling squirm of guilt at being inside on such a fine day. It would never have been tolerated at home.

Shortly after the house lights dimmed for the supporting film, a young woman came down the aisle, paused by my row and then, appearing to make up her mind, edged between the seats and sat down right beside me. I had to move my duffel bag to make room for her. After she made herself comfortable her elbow began, quite obviously and deliberately, edging mine off the armrest between us. I paid no attention, simply gave way and shifted in my seat.

It couldn't have been that long afterward when I became aware of her turning and watching me—sometimes long and hard, other times just a glance that I felt was somehow irritated, impatient. Thinking she might not like the smell of my tobacco, I took one last, long, defiant series of puffs that set the tobacco crackling in the bowl before putting down my pipe.

At this point I began to feel not a little indignant—I'd moved my duffel bag to make room for her, I'd given way on the armrest and now, with those penetrating looks, she had made it plain she objected to my smoking. If it bothered her that much, I remember thinking, then she should have found somewhere else to sit. After all, I reasoned, she had the whole cinema to choose from. But my compliance, it appeared, failed to satisfy the lady, for the looks continued. She was also, I was convinced, moving closer, leaning an altogether unreasonable amount over the disputed armrest until I could actually feel her shoulder pressing against mine.

The moment she began crossing and uncrossing her legs, some-times even touching my leg with her own, her real intentions be-came at once horrifyingly clear. No longer was I filled with indigna-

4

tion, simply with paralyzing disbelief at the situation now confronting me. I wasn't sure whether I should get up and sit somewhere else; just pretend, in as grown-up a manner as possible, that I was unmoved by her advances; or leave the cinema altogether. The possibility that I might take advantage of this encounter had still not even registered as an alternative. My first inclination was to find some means of extricating myself from such an embarrassing situation. I just sat there, staring straight at the screen, trying to decide on the least involving course of action. Suddenly, all too clearly, I understood my parents' concern.

But the continual crossing and uncrossing of her legs, coiling and uncoiling like sinuous black snakes, and the sound of her stockings sliding together (the most arousing sound I had ever heard) gripped my attention—a mouse enthralled by a cobra. In the darkness, very slowly, almost unwillingly, I leaned back in my seat and glanced down at her legs, then sideways at her. She was pretty, no more, and blond, in her late twenties I guessed. She was watching the film now with a soft, satisfied smile.

Throughout the intermission—which came as something of a relief—we sat side by side without a single word spoken or glance exchanged. She read a paper, I leafed unseeing through my film magazine. For some absurd reason I began to long for an ice cream but didn't dare disturb her to get by. Instead I watched covertly as a bored usherette with an illuminated tray walked slowly past us. It was at that moment I finally had to admit to myself that I was frightened she might leave, find someone else. I was suddenly curious, eager even, to find out what would happen next.

As soon as the main feature began, the maneuvering started up all over again. Her legs entranced me; the soft sound of her stockings, the occasional fleeting touch, the closeness of her perfume making my stomach churn one moment with desire, the next with faltering indecision.

I don't remember actually stretching out my hand and placing it lightly on her knee, nor the soul-searching, the twisting up of courage that must have preceded the act, but when I saw it there, as lively and conspicuous as a dead white fish, I expected—despite her advances—a combination of screams and lights, the film ending abruptly in a blur of dialogue and melting celluloid, the people down at the front turning in their seats, the manager being summoned, immediate accusation and scorching shame. For certain someone would contact my parents.

To my amazement, there were none of these things—just a slow uncrossing and slight parting of her legs that left the dead white fish stranded quite high on the inside of her thigh. That parting of the knees with its implicit message of surrender, like a dog rolling onto its back and baring its throat, stunned me. Never before had a woman conveyed to me such a clear signal of intent, responded to me in such a willing manner.

For the first time our eyes caught and I made a passable attempt at a kiss (all lips and teeth), which I considered the next most conventional move, but which she seemed little inclined to continue. Instead, her arm slipped off the disputed rest, a hand squeezed my legs, slid onto my lap and found my zipper. I remember her hand was surprisingly warm, and confident, like a doctor's, familiar with the terrain it covered with cool fingers, and I remember too an immediate sense of shock, undeniably pleasurable shock, at being touched like this for the first time—skin to skin. To me, then, it was something I felt had to be wrong despite, perhaps because of, the pleasure. But I did it, let it happen all the same. Like being in a cinema on a sunny afternoon.

So intense, so involving was the experience that at no time did I question her motives or consider the fact that this woman, older than I by several years, was a total stranger. It was as if our shadowy intimacy was sufficient in itself to bridge such a gulf. I hadn't spoken a single word to her, didn't know her name, her family, where she came from—none of those things I naïvely believed were necessary for the pursuit of that pleasure I now enjoyed at her hand. Rather, I responded instinctively by sliding my hand very slowly, very cautiously (just in case) up and then down her leg until, with some impatience, she slipped forward in her seat and I could feel the top of her stockings, a smooth metal clip and the hem of her dress tight against my wrist. Her skin was soft and pliable like Plasticine, plump at the stocking top, smooth and warm—wet too from the sweat of my palm. And, if I leaned forward a little, I could feel, a little higher, a rough laciness. I could hardly breathe, my heart and Adam's apple seeming to change places with each breath.

But at no time would she allow me any further. If I strayed too close (and I was becoming braver by the minute) she would squeeze her legs together (arousing in itself) or squeeze me (not so arousing) until I retreated. I recall thinking that, given what she held in her hand, this reticence on her part was a little unfair. But it was enough.

6

Like drivers in the night our eyes rarely left the screen, while our hands went through the motions like drivers changing gears. Occasionally, usually at my instigation, we would turn and kiss. Occasionally too, I would reach for her wrist, stop her.

Then, shortly before the end of the film and without any warning she released me, pushed my hand away from between her legs and sat up in her seat. I tucked myself away as best I could and, not sure how to react, what to expect next, continued to stare ahead. Once again she began looking at me, more pointedly this time, waiting for some response after our intimacy—as expectant as a grocer certain of a sale after the fruit has been handled. When it dawned on me that she wanted me to get up and leave with her, to finish our business elsewhere, I felt suddenly afraid, anxious. It had been all well and good in the cinema, in the darkness, but . . . but now, to leave with her, well that was a different matter. And my money. There was no way I could afford what she was offering. I had only my train fare home and the money I had saved by hitching up. Then worse—was I being drawn into a trap? Would there be some man at her home, waiting to threaten whomever she brought back with her? Rob me? Beat me up?

But beneath all these wild imaginings lay simple inexperience. What should I say to her? How should I treat her, outside in the bright sunshine? I decided categorically, and thankfully, that I was best advised to remain where I was.

It seemed forever that she watched for some sign from me, but she never said a word. Simply looked one last time, gathered up her things and left her seat. It sprang up behind her, making my heart leap. I waited a few moments, then turned. She was already gone —the black velvet curtains behind the red EXIT sign swinging closed behind her.

More than a dozen years later that incident remains one of the strongest memories of an otherwise ordinary and predictable youth, a reel of images—her black stockings, that warm darkness, those swirling velvet curtains—as clear and vivid today as on that hot summer's afternoon so long ago. Perhaps too, it was a most significant incident, though I'm loath to draw such ambitious conclusions. Just as I would be cautious about citing the fact that I am an only child, that I was educated at a private Catholic school, that I live alone. All I am prepared to state with any certainty is that this initial encounter was the start of something that culminated in the researching and writing of this book. For the fascination I felt then, when at last I ventured out of that cinema and made my way home, a schoolboy's wonder at so anonymous, so transient, yet so arousing an encounter, I have felt many times since—as an Oxford undergraduate on a working holiday in Australia, in Hungary when I first started traveling professionally as a magazine writer, along the roasting-coffee-scented streets of Dublin, beneath the neon blaze of Las Vegas and Hong Kong, along the shores of Manila Bay and around the docks of Bahia; never particularly sought out, more often than not accidentally found (as in the cinema) and either accepted with a handful of notes or rejected with a smile of regret.

But there were many other factors, in my opinion more significant, that played a part in this undertaking; that combined, made this present work almost inevitable. Perhaps most important of all was the fact that I became a professional traveler after coming down from Oxford, moving regularly from one city to another, from climate to climate, from one hotel to the next, spending most of the time alone. Had I chosen law as a profession, become an accountant, a banker, a doctor, I might never have had the opportunity, the need, or inclination to repeat that early experience. As it turned out, circumstances made repetition almost unavoidable.

Having traveled extensively also made the task of research all that much easier. I knew where I was going, knew the cities I visited, had many friends along the way with whom I could rest up and seek help and company from when necessary. I had also become used to a near-nomadic lifestyle and learned early on that any personal or social life could never be anything more than staggered and secondary. That, too, is significant, for very quickly I lost touch with all but a very few old friends. I missed parties, birthdays, shared holidays, weddings, at which I was either a name on a telegram or the subject of a brief inquiry—all this "separation" before I had even thought about writing this book. When the time came to begin there was very little to give up, to leave behind. I had no responsibilities to tie me down—no wife, no children—and as far as my career as a magazine writer was concerned, the time had come for a change; it was time to move on. This book represented little more than the next step—a simple progression—the chance to write about something I knew well. Had I been a mountaineer, I would have written about mountains; had I been a yachtsman, I would have written about sailing. As it was, I knew a great deal about traveling and something of prostitution. The idea was as simple and as elementary as that.

The story that follows is not some philosophic search, no learned sociological treatise, nor, more importantly, does it set out to be a definitive guide. Indeed, all the names and many of the places that appear in the following chapters have been deliberately disguised, though there would be no difficulty in locating their counterparts in any city in the world. Everything that I did could quite easily be done by anyone with enough money to pay for air fares and other more obvious expenses, and the requisite nerve or foolishness—call it what you will. It is, quite simply, the record of a journey that lasted several months during which time I deliberately sought out and allowed myself to be drawn into any professionally sexual situation which offered itself. This time I was determined not to keep my seat, allow good sense or better judgment to prevail, a schoolboy's fear to intimidate. This time I would follow behind, past those swinging velvet curtains of my youth.

The choice of direction and destination was arbitrary; neither, for me, as important as the characters I found along the way—the opportunity they afforded to explore, more fully than ever before, an obsessive curiosity; an abiding fascination. For this is, primarily, a story about a particular type of people—the way they live and work, rather than the place they live and work in.

It is also, on another level, about myself and my reactions, favorable and not so favorable, to a way of life I had so far only glimpsed (though at the start I imagined I knew all there was to know), a record of my impressions and responses both physical and emotional in a world I had only touched at the fringes.

I have tried neither to condemn nor to defend those people I met, nor to incriminate them (hence their anonymity), nor to sensationalize their bizarre profession—simply to observe and report, from the inside. Perhaps you could call it a vindication—theirs and mine.

Some of those I met during the months away were crude and loathsome; some, like the woman in the cinema, I shall never forget. There were times of fear, disgust and desperate loneliness when I would gladly have given up my wanderings and come home, when I doubted my own ability to cope with what I found, when I was filled with guilt at my own deceit. But there were times too when I honestly believed I had never enjoyed myself more—in the company of pretty women who laughed and cried and drank with a passion, and sometimes, sometimes, loved with a passion too. More than anything else, I am grateful for the opportunity they gave me to work out my own private fascination, to satisfy my curiosity, to follow through such a strange attraction.

To all of them, for their stories, their memories, their confidences; for their friendship no matter how shallow or short-lived; for their small kindnesses, cruelties and deceptions too, my thanks.

London, February 1982   Martin O'Brien

Part One

Roll
the Cameras

Scalotti was Italian, Manuela Spanish—the single exception in his otherwise excessive prejudice.

His adopted city of Buenos Aires was as good as its name the day I arrived (a name he would have romanized given half a chance), the air as crisp as a new peso note and the sky as milky blue as the twin blue stripes of the national flag, tugging at its pole above the air terminal of Ezeiza and above all government buildings in the city.

It was spring and everything seemed to crackle with freshness. Crisp, fresh, crackly like that peso note, but chill also—that still-indeterminate season of brisk sunny weather when you bury your hands in your pockets and brace your shoulders against the shreds of a winter cold; wet scarf weather when you lean forward into your collar to trap the warmth of your breath. The kind of cold that, if you haven't a scarf, can turn your teeth brittle as glass, burn the curled tips of your ears, and hit you so hard in the back of the throat that you think you'll strangle with each new breath.

The day I arrived was a tubercular's paradise, a lung-aching freshness everywhere.

Given the choice, it was exactly the weather I would have chosen—raw, frosty mornings so clear the outline of the sun was razor sharp; short, golden afternoons that steadily stretched my shadow as I explored the new city; and pleasantly brisk evenings that had the *whiskerías* beckoning with their steamy, chattering warmth. A week before in New York the heat had been crushing, relentless, the air as thick as cheese, as damp as doss-house bedding.

Buenos Aires was like learning to breathe all over again.

Scalotti was flash—from the tips of his varnished fingernails to the two clipped wings of his corona-thick mustache. He wore a tan camel hair coat slung hussarlike over broad shoulders, a light gray suit that looked as if it been put on new before leaving the office and shiny stiffly laced shoes freshly buffed by the *lustrador* who squatted by his box of brushes in the doorway of the whiskería. The toe of one he tapped tunelessly on the tiled floor, the heel of the other he hooked back over the bar of his stool. His cuffs were properly shot and linked, and his tie knot slim and immaculate.

When I first saw him, it appeared he was part of a large group gathered at the bar, but as we talked it became clear it was their proximity, almost rubbing shoulders, that made me think this. Though the men beside him had probably never seen him before, Scalotti seemed to blend in with them—one of the crowd of executives sharing tots and conversations at the end of the day, before the long drive home and the long evening ahead. In truth he was quite alone.

Although I sat some stools away, with all the cold reserve and pretended occupation of an Englishman on foreign soil (I was still reading the *Daily Mail* I had bought the week before in London), Scalotti had no hesitation waving me over, starting up an exploratory conversation. In the best Italian tradition he was warm, generous and expansive. And I, imagining him to be one of this larger group, had no hesitation in moving across with an empty coffee cup and glass of water still attached to its paper coaster. Strength in numbers, confidence in a crowd. Even when it became clear the men beside him were a separate group altogether, I was warmed enough by his company and trusting enough of his motives not to care. Anyway, apart from conversations in schoolboy Spanish and pidgin English with porters and desk clerks and disinterested taxi drivers, I had spoken to no one for days. Certainly no one who attacked my language with Scalotti's enthusiasm. If being in Buenos Aires was like learning how to breathe all over again, then being with Scalotti was like learning to talk all over again. And at this time of day, when the inner city was emptying and people were draining away into the suburbs, good company—any company—was a fine and valuable commodity. A bright blue start to the day would get me through the morning, a pitcher of wine at lunchtime would lend a certain swing to my afternoon wanderings, but as shadows lengthened and the first evening chills settled on the streets, my interest in the new sights and sounds, along with the effects of the wine, soon wore away. Company and a good warm chat was the only cure. So Scalotti, or anyone like him, his laughter, his questions, his interest, was a blessing.

For the first time I had felt badly frightened. And more alone than ever before. To begin with I wasn't that surprised, for a sense of fear, a reaction to what lies ahead, has always been a part of that general excitement preceding departure. And some measure of loneliness is unavoidable as you separate yourself from the familiar and the safe. What had startled me this time was the degree of that fear and loneliness—how strong and how positive they had grown. That last morning in London, as I leaned over the sink and brushed my teeth, I felt my gorge rise in a spasm of empty nausea and recognized that this was no familiar predeparture symptom. This was something very different. And in the bar at the airport, the loneliness. I sat at a table with four empty chairs and instead of their attracting company, one by one they were dragged away: "Is anyone sitting here?"; "Can I take this?"; "Is this seat free?"; "Do you mind?"; until I sat alone at an empty table like someone clinging to a life raft. In that huge, crowded, noisy departure hall I was the only person who sat alone, my bag at my feet. Not even the newspaper I had bought (which I kept with me for days as a kind of link with home) could distract me. That Polish strikers were earning more concessions was of no consequence; that the jobless in England now numbered two million or more; that coachloads of British tourists in that summer of 1980 were stranded on the borders of Austria after their transport had been found to be defective—none of these things concerned me, elicited any response that foggy morning I waited alone for my flight to New York.

Nor did the situation improve. There had been a time I could still remember, in those early days of traveling on assignment, when I used to wish the flight would never end, the plane never land. I wished it again as we made our final approach to John F. Kennedy.

In New York, waiting for my connection to Buenos Aires, everything seemed to conspire against me, increasing my discomfort. The sudden heat for one thing, pressing down between the skyscrapers of Manhattan like a mechanical factory hammer stamping onto a mold, prickling at my scalp, trickling down my chest and back, making my trousers heavy round my legs. On my way to Bloomingdale's, where I bought a larger suitcase, I passed a kind of

15

makeshift scoreboard attached to the scaffolding of a building site on a corner of Madison Avenue proclaiming that the hostages had been in captivity 280 days. Each morning, one of the workmen climbed up and increased the number. It was a measure of how cruel the world could be. But all I could think of was that dark, morbid incarceration. The cells, the bars, the stifling claustrophobia. Across the street from Bloomingdale's a line was forming for *Caligula,* but the poster, with its bleeding Emperor's eye, made me turn away. Nothing could have persuaded me to step into that or any other cinema, to see that or any other film. Darkness, confinement. Even the lift in Bloomingdale's bothered me.

Back at J.F.K. I still hadn't shaken off this unease. Having my ticket endorsed for the onward flight to Buenos Aires I insisted on an aisle seat and, before boarding, left a bookstand empty-handed, shying away from the shelves of paperbacks—from the blood, the dripping blades, the silent screams of cover characters. I had my own fears to contend with, without adding anyone else's.

The coffee they served at the whiskería came in tiny cups, scalding hot and gritty. Once the coffee cooled it disappeared in one modest gulp. While I swallowed the water that came with it as a chaser, Scalotti, mustache seesawing, sluiced it round in his mouth, rinsing away the grounds from between his teeth. With my second cup I followed his example and he beamed his approval.

"You learn fast, my friend."

"I have a good teacher," I replied, reaching for my pocket and money for another round. But Scalotti, who had paid so far, seemed at pains to continue doing so, catching my hand in a strong grip and placing it firmly on the counter. Once again the barman was summoned and more coffee ordered, but this time Scalotti waved toward a shelf of bottles beside the cash register.

"Now we have a little something extra, eh?" he said, and the water was replaced by two smaller glasses filled with an inch of amber liquid. Without waiting for the coffees Scalotti tossed his back, brushed his mustache with a napkin, then watched me finish mine. "Good teacher, eh? Good teacher, eh?" he cried, slapping my leg.

Though he looked every inch the successful businessman (electronics, he had said)—as well-dressed, as mannered and confident as any of those standing around us—I noticed, as we talked and drank, a certain roughness about him that his fine clothes could not altogether conceal. His eyes were cold and brown like hard winter soil, the lashes short, the eyebrows thick and angry, and his hair, a coarse curly black, waved back from a sharp peak in a forehead that looked flushed and red as if from heavy work, country work. And despite the varnish, his nails were stubby and uneven, threads of cuticle peeling away from the base and sides like tiny white splinters. There was something of the workman in him, coupled with the charm of a salesman—the strength of a laborer, not a polo player, the habits of a peasant thinly disguised beneath an assumed elegance. When he took a cigarette from me, he tapped both the head and filter on the marble counter, and after each whistling inhalation let the smoke escape with small spitting sounds as if trying to get rid of nonexistent snakes of tobacco. Scalotti, I decided, was a man who had been used to rolling his own. But I liked him nonetheless. He had done well, I thought, and good luck.

What surprised me most in the course of our conversation was how large the Italian community was in Buenos Aires. If he was to be believed, Italians counted for almost one-half of the population. Yet driving through the suburbs of Ezeiza the morning I arrived and then into the city with its wide boulevards, dusty plane trees, Spanish street names and shop signs, and in all my subsequent wanderings, I had been reminded time and again of a Spanish capital—a Madrid, a Barcelona, rather than a Rome, a Florence.

I was also a little surprised that being second-generation Italian, born and bred in Buenos Aires, had in no way diluted Scalotti's nationalistic pride, his almost ruthless prejudice. He was, he proclaimed, as different from the Argentine Spaniard as it was possible to be. And when I admitted, rashly perhaps, that I found it difficult to tell the difference between the two—Spanish and Italian—he set about explaining it with a practical demonstration. In a frightening stage whisper, he began to itemize the various national blemishes of the Spaniard, taking as his examples certain individuals in the bar who best represented each one.

"There, that one, look at that nose, eh?"

"And there, those skinny shoulders, eh?"

"And what about that face?"

"Or him. Look at him, by the door there. Could you trust him further than you make water, eh?"

"You see now, or you want I show you more . . . ?"

"No, no," I interrupted; "I think I see what you mean."

We stayed no more than an hour at the whiskería, until the

steamy bellowing of the coffee machine and the clattering of cups grew louder than the hum of talk around the bar and at the tables. People were starting to make their way home. As we too made our way outside, I felt once again that crush of dread close in. For days now I had postponed that business which had brought me to Buenos Aires. Tomorrow, I would say to myself, I shall start properly tomorrow. It was like standing on the high board but not having the nerve to dive. One afternoon I had strolled along the dreary, daytime-dead streets bordered by Reconquista and Tucuman as far down as the rail tracks and docks where the seamen were said to swarm like flies over dead meat. But that was all. I had yet to return there at night, or somewhere like it, when the doorways would rustle with bodies. There was something unnerving about such cold premeditation. I wished it would just happen, as it always had in the past.

"For certain it will rain tomorrow," observed Scalotti as he turned to face me on the pavement. I looked up at the darkening skies, the stars already bright above us.

"Looks clear."

"You do not understand yet, my friend. You see, tomorrow is the feast day of Santa Rosa. And on that day in Buenos Aires, it always rain." He pushed back a white cuff and glanced at his watch. "We have time for another drink someplace, someplace better, if you like?" The invitation took me quite by surprise. I imagined we would part company and each go our separate ways. Feeling as I did, I needed little encouragement.

"You're not busy?"

"If I am busy, you think I say come and have another drink?" he asked, sliding his arms into the sleeves of his coat and turning up the collar. "Eh?" There was a place he knew not far away and together we set off up the street. As we walked, he explained that he had a dinner engagement, that he was sorry but he couldn't change it. But there was still time for a drink.

Or two. Or three. In the dark, paneled bar of the Claridge Hotel we sat at a table by the window and drank expensive whiskey— Scalotti's with ginger ale, mine with water. He drank as though from a well, gulping through the ice as if to quench an enormous thirst, belching occasionally into a closed fist.

"If you don' mind me asking, you married?"

"Used to be," I lied.

"You look too young, you don' mind me saying."

18

"That was the trouble."

Scalotti laughed, belched into his fist and then punched my arm with it. "Is a most difficult thing to get married."

I asked him if he was married. It sounded as if he was.

"One time," he replied. "Now I have girlfriends." He used the word as though he was unsure of it, uncomfortable with it.

"They can be just as bad."

"Oh, you are right, you are right. They drive you crazy with all the problems." At which point we ordered another round.

But time was clearly pressing and I could see Scalotti was ready to go. When he finished his drink he pushed the empty glass away from him, rather than holding onto it.

"I am so sorry, but really now I must dash . . . that is the word, eh?"

Yes, that was the word, I told him. It rather suited him. I paid the waiter and the two of us left. I was not yet so drunk that I didn't notice the size of the bill, nor the fact that Scalotti was not as swift with a hand into his pocket as he had been at the whiskería. But I didn't think anything of it. I had enjoyed myself immensely. Perhaps I would even take a cab down to Reconquista when we parted.

"My car is in the next street. You want I give you a lift to your 'otel? Which 'otel you say you are in?"

I tried to work out how far away we were. I hadn't been to the hotel since lunch and didn't recognize the street we were in. I supposed I could retrace our steps to the whiskería, then make my way on from there. But it was cold and the offer of a lift, the chance to extend our companionship if only for a few moments more, was hard to resist. On the way back I might even ask him about Reconquista, quiz him about the city and what I was looking for. I told him the name again.

"Good 'otel, my friend. Best in town, no question, eh?" It was not that far, he continued, but he would be glad to give me a lift all the same. He had enjoyed meeting me. I returned the compliment.

The hotel was closer than I thought—such a short distance that the lift had been scarcely necessary. We had been no more than six blocks away, less had I walked and avoided the one-way system. Scalotti pulled over and stopped outside the hotel. I thanked him, we shook hands and I made to get out. It was then he reached out and held my arm. He looked a little embarrassed, uncertain.

"What you gonna do now, eh? You have plans?"

19

I shrugged. "Nothing really," I told him. Perhaps I'd change some money and go for a walk, go to a club. I'd heard there were some good ones around Reconquista. Find myself a girl even— *coperas*. Wasn't that what they were called in Buenos Aires?

"Reconquista! *Copera!*" He chuckled and shook his head, even looked relieved. "Believe me when I tell you they are not for you. Listen. I ask you a favor if you don' mind. This girl I have dinner with, Manuela is her name, if you are not occupied, join us. She is an old friend, you understand. I promise I take her to dinner but I know she will make things difficult for me. And I have someone else now, you see. You will help me a lot. And you will have better time with us than you find in Reconquista." Scalotti paused, squeezed my arm.

"Well . . ." I began, sorely tempted by the offer.

"I take her to La Boca. You seen La Boca, eh?"

I shook my head.

"Oh, you like La Boca very much. Is the very best food in all Buenos Aires. In all Argentine. Is Italian food. Eh? What you say?" He now looked excited, knew he had me hooked. Tomorrow, I could start tomorrow. One more evening would make little difference. As if making up my mind for me, Scalotti leaned across, caught hold of the door and slammed it shut. "We have good time, yes? We have great time." He threw the car into gear and squealed away from the hotel.

This time the drive was much longer. In his old but immaculate Fairlane 500 we sped down from the center of the city toward the River Plate—somewhere on our right, but now hidden in darkness —and followed the signs for Olivos. I could see the area we were driving through was parkland, with buildings crowding its farthest edges. There were trees too and their leafless branches made the lights in the distant apartment blocks wink like stars. Apartment blocks! Buenos Aires was filled with them. They looked like stacked pigeon baskets at a homing meet. Manuela's, when we finally arrived, was no different from all the rest.

The glass door of the Edificio Areco, where she lived, was overlaid with an intricate and protective pattern of black metal twisted into the shape of a vine. In the lighted hall beyond I could see the first flight of stairs winding up around an ornate lift cage. Beside the door and set into the wall was a small grille the size of a postcard and an enormous bank of buttons with a number engraved below each one. The grille, the buttons and the backplate were all brass and the wall around it stained a dull coppery green from careless polishing. Scalotti quickly found the number he wanted and pressed the button.

"You will like Manuela; we have good time, you see," he reassured me as we waited for her to answer. The voice, when it came, was accompanied by a barrage of static. It sounded as though the person at the other end was gargling with a mouthful of metal filings. Scalotti replied in Spanish, lips almost touching the grille. There was a prolonged buzzing from the lock and a loud click as he pushed open the door.

"The apartment is on the tenth floor. We take the lift, eh?"

"Preferably," I replied, and Scalotti chuckled.

The moment the lift jerked to a stop, Scalotti hauled back the doors with a clang and I followed him down the corridor. Manuela was waiting for us in the doorway of her apartment. She was barefoot, wore a pair of faded jeans and a long, loose T-shirt with a stylized computer print of Debbie Harry on the front. Her hair was shoulder-length, blond and dyed, the roots in the center parting brown and bruised looking. Her face had broad Spanish features, large, lazy eyes that looked too heavy for her cheeks to support, and full, thrusting lips that parted slightly as Scalotti hugged her to him. Hardly Scalotti's type, I thought. And Spanish too! After what sounded like a brief and apologetic explanation, he turned, switched to English and introduced us. Her hand was cold and bony—like brittle twigs wrapped in cloth—but her grip was strong and definite, drawing me toward her. I could see she was not altogether happy about the company, but she hid it gracefully.

"How nice to meet you," she smiled, her English clear and precise save for the slightest rasp on the "h"—quite unlike the voice on the intercom. "Please, come in."

Her apartment was warm after the night air and chilly corridor, and sweet-smelling as though she had recently used a fly-spray or air-freshener. Talking now to Scalotti, in what I judged to be a rather piqued Spanish, she led us down a narrow hall, past a brightly lit kitchen and into a large living room, carpeted in a deep woolly pile and dominated by a curtained picture window. In daytime, I reckoned, the view would be extraordinary and almost completely unobstructed—a clear sweep over the river to the distant banks of Uruguay. Across the room was another door, leading, I presumed, to the apartment's only bedroom.

Although the room was large, it was lightly furnished. A glass-topped dining table with four straight-back chairs stood by the window and a matching glass coffee table separated a three-seat sofa and two armchairs. There was a narrow, shelved recess holding two rows of books, a television and hi-fi; two speakers with a small potted plant on each; and in between them, where the fireplace should have been, a heavy-looking carved Spanish sideboard with a tray of bottles and glasses. On the three remaining walls there were a number of gold-crusted portraits and river scenes, a few unframed but glazed theater posters and, stacked by the bedroom door, waiting to be hung, prints of fragile-looking plants. I suspected Manuela had only recently moved in.

"Sit, sit down, please," she said, catching my elbow and directing me to the sofa, while Scalotti chose one of the armchairs and plumped himself down in it. "Will you have a drink, please? Whiskey, wine?" Crossing to the sideboard she poured the drinks we asked for and handed them round.

"We decide to take you to La Boca for dinner," Scalotti told her.

"How nice," she replied. "Have you visited there yet?" she asked, turning to me. "It is very pretty. Very good food. But," looking down at her jeans and T-shirt, "I think even for La Boca I must dress. You will excuse me, please."

As soon as she had disappeared into the bedroom, Scalotti spread his arms as if to say—What a place! What a woman, eh? and I nodded in agreement, wondering if Manuela knew of Scalotti's philandering. I thought not, though she was probably suspicious. There was a certain coldness in her manner, a brusqueness toward him, an attempt at indifference—as if she didn't care.

For a few minutes we sat in silence, listening to Manuela rummaging around in her bedroom, sliding drawers open, snapping them closed, and then Scalotti started talking of La Boca, how that was the place where his family had first arrived by ship from Genoa and where they had first set up home. La Boca, he told me, was the center of all Italian life in Buenos Aires, in all the Argentine. I asked if he had ever returned to Genoa, but he shook his head mournfully, as though for the loss of a close friend, his mustache dipping down dramatically—"One day, one day I go back." Just then, Manuela passed in front of the open door and into an adjoining room. As she closed the second door behind her a length of mirror flashed into view. In its reflection I could see part of a line of cupboards and a corner of her bed.

Scalotti swallowed down his drink and got up to fix another.

"You have one more before we go?"

I shook my head and held up my half-filled glass. "The water makes it go further," I explained. I tried to remember how many drinks we had had—certainly a few—but I felt no ill effects; and Scalotti seemed steady enough on his feet, though perhaps a little more flushed than earlier. Back in his chair, he looked at his watch and shouted something in Spanish over his shoulder. A muffled voice from behind the closed door answered impatiently, then the lock turned and Manuela reappeared, her jeans and T-shirt now replaced by a long white dressing gown.

"Only two minutes more," she promised.

Scalotti didn't turn, simply waved his hand for her to hurry and continued his monologue on the various high points of Italian life in Buenos Aires, and the clear superiority of that race over the resident Spanish. But I was only half-listening. Instead, I watched with horrified fascination as the bathroom door began to edge closed, as if on a spring. And there, as it clicked shut, reflected in the mirror, was Manuela in her dressing gown, sorting through her wardrobe. Sitting where I was, with Scalotti almost directly in my line of vision, I had only to move my eyes a fraction and readjust the focus—short for him, long for her—to see the mirror on the bathroom door and Manuela's reflection in it. Even when I had my eyes fixed on Scalotti I was still aware of Manuela's movements— so long as she stayed within the narrow frame of the mirror. I felt I ought not to look, but there seemed almost no chance of being caught out; and anyway, the temptation was irresistible. Covertly, nodding at Scalotti as he rattled on about La Boca, I watched her unhook a black dress from the rail, drop it onto the bed behind her, then reach down to untie the belt of her gown. But just as it slid from her shoulders she stepped to one side and was gone.

"In La Boca, you eat the very, very best Italian food in all Buenos Aires," Scalotti was saying, "and if you want to dance, you dance the tango. You know the tango? Hum hum hum hum, hum-hum-hum-hum-hum. You know it? Eh?" With this he pulled himself to his feet and went round to Manuela's record collection, stacked in the far corner by one of the speakers. "I find some tango music now and we play it while our friend gets ready—yes? What do you say?" Absolutely, I agreed. Now that Scalotti had his back to me I was able to focus all my attention on the mirror, even shift a little in my seat to widen the angle. But still no Manuela, nor any sound from the bedroom—not even a shadow. Meanwhile Scalotti

flicked his way through the pile of albums, like a clerk after a file
—picking one out, glancing at the title, then sliding it back; then
another, and another. "No good . . . no good," he said each time.
"I know there is better someplace."

Then, suddenly, Manuela was back, sitting down on the corner
of the bed and lifting her leg to draw on a length of black stocking.
She was sitting almost sideways on to me and I could see the side
of a breast press against her leg. As soon as the first stocking was
fastened, she cast around for the second, and for an instant turned
directly toward the mirror—and my reflection in it. I looked away,
praying she hadn't seen me, and when the door didn't slam shut,
I risked another look. Apparently still unaware she was being
watched, she was gathering up the second stocking and fitting it
over her toes. I watched as she pulled it up over her leg, letting the
material draw through her fingers. Scalotti was still engrossed with
the records, saying he had a favorite and it was there somewhere.

"It would be nice if you could find it," I encouraged him,
Manuela now standing with her back to me and struggling into her
dress, but he seemed to have lost interest.

"Hey, Manuela, it is time to go," he cried, standing and moving
toward the bedroom door. I reached forward and picked up a magazine from the coffee table. When I looked up again, Manuela was
standing behind the armchair, with Scalotti fixing a bracelet around
her wrist.

"If we are ready," she said, smiling at me, "let us go."

La Boca, the Mouth, was much darker than the rest of the city
—fewer street lights, no brightly lit shop windows, and on our left
a yawning blackness where the shapes and silhouettes of cranes and
gantries, and the stacked walls of containers, were only visible as
dark, shadowy cutouts against the starry night sky. Through the
open window of Scalotti's car, beyond the scent of Manuela
squeezed beside me, I could smell an oily, dirty imitation of the sea.
Turning abruptly from the docks, Scalotti hurtled up a narrow,
high-sidewalked street—so high a pedestrian could have stepped
from the footway onto the roof of a parked car—rarely stopping at
any of the intersections, slowing only minutely with the ball of his
fist flat down on the horn, before careering across them. When we
finally reached our destination—two long, lighted windows with
long, cinched curtains and a wood-cracked, weather-beaten door
between them—Scalotti parked so close to the wall we all had to

scramble out on his side, catching hold of the wheel and hauling ourselves over the seats.

The noise in the restaurant was spectacular. Plates clattered, chairs scraped, waiters shouted, customers shouted, fists banged tables, feet stamped on the wood floors, every sound—even snatches of song—rising and echoing under the high, dark ceiling while a *bandoneon* player wheezed and hummed and sawed along as a minor accompaniment to this great orchestration of noise. If someone had wheeled in a motorbike and given it full throttle, hardly anyone would have noticed. Not even the fumes from the exhaust would have bothered these customers, for the room was already thick with smoke from the kitchen, from a thousand cigarettes, from the smeeching candles on every table.

If Scalotti had been alone and unknown in the whiskería, then he made up for it here. Apart from an old man sitting by the door, a stick hanging from the back of his chair and a pair of horn-rimmed glasses with emerald green lenses resting squarely on the bridge of his nose, it was evident Scalotti knew everyone. Even the man with the squeeze-box bandoneon strapped to his hands shouted out a silent, wide-mouthed welcome, swinging his instrument dangerously high above his head in salute, while the waiter who set our table slopped red wine onto the paper cloth in his haste to see us properly and happily settled. None of us had ordered the bottle, it simply appeared with a flourish of stained napkins, a corkscrew plunged into its neck and the cork withdrawn with what would have been a healthy plop had we been able to hear it. Before we had lifted the glasses to our mouths, the fat *padrone* came over, arms wide for Scalotti, fingers and teeth nuggety with gold, with his wife, shorter, wrapped in an apron, and proportionately overweight, waddling up behind, taking Scalotti in her bulbous arms and smacking him with kisses. There was much pumping of hands, slapping of backs—Scalotti and I standing to meet the onslaught, Manuela seated behind us. It was like being with someone's favorite son, a soldier home from the wars, the conquering hero returned. For the first time since leaving London, I was enjoying myself.

But Manuela was not. Elbows on the table, jaw jutting out on linked fingers, she looked bored by the proceedings, resigned, as if the evening was already showing signs of following a familiar pattern. Nor did she seem to care how many people noticed. The fat padrone, for instance, was coldly received, while his equally fat wife earned little more than a nod in answer to her greeting. She was sulking, smoldering gently, her already heavy eyelids drooping with a mixture of boredom and disdain. I recalled her frosty enthusiasm in the apartment when Scalotti informed her we were eating in La Boca. If she knew what was in store for her, I wondered why she had taken the trouble to dress up, look good. Why had she bothered?

But Scalotti seemed not to notice her mood. Or if he did, he ignored it, more concerned with friends waving and glasses tilted in our direction. It was, I decided, a sound choice that Scalotti had made—a crowded cantina filled with friends—and I could see why he had wanted me to come along. This was where I began singing for my supper, keeping Manuela occupied and letting him off her hook. If there was to be any confrontation between the two of them, then it certainly wouldn't happen here. My presence, and Scalotti's absence, would see to that. For more and more, the two of us were left alone—Scalotti implored away by friends to join them for drinks, for a round of hand-shaking, for hugs and kisses.

For most of the meal that followed—unordered—the two of us were quite alone. At first Manuela seemed to brood, as if planning her campaign, picking at each course, stirring her fork through the creamy pasta and not really listening to my attempts at conversation. I began to wish I had spent the evening in Reconquista, and certainly she looked as if she would have been happier somewhere else. Without Scalotti as the common denominator, we were like a child's top with no string to spin us. But as the meal progressed and as we drank our wine, she began to loosen, brighten, even smiled once when I had to shout extra loud to be heard.

Occasionally, Scalotti would make a brief appearance at our table, scooping up forkfuls of lukewarm spaghetti, winking at me and talking away to Manuela in a stream of Spanish that was impossible to fathom. He had taken his coat off and his tie knot was loose in his collar. A drop of cream from the sauce clung to the bristles of his mustache like a pollen sac on a bee's leg.

"Is a fine place, eh?" he would ask me. Or "Good friends all these people." Or "There is man I must see," when he wanted to move on. Then he would give me a final wink, squeeze Manuela's arm, and tear away.

Coffees came and went, even hotter and grittier than those in the whiskería, and then two large glasses of flaming Sambuca appeared that we hadn't ordered. I was explaining this to a mystified waiter when I spotted Scalotti waving to me across the room, filling his cheeks and making dummy puffs at the curling blue flames in his own glass—like a child preparing to blow out the candles on a birthday cake.

When we finished these drinks, and had chewed into grounds the beans that had toasted in the flames, I was not altogether surprised when Manuela suggested I see her home and leave Scalotti to his friends. I looked around for a waiter, but Manuela shook her head. Let Scalotti pay. Outside, waiting for a taxi, she took my arm and huddled close.

I felt like a savage seeing himself in a mirror for the very first time. Our reactions would have been identical. Like him, I experimented: I raised my arm, the figure I watched raised his; I scratched my head, the figure did the same; I did it faster, the figure kept up with me; I stopped, he stopped; started again, he started again. But what I was looking at was no mirror reflection. For one thing, the figure had his back to me, like a Magritte alter ego. He was also much smaller—I could have held him easily in my hand. I was seeing myself from a whole new angle—and in miniature too.

The television was on a shelf at the head of the bed, the video camera on a tripod directly behind me. As a result, it was impossible to make an accurate identification: if I turned to face the camera, I could, of course, no longer see the screen. I climbed off the bed and, kicking the wires out of the way, moved the camera and tripod around to the side, setting it up by the window about six feet from the edge of the bed. I squeezed between curtains and camera and squinted through the eyepiece. It was still in focus. Back on the bed again, the screen showed the same scene but from a different angle —I was now a profile and not a backview.

Slowly, keeping my eyes fixed on the television, I turned toward the camera until they began aching in their sockets. And there, turning toward me on the screen, was my own face, a little contorted, and my chest, my abdomen, and, God . . . it was the strangest thing to see oneself naked on television. I felt curiously exposed— as if the rest of Buenos Aires had only to tune in their own sets to see me naked. They couldn't, of course. This was a closed circuit. But that was how it felt. Seeing oneself on TV was completely different from seeing oneself in a mirror. The bathroom door opened and Manuela appeared, wrapped in a towel.

"Jeez, I've never done it like this before . . . it's incredible," and the two of us—me and my screen persona—started to shake with laughter. Manuela joined me on the bed, kneeling behind me, and together we looked at the screen, at our two tiny profiles. I watched her arm move, saw her hand touch my shoulder, slide down to my elbow. I watched her lips brush my skin, then saw her sink back onto her heels, her hand reaching down into that grayish area that had so surprised me a moment before. As I watched myself respond, I saw her turn to the camera, then smile at me from the screen. From that point on, I was a spectator at my own seduction.

I woke long before Manuela. Her breathing was steady and deep, each breath drawn in along the edge of a snore but never quite connecting. Her exhalations were like sneers, as much through her nose as her mouth, her lips curled against the pillow. I looked past her and saw the camera staring blindly down at us, and on the shelf behind me the TV screen was dead. I couldn't remember anything being switched off; I must have fallen asleep immediately. The curtains were closed and only the thinnest line of daylight slipped through to streak the opposite wall. I slid silently out of the bed, gathered up my clothes and shut myself in the bathroom to dress.

In the living room, the curtains were open and the place filled with light, the lace netting softening and diffusing the glare. I walked to the table and picked up my cigarettes. Outside it was raining, large drops smacking against the glass in a steady downpour. I parted the lace but heavy gray clouds obstructed the view. I wondered whether I should stay until Manuela woke, or call her later from the hotel. Or perhaps I should go back into the bedroom and wake her myself.

"You have umber-ella, eh?"

I spun round to find Scalotti leaning against the doorframe. He was wearing his suit trousers and shoes and a vest tucked tightly into his belt. The vest made him look broad and more muscular. The tops of his arms were covered in eddies of fine black hair that disappeared under the short sleeves then reappeared at his neck. The muscles in his arms fidgeted under the skin as he dried a coffee mug. "I tell you las' night," he continued, "today is feast day of Santa Rosa. On this day in Buenos Aires, it always rain." I was relieved to see he was grinning hugely, his mustache stretched to its full span. But whether he was grinning at the outcome of his weather forecast, or the way things had turned out between me and Manuela, I couldn't decide.

Yes, I said I remembered him telling me. And no, I didn't have

28

an umbrella. From there on, I wasn't at all sure how best to proceed.

"You enjoy Manuela? Good girl, eh? Very good with the *coglioni.*" He drew this last word out as though eulogizing over a particularly luscious pasta, and then began fanning his crotch with the dishcloth. "Eh? Eh?

"And film show? You like film show, eh? Superstar actor, eh?" He began to laugh softly, as if to himself; a jeering sort of laugh as if somehow I had made a fool of myself; a kind of tut-tutting laugh —admonishing. It was too early for this kind of thing, too soon after sleep to understand what was going on, what Scalotti was doing there. After all, he couldn't be that surprised—he'd as good as laid it on for me, forced Manuela and me together. He had no one to blame but himself.

And then, clearly, the bright light of comprehension. The pattern, often repeated, smooth as silk with practice. The accidental meeting, the exploratory questions, the eventual invitation, the setup. And now? The denouement? As if to confirm this, he continued, an edge of malice seeping through his words: "I hope so. Film show very 'spensive. Manuela very 'spensive." He went back into the kitchen and returned a moment later with a tray and two mugs of coffee. "You want coffee. Coffee while we discuss, eh?" He set the tray on the table and drew back two chairs. The glass in the window creaked and cracked as the rain hit it. "Coffee no charge, eh?"

"How much then?"

Scalotti shrugged. "How much you got, eh?"

The gratitude I came to feel toward Scalotti and Manuela grew slowly. Certainly it made no appearance that feast day of Santa Rosa—a bitter bedraggled day when heavy clouds lumbered over the rooftops and lashing rain squalled through the city as if not sure which street to take. But my depression lifted with the weather, the next day as bright and as blue as the day I arrived—as if the rain had washed away the clouds like suds down a drain and emptied the sky of all but its purest element. It was a day for the *domingueros,* the Sunday people of Buenos Aires, and crowds filled the parks of Palermo, the *galerías* and ristorantes of San Telmo and the market stalls of the Plaza Dorrego. Kites flew and tugged at the last winds of the storm as if mocking their retreat, bravura gestures at the back of a foe; sidewalks swarmed with roller skaters; traffic jammed the roads; and windscreens and chrome fenders winked in the sharp sunlight like a thousand flashing heliographs.

And even when the sun set and the mists over the Rio Plata gathered into a golden Turneresque smudge—as spectacular as any of the scenes on Manuela's walls—my spirits stayed as high as the kites, brave after the storm. There was no crush of dread now, no loneliness or despair. Instead a flow of confidence, a burst of energy and enthusiasm. Between them, I realized, Scalotti and Manuela had toppled me from the high board and christened, if not altogether blessed, my adventure. I was bloodied, baptized. Out of my depth perhaps, but still swimming. Singed a bit but not burnt. And, most of all, grateful. I even considered returning to the Edificio Areco, seeing them both again, doing the whole thing over. And I would have had I had the money to spare. For, true to his word, Scalotti had relieved me of everything I carried, a little under four hundred dollars rolled up in a bundle of peso notes.

"What if I refuse to pay?" I had asked, before pushing the roll between the coffee cups.

"Don' be silly," he replied, with an indulgent smile.

"Or go to the police?" I continued, as he leafed through the notes.

"You go to the police, that would be mistake. Better be friends, eh?"

With Scalotti, it was an effort to be anything else. "Now that you have all my money," I said finally, "how am I supposed to get back to my hotel?" I expected him to peel off a few of the peso notes to cover the taxi fare. Instead he looked surprised, as if I should have known better.

"I drive you, of course."

Coke
and Cariocas

Of the two, Frankie, with her hair drawn back into a lumpy knot, was the more immediately attractive. She was tiny as a pixie, her eyes dark and wide and swift, her hands small—fingers ringed and wrists rattling with a tangle of bracelets. She was never still for long—always darting about the room, twisting and turning in her seat, ducking above and below the people around her like a tin target in a shooting gallery. She had a way of straightening her back and smoothing down her hair with both hands that reminded me of a swimmer at the end of a race. When she wasn't talking, she would sink her chin into her collar and fix you with staring eyes, or push her face so close to yours you could feel her breath tickling your lips. At no time did she appear to take any account of what was being said. It was simply an opportunity for her to inspect you more closely—her eyes flicking from your lips to your hair, your eyes, ears, chin, cheeks. Sometimes she would reach out a hand and trace the outline of your lips as you talked, or run a fingertip down the center of your face. When she grew bored, she would pinch the skin on your hand or clamp your nose between finger and thumb until you stopped talking.

Emerald, on the other hand, was slower, more lethargic—the negative element to Frankie's positive charge. She sat in her chair and lounged across the table as though she were melting. She was much taller, longer, broader than Frankie, but her slothfulness made her appear smaller than her companion. Wherever Frankie went, Emerald followed behind with an extraordinarily doltlike compliance, usually chewing gum with an open mouth; whatever Frankie said, Emerald simply repeated, as if she had no will of her own. When I asked what they wanted to drink, for example, Frankie growled "Whiskey" as though her tonsils had been pickled in it, but Emerald, when I checked with her, just shrugged her shoulders, stuck out her tongue, giggled, looked at Frankie, shrugged again and asked, "Whiskey?"

While Frankie was just healthily tanned from the beaches of Ipanema and Leblon, Emerald was mulatto—her eyes black, the whites and edges of her pupils laced with brown, her skin a smoky cocoa color, her lips tubular and glistening. Her hair, the texture of carpet, she had plaited close to the skull like the ribs of a pine cone, accommodating the extra length in a ponytail of tightly beaded braids. When she swung her head, the ponytail lashed from side to side, creating a draft of air that rang with the clicking of beads. When she smiled, often and blankly, her teeth shone white in a wide pink mouth kept constantly fresh with gum. Though her nostrils flattened when they flared, the rest of her nose was straight and true, rising into startlingly arched eyebrows. Her hands were, quite simply, the most beautiful I had ever seen—slimly knuckled and long-fingered with arrowhead nails painted an eggshell white.

I asked how old they were. Frankie told me she was twenty; Emerald rolled her eyes, stuck out her tongue, then suggested she might be the same, or younger. She didn't appear to care.

The club was basement level, and a cabaret was promised at three o'clock every morning on a small stage at the far end of the room. Frankie and Emerald were just two of the girls who worked the joint, joining customers at their tables, stroking their thighs rather than twisting their arms to order more drink, and taking turns dancing on small platforms, in front of long mirrors, in tiny sequinned briefs. Above each platform a small wooden bar, six inches long, like the rung of a ladder, protruded from the ceiling, and to this they clung for twenty minutes at a time—gyrating, swaying, pumping their sparkling crotches into the glass.

Frankie was too short to reach the bar so she never danced, but every hour one of the other girls would tap Emerald on the shoulder and off she'd slope to change—grinning as she chewed. But if she was slow and dopey at the table, she was long, lithe and energetic on the platform, a whisper of black thatch brimming over the top of her briefs. While her arms hung listlessly from the bar, like a sloth's from a branch, her body twisted and pumped to the music until it shone with sweat. Her breasts were large and tipped with tiny brown nipples that reminded me of the chocolate buttons I was given as a child whenever I had an injection. When she caught my eye, she pushed forward her hips and poked out her tongue.

This was my second visit to the club, my second night in Rio. It's a city I've never really come to trust. There's something menacing about the place—the voodoo candles of *Makumba* glittering on Copacabana, the tumbling hillside *favelas* that stink, when the wind is right, of stealth and shadows and drawn steel, the downtown buildings that peel and perspire with a decadent decay. It's an insidious sort of menace that, like the heat, slides into your shirt, trickles into the palms of your hands and prickles at your scalp. It always makes me think of the jungle—always growing, rustling, creeping closer, hemming me in. Being in Rio is like being on a beach where the tide can rise so swiftly that before you know it, you're engulfed. I always walk fast in Rio, as if I'll be cut off at any minute—stranded. But I've learned too that there are ways to ease the condition, stem the tide. With the belting rhythms of samba or with a numbing shot of cashassa, the sugar cane spirit; with a joint or two of Colombian grass or a snort of bluish white cocaine. Or best of all, to lose yourself with some obliging carioca who'll wrap her legs around your waist and fill the dark silence of your room with a breathless panting and the sound of slapping, sweating bellies.

From the very start, I wanted them both. The black and the white, the short and the tall, the negative and the positive—both together.

The first night I was too late, Frankie and Emerald and the other girls already huddled over bottles of Scotch with their clients. So I sat alone at my table and just watched them—planning, scheming, like an animal staking out its prey. And when they left with the two businessmen whose faces glistened with anticipation, I followed. Frankie walked ahead with her man, Emerald a step or two behind, a good bit taller than her companion. And then me, ten yards back, matching my pace to theirs. It was exciting to stalk them like that, without their knowing—to suddenly become a part of that shadowy menace which I so feared. After the deception in Buenos Aires I wanted to be sure—ready and prepared. I could hear their laughter and chatter, grunts from the two Germans, the scuff and scrape of their shoes on the patterned pavements of Atlantica. I could even smell their scent. But I didn't realize the extent of that exhilaration until, at the end of Copacabana, Frankie stepped out into the road, hailed a cab and the four of them squeezed in. I stood in the shadows and watched until the tail lights disappeared down a side street. All that was left was the salt-smell of the sea and the sound of breakers rolling onto the beach. Feeling lost and empty, I turned and walked quietly away. Those were the two I wanted.

Frankie and Emerald arrived at the club shortly after me on the second evening. They were alone. Frankie wore a tight pair of corded jeans and a silk blouse and Emerald a short-short pleated tennis skirt wrapped around a mauve Spandex leotard. As they sauntered past my table, Frankie looked down and smiled. Perhaps she had noticed me the evening before, or was just on the lookout for some custom. They chose a table across the room from me in a dark, banquetted corner. As soon as they were settled, I made my way over and joined them.

"You like coca?" asked Frankie after we had been talking and drinking for a while. Under the table, her hand was stroking my thigh while Emerald, who had just returned from the dancing platform, clasped her feet round my ankle.

"Coca?"

"Coca, coca. You know, coke," she whispered, pronouncing the last work like "cock."

"You have some?"

"If you like I get you some." Her eyes were wide and sparkling. Beside us, Emerald stuck out her tongue and sniffed conspiratorially.

"Tonight? Here?"

"You give me thousand cruzeiros, I find some. No problem." I gave her the money and watched her dart away through the door the dancers used. For the hundredth time that evening, Emerald rearranged her shoulders and poked out her tongue.

"Coca good. Very good coca, here Brazil," she informed me.

Although I had decided to take both of them and was still determined to do so, Frankie's absence left a gap that I hadn't felt when Emerald was away dancing, and it made me realize that my affections were no longer equally divided between the two of them. Even after the short time we had spent together, I was suddenly aware that an edge of preference had begun to creep between us. While I was intrigued and excited by Emerald—by her size, her color, by her wide pink mouth and incredible tongue, I was more readily attracted to Frankie—her roughness, her vitality, her zest; there seemed so much more to her. I liked the way she fixed me with her glittering little eyes, maneuvered her tight, tiny body against

34

mine, pinched my hand, traced the outline of my lips, but most of all I found myself drawn to her Europeanness—this last not so much racial prejudice as racial ease, familiarity. I felt more comfortable with her, more attuned, and since her English was far better than Emerald's, it was altogether easier communicating with her. Whenever I spoke, whatever I said, it was always directed at her—for her to pass on if she saw fit. Had I spoken Portuguese, it might have been the same with Emerald; but as it was, our choice of subject was limited.

"You know, Emerald, you have the most astonishing tongue I have ever seen," was all I could think to say the whole time Frankie was away. Not surprisingly, Emerald looked puzzled, as if searching for the connection I seemed to have made between her tongue and cocaine. When she failed to find it, there was little she could do apart from open her eyes impossibly wide and shoot out her tongue like a jack-in-the-box, wriggling it between her lips like a severed pink worm. We were stumped, the two of us, willing but unable to connect.

When Frankie returned, hips swinging between the tables and looking smug with success, a feeling of balance was restored. As soon as she was comfortable, she drew the table toward us and, using it as cover, opened a small paper envelope she had taken from her bag. A moment later she turned to me and pushed the tip of her little finger up into my nose.

"Make you better, make you happy," she whispered as I closed one nostril and sniffed deeply on the other. She repeated the operation for Emerald, a tiny pile of white powder held in the scoop of her fingernail, and then a third time for herself.

By now the club was filling rapidly and I decided the time had come to open negotiations. Already I had spotted a number of unattached men looking in our direction—probably thinking to themselves I would be as happy with one of the girls as I appeared to be with both. Any minute I expected one of them to come across and join us.

"Is it possible to leave here?" I asked Frankie. "Go on somewhere else?"

"Which one you want?" she replied with a matter-of-fact sniff, nuzzling closer and trailing a hand up into my crotch. Not wishing to be left out, Emerald tightened her grip around my ankles in an unexpected show of enthusiasm.

"Both."

"Both?"

"The two of you," I said. Frankie looked surprised, Emerald giggled.

"You want two girl same time?"

"Yes." The two of them looked at each other.

"Six thousand cruzeiros," she said.

"Six thousand!" I pretended to wince. I wasn't sure whether she meant six thousand each or for both, but I lost nothing by appearing shocked.

"Okay, five thousand," she replied without bothering to consult Emerald, who was busy licking the end of her nose.

"For both?"

They looked at each other and nodded. "For both."

"And what do I get?" I asked, wondering whether I would have to pay something to the club as well.

"Both," growled Frankie. "To-tal!"

I counted out the notes and gave them to Frankie, called for the bill and a moment later we were climbing the stairs to the street. At the door Frankie insisted I tip the doorman a further two hundred cruzeiros.

Outside, the warmth of the night air seemed set at just the right level and the girls fitted snugly on each side. The deal was done. They were mine. I had paid for them and could have them whenever I wanted. The feeling of power was as intoxicating as lust. I tried to say something but a salty, ammoniac taste in the back of my throat made me swallow and seemed to numb my vocal cords. My eyes felt as if they had been set in bowls of ice. Quite suddenly I began to feel an enormous affection for Frankie and Emerald, and a tremendous, devouring excitement at what the evening still held in store. The world, quite simply, was a wonderful place and I was enjoying myself immensely. Nowhere else in the world, I was convinced, could be quite as nice as it was right here in Rio, right now. Arms entwined, we seemed to swing across the street and with every step I could feel Emerald's luscious breast on one side crushing softly against me, and on the other side Frankie's hip rolling against the top of my thigh.

Just as she had done the night before with the Germans, Frankie hailed a taxi and the three of us bundled in. I suggested returning to my hotel, but when I told them which one Frankie shook her head, rubbed her thumb and forefinger together and muttered "muito, muito." She said she knew somewhere better and of course I was content to leave the choice to her. The taxi sped off in a direction I didn't recognize. But it didn't matter; I had an overwhelming trust in my two companions.

When we arrived at our destination, by my reckoning some half-dozen blocks away from Copacabana, I handed Frankie a roll of notes to pay the driver. She haggled unmercifully with him, as if the money were her own, then gave it back to me with a handful of silver in change. She hadn't even tipped him.

The building she led us to was narrower than its neighbors and not so tall, squeezed between them like a slice of cheese in a thick sandwich. A single line of windows, all shuttered, marked out the floors. Beneath each one was an air-conditioning unit; in the silent street you could hear their metallic whirring, and the smack of water that dripped onto the pavement from each of them.

The three of us tumbled up the steps and pushed open the doors. A Negro with graying hair dozed behind the reception desk. From the entrance you could only see his hair—like a dirty sponge on polished wood. Behind him, instead of a rack of keys and tidy pigeon holes, an enormous Akai stereo tape console covered most of the wall—reels the size of dinner plates revolving slowly on their pivots and a line of needles quivering and shaking dumbly in tiny lighted windows. Without even appearing to wake from his doze, the Negro reached under the counter and slapped down a key. Beyond reception we stopped for coffees at a small bar at the foot of the stairs, everything passing me in a rush of startlingly vivid images: Frankie's tight, corded trousers; Emerald's swinging, beaded ponytail; the thick china cups we drank from; jets of steam whistling from the percolator; Frankie fingering the glass of her Dior watch and complaining it was scratched; Emerald's tongue flashing across her lips, her wide pink mouth glistening like a sugary cave; the sheen of her Spandex top; the pleated swirl of her skirt; and then the smooth polished banister rail Emerald and I clung to as Frankie led the way upstairs, swinging the key as she went. We followed her up three flights of stairs (normally I would have searched for a lift but that night I seemed to float up without drawing breath) and along a dimly lit corridor which at intervals widened into cramped landings open to the sky. Each one was crowded with pots of geraniums and trellises of tangled ivy. The floor was tiled and our footsteps echoed up the lightwell. High above a square of stars punctured the night sky like pin pricks in a dark-room screen. From each of these landings half a dozen steps with a pot on each led to a closed and numbered door. Emerald and I followed Frankie up the last of these and waited while she unlocked the door. We were clinging to each other, racked with laughter and giggles and good feelings. Her head rolled so much and looked so loose on her shoulders I was certain it would drop to her feet and bounce all the way down the steps. I tried to warn her but there wasn't enough breath in my body to form the words.

Despite the air-conditioning the room was hot, the only furniture a large double bed with two side tables set into the headboard. Laid out on the mattress was a thin pile of bedding and towels. The walls were covered with a pattern of black flock over silver paper, and one of them, the one facing the bed, with a large tinted mirror. There were four spotlights, one in each corner of the room, all directed at the bed. Without a word, Frankie disappeared into the bathroom and left Emerald and me alone. While I sat on the mattress and watched, Emerald swayed over to the window, drew the curtains and fumbled with the air-conditioning. It stopped, started again, went faster for a few moments pumping cool air into the room, then settled back into its old pace. From a line of knobs on the bedside table she dimmed the lights, and switched on the music —piped up from the Akai console in Reception. Adjusting the volume to suit the lighting—now low and glowing—she flicked through the choices for me—samba, country & western, pop, classical, opera, Muzak. It was like an airplane's program. I wondered if anyone chose Kiri Te Kanawa to accompany the action, or the Berlin Philharmonic. Perhaps someone knew something I didn't. I asked her to go through them again and settled for pop; at that very moment Gloria Gaynor was singing "I shall survive"—it seemed appropriate. It was the last song I remember hearing over the next few hours, the ones that followed simply a background rhythm I could feel but not hear.

Emerald didn't bother making up the bed, just swept everything onto the floor and unhitched her tennis skirt. Eyes rolling and tongue licking lips she pushed me down and lowered her long mulatto body in its mauve Spandex leotard onto me. Her mouth was large and cold and her tongue, burrowing its pink length into the back of my throat, tasted of peppermint. She hadn't seen fit to remove the chewing gum. I found it a moment later with my tongue, secreted in the corner of her cheek, and dislodged it. Without a word she leaned over and pressed it to the edge of the bedside table. Her kisses were langorous and lasting, her body squirming over mine

38

like a trapped lizard trying to shake off its tail. With every movement the Spandex slid between my hands as smoothly as scales. She pushed herself up on an elbow and untied her ponytail. The loosened braids swept over my face. It was, I decided, like making love to a beaded curtain.

We had done no more than kiss and explore when Frankie emerged from the bathroom, balancing another fingernail's-worth of cocaine. Emerald went first this time, taking almost the whole first joint of Frankie's finger into her nostril. I waited while she scooped out another pile for me. Then she took some herself. The three of us sat there on the bed, heads tipped back, in the glowing spotlights, with music pumping in time with my heart. In the mirror we looked like test patients sniffing away in an experimental influenza laboratory.

Frankie had let her hair down too but, unlike Emerald's, it was much finer and had been tied so tight it still waved back as if held by an invisible clasp. She had also removed her makeup, which made her face look sharper and more pinched, and her corded jeans. She wore only a red satin tanga—a G-string of a bikini bottom much favored on the beaches of Ipanema and Copacabana—and her blouse, crumpled around the edges where it had been tucked in. Still snorting, like a pig with a pellet of mud in its snout, she crawled behind me and began massaging my shoulders. Emerald, unconcerned by the changeover, took her turn in the bathroom.

"You like fuck?" growled Frankie into my ear the moment the lock turned. I nodded under her probing finger, adding a sniff for emphasis. "Me, I like fuck," she continued, leaning back and rubbing herself against my spine. Once more I sniffed and another large gob of white, powdery phlegm slithered down my throat. She let me lie back, my heart thumping in the center of my chest. Still kneeling, she looked down at me and smiled—not softly, but a hard smile clenched like a fist. I lifted a hand and rubbed the front of her tanga. Her teeth bared and she rocked against my knuckles. "I like fucking; *muito* fuck," she repeated. Then she was off the bed, hauling the shirt from my shoulders and dragging off my trousers.

"You good?" she asked, throwing the clothes to one side and leaning forward on my thighs. "You good fuck?" She ran a hand down the length of me, the whole of her weight now transferred onto the one leg. The muscle began to burn. "You fuck Frankie good with this? *Muito? Muito?*" Her hand had slipped between my legs and encircled me, rolling me harder and harder between her fingers

—like Captain Queeg, I thought, in the Caine Mutiny, with his steel ball bearings. Only I didn't have steel ball bearings, and gradually a dull aching spread up through me. I should have told her to stop but I didn't want her to think I couldn't take it. I wanted to be able to match her. She would stop in a minute anyway. I hoped it would be soon. I could feel myself softening as though she were hand-pumping all the blood back into my body.

"Which one you fuck? Emerald or me?" Neither, I thought ruefully, if you carry on like that.

"Both," I replied bravely. For the first time I wondered whether they had worked like this before, the two of them with one man.

"But who you fuck first?" The question startled me, the emphasis falling heavily on the last word. I was astonished I hadn't given the matter any thought at all. At no time had I considered which one—first. All I had thought was, both of them, together, without any definition of the act itself—what, how, who and in which order. With coke-inspired clarity I began to suspect my answer was more important than I might like to think. It was ridiculous there should be any rivalry between them—jealousy from either side. After all, I reasoned, both were professionals, both had been paid to do a job and it shouldn't worry them. But they were also women, I told myself, and presumably prey to the same emotions whatever the situation.

As if to help me decide, Frankie unbuttoned her blouse and let it slip from her shoulders to the floor. Her breasts were much smaller than Emerald's—each marked with a faint triangle of lighter skin from her bikini top. She held them in her hands, pinching the already distended nipples, giving herself a double chin as she peered down at them. Now that her hands were occupied elsewhere, my ache was subsiding and I began to respond as she ran her fingers over her tight little body in a kind of stretching self-adoration. She noticed too.

"You like?" I smiled. "I think now you fuck Frankie first. Fuck me? *Muito?* Yes?" Stepping out of her tanga she pushed her way between my legs and we rolled over into the center of the bed, where she began nipping at my lips and roughly fumbling for me. I couldn't decide whether it was this haste before Emerald returned, her roughness compared to Emerald's slower, more sensitive approach, too much drink, or the cocaine, but I knew at once it wasn't going to work. The more she grabbed for me, pulled me toward her, maneuvered me into place, the more I shrank away. Despite the attraction I felt for her, ultimately, in preference to Emerald, I suddenly found myself quite unable to express that affection. Mentally I was equipped and ready, but physically . . . I tried to concentrate my attention on the problem, bombarding the area in question with positive thoughts and colorful fantasies (perhaps I should have chosen Kiri Te Kanawa). But her snapping little bites and urgent fumbling, like a turtle burying eggs, had much the same effect as her squeezing earlier on.

She stopped moving beneath me. *"Brocha,"* she muttered, pushing me off. *"Brocha,"* she said, more loudly this time, sitting up and pointing at me. Emerald came out of the bathroom and peeled off her leotard. Almost to herself, like a chant, Frankie kept repeating the word: "Brocha, brocha, brocha, brocha." Though I could only guess its meaning, I felt no alarm, embarrassment, discomfort. Everything, I was confident, would work out.

"He no good," Frankie was saying, "we go now. He too much drink, too tired—too much the coca," and she wiggled me about to illustrate her point. But Emerald, like a gardener examining a wilting bloom, sat beside me and inspected me gently, fingers cool and soft. Reaching for her bag she drew out a tube of flavoured lip gloss. It was thick and bubbly like glycerol. She said something to Frankie, but Frankie wouldn't answer; then she leaned forward and began smearing it onto me. I watched her lie down between my legs and her tongue lick out at me, her braids clicking against the insides of my thighs. There was a job to be done and Emerald was not leaving until it was. After only a few minutes, she looked up delightedly at Frankie, who had been tweaking my nipples distractedly. When she saw what Emerald had achieved, she gave my nipple a final, aggressive twist and turned over on her side.

"So, fuck Emerald," she snapped angrily, grabbing up a sheet from the floor, wrapping it around herself and curling up as if to sleep. "I tired. You no good fuck."

Eyes rolling at Frankie's show of temper, eyebrows high and wide, Emerald drew herself up on her knees and then settled down on me like a bird on its eggs. Like her mouth she was large and cold. Gently coaxing she began to sway to and fro, taking my hands and resting them on her wide brown hips. We were like a ship in a storm —Emerald the mast and me the hull—and together we rode the waves. But this time, though physically reponsive, I knew there was no way Emerald would be able to steer me to port. I was like a nerveless rod, there to be made use of and then discarded. It was as if a rubber band had cut off the supply. Once more the fantasies, the positive thoughts, Emerald's swaying breasts—but none of these could draw anything from me. At last she pulled away from me, swung off the bed and disappeared into the bathroom. I heard the shower start, its regular beating on the tiles interrupted as Emerald stepped under it. Beside me, Frankie made no move, still curled up in a fold of sheet. Next door the shower stopped. I could hear wet footsteps on the tiles, a tuneless humming, and then the door was open and Emerald was back in the room drying herself off. She grinned at me as she bound her braids, poked out her tongue and rolled her eyes at my still-aroused state. "Coca," she said, nodding at me. "Coca do that."

As she dressed, she called softly to Frankie, but the pile beside me remained still. I wasn't surprised she was getting ready to go. She had done her best—there was nothing more she could do. When she was ready, she leaned across the bed and shook Frankie, but all Frankie did was shrug off her hand and burrow deeper under the sheet. With the amount of cocaine she had taken it was unlikely she was sleeping, but she seemed in no mood to leave. Emerald, on the other hand, was impatient to go. She shook her again, longer this time, until Frankie whipped around with a burst of angry words. In her strange singsong voice—as if speaking Portuguese with a Welsh accent—Emerald answered back just as angrily. She walked to the door and stood there waiting. From the bed Frankie waved her away. Finally she turned out of the room and slammed the door behind her. Tugging the sheet over her shoulder, Frankie settled back onto the bed.

I lay beside her for a long time without moving, unable to sleep, listening to the hum of the air-conditioning and the sound of early morning traffic that rose steadily from the street. When I switched out the lights, the curtained window was gray with dawn. Reaching over, I drew back the sheet and looked down at Frankie. She was lying on her stomach, arms flung round a pillow. I couldn't decide whether she was asleep or not—or just waiting. I touched her shoulder. There was no response. Then I ran my hand down her spine. Again, no response. I pushed the sheet lower and leaned down to kiss the hollow of her back. I could feel warmth beneath my lips and the tiniest hairs. I felt her squirm slightly and then, pushing aside the pillow, she turned over, her eyes half-closed, smiling sleepily. With a warm growl of intent like an animal roused from its lair, she reached for me, pulling me down onto her.

"So now you fuck Frankie," she whispered.

"Now I fuck Frankie," I replied.

Girls
Will Be Boys

The car they drove made no sound save for the hiss of white-wall tires on the rain-slicked streets of Sabana Grande, and the occasional creak from a complaining suspension as the long, lumbering Lincoln bounced through some unseen pothole in the road. Sometimes they were hard to spot, these rain-filled depressions. On a level stretch, where the rain water rose exactly to their brims, headlight beams bounced off them as if the black liquid surface were part of the macadam, and it wasn't until the car lurched down to left or right that you realized the deception. Only on a rise, say on one of the roads that led up the side of the valley that contained Caracas, could a driver hope to make out their ragged shadows and take appropriate action.

The two girls were almost identically dressed. Both wore black. Carmenita, who was driving when I met them, preferred a modest, tightly buttoned bodice that clipped together in a high collar around her throat, with a full skirt that reached over her knees. She had kicked off her heels and was driving in stockinged feet. Her passenger, Consuela, was more daring and, I guessed, a few years younger. Her skirt was full like Carmenita's, but rather than a high front, hers was slashed. She wore a halter over bare breasts, and held a small clutch bag in her lap embroidered with jet bead patterns. They were both blond. Carmenita's hair was probably the shorter, but still long enough to justify a bright purple bandeau that covered the top of her forehead and hairline. She reminded me of a very young Susan Hampshire in an early Cliff Richard movie. Her passenger's hair was more curly and unruly, falling past her shoulders in a tangled mess.

Both wore heavy, blatant makeup around their eyes and lips.

Consuela saw me first, walking toward the car, just outside the spill of their headlights. Carmenita was concentrating on the road on this level stretch. I had my hands in my pockets and was squinting ahead, past the oncoming lights, for a taxi to take me back to my hotel. They pulled up just ahead of me and as I drew level Carmenita buzzed down her window and said something to me in Spanish. But so intent was I on finding a taxi that I didn't really hear what she said. And anyway, my Spanish was not up to giving directions—especially in a city I hardly knew. I bent my head toward her, smiled and said *"No comprende,"* walking on with hardly a pause.

My first evening back on the streets had been, not surprisingly, disastrous. For the last five days I had been out of sorts and had stayed with a friend who lived up in Colinas Bella Monte. We had studied at Oxford together and he was the first old friend I had contacted on the journey. I was glad of his company and grateful for his hospitality. As for feeling out of sorts, it was difficult quantifying the symptoms. A great deal, I was certain, could be put down to loneliness and homesickness—I still worked out the time difference between South America and home, for instance, wondering what my friends were up to on the other side of the world while I trudged down darkened streets—but there were more positive signs too. There was a definite swelling of glands round my throat, a dryness and discomfort whenever I swallowed and a breathlessness that made me feel guilty about the number of cigarettes I smoked a day, but that I conveniently, if incorrectly, attributed to Caracas, some three thousand feet above sea level.

That morning my friend had returned to his office and my "illness" had so far subsided that I rang him to say I would be moving out that afternoon and continuing my journey. I had checked into the Caracas Hilton and had been shown to a shoe box of a room on the fourth floor. Through the window I could see line upon line of foothills rising up into the mountains that flanked the city—climbing depressingly higher and higher above me. I ate a solitary meal in the restaurant followed by beers in the bar, then reluctantly surrendered my key to the concierge and headed out into the city that for the last few days I had viewed from a distance, from a flower-fringed balcony high in the hills. Even now, my friend would be standing there, gazing down on the Christmas glitter of Caracas. Tonight I was alone again.

Caracas is not an easy city. It stretches east to west along the floor of a valley, a jungle of chalky colored skyscrapers with no definable center. It is really a number of small towns that have grown and commingled like microscopic organisms to create a single unit. To make things worse, the major thoroughfare, the Autopista del Este, rarely touches the ground and you have to drive down from its laned flyovers into the roots of the city to search out its soul. I had spent the whole evening scouring an area known as Sabana Grande where, judging by the lights at least, the most activity seemed to be concentrated. I had drunk many beers in many bars, eaten scalding pimientos verdes in a *marisquería* I had thought might offer more, but finally had given up, happy to postpone further wandering until the following night.

At first I didn't recognize the Lincoln as the same car I had passed with a semi-articulate bow not five minutes earlier. It was parked in a side street, directly across my path. I walked toward it, still searching for a cab, unaware that the car was waiting for me and that the driver's window was already down. Twenty feet away it was impossible to ignore the pretty, smiling face that watched me approach. At last, recognizing the car, I smiled back.

"American?" asked Carmenita, in English this time, with a kind of deep-throated enthusiasm—as if the two of them had struck it lucky. I nodded, realizing they were not too concerned about finding their way home.

"You want ride?" The invitation was pleasantly interested, delivered as if I had been hiking along a country road and they had stopped to give me a lift. As a means of gentle persuasion, Carmenita leaned over and lifted her passenger's skirt. So high was the sidewalk that from where I stood it was not possible to see Consuela's face; the roof of the car cut her off at the neck. But in the poor light I could see the tops of her stockings, white thighs, the thin black strings of her garters and a shadow of black where she held her bag in her lap. As I stared the legs began to move, one against the other, and part slightly.

"How much?" I asked, anxious to get the ground rules settled before continuing with the game. Carmenita turned to her passenger and repeated my words in Spanish. There was a thin trickle of laughter and, pushing down her skirt, she bent to look at me.

"Fifty dollars," replied Carmenita, though I sensed the figure was an arbitrary one. There was obviously room for negotiation, but

I was too tired to haggle. Carmenita nodded to the back seat and I climbed in.

There must have been a dog in the family, for there were muzzle prints on the side windows and a gamey animal smell that the air-conditioning couldn't budge. Silently the Lincoln pulled out into the traffic and we were on our way. For a few minutes no one spoke, the two girls watching the road ahead through a windscreen dusty with dried rain. Although I had no idea what to expect, how we would proceed, I was confident I was in no danger. The fixing of a price had, for me, authenticated their motives. Perhaps, I thought, we would return to their apartment, perhaps to my hotel, or find some quiet street in one of the city parks. Whatever they had in mind I was quite content to follow along.

Consuela switched on the radio and turned in her seat. She said nothing, just swung her arm toward me and traced her fingers over my knee.

"So, Americano?" she asked at last.

"New York," I lied.

"I stay some time in Miami."

"Great place, Miami."

"Miami steenk."

I shrugged. Consuela's face was lowered, her eyes following the pattern her nail drew on my trouser leg. Her hand moved higher, her eyes moving with it, until we were looking at each other. They were strong, strangely familiar eyes—that looked at me as if they knew me well.

"What is your name?"

"Alex," I lied again.

"I am Consuela, and my friend is called Carmenita." She took her hand away and placed it affectionately on Carmenita's shoulder. Then she leaned to one side, feeling for something between the seats. Slowly, her seat sighed back until the top was resting on my leg.

"Fifty dollars," she said, holding out her hand. I counted out the money and she took it and pushed it into the glove compartment. As she turned back, she slid over onto her stomach, maneuvering herself in the speeding car up and over the top of the seat so that she came to rest midway between my thighs. Taking my hand she pushed it into the deep cleavage of her dress. Her skin was as damp as the night air spilling in through the window and tight too, as if stretched like a silk screen over the ribbing I could feel between

47

her breasts. Up front Carmenita adjusted the rear view mirror, her nails long and a deep red, the fingers thick and knuckled, until I could see her eyes sparkling back at me. The car lurched heavily into a rut and Consuela, taking advantage of the sudden movement, contrived to shift herself so that a breast filled my open palm. It was hard and firm like a muscle and seemed not to give in any way as she pushed herself against me. When she pulled open my jeans and began her practiced ministrations I turned away and stared out of the window—at the cars passing on either side of us and at the people on the pavements.

I didn't recognize the part of town we were in but I could still see, above the rooftops, the familiar neon signs I had watched for the last few nights from the balcony in the hills; the letters P.O.L.A.R. advertising the local brand of beer, changing from yellow to blue when the word was complete; *El Mundo,* the daily newspaper, spelled out in red; and on top of the pyramidlike PREVO-SORIA building a digital readout display informing me the time was 11:57 and the temperature 24° C. The Lincoln swept up a ramp, pushing Consuela further onto me, and began speeding toward the hills. In a quiet, residential street a few blocks from the highway, the car slowed and stopped and with the engine still running the two girls changed places. Consuela legged it between the seats, tidying the makeup around her mouth with an almost affected delicacy in the rear-view mirror, while Carmenita ran around the car and slipped into the passenger seat. As her door slammed shut, Consuela released the brake, shifted the transmission into drive and we moved off.

Carmenita was altogether less gentle than her friend. Her strong hands gripped my thighs unreasonably tightly and I could feel her teeth sliding over me. For a moment or two I felt just a little uncertain—not that she was being too aggressive, it was just that her teeth served to remind me that any sudden lurch from the car and those teeth could clamp together. I was relieved when the next change came and Consuela took over.

We were heading back into the center of town again, slipping down off the sides of the valley like a skateboard spilling off the walls of a rink into the concrete bowl. Twice more the girls changed places, each occasion accurately timed to keep me at a pitch of anticipation. Then it was Carmenita again, bent over my lap, pumping saliva all around me with monstrous sucking sounds that made

Consuela roar with glee. I hoped she was keeping an eye out for potholes, as well as cheering Carmenita on.

It is difficult to remember at this point the exact sequence of events. I know we were quite close to the raised Autopista del Este and I recall Carmenita's head bobbing faster and faster between my legs. I remember putting my hands on her head to steady her movements, and the car slowing down to stop. I remember too that her hair felt surprisingly coarse, and thick. Then I had both hands on her head and was pressing down only slightly when all at once the hair seemed to give on her scalp, slide, like a rug on a polished floor.

She sprang away from me, screaming furiously, kneeling on the front seat, hands flying to her hair. But it was too late. The bandeau had loosened, slipped forward, revealing the edges of her makeup and a line of black hair beneath. In horrified disbelief I began zipping myself away and then reached for the door handle. But she flung herself back at me, swearing viciously, pummeling at my chest and legs with clenched fists. Consuela had turned in her seat by this time and was howling with laughter at the spectacle—a deep, chesty laugh which certainly didn't improve Carmenita's mood. She was now clinging desperately to my leg as I tried to tug it free from under her seat. At last I pulled clear, my knee hitting her in the chest as I did so, drawing a heaving male grunt from her and sending her sprawling between the two front seats. As she fell and I struggled with the door, the wig and bandeau finally parted company, the bandeau sliding around her neck, the wig slipping sideways to hang obscenely from two persistent grips above her ear. The hair beneath was short and black and covered in a fine netting.

The next moment the door was open and I was hurtling backwards onto the pavement, but as I fell she snatched out and grabbed a trouser leg, holding on grimly as I tried to kick free. I could feel the wet pavement soaking up through my shirt and pieces of grit and stone scraping across my shoulder. Her grip was frighteningly persistent and for one, long, terrified moment I imagined her dragging and hauling me, hand over hand, back into the car.

But then she let go and my leg was free and as I shoveled backward away from the car I felt the toe of my shoe catch her smartly on the point of her jaw. I was on my feet in a moment and running as fast as I could.

They caught up with me a hundred yards ahead, Consuela laughing and shrieking, Carmenita leaning across her and grinding out abuse. One minute the car was ahead, then behind, then level with me.

"*Chico, chico,*" cried Consuela.

"*Coño, coño,*" shouted Carmenita.

Searching desperately for somewhere to escape their taunts and threats, I ran on. Up ahead was a T-junction, and without thinking I sprinted down to the left. Behind me I heard the car squeal to a stop, then tear off in the opposite direction. I turned to see them speeding away from me, taillights blazing as they braked and swung up a side road. Without realizing it I had run into a one-way street and chosen the way they couldn't go. Now they would be doubling back a few blocks so they could catch up with me again. I dashed across the street and down an opening between some shops. In the darkness, I stood panting, waiting, watching the road. It seemed an age that I waited there and had all but convinced myself that it was clear when I saw their headlights beaming toward me and the Lincoln cruise past, Consuela and Carmenita searching from side to side. But somehow they missed me. When I had my breath back, I hurried down the alley and into the next block. I had not the slightest idea where I was, except the Autopista was behind me. All I wanted was to find a taxi and get as far away as possible. Running from street to street, looking fearfully at every car that passed, I eventually found a cab, pulled open the door and jumped in. Even then I lay low in the seat, expecting every moment to see the Lincoln cruise alongside and the grotesque Carmenita scream at me in the hot Caracas night.

I never saw them again. The following morning I slept late, ventured to the pool for an hour or so in the afternoon, and then made arrangements to catch the next flight from Maiquetia.

Nighttime Lucy, Daytime Lucy

I was never altogether alone. The district commissioner slept on the sofa beside me, curled up like a marmalade cushion while Benji, his coat as black as a coal fire with glowing embers, preferred the floor, stretched at my feet in a shifting square of sunlight. A stiff breeze had been blowing down the Parramatta for the last three days, rattling the windows whenever it veered toward the house and chopping up waves on the usually calm Snails Bay, a small protected backwater in Sydney Harbor. On the edge of this backwater, looking out over a line of metal-ringed pilings and a narrow gray jetty that swayed whenever anyone walked on it, stood the house.

On the land side, from the road, it looked like a long, squashed bungalow built of wood with a steep little garden the size of a tablecloth, but from the water, with the incline in its proper perspective, you could see the house had two floors and more generous lines. At ground level there was a pillared stoop running the length of the house and three high sash windows with slatted wood blinds. A tidy garden with brown grass sloped right down to the water where a small rowing boat was moored to a wooden step. For three days now the boat had been bobbing wildly on the swell, tugging at its painter like a mad dog on a chain.

At some time, someone had enclosed the first floor balcony to make an extra room. You could see the wood was a different color from the rest and the windows were much wider. There were two old armchairs and a lumpy sofa in this narrow addition, all three covered in dun-colored rugs and tiny cat hairs. As it was the top floor, the view across Snails was unobstructed save for the highest branches of a gum tree that grew in the next garden. Its young, fleshy branches bent and its spear-shaped blue-green leaves thrashed with every gust of wind. It was the perfect place to sit and lick wounds.

I was still smarting from my encounter with Carmenita and Consuela—or whatever their names were. It was my first serious shock and I had reeled under it. If Scalotti had been a splinter of deception, then the two men in Caracas had been shards of shrapnel. I felt cheated and cheapened, and foolish for it, like a tourist who pays for jade and comes away with colored quartz. Nor was there any satisfaction to be had from the memory of our struggle —my knee knocking the breath from Carmenita's body, my foot lashing out as I fell backward and connecting with his jaw. Sometimes I wished, looking out over Snails, that those blows had been deliberate, both more accurately, more effectively delivered—with clenched fists rather than a clumsy, if lucky, kick. Nor could I derive the least amount of pleasure from his humiliation—lipstick and rage smeared across his face, his wig hanging from his ear like some tawdry Christmas decoration.

For three days I sat on the lumpy sofa with the district commissioner at my side and Benji at my feet. Gradually my resentment lessened and the memory of men's hands on me, men's lips on me, men's teeth, faded. While the cats slept I listened to the windows rattling like chattering teeth, watched the gulls soar on the wind and followed the progress of aggressive little tugs as they maneuvered vast red-bellied tankers through the gap that separated Snails from the main harbor and deeper water.

On the fourth day I packed my bag, bade my friends farewell and moved out.

Jim was the "Quacker," the talker. But more important, he was the fixer. He listened carefully to the voice on the end of the line and decided the caller was South African. The name meant nothing —the Irish were everywhere. The voice was just a little sharp, a little too European for an American. And yet, not quite English either. A strange, diluted sort of voice, a voice that had traveled and picked up traces of many languages, tones, accents. He was probably one of those mining engineers passing through from the Pilbara. One of those tall, blond ockers with more hair on their forearms than they had on their heads. The tin hat brigade, he called them.

"Yessir, I have that . . . eight-thirty in the bar. Yes, I know the one. In fact there is only the one. I'll call you back in a few minutes with the details of your companion for the evening. . . . Yessir, speak to you then."

He hung up and studied the notes he had scribbled down, then reached out for that evening's list of available names and numbers. A moment later he picked up the phone again and dialed, listened to the connection being made and heard the soft buzzing start up in the rather comfortable, oceanside apartment on Pacific Avenue.

Ten minutes later he was calling the hotel.

"Hello again, sir, just to let you know the young lady joining you this evening will be Lucy. . . . Lucy, sir. That's right. Charming girl, sir. Very intelligent, a very stylish dresser too." Jim nodded into the receiver. "That's right, sir . . . blond, fairly tall, twenty-three . . . no, sir, just leave everything to Lucy. She knows the city well. Just leave all the arrangements to her. Thank you, sir. Bye bye now, have a nice evening."

I put down the phone, and a shiver of relief, then excitement, replaced the persistent sense of dread that had followed me from Snails Bay. It was so much simpler this way. I felt I wanted to start everything all over again. I had been too much out of my depth, too soon. Around teatime I had walked up through the Cross before the trade-filled doorways and importunings whispered across the pavements. Dejected by the prospect of taking to the streets in Sydney's red light district, depressed and lonely beyond words, I had hurried back to my hotel. I called home, called friends and then, when the phone seemed a little more comfortable, friendly, I called the agency and spoke to Jim.

I made a point of getting to the bar early so I could find a suitable table, in a corner preferably with a clear view through to the reception hall beyond. It was still only a few minutes after eight o'clock but, to my dismay, there were already four blondes in the bar—three together at a table and one perched on a barstool and talking to the barman. It was unlikely any of them would be Lucy this early and none of them appeared to take particular notice of my arrival; nevertheless, the realization that, apart from her being tall and blond, I had no clear idea of what my companion looked like, shook me badly. Why, oh why, had I specified a blonde? Everyone in Australia was blond. It would have been much more sensible to have asked for a brunette. On the phone I had imagined a tall blonde would stand out like a beacon, yet here I was with twenty minutes to go surrounded by them. I didn't even know what she would be wearing. They were all "stylish" dressers at this hotel. Two more blondes sauntered into the bar and sat at a table near me. I was in despair.

Half an hour and a couple of drinks later I had begun to relax. The girl at the bar had left soon after my arrival with hardly a glance in my direction, the three sitting together were still huddled in a tight conversation, while the other two a couple of tables down from me had been joined by two middle-aged men. Judging by the time, the chances were the next blonde to come in alone would be Lucy. To pass the time, I wondered what she would be like. Whether I would like her. Nice name, at least. She would be pretty of course, but there were levels of prettiness. Would I find her attractive? Would I particularly want to sleep with her? Or would there be something—some blemish—that would put me off? Thin lips perhaps. I've always disliked thin lips. Or heavy black eyebrows? No, not with this one, she was blond. Or a nose that was just too pudgy. Or lumpy hands. Hands were so important. I wondered too, whether she was a nail-biter. I'd once spent an evening with a girl whose fingers were always creeping to her lips; she would pretend to be holding her chin in her hand but I knew it was so that she could nip at her nails. I hated bitten nails, probably because I had once bitten my own. Would I have the nerve to send her away if she didn't appeal to me? There was nothing to stop me. And then, would she like me? Admittedly it didn't matter one way or another. But it was always nice to think there was some mutual attraction. I didn't think I could sleep with someone if I suspected I revolted them. Even when I was paying. Almost as an afterthought I wondered whether I might catch something from her.

I knew it was her immediately. A helmet of blond hair, tall, making for the bar, a small black bag clutched under her arm. She slid onto a bar stool, then caught my eye, slipped off just as easily and came over. We shook hands and she squeezed in.

"Hi, you're Martin?"

"Right. Lucy?"

"Right."

No one looked at us. We could have been friends, business acquaintances.

"Can I get you a drink?"

"Aah, whiskey sour, thanks." She said the last word as though it were spelled with an "e" not an "a."

At first I was disappointed. It wasn't that she was unattractive

—just that she didn't fit in with what I had imagined. She was pretty and tall—but a heavy, not a willowy tall. Had she been any shorter, her appeal would have diminished accordingly. She wasn't the kind of girl I would normally have been drawn to, approached at a party. There was a sturdiness, a stubbiness, almost a clumsiness about her that her height, fine clothes and clever makeup camouflaged rather than concealed. Her hands were small—the wrinkles of her knuckles red and pronounced as if she had washed up in too strong a detergent, the skin shiny as if she had been buttering bread—and her fingers not long enough to wear rings gracefully. Her nails were not bitten but clipped short.

But I enjoyed the strong body sense that came from her, a kind of implicit physical awareness that thrilled—when her leg touched mine, when she laid a hand on my arm, when she leaned forward for her drink so I could see the slope of her breast, when she looked at me, eyes suggestive and inviting and knowing. It's so strong you forget it's something you've paid for—a look that puts you at ease, that puts you to bed. And Lucy had it in full measure.

She was also breaking in new shoes. When we left the hotel she caught hold of my arm not simply because it was expected but to ease the weight off her feet. Nor did she try to hide the fact.

"Glad the restaurant's close—these shoes are bloody murder." It may sound odd, but sharing this intimate detail was arousing. I suggested we take a cab but she shook her head, tiptoeing on like a cat negotiating a glass-topped wall. At dinner she smiled secretly at me and eased off her shoes, placing a warm, stockinged foot over mine.

"Isn't it funny," she said when the waiter had gone. "The two of us are done up like Christmas turkey when we'd have been just as happy in jeans and T-shirts, having a pizza somewhere." Lucy had a way of including me in everything she said. "It's as if someone has put us both here like this. We're doing what they expect us to do. Playing these parts. When really we'd be more comfortable just, you know . . ." And as she played with her food, she glanced up at me. She wasn't even hungry, I thought to myself, just picking at her meat, leaving strips of flesh on the discarded bones. But I didn't resent the fact we were there, instead of having gone straight to my room. There was a quiet intimacy over the stiff white cloth, a warmth in the wine, a closeness beneath the dim lights. I doubted we would have found anything like it in some pizza palace, but with Lucy, who could say?

There was a contented homeliness about her that I was growing to like. She was the kind of person you want just to curl up with in front of a fire. She was honest too, and plain, in a country sort of way. Apart from two thin ivory rings, she wore no jewelry. It was as if she knew the glitter and sparkle would only emphasize what some might have called her dullness.

"Don't you love being in love?" she asked as we finished our coffee. "I mean, it's such a high." The question surprised me. But it suited her. She was Aquarius, she had told me, a dreamer, adept at building wispy castles in the air.

Later, pushed together in a dark crowded club, we had to talk into each other's ear to be heard. I found myself saying anything just to get an answer from her, to feel her lips close to my ear, her breast against my arm.

"Shall we go back to the hotel?" I asked firmly.

"Let's."

We walked back through the Cross. The darkened doorways were now filled and bored offers, cheap insults, hard glittering looks, sometimes soft whispered promises drifted through the night like the oily, sweaty, insinuating smell of a fairground. She held my arm tighter—as if she were a stranger to all this.

"You know, I've never felt like a hooker. I've never felt that this has anything to do with me." I realized, to my surprise, that I no longer thought of her as a hooker either. I told her this. She squeezed my arm, laughed a little and we walked on.

In my room, she asked if she could have a bath. I lay in bed and waited, watching James Cagney in RAF uniform win the Battle of Britain single-handed.

"There's something we have to clear up first, you know," she said, wrapping a towel around herself and sitting on the edge of the bed.

"Pass me my jacket."

"It's sixty dollars for the evening and one-forty for me."

I counted out the money and then, in disbelief, counted it out again. Somehow I was twenty dollars short, but before I could say anything she had taken the fold from me.

"So let's not argue over twenty dollars." She picked up her bag and pushed the notes away. "Do you mind if I make a phone call?"

"You can make it long distance if you like."

She dialed a number from her address book.

"Hi, it's Lucy . . . yeah, thanks . . . look, I'm just ringing to say I'm not going to be able to make it . . . yeah, that's right . . . yeah, he's rather nice," she turned and kissed my shoulder. She smelled of Imperial Leather. "Yeah, I'm sorry too . . . thanks anyway, see you."

"If I hadn't been nice, would you have still come back with me?"

"No bloody fear."

"And the money?"

She shrugged: "It's not worth the hassle, if you don't feel right about the bloke." She drew up her legs, then slid them down into the bed beside me. They felt as though they needed a shave, but somehow it fitted. Almost to be expected. "Mind you, you men don't seem to worry about that a lot."

I almost replied that not many hookers felt like that either.

"Should have shaved my bloody legs," she murmured, as she eased herself over me.

Not once did Lucy look at me. Only when we finished and she pushed me over, rolling with me and planting her elbows either side of my head.

"How to soothe the savage beast," she murmured, flicking the hair out of my eyes.

"If it's a nice day tomorrow," she said as she dressed, "I was going to the beach."

"Is that an invitation?"

"If you want!" She collected up her things and stood by the bed. "I'd stay, you know, only I hate leaving hotels in the morning dressed like this."

I nodded. In a way I was glad she was going. I could have the bed to myself. I was tired—a savage beast soothed. She switched off the TV and lights.

"I'll call in the morning," she said. I don't even remember the door closing.

It was as if the night before had never happened. As if we had never touched, talked, grown close; as if her cheeks had never hollowed as she sucked me into her; as if I had never slipped between her prickly shins.

When I arrived at her apartment a little after lunch, there was no acknowledgment, no sense of complicity—nothing beyond the simplest acquaintance. She had decided it was too windy for the beach so we walked together from Tamarama to Bondi along the cliff path that separates those two bays—shelving cliffs gouged out by the wind and sea like scored Gruyère, the path trembling under-foot from the crashing, massive Pacific swells. She wore rope-soled espadrilles and cotton drawstring trousers so light you could see the fold of her tucked-in T-shirt beneath. She explained the rip currents to me, stopping to point out the clear smears of treacherous water that scarred the sea like stretch marks. "Get into one of those and you just get swept right out." Git swipt raht e-out, was the way she said it.

Her skin looked rougher in the daylight—but in a country way, and under her chin was a small mole with two tiny black hairs sprouting from its center. I had neither noticed nor felt it the previ-ous night. We walked side by side, only touching by chance if a gust of wind pushed us together or when we drew close to let people pass. It was as if, by some silent and mutual agreement, we had decided to start over—our actions the previous night forgotten, our intimacy replaced by a kind of childish, bashful masquerade of courting. It would have been harder for me to reach out and touch her, put my arm around her, than it would have been for some adolescent on his first date. In some subtle way, she had conveyed to me that she did not want to be reminded, and that even if I did say something, she would look at me blankly as if she didn't know what I was talking about. Her allure was like the beam of a torch —strong and clear at night, but invisible by day. It was as if she were two people—the daytime Lucy not even remotely aware of what the nighttime Lucy did. I knew it was in my power to tip that balance but she made it clear I shouldn't try.

At Bondi we bought fish and chips wrapped up in the *Sydney Morning Herald* and sat on a bench to eat them. By the time we had finished, a crowd of gulls surrounded us—cawing and flapping and flicking their hard little yellow eyes at us. There were two that caught our attention—one with a leg missing, the stump waving nervelessly like a thin red twig, the second with a fishing hook pierced cleanly through its beak, the eye of the hook still trailing a length of nylon line. Every now and again a webbed foot would stamp on the line and jerk the beak down. I was sure there was no way the second gull could eat, that it would slowly starve to death, but when I threw him a lump of fishy batter he seized it and tipping back his head swallowed it down, the beak wrenching against the hook, the length of his white feathery neck ululating like a belly dancer. His companion managed equally well, hopping into the scrimmage for bits on his good leg and waving the other about like a kind of balancing rod. Lucy and I agreed they probably worked a partnership, showing their wounds and hoping for sympathy. They would probably live longer than their companions.

On the harbor ferry across to Cremorne and Taronga, we sat outside on the top deck watching the Sydney skyline. We had bought ice creams at Circular Quay—"Not gelato, I hate gelato," she had said—and were taking our last bites when she suddenly turned to me, her hair whipping about her face. "You know, it's so much easier for you blokes. I mean, women have to cram it all in. Make the best of just a very few years. But you men have all your lives. You get better. You're so lucky." Then, looking back across the harbor, she added, "I want so much to have as full a life as I can manage." It was simply a statement. Perhaps there was an edge of resentment, a suspicion of explanation, but there was no malice. Whether she felt it was unfair, whether she wanted me to deny it, I don't know.

We didn't get off at Taronga, just waited until the ferry turned for the trip back. "I can't bear to see all those caged animals," she explained.

It was a sparkling clear day and high above, like some thin, distant cloud was a ghost-white full moon. As we moved away from the shore and picked up speed she told me about the first man she ever loved. He was a craw fisherman in the south island of New Zealand. She made him sound like a character in a fairy tale.

"Do you ever see him now?"

"Oh, yes, whenever I go back." She was silent for a moment. "But I haven't seen him for two years. Still, that doesn't matter. It's always just the same when we do."

"You'll probably marry him one day." I don't think I meant it seriously, but she nodded.

"Yes, probably will."

"Does he know . . . you know . . . ?"

"He bloody well should do." She looked at me and smiled.

"Oh?"

"I used to charge the bugger." It was the first time daytime Lucy had acknowledged nighttime Lucy.

As we walked away from Circular Quay, looking for a cab, I asked if she would have dinner with me again—out of the company's time. She said she would love to, but she had to go to a party first. "I'd ask you along, but it's invitation only." I felt a little disappointed. "Tell you what, I'll call you after, how's that?" I brightened at the prospect.

I was sound asleep when the call came through. It was past midnight.

"Hi, Lucy here."

"Hi, how are things?"

"Fine, thanks . . . look, I'm just ringing to say I won't be able to make it after all. The party went on much later than I thought and I'm back at Tamarama, and I'm exhausted."

"That's a pity."

"Yeah, I'm sorry, you know."

"Is he nice?"

There was a long pause at the other end of the line, and then quietly she said: "Yeah, he's rather nice."

Flaky
Pastry

I hated Melbourne on sight—precise, provincial, Protestant Melbourne. As staid and stuffy as a Sunday prayer meeting; as upright, as inflexible as a church steeple; as chill as pulpit marble. I hated the clipped, rinsed voices; the studied, mannered poise of respectability; the scones-for-tea, collecting-for-the-blind, church-bazaar wholesomeness of it all. It made me want to do or say something scandalous and loud, offend the city's precious sensibilities, rock its steady precocity.

I wish I could be so positive about Melissa—one way or another. Even now, from a distance, I can't quite make up my mind about her.

In her mink, her conservative, square-cut cocktail dress with its short-sleeved matching jacket, the pearls she wore in a double string, she was a lot like the city she lived in—a little superior, just a little preposterous, all dressed up with no place to go. There was something matronly about her and it wasn't just the way she dressed. She had about her an air of tolerant disdain, a kind of smug self-righteousness like some holier-than-thou do-gooder there in my room to perform an unpleasant but necessary social service for the good of the community. She could have changed my bandages while she was about it, she had that kind of look to her. She was also a bit of a fusser. This was the Melissa I didn't like, the one I wanted to take by her string of pearls and shake the stuffing out of. And through Melissa—Melbourne.

When she knocked at my door, at eight-thirty precisely, her punctuality rankled. In Melbourne, of course, it wouldn't do to be late. I was prepared to dislike her before I even opened the door.

This time I had asked for a brunette—which she was, right down to the roots of her hennaed hair. I had also stipulated that whoever the agency sent be under twenty-five—and she was, by a long way. She stood snugly in my doorway smiling up from the deep, wrap-around collar of a ranch mink coat that reached well below her knees. She introduced herself in a cheerful voice and walked into my room with all the confidence and practiced ease of a family doctor calling on a patient. She slipped out of the coat and gave it to me to hang, then sat at the table by the window as if waiting for tea to be served.

"Hiv you bin in Milburn long?" she asked, with polite lack of interest, tipping her head to one side as if talking to a child. Had she worn gloves, I decided, this was the moment she would have drawn them off—finger by finger.

"I arrived this morning, from Sydney."

"Would you mind dreadfully switching off the television?" she said, as if I hadn't spoken. "I can hardly hear myself think."

As we left the room a little later for dinner she turned to me at the door and said: "Don't you think you had better take a jacket? It'll be cold later." I suspected it had nothing to do with the cold, just that she wanted me to look a little more presentable. After all, she was wearing mink.

And then, at dinner: "My, all that traveling. It can't be good for you. High time you settled down." This, from someone a good ten years younger than me.

And finally, over our coffees: "You should try to get to church a little more often, you know. I'm not that regular myself," she pronounced it "rigulah," "but when I do go I feel much, much better for it. . . . And you ought to stop that smoking. Did you know, you've smoked eleven of those things so far?"

Then there was Melissa the businesswoman: brisk, calculating, totally in command of the situation. The conditions, the rates of exchange—a kind of calculated coldness settled on her as if she were reading the minutes of the last board meeting. The take-it-or-leave it, let's-get-down-to-essentials Melissa who made me feel as if I had just been handed an inter-office memo with instructions to act on it without delay. Time is money. Money is time. The office boy and the managing director.

A preliminary round of conversation. Had I ever been to "Milburn" before? No. How did I like it? Hated it. (I was in my most offensive mood.) Where did I come from? Chicago. (I knew nothing about the city except that it was windy and hoped she knew no more.) What I did for a living? I was a—photographer. (Always sounded glamorous.) Then she turned abruptly to business, fingering the twin line of pearls as she did so.

"I meet with you here in your room and tell you this now so there's no argue . . . I mean, misunderstanding" (a sharp little laugh) "later on. So I don't waste your time and you don't waste mine."

I nodded, rather subdued by the level, professional manner in which she delivered her lines.

"Do you mind telling me if you have used a service like ours before?"

I told her I had.

"Very well then. May I ask in what form you propose to pay? I take American Express, Diner's, Visa, Carte Blanche. . . ."

"Cash."

"I see. And for how long will you require my services?"

"For dinner certainly and . . . let's say, until about oneish?"

"From now until," she consulted her watch, counting out the hours on her fingers like a little girl doing a sum, "until one-thirty —call it four and a half hours—that'll be two hundred and eighty dollars." That accounted for the mink and pearls, I thought.

"I was told two hundred dollars," I said, a little reluctant to question her arithmetic. She just shrugged, made a little moue but said nothing.

"You'll have to take traveler's checks."

"English, American or Australian?"

"American," I replied. "I'll just work out the exchange." Now I've never been particularly gifted at mathematics but this seemed straightforward enough. I multiplied the amount she had asked for by the going rate, scribbling it all down on my breakfast order form, shuffled around the decimal point and showed her the result like a schoolboy handing in his prep.

"That doesn't look right to me," she said, taking the pen and order form from me. Her nerve astounded me. "Now when I was at school we were taught to do it like this." Melissa preferred fractions and I watched carefully (as carefully as you can upside down) as she worked it all out. The figure she came up with was some sixty Australian dollars higher than mine, but I didn't have the gall to double-check her calculations, simply tore out the requisite number of cheques, countersigned them and determined that in future I would carry out all my financial transactions in fractions. Much to my relief, Melissa the businesswoman made no further appearance until after dinner, when she asked if she could keep the bill.

There was something of the child in Melissa too, her youth parceled up in clothes her mother would have been happy wearing to a Melbourne fund-raising—puzzling but instantly provocative; deliberate or accidental I couldn't tell. It didn't really matter that much. But beneath the clothes, beneath the businesslike manner, there lingered a calm, terrifyingly childlike presence. She made me feel like a doting uncle taking his niece out from school. I loved her naïveté; was charmed by her gaucherie; amused by her narrow determination and blinkered certainty. She was a little girl at her first grown-up dinner party—enchanting, engaging and insidiously beguiling.

Melissa had booked a table for dinner in my name at a plushly pretentious restaurant that presented the ladies with a silver-foiled, ferned carnation. Melissa immediately put it in her bag. Strangely, I felt touched. But then I was rapidly becoming as soft as a punc-tured soufflé. I noticed her hands were fat, with dimples as knuckles. As we ate, as if it had been learned like a lump of verse from a school text, Melissa expounded her personal philosophy. It all sounded so easy, so uncomplicated—so childish—I almost envied her igno-rance. She would marry a rich man—would have to marry a rich man. She had ordered a rough pâté en croûte, I had chosen the mousse. When it was served, she picked a square of toast from its napkin hollow, buttered it neatly, then tried to spread the pâté—crust and all—in the same way. I could see her knife bend with the effort but the pâté resisted all attempts to flatten it. It crumbled and the pastry flaked—both refusing to stay put on the toast except for a single crumb stuck in the butter, which she bit off daintily. It was clear she had never eaten anything like this before. I watched her repeat the operation as she insisted that love—which I had churl-ishly (and rather complacently) introduced as a possible foil to her ambition—was all well and good but in her considered opinion an unnecessary and expensive luxury.

"I mean, two hundred and eighty dollars a night, it's a lot to give up, you'll admit," she whispered across the table. It wouldn't have surprised me if she had added that love was soppy. "I'll just have to marry a rich man. Love's okay but it's not much use when you're both scraping to raise the rent" ("rint," she pronounced it). "No, I'm going to marry someone rich. Very rich." Once more pastry and pâté exploded in a shower of flaky crumbs.

Her plate was now littered with debris. I offered her some mousse in exchange for a taste of her pâté. I wasn't going to say anything. I just thought she might take a peek, see how I coped and act accordingly. I cut off a corner of the pâté, balanced it on some toast and popped it into my mouth. But the demonstration went unheeded. The mousse behaved impeccably under her knife but a moment later she was still trying to mash the pâté.

She was now telling me that men were boring, probably even rich men, she conceded, and that without question she preferred making love to women. "I'm bisexual, you know?" I couldn't decide if she meant what she said, whether she was telling the truth, or just thought it was the thing—a grown-up kind of thing—to say. A let's-shock-the-adults sort of thing.

Melissa didn't play her real role, her trump card, until last. Melissa the whore. A kind of trinity—all three rolled into one, spread across my sheets. Melissa the Melbourne matron in her uniform; Melissa the businesswoman sparing a few precious moments in a busy schedule; and Melissa, the innocent, submitting to her first lover.

In the taxi back to the hotel, she put her hand onto my leg. It was the first deliberately physical contact of the evening. And as we walked through reception to the lifts she slid her arm through mine. The desk clerk didn't even look up. The clock on the wall behind him showed it was eleven thirty. Two hours, I thought. Up in my room she sat on the bed and not at the table. I switched on the bedside lights.

"No, not those—that one in the corner is best," she said, slipping off her jacket. I did as I was told, the pool of light narrower in the corner, the room darker, and joined her on the bed.

"Would you like a drink?" I asked, uncertain how to proceed.

"I'd die for a port."

I dialed thirty-seven for room service and waited for them to answer.

"If you can't get through on thirty-seven, try nine."

I pressed down the pips and tried the new number. I was through after two rings, and put in the order. The lights first, then room service—Melissa, for all her apparent innocence, knew this hotel quite well.

I touched a hand to her face, pushed my fingers through her hair, kissed her cheek. At first she didn't move, respond. Then she turned and brushed her lips to mine.

"Min' if I use your bathroom?" she asked as her mouth floated past my ear.

Room service called and left a tray. "Sorry, sir, the bar was closed. Will a bottle be all right?"

Melissa reappeared, leaving a flushing lavatory behind her. She closed the bathroom door so the noise diminished to a soft hum of falling water (the Melbourne matron in her had probably lowered the cover before flushing). She took the port I poured for her and sipped it as if it was a special treat. For a moment I was confused —one minute she was a whore, the next a pretty little girl being daring.

As we lay back on the bed her dress rode up over puppy-fat thighs. We kissed silently, her hands above her head as if she were being held up at gunpoint. Taking this pose as an invitation, I put a hand on her breast and stroked gently, not wishing to appear too rough. Then, abruptly, she pulled away and leaned over onto her side, pushing up her hair and showing me the zip to the cocktail dress. Turning back, she held out her arms to me and I peeled down the front of her dress, letting it drop around her waist like an apron turned inside out. I had never seen anything like her nipples—they were shockingly, almost transparently pink, too-tender-to-touch-looking; as uncreased, as unwrinkled as perfectly shaped rubber teats. They could have been pressed in the same mold.

We stood to undress, then lay back on the bed. Where I had lingered a moment before with care and tenderness, Melissa now gripped tightly and kneaded. While I concentrated my attentions on the insides of her thighs, she began wrenching at her breasts as if they were nerveless lumps of clay and looking up I could see the flesh pinched white beneath her fingers. Her eyes were closed, and her lips parted—the intensity of her response, and her ferocity, surprised me. From her breasts, her hand then pushed down between her legs, two fingers digging into herself, sliding back and forth. Like a child who has just dipped into a mother's mixing bowl, Melissa lifted her fingers to her mouth and licked them clean. Then down into herself again and back to her mouth. The third time she sat up and slid her fingers into my mouth. They were plump and tasted sweet and oily. The change was now complete, Melissa the whore pure and simple.

It also became clear that she was reacting far more to her own stimulation than to anything I did. I joined in as best I could but it was like playing against the computer in a TV tennis game, a computer programmed to go faster and faster. In the end I was left way behind, simply turning the knobs and hoping some lucky connection was made—a service returned.

At one-twenty she went and showered. And a few minutes before one-thirty she slipped on her mink coat and kissed me goodnight, straightening the bed clothes around me. I felt like a little boy being tucked up.

Part Two

Bogeymen
and Bruisers

There was absolute clarity—no smudginess at all, no ragged edges. Color was steady and well defined, the sound precise and level, the whole scene incredibly detailed.

The room, so far as I could judge, was almost exactly square with a high ceiling that sloped into the walls. It reminded me of the sitting room in the house at Snails Bay. In one corner just below the window was a patch of damp that looked as if it could easily be furry—a gray stain laced delicately with streaks of yellow, like some gross wound that, unobserved, untreated, had begun to suppurate. The doctor was tall and faintly familiar. He stood by the window looking into the garden below, hands pushed deep in the pockets of a short white jacket.

"It'll have to come off, of course," I heard him say. I watched him close the shutters. Sunlight, split by the wooden louvres, fell in a grid pattern across the floor and his desk. Above us, two fans rotated lazily, their wide, batlike blades slicing at the heavy air but making no appreciable difference. It was uncomfortably hot. The doctor was now at his desk, sitting down in front of me. "It'll have to come off," he repeated.

"Off?"

"And as soon as possible, no delay." He leaned forward on his desk, hands joined, fingers flexing. His desk was large, strewn with shiny chrome instruments that looked vaguely sinister, cloth-covered enamel bowls and heavy black and gray X-ray sheets clipped to metal hangers. The corner of one of these sheets was bent awkwardly under his elbow; I wanted to straighten it. On my side of the desk and just within reach stood a rack of vials, each one filled with gloriously colored mixtures. They looked like test samples of exotic cocktails.

"But off?" It sounded like the old joke I had heard a hundred times before in a hundred different bars. He couldn't be serious. I had imagined an injection or something.

"It's for the best. Please believe that."

"Well, look . . . I mean, isn't there something a little less, you know . . . radical, drastic?" I was stumbling after alternatives. "I mean, isn't there an injection you could give me, a course of pills . . . ?"

The doctor shook his head.

"I don't want to sound disrespectful or anything," I continued, "but I really would like a second opinion on this. I mean, Jesus. . . ." I was beginning to panic.

"You are, of course, quite at liberty to do that, my dear fellow," he spread out his hands, "but good God, you just have to look at it. It's green. Any of my colleagues would have no hesitation prescribing the same treatment."

I could feel the swollen beast begin to stir—heavy, sated, lugubrious, like some scaly reptile on a full stomach. For a moment it had life of its own. But it did no more than stir, like a cat settling itself more comfortably in front of a fire.

"I'm afraid," he continued, "the condition has been left far too long. The infection must have set in weeks ago. There's no telling how far it's spread. Why on earth didn't you come to us sooner . . . ?" Because I thought it would go away. But my attention had wandered to the gray, furry stain by the window, with its suppurating streaks. I thought back over the last few weeks and remembered their faces—smiling, guileless, eager. Manuela and Frankie and Emerald and Lucy and Melissa (at least I couldn't have caught anything from Carmenita or Consuela). Which one had it been? How long had this germ of rot been at work on my system? The thought that I might have passed it on was of no consequence to me.

The beast moved again. I tried crossing my legs to restrain it, but the slightest pressure was painful. Instead I laid my hands gently in my lap, lightly, trembling, not wishing to place too much weight on the creature. I seemed to sit there for long silent minutes, staring at the doctor. He stared back, shaking his head, flexing his fingers, shaking his head, flexing his fingers, flexing his fingers. . . .

The dreams had been going on for about a week and were just one symptom of a mounting hypochondria. Sometimes I was alone, sometimes with a doctor, a nurse—sometimes whole teams of physicians surrounded me, delicately examined me. And always I was somewhere that reeked of ether—I could actually smell it in my dreams: the chemistry lab at my old school, in a doctor's surgery, in a hospital bed with a hooped frame about my middle, in a sterile, white-tiled room where the green beast hung like a sulking gherkin. I knew the dreams were ridiculously exaggerated when I woke— nightmares that fled with consciousness. But I also knew their cause.

It had started at Tullamarine airport in Melbourne. I was queuing to board the plane, my case at my feet, when a swift, sudden jab of fire—as thin and penetrating as a red-hot needle—passed clean through my vitals, leaving a gradually subsiding tingle in its wake. So unexpected, so immediate was this flash of pain that, had it not been for the afterglow, I might easily have thought I had imagined it.

As soon as the plane was airborne, as soon as the seat belt sign blinked off, I was up and out of my seat, locking myself and my pounding heart in the nearest lavatory. There I sat, for most of the flight to Hawaii, examining myself as anxiously as an adolescent scanning his face for incipient pimples. At first I could see nothing wrong, but the more I looked, the more unfamiliar the thing seemed. I tried to remember what it had looked like before the trip—had it changed in some subtle way that I was unware of? Had this always been there? Had that looked the same two months ago? Was that a swelling or a fold of skin? Was this a different color? Should this be like that? Or was it just the light above the mirror? I turned myself from side to side trying to pinpoint some difference, trying to establish something amiss, something that might explain the cause of the pain I had felt at the boarding gate.

Mine was the most disturbing hypochondria, my first week in Hawaii total and unremitting misery. I would sit at a bar, look at the people around me and wonder what their reaction would be if they knew of the leprous disease I nurtured. I would put off going to the lavatory as long as possible, dreading having to look at it between my fingers in case it had suddenly metamorphosed, fearful that the once mindless, simple exercise of urinating might have turned into torture—a stream of liquid glass tearing me to pieces. On the beach, in shops, walking down the street, I feared imminent discharge of the grossest kinds, and planned how best I could double back to my hotel room without anyone being the wiser, without anyone suspecting the condition I was sure would erupt at the next DON'T WALK sign, before I left the store, as I struggled out of the surf at Waikiki.

So far mine was a private purgatory. As soon as something visible came to my attention, I would seek medical help. But until that time, it was up to me.

Beyond my hotel there was a two- or three-hundred-yard stretch of pavement that ran along the land side of Kalakaua Avenue, between Kealohilani and Lewers, where trade was readily available in all shapes, sizes and colors. Along this stretch the girls prowled and swaggered at night, whispering "Fuck me, fuck me" as they passed. Whenever I left my hotel I had to run this gauntlet but I was like a eunuch in a harem. I also felt the most grinding resentment, which I had to try hard to disguise. If not for them and their sort . . .

Most of the time I spent in drugstores, reading the instructions on tiny brown bottles, noting what particular ailments the various creams, oils and ointments promised to reduce or cure. Having decided against medical help for the time being, I was my own general practitioner. I bought bagfuls of these lotions and scores of dermatological soaps—"Superfatted with Lanolin" and endorsed by leading physicians—which I tried out in the shower, in the bath, dangling in the wash basin, working up the most wondrous lathers. Without question, I had the cleanest testicles in the whole Pacific.

I also experimented with underwear—loose cotton pants, baggy Y fronts, jockey shorts, no underwear at all, my mind constantly absorbed by what was going on in my crotch.

I even began to list the various feelings that afflicted the area, the times they occurred and their frequency. I dreaded the return of that needle-sharp pain and would freeze whenever I felt the slightest tickle. Most frequent was a steadily increasing tingle similar to the one that had followed that exquisite needle of fire, a blunt sort of sensation not exactly in the pain bracket but persistent enough to make its presence felt. Then there was a prickly, sweaty discomfort that I eventually attributed to the heat. A steady throbbing was a further symptom, and a sensation of tightness another. Almost as frequent as the tingle was the itchy feeling—something like an insect bite—that yearned for fingered relief, a quick satisfying scratch. I tried to resist the temptation as possibly worsening the condition (I remembered chicken-pox scars), but often I would dig my hand into my pocket and, as discreetly as possible, skirt around the edges of the itch, taking care not to irritate it more than necessary. I was convinced that sooner or later a rash of sores would put in an appearance.

My hotel room was the center of my life in Hawaii—doubling as a temple of remorse and personal surgery. The room was on the thirty-second floor. I shall never forget those journeys in the lift, watching the numbers fly by, getting nearer and nearer until that pneumatic pause as the lift slowed to my floor, and then the ten-yard bowlegged hop to my room where, quaking with apprehension, I would lower my trousers for a fresh examination.

True hypochondria started ten thousand feet above Melbourne's Yarra River, peaked overlooking Waikiki and ceased, strange to say, in the most extraordinary manner.

It was late at night. I had spent almost an hour examining the display shelves in an all-night drugstore reading labels and matching symptoms, and was on my way back to the hotel with a new supply of medicines to try out—a Finnish cleansing liquid with a high pH content recommended for "intimate hygiene and for gentle cleaning of skin-fold areas"; a lotion that promised to "dissolve and clear away scales and crusts"; and a tube of cream for sixty-nine cents that guaranteed "to promote healing of chapped, chafed and inflamed areas." I had cut through a side street that I was certain would bring me out only a few hundred yards from my destination. Up ahead, a youngish man was walking toward me, head down, hands in pockets. We drew closer, he looked up, and the two of us began that embarrassing shuffle that always seems to bedevil two people trying to get past one another. Weight onto the left foot, then onto the right, then the left again, choose the side you want and go for it. Usually each protagonist passes by without so much as a shoulder brushing. But not this time. We collided with each other. I was about to apologize when the stranger's fist hit me high in the chest—a little below and to the right of my breastbone. The shock of the blow drove the breath from my body in one whopping gasp. My eyes clenched shut and I doubled up, my forehead scraping the buttons on my assailant's jacket. Almost immediately one, two, three, or more blows came from behind crashing into me in the space between my hip bone and ribs. I put out a hand to steady myself and gripped the arm of the man in front of me. I could feel almost every thread of the material in his jacket—rough and damp

—see in my mind the pattern of the weave. I could also smell him, and his friends behind me, with astounding clarity—a stale, beery warmth on their breath, a strangely sweet smell on their clothes. By this time I was desperate to fall to the pavement, to avoid more blows, but I seemed supported between them. I took two more crashing punches in the back and two, maybe more, from the man in front before I felt them step back, letting me slide to the ground, a fluid warmth streaming down my legs, soaking through my jeans. After the strained tension in my crotch over the last few days there was a sudden lessening, a muscular release, a comforting relaxation. So total was this release there was no way I could stop myself peeing. With no breath in my body I could neither speak nor shout out for help but I could see in my head, spinning around like a carousel, the words "Shit, shit, shit." It seemed years before I hit the pavement, curling up when I did so, like some premature fetus. Beneath me I could feel my bag of medicine. Once I was down, a hand riffled through my jacket, snatched a bundle of notes and sent a spill of coins ringing into the gutter. One of them lifted my arm, struggled a moment with my watch, then slipped a blade between strap and skin and cut through. I remember a volley of hefty, healthy kicks in my back and sides and one numbing boot burying into my thighs. I curled tighter, waiting for more, but all I could hear were footsteps running off. My eyes had been clenched tight throughout; it was difficult to open them now it was all over. My trousers were warm and wet and suddenly I began to shiver, not from the cold, but from a suppressed and delayed fear. I thought I would never stand again. Every muscle began a slow and insistent ache of complaint.

It wasn't until the following morning that the real effects of this beating began to show themselves. I had reached the hotel surprisingly easily, numbed a little but otherwise in one piece, and slumped into bed without delay. But when I woke up I could hardly move. It was impossible to sit up and I had to roll slowly to the edge of the bed, slide my knees to the floor and then drag myself to my feet. I had never been beaten up before. I could hardly believe the pain. One leg was almost entirely dead, aching abominably at about mid-thigh. I began to wonder how I had ever slept a wink. I limped into the bathroom—my head surprisingly clear—and looked at myself in the mirror. It was a substantial shock. On both sides of my body stretching almost from armpit to waist were livid black bruises. One leg was also badly bruised and my back was stiff as a surfboard. But worst of all, though there was hardly any bruising, was my stomach. It felt as though every muscle there had been torn like damp tissue paper. Every movement—arm, leg, hand—sent a flash of pain across it.

Dressing was a nightmare. That first day I gave up and stayed in bed, gently feeling with my fingers over each rib to see if there was a break. The following day the bruises were larger still but less livid, and although it was a little easier moving about, it was still impossible to dress. Putting on a sock was like trying to topple the World Trade Center. On the third day I woke feeling a great deal better. I spent the morning sitting on my balcony, even managed to dress and make it down to the bar—very stiffly—for a drink that evening. The following day I felt just about fit enough to leave Hawaii forever.

As I boarded a plane bound for Tokyo, I realized I had totally forgotten the "illness" that had racked me during the first part of my stay. And more, there was nothing to make me aware of it. Though I was aching still, it was the most enjoyable flight I have ever taken.

No-Name

The relief, as I boarded the plane in Honolulu, lasted clear across the Tropic of Cancer, the International Dateline, and out over the wide, blue spread of the northern Pacific. An hour out of Oahu, after most of the passengers, American and Japanese, had sated a morbid curiosity with an aerial peek at infamous Midway Island passing some forty thousand feet below us (such a tiny, insignificant scab of land), I sated my own in the cramped confines of the john with one last examination of the "coglioni." As usual everything was in order, only this time I didn't leap to fanciful conclusions. I packed away my mental medical dictionary and pressed the flush pedal. Apart from the odd ache in my ribs and puddles of bruising, I was purged.

The weightlessness of relief had calmed into a soft glow of complacence and well-being by the time we landed at Narita. It was foolishness to take a taxi into the city, seventy dollars of foolishness, but I wasn't in the mood to care. Splash out, celebrate, treat yourself, I thought.

But as I lay on my bed in my hotel room planning the evening ahead—a real sushi dinner, a trip to the Ginza and who knew what else—I slipped into a light doze. When I woke the following afternoon—curled on the bedspread fully clothed—I felt more refreshed than I could believe possible. It wasn't until I stood under the shower that I remembered I hadn't dreamed.

I never learned her name and I never saw her body, but the white Dutch rabbit she kept in a bird cage at the foot of her bed was called Misha. Or Mija. The name sounded more Danish than Japanese. Taken in proportion the living quarters of pet and owner were equally confined. There was just enough room for Misha, or Mija, to juggle himself (or herself) round in the cage, and between the bed and the wall just sufficient space for two people to stand side by side.

The apartment was approximately twenty feet long from door to window and about half that across, one corner boxed off to accommodate a cupboard-sized bathroom. It was like a comfortable prison cell—no more. I couldn't decide whether she actually lived there or just used it for work; but I suspected the former and was mildly appalled.

The bed was somewhere between a single and a double, and unmade—a gray tangle of pink nylon sheets, frilled pink pillowcases and a gray-pink nylon spread. The headboard had probably been much admired—a width of cream leatherette pinched and buttoned into what looked like a neat row of navels. But some of the studs were now missing, leaving only lengths of thread trailing from the holes like untied umbilical cords. It looked grimy and a little sticky.

In one corner, next to the bird cage, I could see the curved handle and wired stem of a Hoover, and in the other corner stood two narrow wardrobes with a length of green checkered cloth hung between them. The cloth concealed a mirror screwed to the wall and a narrow shelf piled high with cast-off clothes, a stack of magazines that looked as if their insides had been cut up with scissors, and four or five red leatherette photo albums. There was only one other piece of furniture in the room, a small bedside table that held a green marble lampstand with a red frilly shade, a hotel ashtray filled with hairgrips, and a round-faced alarm clock that ticked tinnily. Beneath the table was an electric kettle and hotplate, both tethered to a wall plug; one plate, two cups, a biscuit tin, a transistor radio in a black leather jacket, and a single Japanese pear—perfectly round and textured, like a cooking apple without the shine.

There were three pictures tacked to the walls, unframed crayon sketches of Trafalgar Square, Piccadilly Circus and Kensington Gore. They were winter scenes, gray and slanted with charcoal rain, and they made me instantly sad. I could smell the rain on the pavements, see the lights glisten, feel the drizzle and the cold. For a long moment I remembered London.

But it was Tokyo outside, not a gray, rainy London. The neon glare over the rooftops belonged to Roppongi, not Piccadilly, and the lady who had brought me there was no brisk Cockney but a haunted-looking tubercular Japanese who talked to herself more than she talked to me, in a squeeze-box wheeze that suggested that she had to pump up her vocal cords before getting out a simple word.

More than anything else it was her age that intrigued me. She was easily twenty years my senior and I was simply curious, in a strange way attracted to her because of it. She could have been the mother of any one of the friends with whom I had spent that evening in a second-floor club where we drank beer, ate nuts and popcorn and played endless, high-scoring electronic games.

When we met, in a sloping alley behind the district known as Roppongi, my head still buzzed and popped and exploded with computer noises, and my eyes danced with mauve and green and yellow and blue blips. I was sitting on a low wall when I first saw her and I knew instinctively that she would stop when she reached me and start talking, repeating that strange, almost comforting litany of inquiry.

She wore a long ribbed cardigan that reached to her knees, corduroy jeans that seemed a little baggy at the waist, a black polo neck sweater and a single gold necklace that hung over a flat chest. Her voice was dry, a little choked and in the light from the windows above us I could see powdered wrinkles and rouged lips—the red lipstick working its way up through the creases. She was going home. Would I like to join her? It wasn't far. She would make me feel comfortable. She was a wonderful masseuse, she told me, but she didn't look strong enough to crack a finger joint.

The road she led me along had narrow pavements and at one point, when I dropped behind her to let a car pass, I noticed she wore a curved, coral-colored hearing aid behind her left ear. Farther on she stopped at a Coca-Cola machine that shone a bright red in the shadows and fed in a handful of yen. When she pressed the button there was a whirring sound not unlike the ones I had been listening to all evening and a loud clunk as the can dropped into the metal basket.

As we walked, she asked me where I came from. London, I replied. She nodded (I thought perhaps she hadn't heard and that I should repeat it louder this time), but she caught my arm on a wider stretch of pavement, drew me to her and told me that she would soon be in London. She had friends that she could stay with in Knightsbridge. She pronounced it "Nicebeerage." The word, the image of that far-off place, the fact that she should be staying there struck me as absurd, ridiculous, inconceivable in this grimy, unlit side street. How could anyone get out of this and end up in Knightsbridge, I wondered. She had almost saved enough money, she continued, but it was very expensive to fly from Tokyo to England. It was pretty expensive just taking a taxi to the airport, I thought, but said nothing. How much would I pay her, she then asked? As I walked I shrugged, lifting her arm a little as I did so. I didn't know, I replied. How much was it usually?

"I don' charge Europeans as much as Orientals," she lisped.

"So how much is that?"

"I give you a good bro job eight thousand yen—massage better so fifteen thousand yen. Okay?" It struck me that she must have got the rates in the wrong order but I agreed to her terms nevertheless, and we walked on.

Soon she pointed out a block of flats up ahead. The place where she lived. There was a short rise to the gate, no more than a few yards, but she was panting when we reached it and still breathing heavily in the lift that took us to the fifth floor. She tried to disguise her condition by asking me questions—as though being out of breath was nothing, didn't bother her, I shouldn't be worried by it. How old was I? she asked, as we walked down the corridor to her apartment. I said thirty. In between breaths she told me she was twenty-six. It was a ridiculously transparent lie, but I made no comment.

She buzzed around the confined space like a housefly fretting at a window pane. She seemed nervous—picking things off the floor, putting them down again, drawing the curtains, adjusting the lights, burrowing into one of the wardrobes. I wondered how many men she managed to lure here a night. I couldn't imagine she attracted many customers unless they were old and poor like her. I was neither frightened by her nor disgusted, simply intrigued as I have said. But concealed in that curiosity was a frisson of excitement, a decadent, debauched excitement.

She turned to me as if she had just noticed I was there and told me to take off my trousers—as unconcerned as a doctor about to examine a patient. I did as I was told, equally unconcerned, and sat on the edge of her bed in bare feet and shirt tails. I watched her rummage in her shoulder bag and draw out a nasal inhalant that she inserted into each nostril, taking a heavy snort each time. Then she sat down beside me.

"You nice gennerman," she said, and patted my leg. But when

I lifted a hand to touch her, she stood up quickly and stepped over to the wardrobe. There was a rattle of hangers and she produced a black and white ivy-patterned *yakata* that she laid at the end of the bed. When she took off her cardigan and polo neck she turned her back to me so I could see only the shadowy ridges of her spine, covering her thin breasts with an arm as she stooped down to pick up the cotton gown. As soon as the belt was tied she unzipped her trousers and stepped out of them. I was puzzled that she did not want me to see her body. Perhaps she thought it might give away her real age. I wanted to say to her don't worry, let me see—but I didn't.

She sat down beside me again, pushed me back and lifted my shirt. Like a housewife examining Tupperware she took me into her hands and tut-tutted, wheezed, mumbled, muttered to herself as if searching for some design fault. The next minute she was up and away and locked in the bathroom while I gazed up at the ceiling feeling the nylon sheets grow clammy beneath me. Suddenly, ludicrously, as I followed a crack in the plaster above me, I thought of Shakespeare saying how the beds in the East were soft. In the classroom I had imagined plump, down-filled pillows, warm, body-scented sheets and heavy, luxurious blankets. Yet here I lay, beginning a small sweat on a stretch of crumpled pink nylon. Oh, Shakespeare, if ever you had come East!

"I make you come twice," she promised when she returned from the bathroom. "First time after an hour, then massage, then you come ten minute later again." I must have looked doubtful, for she set about reassuring me: "True, I know, you listen to me, I know." Between each group of words she took deep, deep breaths like a bladder filling up with air. "The longer it take you," she wheezed, "the more spunk you have here," and she squeezed me there tightly before going down and lapping them up.

The old lady never got on the bed but knelt on the floor between my legs the whole time. Once she took my foot, slid it inside her gown and rubbed the sole against a damp corrugated breast. Occasionally, she would reach for her bag, take out the white inhalant tube and push it up a snorting nostril. Most puzzling of all, she bent under the bed and pulled out a circular hand mirror, which she gave me to hold. Taking my hands she showed me how she wanted it held, the rim resting on my belly, the glass pointed down at her. I tried to imagine what she must see in the glass, what she must think. But more, why she did it? Did it excite her? Did it help her somehow? On she snorted, her mouth full, her face glaring back at her from the beveled glass.

She pumped and she sucked and she salivated. Suckled, lipped and tongued. She held me tight between finger and thumb, bent me, twisted me as if wringing out a dish cloth. These extra displays, refinements, had begun, I noticed, with the introduction of the mirror, as if the performance were more for her own delectation than my satisfaction. She even pulled open the can of Coca-Cola, took a mighty swig, then bent down again, cheeks swollen. At first it was so cold there I thought I would shrink away, but she began sluicing the bubbling liquid around in her mouth until it warmed and tickled and exploded in tiny bursts all over me. She did this three or four times, swallowing each mouthful, until she sat back and belched loud and long—the rumble coming from deep down in her tubercular chest. Wheezing and laughing, down she went again.

According to the clock on the bedside table she came close to keeping her word. The bedsprings creaked, the cream, leatherette headboard bucked against the bathroom wall, and give or take five minutes, she did what she said she would. Each time, she disappeared into the bathroom where I could hear her gargling energetically, splattering the results into the sink. At the bottom of the bed, Misha or Mija stretched out its forepaws, pushed up its rear like a lazy dog, then settled back into its straw.

Afterward, while I dressed, the lady with no name plugged in the kettle and brought the red bound albums to the bed. When the tea was made she handed me a cup, sat beside me and opened up the albums. I remember the photo of a much younger woman standing in a garden in front of a large, Tudor-timbered house, its roof cut off by the photo's white border.

"Guir'ford," she lisped, pointing at the picture. The young woman wore tight, laced white boots that had been fashionable in the early sixties and a short fur coat from the same period. It could easily have been someone else. The photo was old. Like the Japanese pear, it had lost its smooth shine.

There was another picture too that I recall, a few pages further on. The woman in this one wore the same boots, but a different, longer coat, her hair tucked up under a black cord cap.

"Eyerif Tower," she told me, running a nail along the metal frame supports that made up the background. I wondered if the same person had taken both pictures. I asked her if it was a man, but she seemed not to hear, content just to turn the pages, to point, mutter something, delighted by this panorama of her past. What had happened on the bed behind and beneath us was a world and more away.

The second album she showed me was filled like a scrapbook with pictures of models cut from the pages of the magazines I had seen earlier. On one page she would point out the girl's eyes, on the next page her lips ("Look, look, very fine, very good"), a face here, legs there—each page, each girl, something she admired. It was all rather sad the way she gazed at these magazine models, showing them off to me as if they were pictures of herself, of friends, family, children. I felt the least I could do, as I sipped the tea, was indulge her.

The third album was more surprising still. Only one model appeared throughout, the scissored edges either cut straight or decorated with squiggles. On one page she was in underwear, in a fur coat the next, modeling jewelry, lying on a beach. It was a very familiar face. I had even met her once.

I told the woman I knew her. I told her the name. Said she was married to a famous photographer. But the old woman didn't seem to hear, or if she did, she wasn't interested. She just kept turning the pages, faster and faster, with a rapt and fevered concentration. The time, I decided, had come to leave. All at once there was a feeling of frightening unpredictability in the room.

I got up to leave, counted out the money I owed and held it out to her. She was still turning the pages, but paused when she saw the fold of notes. Almost sadly, she put the album down, buried the money beneath a pillow and stood to see me out.

"You understand I have to take money. So sorry. Very expensive fry to London. But you very genner man, very good man," she told me, wheezing as she bowed, as if the movement forced the breath out of her. "No hug hard like many men, or hurt me."

She watched me to the end of the corridor, to the lift. As I waited, I turned back to look at her still standing by her door. And twenty yards apart we bowed simultaneously.

Hairy
Metal

Takanosato, the number-one Maegashira, had cause to celebrate. He had won Jun-yusho for the second straight Basho, been
awarded Shokun-sho for the first time, received Kanto-sho for the
third time and assured himself of promotion to Sekiwake for the
Kyusho Basho.*

But his friend Yokozuna Wakanohana had the supreme sumo
title, held the Emperor's Cup in his thick paws and was ultimate
champion of the Aki Basho. The spectators in Tokyo's Kuramae
Kokugikan stadium rose as one with a roar of satisfaction and
frenzied applause. This was Waka's fourth Yusho, a worthy champion indeed, and in a month he would marry the eldest daughter of
his coach and team manager, Futagoyama Oyakata.

In the final bout he had cunningly tripped up fellow Yokozuna
Kitamouni at the precise moment Kita thought the match was his.
It had been close, the crowds silent as the two men circled each other
like massive, naked bears, casting ritual salt around the ring for the
last time. They bowed formally, squatted down and leaned forward
—hands on knees. There was a rustle of silk from the umpire, the
minutest click of his black fan and the two giants clashed together
like greased battering rams. The knotted buns on their heads wobbled with the impact. Back and forth they charged, locking shoulders, arms flailing for a grip. At one point, Wakanohana latched

*Maegashira, Sekiwake, Yokozuna: various levels in the sumo ranking system;
Basho: tournament; yusho: title; Jun-yusho: runner-up; Shokun-sho: prize for
outstanding performance; Kanto-sho: prize for fighting spirit.

both hands onto his opponent's black belt and spun him around in an attempt to throw him off balance. But Kita countered, slipping a pudgy hand between the rolls of greased flesh and Waka's own belt, and tried to lift the mammoth weight out of the ring. Whether Waka had planned for Kita's countermove would be a topic of heated discussion for days to come, for the champion was ready. As Kita tried to execute this ambitious arm throw, Waka fell short at the very edge of the ring, swung out a leg and brought off a devastating sotogake that sent a startled Kita sprawling into the clay. The men beside me shouted their approval at the screen.

The five of us sat around a low table in the industrial suburb of Kawasaki, some forty kilometers from the stadium in Tokyo. The television stood on a long dresser against the opposite wall. All of us wore ceremonial slippers, held a numbered plaque, and were waiting our turn. Tea had been served earlier in china as thin as the brew and five cups stood empty on the table. It had left a briny dryness in my mouth and the cigarette I smoked tasted foul.

I had caught a late-afternoon train from Shinbashi station near the Ginza, but not so late that the conductors with their white gloves had had to push me on—like butchers stuffing a steel sausage. From the center of Tokyo the train followed the course of the Sumidagawa river, then took the commuter route for Yokohama. On either side, the view was gray and black and unrelieved, a dusky, dusty landscape shrouded in a pall of factory smoke. It was impossible to see ships or the sea, just a black trelliswork of cranes. A wind along the Sumidagawa had channeled the fumes low over this monotonous scene and as we drew into Shinagawa every face on the platform was masked—a team of surgeons waiting for the patient to be wheeled in. The door slid open like a gaping wound, then hissed shut as cleanly and as tightly as a sutured wound.

I had this picture in my mind: The house would be low, its shingled eaves barely visible above clipped box hedges and tutored shrubs. There would be a moat of finely raked sand, like the dry garden at the Zuiko-in temple, rippled around boulders of red jasper; a stream through the gardens; a delicate stand of tatsutu maples just turning the color of the jasper; and a delicate willow-pattern bridge. I could see a small lake stocked with whiskered carp, a jigsaw of stepping stones, a banked cascade, and beneath the surface smooth round pebbles arranged in pleasing groups. Powdery Japanese pine would stand supported, like frail old men, on bamboo poles, there would be ferns, and fallen petals pinkish white from laden camellia trees.

Inside the house, there would be many waiting rooms and screened reception parlors. There would be hushed chatter and tinkling laughter, as if heard from a distance, and delicate geishas swooning and bowing, wrapped like gorgeous Christmas gifts in silk kimonos and heavy bustles. My clothes would be taken, a light *yakata* bound around me and plates of my favorite tamogoyaki served. I would be led to a room where the water bubbled from a natural spring and steam rose in perfumed waves. There they would soak me and rinse me, pat me dry with towels as thick as angora blankets. I would be anointed with slippery ointments, my hair would be combed, and then, in dizzying sequence, one after another . . .

Reality can be a startling disappointment. When I left the train at Kawasaki there was no screened house in sight, no willow-pattern bridge, no stand of maples—the dreams faded as the neon flickered into life against the darkening sky. The suburban town was flat, mechanical and ugly. Not a box hedge in sight, no trees, no tidy raked gravel crunching underfoot. The station square I found myself in also served as a bus terminal and the air was filled not with waves of perfume, but with fumes of blue exhaust. Pachinko arcades rang with the metallic chuckling and groans of one-armed bandits, cars hooted and pushed their way through the crowds, and in shop windows plastic plates of dummy sushi glistened under their coats of gelatin. With a heavy heart I stepped into a side street and wandered off into the evening gloom.

Hiroyuki sat on his bar stool like a fat frog squatting on a water lily. His hair was jet black and spiky, and on the back of his neck, beneath the stubble of his short back and sides, were large red welts with black pinhead scabs. A few angry spots clustered around the corners of his mouth. His eyes were thin and emphatically slanted as if pulled back by invisible fingers. He was the only person in the bar who spoke any English, though I had to wring each word out of him, each repeated several times before the meaning became clear.

"You're rike heary meral?"

"Sorry?"

"Heary meral?"

"Heary . . . hear . . . ?"

"HAIRY ME'AL!"

"Hairy Me'al?"

"Yes, yes . . . heary me'al. You rike?" And he started abusing an imaginary guitar.

"Aaah, heavy metal, why yes."

Much of our conversation in this bar was dependent entirely on charades, but Hiroyuki was tireless in his efforts to understand and be understood. His hands, small and pudgy with bitten, blackened nails, were at one time or another airplanes, shovels, birds, beer, whiskey, fish, knives and forks, wallets, even a motorbike—depending how the conversation was going and what particular item was under discussion. He was deferential, pleasant, polite, bowing deeply every time I topped up his glass from my bottle of Suntory special reserve whiskey. With painstaking strokes he wrote his name for me on the back of a beer mat and nodded energetically when I read the name aloud.

"Hiroyuki . . . yes . . . me."

"Hiro-yuki."

"Yessah. Hiroyuki sah."

"Hallo Hiroyuki."

"Herro Ma-rin."

"Martin."

"Maaaarin."

It was Hiroyuki whom I gently approached, after a few rounds, on the delicate subject of To Ru Ko—a bath house. And where, in Kawasaki, I could find one. During my walk through the streets I had scanned every neon sign, shop sign, road sign for characters roughly approximating the ones a friend had written down for me in Tokyo. But I could find them nowhere—nothing even coming close. And only now, in the dim light of this basement-level bar, with Hiroyuki at my side, did I at last summon the nerve to repeat the phonetic sound of these characters.

"Toe ro-ah cow," repeated Hiroyuki, bending closer to catch the words.

"Toh-Ruuu-Koh," I intoned.

"Toh-Ruuu-Koh?"

"Yes."

"Aaaaaah, toruko," he repeated, nodding fervently but then suddenly coloring with embarrassment.

I nodded too. "Is . . . toruko . . . far? Hiroyuki know one?"

He glanced sheepishly round the bar. "Toruko no far, I show."

We spoke very little as we walked, Hiroyuki always a step or two ahead, catching hold of my arm whenever we took a new direction. It was clear there was little I could do or say to restore the warmth of our earlier friendship; it was as if, by asking him to show me the way to a toruko, I had let him down somehow, for he seemed suddenly deflated, disappointed in me. I thought it unlikely he would join me in the toruko but if he did, I determined, then I would treat him.

When we reached the bath house, he sidled up to the man at the door, spoke as if making an introduction, caught and shook my hand, bowed swiftly, then disappeared into the night. There was no time even to call out after him with a word of thanks.

Fujiko was as fat as a tub. She knelt, her nose an inch from the tatami mats, at my feet. My turn had come, my numbered plaque had been taken and I had drawn Fujiko. The moment I saw her I was tempted to ask if there was another girl available but I decided against it. It was unlikely they would understand my request and if they did it was certain Fujiko would be insulted, perhaps lose face, perhaps even her job. She gathered herself up, dipping and bowing, and led me down a long passageway past a line of doors, each with a pair of slippers outside. The last door she opened and bowed me through with words of welcome: "Herro Ohio-san, Irashemase," and pointing to herself added "Fujiko."

The room was tiled and gloomy, the floor wet and sloping very slightly toward the far wall where a huge trough of steaming water overflowed its sides. Against another wall was a long couch in a style much favored by hospital accident rooms—the mattress no more than two inches thick and covered in shiny black vinyl; beside it was a hospital screen, a stool, three plastic buckets and two washing-up bowls. And very little else. The air was thick and sticky and felt like wet towels, and in the window above the bath an air-conditioning unit pumped away the steam. After more protracted bowing and mumbled greetings, she sat me down on the couch and pulled off my slippers—taking them in her arms and putting them outside the door as if to await valet service. It was hardly the most intimate of services, but somehow Fujiko managed to invest this simple task with affection and reverence. The rest of my clothes were removed in the same manner, affectionately and reverently, each item folded and laid in a neat pile on a rack beneath the couch. Then, taking me by the hand, she led me to the bath and indicated that I should step into it. The water was warm, not hot, and deep, so deep that with every breath my body seemed to rise and fall. As soon as I was settled, a folded towel tucked behind my head like a pillow, Fujiko slipped off her kimono and, naked, fetched over the stool and one of the bowls. Her skin looked bloated and podgy and damp like a body that's spent too long in water, her breasts almost indistinguishable from the rolls of fat that hung from her in rings. Her legs were short and stumpy, heavy round the ankles, and the hair between thick and black and tangled like an unruly bird's nest. While I soaked, she dipped the bowl into the bath and scooped out some water into which she grated flakes of soap from a bar the size and color of a wedge of Cheddar. As soon as she had worked this up into a lather she reached for my arm and urged me out of the bath.

The stool she sat me on was unlike any I had ever seen. Cut into the seat was a narrow groove about four inches wide and eight inches deep, which she maneuvered beneath me until I sat with my buttocks on either side, genitals hanging free. Then, kneeling in front of me, she began washing my feet, lifting each one, slipping her fingers between the toes and sliding her hands over the soles until I felt I would die from tickling. Reaching for a sponge, she then moved higher up over my legs and onto my thighs—wet, glistening, suds-covered breasts swinging at my shins. It was then I realized the significance of the gulley on the stool, for her hand and arm and soap-ridden sponge disappeared under me. Catching my eye she smiled and slid the sponge in ever more penetrating strokes between my legs until I could feel the warm lather reaching up to the small of my back. Next moment, the sponge was in the bowl and her hand —as slippery and insinuating as a greased eel—began the most intimate probing. Silently intent on her work, she no longer looked at me.

I was astounded by my response. Up until that moment, I hadn't imagined Fujiko capable of arousing me in this way. But the fact she could produce such extreme levels of pleasure made me feel far more generous toward her than I had at first. I even decided there was something not wholly unattractive in her tubbiness as her hands and fingers circled and teased.

From the waist down I was a sea of white foam. Sliding between my legs, Fujiko now began on the upper part of my body. Arms first, held in her water-crinkled hands and sponged down, then shoulders, back, chest and belly. This last I had discreetly sucked in but she indicated I should relax completely by pushing out her own belly in a grotesque imitation of pregnancy. Unwillingly at first, I followed her example, relaxing all my muscles. I felt almost as fat as Fujiko. We must have looked an extraordinary pair. Gently, with both hands, she began to push and pull at my pot like a housewife kneading dough. It was a startlingly sensuous and releasing massage that made me grow ever harder and more urgent in the gulley. When she saw this reaction she looked satisfied, as if I was behaving exactly as she expected.

The cleaning over, Fujiko sluiced the dirty water down a drain by the bath and then filled the bowl with fresh water, pouring it over me until every scrap of soap had been washed off my body. Then the hot tap was turned on and I was invited back into the bath to soak some more. As the temperature of the water increased—its surface steaming—I seemed to float like some hollow dumpling. Meanwhile, Fujiko was working up another bowl of lather, this time from a green liquid that looked suspiciously like washing-up fluid. Again I was hauled out of the bath, shown to the stool, and the whole operation was repeated—the soaping (sweeter smelling this time), the gentle massage, the probing, slippery fingers, and finally bowls of hot water cast over me until I sat on the stool dripping and bedraggled like a landed Proteus. Back in the bath again, I watched Fujiko open a cupboard and pull down a pile of towels. For the third time I was urged out of the bath and directed to the stool, the drying done just as Fujiko had washed me, but in the reverse order. A towel was wrapped round my head and as she rubbed at my scalp her blubbery breasts slapped at my back. Fresh towels were then applied to my body and I was dried softly and extremely efficiently—Fujiko lingering thoughtfully with warm-towel hands in the gulley.

The black vinyl on the couch was sticky as I lay back, a strip of towel laid modestly over my middle. Now the soaping was over, it was time for a massage. Despite my response on the stool I had no intention whatsoever of making love to Fujiko even though I had paid at the door for that service. But Fujiko had other plans. After an energetic massage that left me aching with a soft, glowing warmth, I felt my towel cover removed and more personal ministrations begun. When I started to get up and voice soft objections, she just giggled and pushed me back. Reluctantly, in that damp, gloomy room, with my eyes closed and water still splashing into the bath for the next customer, I made no further effort to stop her. At one point, as she squatted over me, I reached out blindly and my fingers encountered a shaking, indefinable mass of flesh, quivering, slightly sticky and bloated. I closed my eyes tighter and laid my arms back against my sides.

Once more I was back on the stool, for the fourth and last time, as she sponged the oil from my body. Then she dried me again with great care and helped me dress. Back in her robe, she held open the door and bowed from the waist. I hadn't noticed it before but beside the door stood a small table with a chipped china plate on it. A few silver coins lay there. While Fujiko held her low bow, I reached for my pocket, drew out a one-thousand yen note and dropped it into the dish.

"*Arigato domo, Ohio-san. Sayonara, sayonara,*" she whispered without raising her head. When I reached the end of the passageway, she was still bowing.

Wanchai
Winnie

Winnie had been gone an hour. Down the hall someone was knocking softly at the door of Mr. Lim's apartment. I knew it was his apartment because Winnie and Mr. Lim were the only ones living on the sixth floor. Winnie was 6A and Mr. Lim was 6B. The door leading to the staircase had no number. On every floor, apart from the sixth, there were four apartments, most ridiculously over-crowded. It was like living on top of a termite nest. Apartments A and C on all floors looked through a ribbing of bamboo scaffolding on to the street and were generally regarded as being rather smart. The Bs and Ds were cheaper because they were at the back of the building and had no view to speak of, only a blank wall and lines of washing: blue working overalls, flower-patterned blouses with short sleeves, listless gray sheets and the black cotton pajamas that belonged to the old ladies in 2D, 3B, 4D and 5D. Directly below was a small square of roof that covered the back of the grocer shop on the ground floor and separated our building from its neighbor. Someone had put three pallet beds on it, crammed side by side, and at any hour of the day or night there was always someone asleep down there. The beds seemed to be shared on a rota system by an unknown number of people.

I heard the door open down the hall and Mr. Lim's whispering voice, his slippered feet shuffling back to let in the curious. You had to be curious to see Mr. Lim, and Winnie was more curious than most. She called on him at least once a week, always in the after-noon. For some reason, all his clients seemed to prefer that time of day. All morning you wouldn't hear a sound from 6B, but from

93

three o'clock onward, sometimes until late at night, there would be a constant flow of callers, all sorts of people knocking at his door. But never more than two at a time and they rarely stayed longer than half an hour. You could almost tell the time by his visitors, their comings and goings, each knock striking the half.

Winnie, of course, took longer because she insisted on asking questions to clarify some point she had missed or misunderstood. Mr. Lim always answered but the interruptions seemed to annoy him, break his line of thought. For all that, I suspected the old man was really very fond of Winnie. And I am sure that Mr. Lim was the only other reason Winnie continued to live in that creaky, shaky old house. The main reason she stayed there, of course, was the fact that she was paid to.

The sun had got much lower, somewhere behind the building opposite, so her room was in shadow. Since Mr. Lim lived at the back, the sun never reached him. Winnie thought this suited his profession—dark and mysterious, though she didn't use those exact words—and I agreed.

Mr. Lim was no youngster. He was in his fifties but looked a great deal older. His yellow eyes were almost squeezed shut between swollen folds of skin. His teeth were a blackish gray at the back, and gold up front. He was not quite bald yet, but you could see every inch of scalp under his thinning hair. His hands were quite beautiful, soft to the touch with spindly, pointed fingers and brown-white palms. His nails were almost as long as Winnie's, pink with white tips and perfect white half-moons.

The night before we visited him, Winnie told me a little about him—that when they were both very young he and his brother had watched from a rooftop while their parents and two grandparents were led into a courtyard and shot by the Japanese. A month later they took his two sisters and installed them in a common soldiers' barracks, never to be seen again. And not long after that his brother had been taken for stealing. They shot him too, whispered Winnie, and though Mr. Lim had not seen it this time, he had felt it. "That when he know he is ve'y special ol' man." I tried to prod more information from her but she closed up as if the details were a sacred trust between them. "Jus' ter you, King Size, Misser Lim ve'y special ol' man."

King Size—that was what Miss Winnie called me the first time we met. She slipped into the bed and burrowed up against me, pressing my arms to my sides, her head to my chest. She held so tight it was difficult to move. Then she released her grip and gravely informed me, sliding her hand down between our bodies: "Chinee gir', small gir', Misser. You king-size man, Misser. You be care'ul wiv lirrel Chinee gir'."

It turned out I was no more king size than her, as moist and slippery as a peeled papaya, but the name stuck. When I woke that first morning in Hong Kong she was gone, leaving behind her only the dark, drying stain of her period on the sheet. When it happened she pretended it was me: "King-size man push too hard," she cried, smacking my chest and running to the bathroom. Later she told me the truth. She had not been ready, didn't think it was today—"sorry Misser King, all my fau't." And when I slept she left.

Two nights later, on the ramp leading down to the *Solar Star* ferry, crossing from Kowloon to Hong Kong, we met again, though I didn't recognize her until I heard my name.

"Hi, King Size, how are you? I am better now."

I don't think I recognized her immediately because I didn't believe it could possibly be her. Not Winnie. Not here. Not as easily, as unexpectedly, as this. Surely not? For I had pretty much given up hope of seeing her again. It was the most extraordinary coincidence. When I returned that second night to the cramped club in Tsim Sha Tsui where we first met, there was no sign of her behind any of the small, semicircular bars where the girls worked in pairs, covering themselves with long hair or lace shawls. At the bar where we had talked not twenty-four hours before, no one seemed to recognize the name. Minnie? Minnie? No, Winnie, I repeated, W-W-W-Winnie, stuttering the initial letter for emphasis. Winnie? No Winnie here, they shrugged. Then I tried to describe her—small, I said, indicating her height against my arm; shoulder-length hair "like yours" pointing to one of the girls; and big, very big I gestured, cupping my hands. The girls giggled. I should have known it would be impossible trying to describe one Chinese to another. I said what she had been wearing—tight white jeans, lemon-yellow shirt, and a shoulder bag, with . . . with, I suddenly remembered as if this would clinch it, a picture of the Golden Gate bridge with the name San Francisco stamped beneath? But no, they shook their heads, one of the girls letting her shawl slide open for me, they didn't know anyone like that. No Winnie, no bag of San Francisco. "But what about me, American boy? We have good time, you take me from here," this the one with the wayward shawl. "Much better than

Minnie, tut tut, Winnie I mean. Eight hundred Hong Kong only?"
They were almost the same words Winnie had used on me the
previous night. I finished my drink and left. "Six hundred dollars?"
I heard the girl shout after me.

I repeated my questions, my descriptions, in other bars and
clubs along the notorious neon glare of Peking, Hankow, Lock,
Nathan and Mody roads, with an equal lack of success. But the
more I described her, the more clearly I remembered her and the
more strongly fixed my intention of finding her, though these extra
details were of no use as a general description. No police force in
the world could create an identikit from the characteristics I recalled: the way she kissed me on the cheek, "a Chinee kiss" she
called it, a butterfly of a kiss—but never on the mouth; the tiny
white pattern of stretch marks around her nipples like the contour
lines of a peak on an ordinance map; the thin red worm of a scar
that ran from a point just below her navel into the smallest nest of
black curls; the bloodiness and the stickiness that had arrived without warning—in short her frailty, her vulnerability. Though there
were many prettier girls than Winnie that night, all equally available, I returned to my hotel alone.

Yet there she was, one night later, shaking my hand and coolly
ignoring her replacement, a bar girl called Betty whose offer of
company I had finally accepted, resigning at last my hopes of ever
finding Winnie. As the *Solar Star* docked and the crowd started
forward I turned to Betty, tucked some notes into her hand, and
then hurried after Winnie. Back in my room again, she quoted me
a special rate and stayed until morning, rather pleased, I think, that
I had chosen her and not Betty.

That morning, after ten minutes of exercise—naked, legs apart,
toe-touching in wide, breast-swinging sweeps, she suggested a trip
to Lantau, an hour's ferry ride from the Colony. I agreed, of course,
and at Silver Mine Bay where we landed I hired a grumpy old taxi
for the drive to Po Lin monastery. There we lit joss sticks in a huge,
ash-filled urn outside the temple, ate bowls of almond-flavored
curd for lunch and walked in the gardens.

That night was the first I spent in her Wanchai apartment. And
the last time I paid for her services.

The block she lived in was some distance down the Hennessy
Road, more Causeway Bay than Wanchai, I remarked early on. This
casual observation, however, was smartly corrected by Winnie and

followed by an indignant stream of Cantonese, a language I quickly learned to recognize as a sign of her displeasure.

There was no lift in her building, nor were there any lights or windows to illuminate the narrow staircase that led up to her apartment. Unless one of the landing doors had been left open we had to feel our way up and down in near-darkness. Winnie was, of course, more used to it than I and was always a flight ahead. I would hear her somewhere above or below me laughing in the darkness. All this was especially irritating if all I needed was a pack of cigarettes. Fortunately Winnie was always ready and willing to go down for me provided, of course, I gave her enough money to ensure there would be plenty of change—which she always kept. While I no longer paid her, in any formal sense, she must have salted away a fortune in loose change.

Sometimes she would come back from these expeditions with waffles from Yung See on the corner, fruit from Jimmy Sun on the ground floor, or a basket of steaming, delicious dim sum from the stall down the road. But whatever she bought, the extra expenditure depended entirely on what size note I had given her for my cigarettes.

Elsewhere her behavior was governed more by a genuine and surprising affection for me—more by what she imagined her *tai-tai* (literally housewife) role to be—than by purely pecuniary considerations. The first morning, for example, she came into the bathroom just as I was about to start shaving and exploded into a torrent of Cantonese. She snatched the razor from me, sat me down on the edge of the bath and, despite my objections, proceeded to wipe all the foam from my face. Methodically, as though she had worked in a barber shop all her life, she set about soaking a small hand towel in near-boiling water and lathered up a fresh supply of soap. Testing it first on herself, like a mother with milk for her baby, she wrapped the towel around my face and when it came off a few agonizing minutes later, started brushing the soap onto my chin. Then, carefully pulling back my ears, pushing up my nose, stretching my cheeks and throat, she drew the razor over my skin and shaved me clean. The one time I slipped a hand between her legs she stepped back and threatened me with the blade. As soon as she had finished, the same piping hot towel was slapped back onto my face. Every morning thereafter she bathed me, washed and then combed my hair and shaved me; I was convinced that she would have cleaned my teeth for me had it been at all possible.

The apartment was large—on the floors below two families shared the same space. There was a bathroom, with a shower attachment set so low on the wall that had it worked (it just dripped —on or off) I would've had to kneel to get under it, and the main room. Screened off in a corner by the door was the kitchen (a sink, a two-ringed stove and one cupboard) and over by the windows, squeezed into an alcove, a large double bed. In between the room was sparely furnished—a sofa, a number of straight back chairs, a large and a small table, some rugs on a cement floor (there was no air-conditioning but the floor kept the place cool), a television that Winnie only put on for Chinese feature films and, highlight of the room, a Sony tape cassette player the size of a Rolls-Royce radiator with twin speakers as large as headlights. When Winnie moved in she had painted everything yellow—her favorite color—even the bedframe and the lavatory seat, which always felt a bit tacky on hot days. Outside the windows was a very shaky-looking wrought-iron balcony that she had hung with every kind of plant grown in every kind of container—from sweet corn tins for the cacti, dewy with tiny cobwebs, to plastic washing-up bowls for the more deep-rooting specimens.

The marvelous thing about Winnie's apartment was the roof. No one else in the block used it. For a couple of hours every day, even when oyster skies drifted across from the Peak, we would lie up there with her cassette player and the shoulder bag with San Francisco on it filled with tapes. To save the batteries, Winnie insisted on trailing an extension cord all the way from her room, down the hall, up the stairs and across the roof.

When we weren't up on the roof playing tapes on the Sony or lying in bed listening to the sounds of the street below—the snarl of traffic, the blare of horns, an occasional wail of sirens, the sing-song chant of a thousand voices—there was nothing Winnie liked more than to dress up and go out.

Since there was never anything to eat in the apartment, first stop would be the nearest, and our favorite, Yum Cha, its cramped premises squeezed between an opening in the wall crammed and stacked with black car batteries and a timber merchant. The smell of sawn wood reminded me of chilled retsina—all resinous and fresh—but the scream of the saw set my teeth on edge. In the Yum Cha you could eat standing round the gurgling bain marie they kept on the pavement or, if there was room, sit inside at one of the eight Formica-topped tables. The front of the Yum Cha had a metal blind which they rolled up for business so the whole place was open onto the street. It was like eating in a garage and just as cramped. Hot dumplings were best, round as cricket balls—soft and glistening dough; then two bowls of congee—a watery soup of rice with tatters of some unidentifiable flesh; followed by a selection of dim sum—steamed envelopes of flour filled with nuggets of meat or fish.

Shopping was Winnie's favorite occupation, and the buying of small gifts for her my major occupation. Once I had eaten my fill of dumplings and dim sum, I was happy to be led around from stall to shop to store and after the first few outings began to recognize and then participate in that curious ritual which preceded any purchase. First she would stop at a counter, pick something out, inspect it minutely, then toss it back. If she tossed it back carefully, I was primed for the next stage. We would either walk around the block or go to another shop, but sooner or later find our way back to the first counter. The same item would be examined once more as if she had never seen it before. If it was a brooch she would hold it to her breast, or if something for the apartment, she would hold it out at arm's length like an artist taking perspective. But she would never ask my opinion until the third, even the fourth time we passed by. The more expensive it was, the more excessive the examination.

"Tie goo-why," I would say at last, too expensive.

"Hai, hai, tie goo-why," she would agree, laughing at my attempt at Cantonese. But she never laughed for long, and then her lips would tighten with concentration as she worked out some new strategy. The thing was, I knew she wanted whatever it was, she hoped I knew she wanted it. The question was, would I buy it for her? I knew I probably would, but she didn't. It was all a big game but we played our parts seriously—right down the line.

I would move away, she would stay where she was, holding whatever it was and chattering away to the salesgirl.

"One price only," she would shout after me, as if that was any recommendation. I would take my cue though, nod and walk back, taking the item from her and examining it as minutely, as gravely as possible. She would watch, breathless, hands clenched, waiting for some judgment. I would put it down, then pick up something else. Her round, brown face would collapse like a punctured ball, drop with dismay. "Now that would be nice . . ." I would say, holding up the nastiest thing I could find. She would pretend to give it some thought, but eventually shake her head—slowly, as if it had been difficult making up her mind.

"I think this nicer."

And then, very quickly, I'd say: "Wellwebettergetthebloody-thingthenhadn'tweoryou'llsulkallevening," or some such thing, and she'd stare at me, hooded eyes wide, as if I had gone mad, not understanding a single word. It was the best, the most exquisite moment. But as soon as I reached for my pocket her face would light up and she would clap her hands, or hop from one foot to another, like a wind-up toy.

I also learned that the item itself was of no real importance or value to Winnie. It was soon lost, or broken, or forgotten. What was important was that I buy it for her—the act of giving more signifi-cant than the gift itself—and in front of as many people as possible.

Other times she played guide and we explored the peaked, skyscrapered colony together. One afternoon we took a cable car to watch the dolphins at Ocean Park, another we spent scouring through too-expensive curio stalls along Ladder Street and Morlo Gai; we climbed the Peak, had a smart lunch at Repulse Bay that she said made her feel grand, and crossed to Kowloon for tea amongst the columns and gilt of the Peninsula Hotel.

One day she told me she was going to show me something I could never possibly have seen before and led me along the Des Voeux road, up into a tangle of streets to a snake shop which, ironically, I had visited two years before. But I said nothing, pre-tended it was all new to me. The shop was on a corner, with roller blinds like the Yum Cha, so it was open to the street on two sides —you could walk through it and cut the corner. It smelled of chemi-cals and the stale insides of preserving bottles. The floor was tiled, the squares shining like a pattern of scales, and on the walls hung fading sepia prints of the present owner's forebears. I recognized him straight away, tall for a Chinese, dressed in a long black robe with deep sleeves in which he concealed his hands.

The smaller snakes were kept in wire baskets stacked one above the other from floor to ceiling wherever there was room, a tangle of writhing, coiling bodies and flicking tongues, while the larger and presumably deadlier specimens were stored in a bank of punctured drawers lining the back walls of the shop.

Winnie was determined I try the shop's special gall-bladder wine and she approached the old man with this request. Just as he had done the last time I was in his shop, he pushed up the sleeve of his gown, sunk his arm into a barrel of white sulfur powder, then lifted a hinged lid on one of the wooden drawers. His arm disappeared into it up to the shoulder. There was a moment's groping, then quite clearly a vicious hissing, followed by energetic thumping as the snake he had selected lashed its body against the wood. Dragging its swerving body across the floor, he held it up by the tail for Winnie to inspect. For the next five minutes they argued over a price, Winnie shrinking against the glass-topped counter, eyes wide while the monster slid around the floor. If it went too far the old man jerked it back with a careless flick of his wrist.

As soon as they had agreed on a price, the old man slipped the snake's tail under one foot and the hissing, hooded head under the other; then, lifting and turning the middle section of the body belly-upward, he began to probe with grained yellow thumbnails. When he found what he was looking for, he slid one of them under the scales, pushed, the snake jerked, and a mushroom of pink flesh appeared magically between his fingers. There, like eggs in a nest, lay three black pouches the size of almonds. Pinching them out, he dropped them into a glass on the counter.

The snake was then passed to an assistant in Wellington boots and a leather apron, this last slimy and sticky with gore. As calmly as his boss, the young man stepped on the tail, stretched the reptile to its full length and with a pair of pliers knicked a collar around its neck. With his free hand, in one downward sweep, he stripped the skin from the body as cleanly as a stocking from a woman's leg. Meanwhile the old man had mashed up the bladders, splashed in what looked like white wine and handed me the brew. It was thick and cold and bitter and slid down my throat like the snake it had come from.

On the way home, with a still-squirming skinless snake smearing the inside of a polythene bag, Winnie told me I was now sure of protection from the devils of Tai Phun. I asked what these devils were.

"Oh, bad fever, fru, colds, all kind of winter sickness." I didn't mention I knew of simpler cures, and cheaper ones too. While I cleaned my teeth, Winnie passed in the snake to Mr. Lim as a gift.

Mr. Lim. Old Mr. Lim in 6B. Down the hall on the dark side. Winnie took me along with her one afternoon. Even then, teatime, it was dark in his room. He showed us in and sat us down in two chairs by the slatted window. Tea was prepared, he drew up a stool and the three of us sipped at our cups in the gloom. I remained silent while the two of them talked—the softest, most respectful, most deferential Cantonese I had yet heard; items of news given and received like the flow of responses in a church service. Looking at Mr. Lim I could not imagine him ever raising his voice. There was a tranquillity about him—an aura of peace—that soothed. He sat on his stool with his hands laid on his knees and his body swayed minutely.

"He say snake ve'y good. He share wif a friend." Mr. Lim nodded toward me and displayed his long gold teeth. I nodded back. I had the unmistakable impression there was little I could ever hope to hide from Mr. Lim—the swollen slits of his eyes deceptive.

When our tea was finished and our cups removed, he started on Winnie, pulling his stool very close to her and laying his hands on her face. His fingers pushed up under her fringe, rubbed at her brow, then ran down the sides of her face—once, twice, three times. He spoke quietly and rapidly, and Winnie nodded, repeating his words for fear of forgetting them. Then, like a blind man feeling for features, his fingertips traced her eyebrows, nose and lips, the line of her jaw. More words, more nodding. I began to feel a little embarrassed as though present at a doctor's examination. What they did together seemed so intimate, so private, that I felt I was intruding. But Winnie looked radiant, her face thrilling at every touch, her body tense with excitement. I wondered what he was telling her. Next he took her hands, spread them in his, and leaned forward to study her knuckles and fingers and nails. Pressing the fingers together he held both her hands to the window, squinting, as if trying to see the sky through them. He spoke again, again Winnie nodded. Then he turned them over and peered down into her palms. I noticed she had removed all her rings. First he rubbed at the lines with his thumbs as if to see them more clearly, then clenched her tiny fists in his, one after another, inspecting the wrinkles they made. Gently he laid them back in her lap and Winnie flushed.

Now it was my turn. His fingers followed the same route they had taken with Winnie. He spoke gently, a whisper, and when he paused Winnie translated.

"Ol' man say, we good for each other—make happy couple." Winnie beamed as she waited for his next pronouncement, and I smiled at her. "He say you serfish man. But good man asso in heart. He say not cover . . . " she pointed at my forehead—I told her the word—"foh-head wif hair. Lucky foh-head. Cover wif hair, luck go way. Change hairstyle." Mr. Lim now held my hands in his, rubbing the lines just as he had done with Winnie. "He say you make money

102

fast but lose fast. You fink wif head no' heart. Good fing. All lines in hand ve'y good sep business—better you make money away from home, in foreign place." Continuing his examination, Mr. Lim bunched my hands into fists, spread them open, held them to the light, then let them fall. As if anxious to finish before his next clients arrived, he reeled off a string of Cantonese that left Winnie stumbling after him. She was still muttering to herself as he showed us to the door.

Back in her apartment I quizzed Winnie on the rest of his prediction.

"He ter me your future. He say you have two chirren and live to old age. But warn you too."

"What warning?"

"Misser Lim say free gir' special for you—but no marry any, or much sorrow. He say you know this anyway, but good for someone ter you same thing." Then, quietly, "He say asso we have good time but soon over. Not my fau't, not you fau't. Jus' happen."

As I had thought, there was very little you could hide from Mr. Lim. I wonder now, whether he foresaw the nature of our breakup, the end of our tiny romance.

There was no doubt we were bound for the same place. Their boat had left only minutes before me, was somewhere ahead in the darkness. There were so many lights flickering across the typhoon shelter and so much other traffic it was impossible to pinpoint them precisely, but I could still make out the sound of their engine chugging away as I stepped down into the next walla-walla. The boat boy roped up the outboard and with one swift tug had the motor started. Settling onto his haunches, the tiller in his armpit, he grinned proudly.

We caught up quickly, their speed not so great as the sound of their straining outboard suggested. There were four of them aboard —the boat boy and three passengers—and they rode low and slow in the water, coils of blue exhaust swirling out of their wash. As the two hulls converged, the sea slapped and splashed and threatened to spill over their side. There was a jabber of Cantonese, and my boat boy turned the tiller, swung aside and drew easily ahead. The three passengers turned and watched our progress, two large men with a third and smaller man between them. They looked like policemen taking a criminal into protective custody. Their charge was wrapped tight in a high-collared coat that hid his face, a homburg was pulled low over his brow, and even though it was a warm night, I could see the edge of a scarf tucked round his neck.

The junk looked enormous from the walla-walla. We circled the stern and came in alongside a creaking wood pontoon that looked slick and treacherous and a steep companionway that led up to the deck. I had climbed no more than halfway when I heard the second boat approach and another stutter of Cantonese. There was laughter below and shouted instructions. When I reached the top a young boy, about fifteen, in a white jacket, caught my arm and helped me aboard.

The deck was tented like a summer marquee, a length of striped canvas stretched tight from the high slanting poop to the bows. The boy in the white jacket indicated I should follow him. A moment later he opened a flap in the canvas and showed me into a small, enclosed anteroom. On the other side of the canvas I could hear a low murmur of conversation and squeals of laughter. When I entered, an old woman in a suit of black pajamas got up from a stool and with hands that looked as if they had been pickled in vinegar reached up to take my coat. She also took the square white calling card I had paid for on the dockside before letting me through.

From where I stood, on a raised balcony running the width of the junk, it looked as though the main deck had been cut out or lowered. I was just below the striped ceiling and in shadow—a row of tasselled lanterns, strung from the tent's crossbeam, hanging on a level with my feet. On either side of the balcony a flight of stairs led down into a long, windowless cabin. Ranged along the bulkhead were six gaming tables, three to a side, each with chairs set round it and a single small lantern hanging above. Four of the tables were crowded. I could see the corner of a mah-jong wall and hear the soft thud of ivory tablets slapped down onto the baize. Winnie had told me they played for high stakes. At least I could resist that temptation.

In the center of the room was the mast housing, around which a red sofa had been constructed, and at the end of the room a small bar tended by white-jacketed waiters. Directly beneath me was a bank of cushions held in the arms of the twin staircases, a scatter of low tables littered with bottles and smoking ashtrays, and a number of long, russet-covered couches. There were maybe thirty people in the cabin, most of them girls in uniform satin cheongsams in need of a clean. The men, both European and Oriental, most of them middle-aged, sat at the gaming tables or cuddled up with their chosen companions on the bank of cushions or on the couches. A blue gloom of cigarette smoke hung at balcony level, giving the scene a kind of soft-focus smudginess.

What had seemed a very large room from the balcony turned out to be quite cramped at deck level. At the bottom of the stairs the jowl-bulging old mamasan Winnie had described to me wheeled herself over in her cane chair, welcomed me with a tip of the head and without further ceremony led me over to three girls sitting by themselves. As I squeezed onto the sofa between them, she wheeled herself round and headed back to the stairs—there to await the next and, I suspected, more important arrival.

My three companions, who had at first appeared as a row of identical Eastern faces—"slants," an American friend had once called them—quickly took on more definite and individual characteristics. Nancy, the first to introduce herself, was the tallest of the trio with a perfectly round face and china-doll cheeks rouged a bruised red. Then there was Lee, on my right, with long straight hair that reached into the creased lap of her dress, hair so heavy that the tips of her ears peeked through. But it was Connie, farthest away from me, with her legs crossed and a triangle of thigh showing through the split cheongsam, who drew my attention. Her face was long, cheeks less rounded than her friends', nose slightly more flared and flattened. Her skin was darker too, and I doubted she was Chinese at all. Malay perhaps—eyes hardly hooded, the whole brown iris visible between her lashes. I indicated to Lee that she should make room for Connie and invited her to sit beside me. I saw no point wasting either time or money. Lee didn't bother sitting down again but with a sweep of her hair wandered over to the tables. A few minutes later Nancy, equally unconcerned, joined her.

I had just ordered two beers when I felt a stir pass through the room. Though there was no obvious lessening of conversation, everyone's attention seemed suddenly focused on the balcony where three pairs of shoes had appeared. At the foot of the stairs, the mamasan raised her hands in welcome and for a moment looked as if she might roll backward on the sloping deck. While Connie slung herself round my shoulders, whispering and nibbling at an ear, I watched the shoes make for the stairs. As they came down into the light I could see the two younger men were now carrying their companion. How they had managed the companionway I could not imagine. The old man was seated on their hands and his arms were around their necks. He looked for all the world as if he had just ridden the winner at the Happy Valley races. He was quite bald without the homburg and his head was as smooth and shiny as a berry about to burst. His eyes glittered with excitement and his face was split by the widest grin I had ever seen. When, at last, they reached the deck, the two men lowered him onto tottering feet and retreated up the stairs. For a moment he stood before his hostess nodding at her words of welcome and beaming around the room, then a waiter was beckoned over, a few more words exchanged, and he was guided gently across the room. At one of the gaming tables I saw him pause and whisper to one of the girls. As I watched, she unbuttoned her collar and the old man pushed his hand down the front of her cheongsam. His grin widened and hardened as he fondled her but I could see the girl wince as if in pain. Then he was on his way again, on the arm of the waiter, making for a door beside the bar. As soon as he had gone the room seemed to reassert itself, conversation humming up a gear.

My presence that night on the junk had been nothing more than a retaliatory gesture, an act of uncharitable reprisal if you like. For the third night in a row the other man in Winnie's life had phoned, the benefactor who had set her up in her Wanchai nest. And for the third evening running I was bundled out of the apartment. First I was only mildly annoyed, then angry, jealous, and finally, worst of all, resentful. Cruelly, I waited until the very last moment before leaving, sending Winnie into a panic of apprehension at the thought of her two lovers meeting—one her financial mainstay, the other an itinerant and unreliable companion. As on the other occasions he visited, my case was pushed away beneath the bed and Winnie paced the flat picking up and hiding anything belonging to me. I know now how she must have hated me watching these preparations.

"Time to go, prease," she said, plumping up the cushions around me. And then, when I made no move to go, breaking into Cantonese: *'Jaaw hoy, fie dee*—go away, hurry. Not long, King Size; two, free hour and you come back. Jus' look for blin'." This was our prearranged signal: when the coast was clear Winnie would wind up the blinds and I, usually watching from across the street, would go on up.

But that night was different. If Winnie could do it—I reasoned unreasonably—then so could I. And instead of buying a ticket for the cinema in the next street, I made for Aberdeen.

Winnie had told me about the junk the day we spent at Po Lin, a part of the life story she related as we walked through the monastery gardens. How she had worked there for a year, been one of the girls; how she always wore a yellow cheongsam, making it sound much grander than it turned out to be. It was there that she had met the man who, for three nights running, had taken my place in her bed. I didn't know whether he was old or young—only that he was European, that he must have been quite rich to support Winnie, even in her tiny apartment, and that he wore Paco Rabanne; I could always smell it afterward on the pillows, and distantly around the flat. Apparently he had been a regular customer at the junk I was then bound for, was a favorite with the mamasan, and always chose Winnie. After only a matter of months an agreement was reached with the mamasan (there was always an eager supply of girls from among the boat people to take her place) and Winnie was installed in the apartment, readily accepting his conditions that she should entertain no one but him. To ensure her fidelity she was provided with a small allowance. It was the thought of losing this independence and security that threw Winnie into a panic when I stayed too long.

But later, as Connie and I lay on our narrow bed, listening to the timbers creak and feeling the hull rise and shift on a new tide, I was filled with remorse, acknowledged my selfishness. How right Mr. Lim had been. I could think only of Winnie and the months she had spent there—perhaps even in that very bunk. How damp and dismal and despairing it must have been. And how glad, grateful, she must have been when she was able to leave.

When the knock on the door came I was glad. I slipped Connie some dollars, dressed and found my boatman.

It was dawn by the time I found my way back. Winnie was asleep so I undressed quietly and ran the bath. She was still asleep when I finished. I leaned over the bed and touched a brown shoulder but she didn't move, so I went down alone for some breakfast at our Yum Cha. Time enough later for explanations.

From my table I glanced up at Winnie's window. She would make a big fuss of course, screech away half the morning in Cantonese, but I could handle that. When she calmed down, I decided, I would take her out to lunch and order her favorite roast pigeon. That was sure to win her over.

But when I returned to the apartment, there was no sign of her. The bedclothes had been pulled back, were still warm—but no

Winnie. She must have slipped out without my seeing her. I sat down, picked up a book and began reading. I didn't think she would be away too long, but an hour later she still hadn't appeared. I went to the roof to see if she was there; it was deserted. Then down to the street, fumbling down the darkened stairwell. No, Jimmy Sun hadn't seen her. Nor Yung See, the waffle man on the corner. They both shook their heads and looked at me blankly. As I passed Mr. Lim's door on the way back, I listened for a moment but there was no sound from inside.

Lunchtime came and went and with it all hopes of a reconciliation over roast pigeon. Which made me a little cross. I also liked pigeon; now I would have to wait until dinner. I looked out of the window, wandered around the room, picked up my book again. And began to grow impatient. I was looking forward to telling her about dinner, even if I did have to put up with a stream of abuse first. She was always appreciative.

At three o'clock the lock turned and she breezed in. She didn't look at me or say a word (par for the course), just dropped her bag in the chair and busied herself with bedmaking. The great battle was about to begin. Any minute now the shrieks of Cantonese, the ranting and the raving, the slamming and the banging and the stomping about, the clenched fists, the threats and the accusations, the ridiculous English she spoke when she lost her temper and couldn't be bothered to use the right words or put them in the right order. Then my explanations, apologies, excuses, whatever story was needed or expected. And when I had said all that—then out with the big guns: roast pigeon for dinner.

But it didn't go like that at all. She kept silent far too long and I recognized something cold and detached about the way she shook the pillows into shape, straightened the sheets and cover. She disappeared into the bathroom and came out brushing her hair.

"You come back?"

"Of course—look Winnie, I am sorry about last night . . ." I began.

"Good fing too, but no matter." I felt relief. But then she pulled out my case from under the bed. "You put clothes in now, and go, right?" Relief was replaced by a stirring of panic.

"Well, hang on. I thought we might have dinner, you know, pigeon. Whatever you like."

"No hang on. No hungry. Have anyhow appointment." She picked up her bag and walked to the door.

"Winnie?" I got up and followed her. "Winnie . . . ?"

"No. No more. Time to go. All finish up."

"Look, Jesus, it was only . . . "

"Don' care. Never want see you 'gain. You leave time I get back. I have man wif me. You go now, see?" And with those last words she closed the door behind her. I could hear her heels clacking determinedly down the corridor, and then, fading, down the stairs.

Mr. Lim was busy as usual. I took out and lit my last cigarette. My bag was already packed, lying on the bed. By the time Winnie got back I would be long gone.

A Night
at the "Filly"

The German party, some forty in all, arrived at Don Muang airport an hour before me, flushed from in-flight drinks and startled by the heat. A coach with mud-spattered body work and rain-dusty windows but equipped with an air-conditioning system that worked met them outside Customs and Immigration and desposited them half an hour later in an eager, brow-mopping bunch at the front door of the Philadelphia Hotel, class D, in central Bangkok.

Although it was late, shortly after ten, the temperature had dropped only one or two points below the midday reading and a damp, dismal heat rose in waves from a rain-soaked earth. The week before a massive storm front had gathered over neighboring Cambodia, swept in across Thailand's eastern provinces and caused substantial flooding in the low-lying central plains north of the city, and subsequently in the city itself. The klongs, or canals, lacing the city had swollen at an alarming rate, swirling thick and brown around the stilted shacks that lined their edges while the river, Chao Phya, mother of all waters, broke her banks at successive high tides and inundated the lower districts around Kiak Kai, Tha Charng, Phrasumaine and Banglampoo. I had learned all this from daily reports in the *Hong Kong Times* while Winnie watered her plants or went out shopping. There were pictures, too, of half-submerged cars and sandbagged doorways and laughing, splashing children. I hadn't imagined I would be there so soon. Now, a week later, while the storm raged and squalled its way farther south over the Gulf of Thailand, the flood water was receding, the city drying out. The whole place smelled of wet blotting paper, but at least there was not the usual dust to grit the scalp, the eyes, the ears, the nostrils. But the Germans, sweating generously into their Lacoste sport shirts, were not to know that. By the time I reached the hotel, porters were unloading the last of the baggage, most rooms had been allocated and only a few of the party remained in reception waiting for keys —the rest hurrying away, not to sleep but to shower and change their clothes.

Stranded on a block of land between the Sukhumvit and Petchburi roads and approached down a lane lined with steep grass verges and leaning telegraph poles, the Philadelphia, its name buzzing with blue neon, looked sufficiently solid and impressive beside its ramshackle neighbors to make one wonder at its low classification—a modern, concrete structure rising several floors above a taxi-jammed forecourt and a semicircular driveway that led up to its glass-fronted first-floor entrance. Indeed, its very blandness was reassuring, even misleading. Inside, the ground plan was predictable and unexceptional if a little shabby, identical in layout and character to a thousand other "package" hotels around the world; a clone created with a drop of Hilton, a smear of Marriott and a sprinkling of Holiday Inn. There was a carpeted foyer, a reception desk with the usual pen sets and key rack, and a cashier counter with a grille front, the day's exchange rates posted up against a line of flags. There was also a tourist desk where guests could book day trips to the ancient Thai capital of Aydhya, or arrange longer expeditions to Chiangmai in the north or to Pattaya and Phuket in the south. Faded color photographs illustrated their relative merits. Beside the name Phuket someone had added in felt tip capitals "FUCK IT IN . . ." as an alternative attraction, and no one had seen fit to remove it.

On one side of the reception area, a line of shops selling postcards, souvenirs and bolts of Thai silk led to a dining room only thinly concealed behind a screen of latticed wood, and on the other side were two flights of stairs, the first leading to a barber shop and the lifts, the other down to a large shopping mall, the hotel's nightclub and bar. More than the smoke-dulled mirrors, the worn carpets, the sticky, unpolished woodwork and the tourist graffiti, it was these last two facilities, the nightclub and bar, that were responsible for the Philadelphia's present rating from the National Tourist Board and its past reputation among G.I.s during the Vietnam War. Whether or not the hotel had been directly funded or its construction subsidized by the American government for the use of soldiers on R & R, the "Filly," as it became known, survived the slump after their withdrawal by redirecting its marketing energies into certain other, similar branches of the "package" industry.

In no way could the Philadelphia be regarded as a family hotel. In the German party that had just arrived, for instance, there were no wives, girlfriends, sisters, children or mothers; just forty or so slightly drunk men brought together from half a dozen towns and cities in West Germany. Soldiers from the war front had been replaced by businessmen from the domestic front, army fatigues by lightweight suits and Lacoste sport shirts, Frankfurt am Main rather than Saigon duly noted on immigration forms. In short, the Philadelphia had found another way to keep its beds filled.

Some of the Germans were married, most of them probably single, ranging in age from mid-twenties to mid-fifties. Few, if any, would bother with trips to Ayudhya, let alone forsake the capital altogether for a weekend in Chiangmai or the south. It was more than probable that some of the party would never set foot outside the hotel. The younger ones among them, tall and uniformly flaxen-haired with thin, spiky mustaches that made their lips look blood red, would, finances permitting and with typical Teutonic thoroughness, sleep with three or four Thai girls a day for the next six days, average perhaps the same number of "body massages" in any one of the several downtown parlors, and return home to young wives or girlfriends either diseased or very fortunate. The older and more circumspect—the stolid, sausage-plump family men—would run a close second, taking time out to visit one or two of Bangkok's temples just to have something to talk about when they returned. Wives and girlfriends, friends and neighbors, had been told this was a business trip. Some of the men even took briefcases with them to supplement the deceit. The truth was they had all come to Thailand for one specific purpose and, as with the G.I.s, the "Filly" took pains to provide the relevant facility.

Though it was by no means the general rule, newcomers started with a drink in the bar, found themselves the first available partner, moved on for a dance in the adjoining nightclub, then took the girl to their room. The older the man the more he paid, the older the girl the less he paid. By the second or third day few bothered with the stopover in the nightclub. They simply made their selection in the bar and headed for their rooms. It was little more than acclimatization —sexual rather than climatic.

By the time I reached the bar, the Germans had already gathered in force like a raiding party from the north, clutching bottles of local Singha beer in one hand and a girl in the other. Even with forty-odd Germans, a handful of fat-lipped Arabs, burly English engineers with florid faces and Popeye forearms, and delicately dressed French businessmen, Thai girls were in the majority, forming, as far as I could see, two distinct groups. The older, tougher and more experienced lolled three deep at the bar and accosted, verbally and physically, any man who passed by or tried to squeeze in for a drink. Almost without exception they were bulgingly plump and soiled-looking, their clothes creased and stained, their manner loud and coarse. One, for instance, sitting at the end of the bar, kept lifting her dress to scratch a purple-pantied crotch. If she caught any of the men looking her way while she did this, she pushed her hips forward and rocked to and fro on the stool, spreading her plump brown thighs even wider and pointing between them with a luscious red-lipped leer. Their looks long gone, they relied heavily on making the first move before the man had time to look around and find something better. The second group, mostly younger girls, kept their distance, preferring the shadows and the tables around the walls. Some of the braver ones might approach as close as the jukebox but no further. It appeared some strange pecking order had been established whereby older hands got first crack at the whip, leaving the younger ones to pick at the scraps they left behind.

It was now close to midnight and reasonable enough to assume that most of these older girls would have entertained at least one hotel guest if not more, which to some extent lessened my immediate enthusiasm. Not so for the Germans who, fresh from a shower with damp licks of hair falling across their brows and rapidly dampening shirts, were in no mood to consider what the girls were like, what they had been doing half an hour earlier or indeed with whom. It was enough that first night, after a long flight, that here were girls readily available—as, no doubt, the brochures had promised. And Oriental to boot. It was like a scene from *Attila the Hun.*

One happy result of their haste—worried lest jetlag deplete their strength and initiative—was that the more attractive girls were left behind, concealed as they had been in the shadowy reaches of the room. Strongly discouraged from competing with their seniors and less inclined to join the general mayhem of prying limbs and sweating bodies at the bar, they were just as eager to find a *farang* and earn themselves some *baht.* Soon they began drifting out of the corners, making brief sorties toward the few groups of men left behind after the massed German evacuation. Few made direct approaches, most of them content with covert signalings of their intent: catching an eye, smiling their willingness and availability, dancing provocatively by the jukebox or indicating with a hand on an empty glass their desire to have some farang join them. It was in these more civilized moments that I took up my bottle of Singha and joined three girls sitting alone by the jukebox.

Even in the near darkness surrounding their table it was clear the three of them were little more than schoolgirls—younger sisters of the old pros at the bar—their broad, flat features coated with layers of cheap supermarket cosmetics. Whenever the crowd at the jukebox parted, these masks glowed sickly in the green and blue and yellow lights shining from its panels. They would, I decided, have been far prettier with their faces scrubbed clean and their heavy black eyebrows plucked into thinner, subtler arches. They looked more like dolls than girls, with stiff, curling lashes and uniform caps of shiny, crow-black hair. Pretend faces, pretend behavior. But once I had squeezed between them like a latecomer at the theater, they became as familiar as "spread-legs" and her crew, wasting little time in making clear their intentions. Plump arms slipped around me, hands reached for my legs and warm thighs pressed against mine.

Mena and Vena, the two girls either side of me, were sisters, and Doi, who had taken the chair across from me was their friend. In return for this information the three of them questioned me closely and rapidly as to my name, nationality, age, marital status and duration of stay, each question springing from the last as if they were reading them from a census form. Once these details had been established they seemed at a loss, looking to each other for the next question.

"Sprechen Sie Deutsch?" asked Vena eventually. I shook my head. A long silence followed during which they watched me finish my beer, broken only by tiny explosions of giggles whenever their hands touched under the table or behind my back. Too far away for any close work but determined not to miss her chance, Doi laced her feet around mine; I could feel her ankle rubbing disjointedly against mine.

The notion to take the three of them came from nowhere. It certainly hadn't been my intention when I joined them, but this idea lodged itself in my head, secreted itself in my imagination, as neatly and as finally as the last piece in a jigsaw. Judging by the going rate the last time I had been in Bangkok, money would not be a problem, for it was unlikely that "short-time" with Mena, Vena and Doi

114

would cost any more than "short-time" with one European girl—and by the looks of the Philadelphia bar, a good deal less. The more I thought about it the more intriguing the idea became; it was something I had never done before and unless I paid for it, I reasoned, the chances were I never would.

I turned to Mena first. As I whispered into her cap of black hair her free hand slid round my neck and drew me so close I could feel the ribs of her ear against the tip of my nose. When I finished she moved back and held up five ringed fingers.

"Wa nower," she said. Five hundred baht, about twenty-five dollars, for an hour.

Vena, on my other side, squeezed my leg as I asked her how much, then looked across at Mena. "Same," she replied.

Doi was next. How much "short-time"? I asked her. Unsure, she looked from one sister to the other. All three seemed equally perplexed. "Same also," said Doi finally.

When I got to my feet, the three stayed where they were, looking up at me with apprehensive smiles, waiting for me to choose the one I wanted. Doi smiled bravely and a gold tooth I hadn't noticed earlier glimmered in the light from the jukebox. I pointed to each of them in turn. "Okay, let's go."

"Alles?" asked Mena. Obviously Germans were a regular feature of the Philadelphia. Perhaps there was another hotel down the street where the girls spoke French or Spanish or Italian. In ten years Bangkok had become that kind of city and I felt sure the Philadelphia was only one of a kind.

"Alles," I repeated. The three of them bent their heads together and whispered around me. Then Mena, presumably the eldest sister and the one in charge, held up two fingers. Her nail varnish was chipped and thin. Two thousand baht. Another five hundred added to the combined single rate. So what, I thought. About a hundred dollars. Forty-odd pounds—the price of a business lunch in a good London restaurant, of a vacuum cleaner in a discount house.

Outside the bar I waited while they collected their papers. A security guard with slicked-down hair that showed the comb-marks shuffled through a shoe box on his desk looking for their names, then matched their faces to the photos before handing them over. It was, I thought to myself, a little like taking out library books.

Upstairs a second guard, sitting at a deal desk by the lifts, took these same cards back and slotted them into an identical box. Judging by the number of cards already there, sloping forward like a couple of packs in a Las Vegas blackjack shoe, there must have been at least fifty girls at work above us, and perhaps the same again in the bar we had just left waiting for the opportunity. It struck me quite suddenly that I had never before seen so many girls at work in one place at one time. Before letting us go, the guard opened a fat ledger and taking up a pen asked for my room number. As he noted it down at the end of a long column of other numbers I wondered whether, in addition to the girls' rate, the management had it in mind to bill me for multiple occupancy. As it turned out they didn't, but I never discovered for what other reason my room number was recorded. I can only presume it was in case of a fire, as a means of estimating the death toll in a hotel where the number of residents fluctuated beyond calculation. I could see them poring over the ledger as the remains of the Philadelphia smoldered like a damped-down bonfire: O'Brien, room 517, count him as four!

When the lift doors opened we packed ourselves in with an Arab and two other girls. The Arab wore a cream djellabah that still bore the creases of packing and a cream keffiyeh held in place with two braided red bands. The outfit made him look fatter and darker than he was. We were both considerably taller than the girls and faced each other over their heads. As the lift creaked upward his eyes fixed on mine with a hard, glittering look, and I had the distinct impression he was displeased. I couldn't make up my mind, though, if it was because we had squeezed into his lift instead of waiting for another or because I had one more girl than he. They got out on the third floor, after much maneuvering, and as the lift doors closed I watched his pudgy hands with their pudgy gold rings steer his companions down the corridor.

It was the girls' perfume, but more especially their mixture, that made me recognize the smell in my room. Earlier, as I unpacked, I had been unable to place it satisfactorily, convinced there was something more to it than the kitchen smells that filtered up the airless lightwell outside my window, the damp aroma that newly glued wallpaper gives off and the faint traces of sewage brought alive by the recent flooding. But as I followed the girls into my room and closed the door, it was suddenly stronger, more identifiable, more human—a crushed, stale, old, forgotten mixture like the dead scent that comes when you lift the lid of a clothes basket, scent that has long lost its sweetness but still retains its memories. It was as if everyone who had ever used this room had left something of themselves in the air—their smell, their sweat, the accumulated staleness of their breath; just as the smell of a woman remains on the fingers as an intriguing reminder long after she has gone. The room seemed to have absorbed it all like a gauze dressing over an open wound. So tangible was the presence I was surprised not to be able to hear dim echoes of some past conversation.

Mena took the money, four five-hundred-baht notes (I wondered how it would be split among the three of them), the bath was run and the two single beds pushed together. I thought it odd that the management, considering its major trade, had not seen fit to install double beds. But then my room was hardly in the luxury suite bracket. Despite the air-conditioner thumping away beneath the window the room was hot and damp and the drapes looked shrunken and listless. A strip of wallpaper had started to peel away in a wilting triangle above the beds; on the ceiling, and in a pool of light thrown up by the bedside lamp, were a number of circular, gray-edged stains interlocking like a rather tawdry Olympic Games symbol. It seemed the same dampness was soaking through from the room above.

In the bathroom the girls huddled around the mirror wiping away great smears of lipstick with tissues and dismantling their eyelashes. It was like sharing a dressing room with three of the chorus line. Back in the bedroom clothes were unzipped, unbuttoned, unstrapped and dropped to the floor with little ceremony, or flung onto the bed or onto the single chair the room possessed; rings, bracelets, necklaces, chains and earrings unfastened and piled into ashtrays—everything so fast, so muddled, carried on at the same pace as their chatter, that there was little opportunity to enjoy the spectacle of three girls undressing in my bedroom. I might have found it more arousing had I been outside the room peering in through the keyhole. As it was, I was too close, too much in the middle of things to take particular notice of, savor, the flashes of skin and rapid-movement body images in the room's low-wattage light: a brown leg appearing from the top of a pair of jeans, a squeeze of flesh on the hips, a mole on an upper arm, the slope of a breast, shoulder blades flexing under the skin, a cleavage of buttocks above a blue panty line, a brush of hair in the armpits and in the shadows of a firm belly, the knobbly ridge of a spine; everywhere elbows, knees, tugging limbs and finally—mouths full of grips as they pinned up their hair for the bath—jiggling breasts suspended between raised arms. There were so many details it was impossible to create a sequence, construct a single, seductive picture; a jigsaw of images impossible to fit together into a fantasy. Though it was no one's fault, I felt a little cheated. I was no part of their actions even when I stood beside them undressing myself. Had I not followed them into the bathroom they might well have left me sitting on the edge of the bed, naked and alone.

The bath water was rusty-looking, not even hot (the Germans had probably used it all up) and the soap gritty, but for the first time since they had come into my room I became the center of their attention. Their hair pinned up, their lips brown and thick, their eyes smaller and clearer without the heavy fringe of lashes, the three of them knelt outside the tub, shoulder to shoulder, breasts resting on the brim, and bathed me thoroughly if a little roughly. They reminded me of peasant women kneeling at the edge of a river to do the week's washing, though judging by their cackles and chatter, they found me a little more interesting than a pile of sodden laundry. It was Vena who started the splashing and soon the three of them were dripping and shrieking. One by one they crowded into the bath with me, sitting, standing, kneeling around me. When I started soaping them, they shrieked even louder, pushing my hands away—ineffectually, like children being tickled. I was certain that any moment there would be a hammering on the door and my companions bundled out. But no sound came.

The towels supplied were hardly larger than flannels (Doi, last out of the bath, had to make do with lengths of lavatory paper which she dumped into the bowl when she had finished with them) and were soon wringing wet. But it wouldn't have mattered if they had been larger or thicker for the heat was so oppressive that no sooner had the bath water been wiped away than it was replaced almost immediately by trickling beads of sweat. I thought this rather convenient, for making love after a bath can be an uncomfortable business, the skin tight and tacky and pinching. The girls, however, had come prepared—sweat or no sweat—and as we lay back on the bed Mena passed around a giant economy jar of Brylcreem, cooling dollops of which they smeared onto themselves and then me, like mechanics greasing the moving parts of an engine. I wondered if they understood the words on the label (probably not) and remembered the story I had heard about the Brylcreem rep who, investigating the reason why his product sold so consistently well in some West African state, discovered the natives were using it as cooking oil. There and then, as the girls set to work, I began composing an appreciative letter to the manufacturers.

118

I was glad the girls only stayed "short-time." For one thing it was too hot in the room, let alone in the bed, for the four of us. And while I had enjoyed their bodies around me and on me—little Doi hovering and plunging, Mena pumping breathlessly away like the air-conditioning and Vena hunched over me like a jockey racing for the post (she was first and I was second)—I felt little for the girls themselves. Once there was no further use for them I was relieved to see them start searching for their clothes without my having to say anything, dressing silently in the gloom, then closing the door behind them. Perhaps if they had spoken better English . . . but as it was there was nothing to hold us. I went to sleep thinking regretfully of Winnie, missing her, but not actually wanting her.

I was even happier the following morning when I went down for breakfast. The dining room was as silent as a funeral parlor, spectacularly silent, heightened and given substance by the isolated sounds of knives scraping butter onto toast, spoons stirring coffee, someone turning the pages of the Bangkok *Post*. For the men who had kept their girls all night, Germans for the most part, now sat stunned and speechless looking across at the plain, unmade-up faces of the girls they had found so irresistible a few hours earlier but were now so desperate to be rid of. As yet, they had neither the nerve nor the knowledge to simply dismiss them, while the girls, not slow to recognize their advantage, were milking them for all they were worth, would continue to do so all day given the chance. By the end of the week, I thought complacently, these new arrivals would grow harder, less sensitive. My friend the Arab, a lightweight replacing the djellabah, was the only other man who sat alone. Over the strained silence we nodded a smug, satisfied "good morning" to each other.

I stayed only the one night at the Philadelphia, which proved to be no great disappointment, leaving in my room for the next occupant a sweet, oily smell of Brylcreem, a choked lavatory and, on the shelf above the washbasin, a tangle of stiff black eyelashes that resembled most precisely a half dozen mating centipedes *in flagrante*.

"Downtown, Upmarket"

Pimsiri liked to say she worked "downtown, upmarket." It sounded as if it might have been taken from the establishment's publicity blurb, had Le Palais been so indiscreet as to publicize its activities, or something a customer might have said to her. But wherever she had heard it, she repeated it with a sense of pride, as well as pleasure, at its patness. Not surprising, then, that she looked horror-stricken when she learned I was staying at the Philadelphia. Unlike other professional classes, prostitutes rarely waste an opportunity when it comes to putting down the competition and Pimsiri was as energetic in her attack on the "Filly" as she was with her "body massage." It was a bad, bad place she panted in my ear, her breasts slapping across my shoulders; with very bad "euggggghh" girls she said, her spine sliding along mine; I should find somewhere else to stay, she advised me as the bone of her crotch rubbed over my buttocks like a scouring pad. In between grunts I agreed with everything she said.

"You sleep fucky-fuck with 'Filly' girls?" she inquired, slithering up and down the backs of my thighs like a lathered eel.

"Of course not," I lied into my elbows.

"Huh . . . some chance," she replied, slapping my backside with a soapy hand—making it plain that she knew better and that it was time for me to turn over.

"Downtown, upmarket," was an apt description of Le Palais. "Downtown" indicated an all-important few blocks from the twin red-light strips of Patpong One and Patpong Two, parallel lanes linking the Surawong and Silom roads; a five-minute walk from the muddy but graceful expanse of Lumpini Park; and a fifteen-minute cab ride from the Philadelphia. As for upmarket, Pimsiri meant four things: at Le Palais the girls were prettier and cleaner; the clientele smarter, richer, more respectable; the surroundings safer and more comfortable; and the charges, not surprisingly, higher than the girlie bars and massage parlors farther down the street. Unlike the Philadelphia, for instance, Le Palais served its Singhas in glasses.

Le Palais, a tall, shuttered building wedged anonymously between a Thai silk emporium and an obscure government office, had been a favorite of mine since my first visit to the city. I even carried, and still carry now, a special card presented to me by the management entitling me to a 50 percent discount on anything ordered in the bar or restaurant, but more importantly on any girl I happened to select. All I have to do is show the card when the order is made. What it really means is, I don't pay tourist rates, just the regular Thai price.

The most extraordinary feature of Le Palais is an escalator between the ground floor and the first-floor reception area. Admittedly it doesn't always work but its installation indicates the kind of place Le Palais is—a symbol, if you like, of being a "downtown, upmarket" establishment. There is something respectable, accepted, permanent about a property that has an escalator. It always makes me feel as though I am visiting a department store and not a bordello. Strengthening this impression, the management has placed a shop-window mannequin just inside the door with a bonnet of black hair, a high-collared silk jacket, and a banded, wrap-around silk *paisin.* Her neck and arms are hung with floral tributes and her plaster hands have been brought together, palm to lifeless palm, in the traditional welcoming *wai.* As she is a symbol of the spirit of the house, it is customary for visitors, even though she is only a dummy, to return the greeting as they step onto the moving, sometimes stationary, stairway—hands pressed together, head slightly bowed.

Le Palais opens shortly before lunch and although there is a bar and restaurant, few men come there just to eat or drink. The main attraction is the fifty or so girls who sit in rows behind a screen of purple-tinted glass that stretches the length of one wall. They all wear regulation cotton or nylon evening gowns, and a numbered badge around their wrists like contestants in a beauty pageant. Some chat among themselves; others, squinting into compacts, repair their makeup.

The customer side of this glass screen is presided over by Samlor the manager and Iris his assistant, a rather plump Chinese matron who wears her cheongsams too tight. Working their way along the length of glass, they chivvy window shoppers with a beam and a chuckle and explain to prospective customers with an air of friendly confiding that the girls on the left with the red wrist badges cost three hundred baht-"sah" for an hour's straightforward hand massage, while the girls sitting on the right with the blue discs cost nine hundred baht-"sah" and specialize in "body massage." "Yes-sah," Samlor will say, "nine hundred baht-sah. But very good-sah. Stir circulation-sah."

The expression "body massage" is misleading only once: for three hundred baht the girls use only their hands, for nine hundred they use their bodies. For the girls it's a vigorous, muscle-aching hour—one long, sliding press-up performed over the customer's naked, lathered body. For the man it's the most exquisite pleasure. They say it's a Thai specialty and to support the notion the girls at Le Palais are expert.

Once a customer has decided which of the two services he requires—or, more accurately, which of the two he can afford—and has chosen a girl, he gives her number to either Samlor or Iris who then repeats it into the microphone each of them carries like a badge of office. Both these microphones are connected to a speaker on the other side of the glass, and when a number is called the girl who wears it gets up, goes to a side door and appears a few moments later to take the customer upstairs. On a busy day it's like a bingo session at Le Palais as Samlor and Iris call out the numbers.

I was neither surprised nor offended when Samlor failed to recognize me, but when I produced my card he beamed, shook my hand and patted me on the back like an old chum. It was gratifying to learn I was still entitled to my discount. Leading me to the glass, he waves his hand at the girls. Which one, he asked, would I like? Now the most demanding task at Le Palais is actually selecting the girl you want. There are so many to choose from, so many variables to consider. Just when you think you've made up your mind, you'll spot another one with prettier eyes, a more luscious mouth, more slender figure, or whatever it is you're after. Knowing the problem I left it to Samlor to make my selection for me with the simple proviso, "Body massage girl, Samlor, big titties and speakee English, okay?" As I followed him to the glass it struck me how much easier it was to say these things to someone who didn't understand the language so well, to someone who knew me in the context of Le Palais. I also noticed how pleased he looked. It was unlikely, I supposed, that many of his customers let him influence their decisions with nine hundred baht at stake. But at four hundred and fifty baht I could afford a gamble.

Drawing me to the glass and covering the head of the microphone he mentioned a number and pointed the girl out. She sat in the front row not ten feet away, staring blankly up at us through the one-way glass like a suspect in an identity parade. She was well built with a low scooping front to her gown and a massive, bulging cleavage—but she looked bored and a little sullen and, suspecting her performance might match her looks, I shook my head. The next girl he picked out for me, also in the front row, was far more attractive. A moment's hesitation gave Samlor an opening for his sales pitch: "Big girl-sah. Strong too, give you lot fun for sure-sah." But we moved on.

Pimsiri was the third girl he pointed out, not in the front row this time but sitting well back with her arms clasped around her legs and her chin on her knees. She wore a pink gown with red-sequin bodice and shoulder straps, her hair was loose and long and her skin a deep nutty brown. The single most startling thing about her was that she wore almost no makeup: her face was broad and flat with no cosmetic shading to soften its lines, her eyes as heavily lidded as a Buddha's, with no false lashes and only a smudge of mascara, and her nostrils like deep, circular holes in the center of her face, the bridge of her nose having sunk between her cheeks without trace. It was a strong tribal face with hard, stretched features that made no concessions to western taste, that challenged selection rather than inviting it. It was as if Samlor had brought her in that morning from some distant hill settlement in the north and had only time to squeeze her into a gown and give her a number. I watched her for a long time, wondering what she was thinking, her chin on her knees, hair streaming over bare arms, then turned and nodded to Samlor.

"Thirteen," he said into the microphone. "Thirteen. Number thirteen pliss."

I watched her stand, stretch slowly as if this was the first time she had moved all day, bend down to pick up a matching pink purse, then head for the door.

At Le Palais there are four floors above the reception area served by a pair of lifts with the same brushed metallic shine as the escalator. On each floor an old lady sits at a desk by these lifts handing out towels, soap, hair grips, lubricants, contraceptives, shower hats—whatever the girl wants—from a cupboard behind her. There is no charge for these supplies, but it is customary to leave a few coins or low-denomination notes as a sign of your appreciation on the folded cloth provided for that purpose. It is also a precautionary move, for up here the old dame rules; it is she who rings the bell in each room when the hour is up and it is she who puts through requests for food and drink. Should a client forget his "obligation," his hour will be up sooner than he expected and his refreshments take longer to reach him than he could have imagined possible.

Each floor is divided by a narrow corridor with six apartments to a side. I have been to Le Palais enough times to know they are all approximately the same size, with the same layout and furnishings. Immediately inside each door is a tiled, step-down area with a bath and airbed side by side. Beyond the "bathroom," the apartment is carpeted and furnished with a table and chairs, a built-in wardrobe, a television, a plush banquette sofa, and in a mirrored alcove at the far end, a double bed with a control console set into the headboard. Press the button marked *sanuk* (the Thai word for fun) and the bed vibrates. Apart from a wood screen around the bath area, there are no other dividing walls. Outside each door there is a red light fixed to the wall above it. As in a recording studio the light goes on whenever the room is occupied. Even when only one or two of the rooms are in use, the corridor glows a warm scarlet.

Pimsiri took me to the fourth floor.

" 'Merican?" she asked on the way up.

"English," I replied. She said nothing more, just turned and watched the floor indicator. When the doors slid open, she stepped out into the hallway, collected a handful of towels from the old lady and led me to the only door with no light on above it. Inside she ran the bath, pinned up her hair under a plastic cap, and undressed. She then bathed me, slid and rolled her tight brown body all over mine on the airbed (complaining about the "Filly" as she did so), bathed me again, and for one thousand baht, the going rate for extras, stretched herself out on the bed, lowered the lights, turned up the radio and pushed the button marked *sanuk.* When the bell rang and our hour was up, we took the lift down to reception. There we parted company, for Pimsiri was only halfway through her shift, arranging over two folded one-hundred-baht notes to meet up later in the bar of the Sheraton. But, she warned me, if I was still at the Philadelphia she would only stay for a drink. I could hardly expect her to go with me to a place like the "Filly," she told me. She was, after all, an "upmarket" girl.

Within an hour of leaving Le Palais I had checked out of the "Filly" and found a room in a more respectable hotel. It cost me more than I had budgeted for and meant a shorter stay in the city than I had planned, but at least it meant I could see more of Pimsiri.

Without any discussion the two of us quickly settled into a routine. Now that I was staying in a better hotel, Pimsiri made no objection about spending the night with me (it was up to her standards; it also, I discovered, charged extra on the room rate). In the morning she would share my breakfast, then go home to change for her shift at Le Palais.

The things I found out about her during this time, I found out in much the same way that a lazy man reads a newspaper—headline by headline, with no real story. I learned that she was nineteen (unlike Mena, Vena and Doi she looked older without makeup), that she was the eldest of four sisters, that her father was a silver-smith (the last thing she took off before a massage or climbing into bed was a silver chain necklace with a small, intricately worked silver Buddha that he had made for her), and that neither parent questioned too closely the source of the money they regularly received from her. This information came slowly, each fact isolated and unembroidered like answers to a questionnaire. On only one subject was she particularly forthcoming: her house on the beach.

It was the one topic constantly recurring during our time together. A few months earlier, she told me, she had spent a weekend with a customer at his home near Bang Saen, a resort south of Bangkok on the road to Pattaya. She had fallen in love not with the customer but with the place. Even before they set out for the journey home to Bangkok, Pimsiri, with not a penny in the world, had determined to go back there one day and buy a house on the beach. She made inquiries and discovered it would cost her close to half a million baht, but calculated that if she saved hard it would take her a year or two at the most before she had enough money. She was still at that early stage of the dream when the sums are repeated time and again, as if each new set of calculations somehow made the result more palatable. For her own benefit more than mine, she would take a sheet of hotel writing paper and work out the sum she must have worked out a thousand times or more since that weekend in Bang Saen, scrawling the figures over the paper in a rush of anticipation, in case this time the result had changed—even a few baht made all the difference.

At the top of the sheet of paper she would write down the capital sum of 500,000 baht and from that subtract the money she had already managed to save since that momentous weekend in Bang Saen. Then, in a laboriously calculated long division sum, she would divide what remained by her average weekly savings. The figure she eventually arrived at was the number of weeks she still had to wait or more accurately work, until the dream came true and the house in Bang Saen was finally hers.

In fact there were two sums, the first one based on an average week's pay with rarely more than one man a day paying Pimsiri the extra thousand baht. According to these figures, it would take her two years, perhaps longer. To cheer herself up, the second sum was more ambitious, calculated quite ruthlessly by figuring the optimum number of men she could handle in a week, each paying the maximum amount—six men a day, six days a week—plus any extra work (like me) that happened along. At that rate—say forty men a week —minus minimal overheads, she could make Bang Saen a great deal sooner. The thought made her laugh out loud and clap her hands.

Of course, she confided one evening, making that extra thousand baht depended on her skill—or perhaps lack of it—on the airbed. This last was the body masseuse's particular piece of equipment, more than the bath or the double bed, the place she could make her money by fair means or foul. While the customer soaked in the bath, the masseuse worked up a deep, rich, warm lather in a plastic bowl, then lifted out the suds, spreading them over the length of the airbed as if buttering a slice of bread. Indeed, the whole process of body massage was not unlike creating one enormous, soapy sandwich. The customer was then laid onto the airbed face down and more lather spread over his back and legs. The last piece of the sandwich was the girl herself, assuming a press-up position above the man and rubbing various parts of her body over his—from his shoulders to his heels. The press-up position, with the girl's arms either side of the man, was the generally accepted mode of operation, but there were multiple variations therein, any of which the girls could adopt. Often, to ease the strain on the shoulders, the girls would sit and slide, toe and slide, elbow and slide, knee and slide—each alternative method providing some new sensation. The first part completed, the man was then turned over and the process repeated. "Most danger time now," said Pimsiri, for if the customer climaxed, she explained, during the massage (not the most difficult thing in the world), spurred on by the warm soap and the touch of her body sliding over his, then she was in no position to offer any extra services. It was too late. If she was lucky she might wheedle a hundred-baht tip out of the customer, but that was all. The trick was to hold him back so that he would gladly pay the extra for her to finish off the job—manually, orally, amongst the suds or on the bed with the button marked *sanuk.*

"But how do you and the other girls hold them back?"

"Easy, easy," she laughed. "Some girl I know wear ugly, ugly bath hat, other girl put tissue between lips to save lipstick—look awful horrible, put man off when he see them. Or, if girl think man close, not let him touch her, and for sure she not touch him there, but leave alone; play some time with foot or shoulder until the wanting goes. Also too, for me, I squeeze tight here," she demonstrated on me, "Yes? You see? Always I pretend for fun but always works good. Or scratch too, or get off to switch music, or make lather with cold water. There are many ways to stop man, to hold man, to make him pay."

"But how do you know when a man is coming?"

"I have to tell you that?" Her eyes opened wide.

"But how?"

"All girls at Le Palais, me too, when we see man first time, we know what kind of man, what we must do. You, you easy man; you lucky too, I think. I know in bath you good for Pimsiri, know very soon you take long time; too much massage not make you come, I think. We have good massage together. No worry for me. I come but you do not know. I know too you want fucky-fuck not massage only. For sure you pay me quick one thousand. Other man I see, I think he come quick so bathe him hard—scrub, scrub, not soft—not let him touch me here or here, do massage quick. Then I make him pay. And many men make funny noise like car or thuck-thuck," (motorized scooter taxi popular in Bangkok) "or like siren. Then I must hold tight—pretend to help but stop him certain. It is easy, easy, but sometime make mistake and all finish. Many men come quick, go quick, no money for Pimsiri—wait long time for house in Bang Saen. Chinee men no hope, so quick. Same Thai. Tourist easy for money. Yankee quickest—in, out, whooooof. That why I ask you Yankee in lift. Sometime Yankee come in bath—no use."

Another time I asked her how she intended supporting herself once she had this house. How would she manage its upkeep? How would she furnish it once she no longer worked at Le Palais?

"Do same thing," she replied. "Maybe, you know, open own place. Be like Iris. Only fatter!"

In Pimsiri's scheme of things there was no room for obstacles. Nothing, I learned, mattered for her except the house in Bang Saen; nothing was as real as that. It made the present bearable, the future bright. Life for Pimsiri was little more than a long division sum and a gradually diminishing number of weeks.

"When I have bad men I don't like—ugly or old or fat or with no leg or no arm or sick, or hurting me," she told me another time, "I think of house in Bang Saen. I think when they go fucky-fuck with me, this man he buy me front door, this man buy me big window that is looking to the sea. This ugly old man buy me nice carpet, this ugly old man pay money for air-condition."

I wondered if all the girls at Le Palais lived on dreams like these. Now I knew what Pimsiri had been thinking that first time I saw her behind the glass, her chin on her knees. She was down in Bang Saen where the sea breeze rattles through the palm fronds, hanging the curtains the last customer had bought for her.

But the more time we spent together, especially in bed, the more her companionship began to grate. It struck me quite suddenly that I didn't really like Pimsiri. It had nothing to do with her job, her ruthlessness, her blind singlemindedness, the way she held out her hand every morning for payment—all these things I understood, even quietly admired. Silently I wished her good luck, hoped one day she would have the money to buy her house. Nor did it worry me that, despite the time we spent together, I represented nothing more than a three-piece suite or fitted kitchen. After all, was she anything more to me than research material? If anything, she was more open and honest about her motives than I—for hers were plain while mine I kept concealed. The problem was much simpler than any of these things, the roots of my disaffection much closer to the surface.

The trouble was that, while the mental aspect continued to improve, with me learning more and more about her work, the physical side of the relationship, those very qualities that had at first so charmed or intrigued me—her nativeness, her orientalness, her differentness—soon began to pall, to irritate and annoy me. The one thing that kept us together, gave each meeting a purpose, was starting to lose momentum.

The hot smell of garlic and spices on her breath, for instance, that had once seemed to me exotic, animallike, so distant from the clinical, toothpaste-fresh anonymity I was used to, now seemed to grow ranker day by day until at last I began turning my head aside whenever she came too close. In bed it was worse—the deeper, the faster her breaths, the richer, the ranker the fumes.

Equally objectionable after a time was her habit of hawking and snorting into the washbasin. Every morning Pimsiri would be first up to run the bath while I lay in bed waiting for that preliminary cough, hawk and gurgle to echo in from the bathroom as she began the ritual clearing out of what sounded like every mucous passage in her body—great gouts of phlegm spat slapping into the basin, sliding and choking down the drain.

Another thing—small too, but telling. In the beginning I had enjoyed her working the joints in my fingers, seeing it as a kind of personal attention, affection for me. Idly, as we watched television or lay in bed, she would reach for my fingers and pull at the joints like a waiter drawing a cork until they clicked to her satisfaction. There was something maternal, reassuring, restful in it—a kind of adult five-little-piggies-going-to-market. But gradually this habit of hers began to annoy me, the dislocating of joints becoming more and more frequent, less and less gentle. Soon the very sensation of bones moving and stretching out of their accustomed place, the sound of them crunching out of joint, began to make me shudder. As in everything else, Pimsiri seemed insensitive to someone else's discomfort. To her it was all a game, to be pursued to the bitter end; part of her nature never to let anything rest. One night, as we lay in bed watching the street lights pattern the wall, I slipped my hand over her breast, rubbing at a nipple with my thumb. I had meant it affectionately, like a goodnight kiss before going to sleep, but she caught my hand and started to tug at the fingers with a sudden and surprising energy. It seemed to me a rough, unwarranted response and I pulled my hand away telling her no. But, like a child intent on having her own way, she wouldn't listen. Wide awake, she jumped astride me and snatched at my hand. Again I pulled it away and tried to hide both of them under my body, glaring at her sternly all the while. But in the darkness she must have missed the warning look and, thinking it all a great game, set about prying my hands loose and getting at those fingers.

"For Christ's sake, will you leave off?"

"Come on, come on, come on."

"I said stop."

"I get hand. I get hand."

"Pimsiriiiii!!"

"Give, give, give."

"I said will you STOPPIT!"

"I find fingers, I find fingers, you see."

At last I gave in, hoping my pretended indifference might make her lose interest. I should have known better. Triumphantly, delightedly, she tugged away at the joints in my fingers until the knuckles throbbed. Then she tried the wrists, and after they stubbornly resisted her manipulations she moved on to my elbows, then pushed and pulled at my shoulders, finally burrowing under the sheet for my knees and ankles and toes until she had my whole body snapping like a pair of castanets.

Pimsiri was never a gentle lover. Not for her the lazy, languorous movements the damp heat of Bangkok demanded; rather a rough and ready physical pounding. She used her sex like a blunt instrument—no subtleties in her technique, no changes in tempo, no troughs or peaks, no gentle maneuverings—just a tight, solid, animal coupling. Nor was there ever the chance to say no, not tonight. As soon as our clothes were off she would attack, grapple me down onto the bed and fuck hard. I told her many times she'd get the thousand baht anyway, just for spending the night. But it was no use. It was as if she was conditioned to equate a fee with a fuck. Worse, she pinched and grabbed and squeezed to the point of distraction and the more I complained, the more I remonstrated and tried to deter her, the more she laughed—paying not the least heed, indeed often increasing the discomfort. If I pushed her away or slapped her, she pushed me back, or slapped me just as hard, then cackled with laughter. I always regretted doing this, not because I hurt her, but in case she decided to adopt it as another game: you hit me, I hit you. Pimsiri was a tough little bastard—there was probably nothing she would have liked more than a good punch-up.

Worst of all were her kisses or, more accurately, her pretend-kisses. As a preliminary to fucking (it is quite impossible to describe what we did together as making love), but more usually in the exhausted lull afterward, she would lean forward, eyes closed, as if to kiss; then, at the very last moment, spring her eyes wide open, bare her lips like a snarling animal (she even snarled sometimes) and bite my face with her sharp little teeth. The more I struggled, the more she persevered, scraping her teeth over my nose or chin, which was bad enough, or actually catching hold of a piece of cheek and nipping hard. Very rapidly it passed from a game into an annoying deception—never knowing for sure whether she meant to kiss or bite, never quite being able to relax, never knowing whether to be on the defensive or not. As with everything else, Pimsiri went too far, content only with extremes, stopping only at the very last moment, sometimes even going beyond the limit of endurance.

This ferocity scared me; her ability to inflict pain and withstand it was quite frightening. Had I ever stubbed a cigarette out on her, I am convinced she would have done it back—then laughed glee-fully at the experience. Just as frightening were my own reactions —the sudden and quite unfamiliar desire to lash out as hard as I could, just to get through to her, to make her stop. I could never make up my mind whether she did these things because she thought it was the kind of behavior that I wanted or, perversely, because she knew it wasn't. Whatever the case, it was becoming increasingly clear that the physical price I had to pay was beginning to outweigh the more practical, research advantage. Like a seesaw, the balance of our relationship was unequally distributed and was rapidly tip-ping us toward a showdown.

I wasn't surprised when it first dawned on me that Pimsiri was a thief. So small and insignificant were the things she stole that I was rather amused by her choice—a couple of T-shirts ten times too big for her, a pair of red socks, a packet of razors, nail clippers, some cassette tapes—and that she imagined these losses went unnoticed. But soon she started taking money. First she selected only odd coins from the handfuls of loose change I took from my trouser pockets last thing at night and left on the dresser. But then she grew bolder, scooping up the whole pile. Even then I didn't say anything—it was my own fault anyway for leaving it around. And Winnie had been as bad. After all, there was the house in Bang Saen to think of.

It wasn't until the chambermaid cornered me one morning after Pimsiri had gone home, led me into the bathroom and demanded to know what I planned doing about the missing towels and flannels and bathmats, that I realized, almost thankfully, that our relation-ship had reached its inevitable conclusion.

That evening I met Pimsiri for the last time at the bar of Le Palais and told her over a glass of Singha that I had booked a seat on the late flight out. This time tomorrow I would be in Tel Aviv.

It seemed a million miles away—from Bangkok, from the time we had spent together. She seemed not in the least concerned, just pouted those wide brown lips, shrugged and finished her drink. Outside in the street, she swung her bag over her shoulder and we shook hands.

"See you again," she said.

"Next time in Bang Saen," I replied with a smile.

"Bang Saen," she repeated, then turned and walked away.

Part Three

A Shabbat
at Zilla's

The storm broke on the eve of the Shabbat. It had been muster-
ing all week somewhere far out at sea, but too far out to be visible.
Those who knew the signs would have remarked on the sun, for
instance, when it set, slithering through a streak of haze rather than
sliding cleanly into the sea. There was the wind too, warm and a
little fetid as though it had stumbled through a slaughterhouse. It
had a blustery, indecisive sort of character like a drunk who's not
sure where he is but makes a point of letting everyone know he's
arrived. Out of the wind, there was a certain flat heaviness, and
those people who had them started switching on their air-condi-
tioners. As the days passed the sea grew darker and the waves
stronger, smacking up against the breakwaters and scalloping between them. For those flying into Lod, the shoreline of the Promised
Land must have looked like the edge of a lace tablecloth.

Friday was fine to start with—the sky a clear blue, shadows
sharp and the chalky sprawl of the city bright and glaring—but
shortly after lunch, as the girls arrived and Zilla's took down its
shutters, a sheet of cloud slipped in from the sea and settled over
the town. Without anyone really noticing it the bluster dropped and
the flags in hotel forecourts hung limp for the first time in a week.
It wasn't the season for sweating, but everyone was.

As usual the girls at Zilla's sat up front in the space left by the
shutters, their bare feet resting on a low Formica-topped table that
was covered with brushes and combs, pins and grips, ashtrays,
cigarette packets and bottles of nail varnish. I had noticed on my
two previous visits that the girls kept their perfumes in their bags.

There were three of them: Rachel, the tallest of the trio, with the frizzy, tobacco-colored hair and freckles; Zena with the wide, dark eyes and bitten fingernails; and Yael, quietest of the three, who always seemed happy enough just looking out across the road at the sea. On a spare chair stood a two-bar electric fire with the safety grille missing, which the girls used for lighting their cigarettes, and on the floor lay a selection of curled paperbacks and old magazines that crackled with sand. None of them looked up as I stepped in off the street for the third time that week. In her usual place behind the bar was Zilla, standing on tiptoes and redirecting the three-blade fan that stood on top of the Electrolux so the draft played directly over her. It buzzed and whirred and hovered like a swarm of bees and at the end of each sweep gave a loud click. In another ten minutes it would move back to its original position like a gyroscope automatically correcting itself.

"One day I take hammer and nail, so help me," she threatened as I approached the bar, watching the fan begin its inevitable journey back across the top of the fridge.

"Amen," chorused the three girls.

Zilla's was at the wrong end of the beach—that section of the Front where the the sand was more like shale, and concrete blocks, shaped suspiciously like antitank emplacements, had been bulldozed up into piles. They had the same air of stored readiness as a stack of gilt-backed chairs waiting for the next reception. People tended to stay away from this part, especially tourists with young children, imagining quite understandably there might still be mines sewn into the sand. It looked the kind of place where a child with a bucket and spade stood a good chance of digging up a live hand grenade. Another reason they stayed away was Zilla's, one of several low-down bars and flyblown sweetmeat shops occupying ground floor premises in a blistering stuccoed block of old hotels whose windows, unlike Zilla's, remained shuttered from one day to the next. The fronts of these hotels, stretching a hundred yards or so along the beach and each painted a different shade of pastel wash, had been built over the pavement and, supported by a line of Moorish-style arches, formed a narrow arcade that provided much-needed shade during the hotter months. Less appealing was the way it caught and held along its echoing length all the smells of the sea, absorbing them into its sweaty plaster—as if the fishermen of Old Yafo used the arcade for storing their nets and pots. Not even a stiff breeze like the one that had been blowing that week could flush them out, nor the assorted perfumes of the girls who worked there.

It was, however, a smell that was not destined to last much longer, for Zilla's, the other shops and bars, the ten-room peeling hotels that had seen better times, even Abe's where the girls sent out for their baclava slices—all were doomed. Already acres of land on every side had been acquired and promptly flattened, leaving Zilla's block the only one still standing. Isolated on this bomb site of redevelopment and taking up valuable real estate along the Front, it had about as much chance of survival as a sandcastle facing a high tide. Whether it was a temporary lack of funds, or more likely, some obdurate landlord holding out for a better price that had so far kept the developers and bulldozers at bay, it was certain that within the very near future Zilla's and its neighbors would cease to exist— reduced, like the land around them, to a pile of rubble. As Zilla herself observed my first night in her bar with admirable if ambitious resignation: "One day soon, this bar will be a smart reception desk in a Holiday Inn, a Hilton, a Dan Hotel maybe." She spoke the words like a mourner accepting that the deceased was bound for a better place.

For the moment, though, it was business as usual.

With its red-wash walls, black ceiling, stone floor and red fluorescent lights, Zilla's was more like an aquarium than a bar, albeit without the fish tanks. Scraps of netting hung from the corners like enormous cobwebs, red and green navigation lamps stood at either end of the bar and there was always sand crunching underfoot. The room, with its few tables and chairs and line of bar stools, felt sticky with salt.

It was never clear whether Zilla owned or merely managed the bar. Although everyone seemed to know it as Zilla's, her name did not appear on the warped sign above the door and there was nothing to indicate her ownership. Nothing, that is, except her solid air of permanency. It was difficult to imagine her anywhere else except behind the bar; when they brought in the bulldozers one suspected she would be reduced to rubble like the building itself, so successfully had she managed to incorporate herself into the surroundings. Zilla supported this impression with her formidable size—the way she maneuvered behind the bar was an extraordinary thing to see. The three times I visited she wore the same flowing caftan with an open V-neck that revealed an expanse of brown mottled skin and the wrinkled beginnings of a cleavage. She was always pushing her sleeves up over her elbows as if to show she meant business, and she slip-slopped around in a pair of worn leather slippers that revealed equally leathery heels. With her hair cut en broche and colored with streaks of gray there was something mightily lesbian about her. Her apparent disdain for the girls in her charge seemed to support this.

For the second day running I was the only customer.

"You again," said Zilla, turning from the fan. "You doing a survey it's so good here? Soon it's only me and Adolf you're left with."

"Take the dog," I heard Rachel mutter across the room, "you'll suit."

"So, a glass of beer, yes?" asked Zilla, ignoring the remark.

"Yes. Please."

"And maybe one of my *tchotchkas* to keep you company again?" This was how Zilla made her money—doubling the drinks and quadrupling the prices.

"There's not a lot of choice," I said, looking around at the girls.

"So it's a supermarket you want now. If you're looking there's one up the road." What she was really saying was, it was my fault the choice was limited. Since neither Rachel nor Zena was talking to me, there was only Yael left. Rachel, the first of the three I had taken to my hotel, was doubtless still smarting from the knowledge that I had paid Zena twenty dollars more than her for the same service (worth every penny—Rachel had never stopped talking the entire time and smelled almost as bad as the arcade); while Zena was sore that I hadn't let her stay the night and hadn't contributed toward her taxi fare home. As she had a hundred dollars of mine in her bag I hadn't really seen the necessity.

Taking her cue from Zilla's inquiry, Yael got up from her seat and walked over to us. While Zilla poured my beer, she hauled herself up onto the stool beside me. She was small and wiry with long, strong fingers and a mane of hennaed hair that looked too heavy for her narrow shoulders to bear. She had a way of lifting it in handfuls and piling it on top of her head. She did this now, the small hairs beneath sodden and stuck to her skin like leeches.

"You buy me drink?" she asked, letting the hair fall back around her shoulders and closing her arm round mine.

"What else should he buy you here?" interrupted Zilla. "If he's looking for a restaurant, he'll find one down the road." Zilla was always saying that anything not available in her bar could be found either up or down the street. It was not her intention to direct customers elsewhere, rather her way of telling you that you should make do with what she had to offer. This was a bar. Here a customer came to drink. If he wanted anything else, he should have gone somewhere else. Up the road or down the road.

Before I had taken my first sip of beer, Yael had already downed the tiny glass of pretend-cognac she had been served the moment I nodded my head, and Zilla was waiting, bottle under the counter, for me to order another. This was the system at Zilla's. After two or three of these, Yael would suggest we might be more comfortable in the back room (just as Rachel and Zena had done before her)—a small, curtained alcove at the end of the bar with one flickering electric candle and a deep, spring-sagging sofa. Once I accepted the invitation, bar prices would soar, Yael, as her two colleagues had done before her, would rest her hand tantalizingly in my lap, and hundred-shekel notes would disappear as rapidly and as resolutely as her drinks. At any time I would be free to withdraw and return alone to the bar, but the object was for the girl to keep me detained, to keep me occupied, to keep me supplying her with drinks. Should I ask her back to my hotel this was only too easily arranged, at an hourly rate, payable to Buba Zilla. Thereafter, negotiations between girl and customer were on a freelance basis. That had been the way with Rachel and Zena and I expected nothing less from Yael. But it seemed she had other plans.

While Zilla busied herself with the fan, Yael leaned close: "You don't have many friends here," she whispered, nodding toward Rachel and Zena.

"I can imagine."

"Tell me, how much you pay Bubele for taking Rachel and Zi?"

I told her.

"You pay me half that, and my money, and I meet with you later, okay?"

"How much and where?"

"Eighty dollars and half Bubele's money. I help you save a lot. We meet ten o'clock in Laromme bar." The Laromme was one of the new hotels that had been built farther along the beach, the kind that would one day replace Zilla's block.

"When do I pay?"

"Later. Buy me now one more drink then go."

By the time I left the afternoon heat had turned to an evening chill. The wind had started up again and sand drifted across the road like flakes of snow, twisting through the arcade and sparkling on the twin bars of the electric fire. As I walked away I could hear Zilla shouting instructions at the girls: "Put up a couple of shutters, why don't you? How many times do I need to tell you the sand gets everywhere. You had to clean it up, you'd close the shutters soon enough."

After all the buildup, the real storm hit the coast much farther north, toward the port of Haifa and the Lebanese border. Tel Aviv was left with the slipstream. As arranged, Yael and I met at the appointed time and after a drink at the Laromme took a taxi back to her home. This choice surprised me; neither Rachel nor Zena had wanted to go anywhere other than my hotel. All along the Front the wind buffeted the taxi from side to side and Yael had to hold my leg to steady herself. When we got out, in a steep street in Old Yafo, the wind picked us up and pushed us along, Yael struggling to keep her scarf on her head and her coattails closed. There was no rain yet, just sheets of stinging sand that seemed to sing off the walls around us. She led me to a green door, unlocked it and pushed me through into a tilting, grass-rutted courtyard. The walls were so high, almost fortresslike, that everything was still. Above us, though, the wind raced on, so strong you could almost see it tumbling over the wall and pummeling into the building that faced us. Arm in arm, we crossed the yard, climbed a short flight of worn stone steps and let ourselves in.

Yael's room was on the top floor, a single door on a narrow landing. Inside, the floors, walls and ceiling were all stone, the walls hung with rugs, the floors strewn with large, yielding cushions, more rugs—tattier this time—and hanging from the ceiling the kind of brass lamp you see above altars, a tiny flame burning in its center. Across the room was a large stone fireplace and standing in its empty grate a low table with a small electric stove. To one side was a large window leaded with hundreds of tiny squares and triangles of colored glass, and beneath it a quilted, rumpled bed. In the morning when the sun came up, the room must have been dazzling. I told her so.

"You pay the money, you see the show." She had started lighting the candles of a branched menorah candleholder. "Don't worry. I am not religious. I think it is just pretty." She went to the door and switched out the light. The nine flames burning in a single straight line made the room seem suddenly warmer and smaller, the stone walls somehow softer and less chill in the candlelight. "You pay me now?" I handed her the money and watched her leaf through the notes. "I am sorry to tell you I need twenty dollars more."

"Twenty more?"

She went over to the bed and started pulling off her boots.

"Come," she beckoned, "sit down, I explain."

"Please do," I said, sinking down beside her.

"It is Rachel. She does not like you. After you have gone, she tells me if I do not pay her twenty dollars she will tell Zilla what I am doing. And I know she will. I must pay her. You understand?"

"Bloody little Rachel," was all I could say, reaching for my pocket.

Yael caught my hand. "It is okay with you? You understand?"

"I suppose so."

"The sun in the morning is very beautiful," she smiled, taking the money and adding it to the pile.

Second
Time Around

"I wonder," I began; the reception manager, with his quick, modern eyes, black knit tie and name-tagged jacket, looked up from the Rolodex. "I wonder if you can help me. I was here in Budapest some years ago, before this hotel was built, and stayed across the river in a very grand sort of place in the center of town. I think it was in Lenin Korut. A very long, wide street anyway. The trouble is I can't remember the name. Perhaps you know it?"

"On Lenin Korut?" mental Rolodex spinning. "That would be Hotel Imperiale, sir?"

"The Imperiale. Of course. Thank you."

I was surprised just how much I had forgotten, how general were the impressions I had so carefully stored away. The Imperiale, for instance, where it all happened. I remembered what it looked like from the street, bulky and looming, but somehow hadn't quite been able to focus on the name above the entrance. It was the same with the rest of the city. I remembered the Cathedral of St. Matthias and the Disneyland ramparts of the Fishermen's Bastion high in the hills of Buda, but had left out along my mental skyline, even higher, the winged statue of Victory on the Gellert Hill and the bare stone cliff beneath. I remembered the Danube, of course, but not the lines of barges that lumbered up- and downstream, the Gothic flanks of the parliament building that shone across its surface, the yellow trams that swayed alongside it or the stone lions that guarded the approaches to the Szechenyi Bridge. I remembered Margitziget but not the thin morning mists that clung to the trees in its park; the ocher wash of the buildings but not their stone lintels; the baroque domes but not the way they glittered like peeled onions; the cobbles, of course, but not the way my taxi jounced and rumbled over them as if its tires were flat. Second time around everything was suddenly clearer, more detailed. It was like filling in the blanks of yesterday's crossword with today's solutions.

The moment we turned into Lenin Korut I recognized the street, knew the hotel was just up ahead on the right. But what I had forgotten were the tram-lines and tram-shelters, the newspaper booths and the people—for some reason my street had been deserted. Seeing it all again was as satisfying as having clear and total recall of a dream. I paid off the taxi and stood, for a moment, looking up at the Imperiale. Bulky and looming. No expression on its face. Just as I remembered it—except for the slanting portico, the curved metal door handles like fat salmon leaping, the doorman's gold braid epaulettes, the wall of heat thrown down by fan heaters just inside the first set of doors. I found myself nodding and thinking "of course, of course."

Nothing had changed inside, but now that I saw it again I realized I'd have got none of the details right had I sat down to draw a picture of it. The general shape and layout yes, but not the finer points—the curtained entrance to the dining room, the red strip of stair carpet with the brass rods leading to the mezzanine, the three lifts—two for guests, one for service—and that particular shade of purple they had been painted; and then that stylized map of the world above the gallery worked in tiny chips of colored stone with dolphins leaping and whales spouting and galleons under full sail with full-cheeked cupids blowing them along.

For the second time in half an hour I stood at a reception desk (just where I remembered it). The man here was older, slower, more like an imperial retainer than the smart hotel executive I had confronted earlier, with a waistcoat of yellow and green horizontal stripes.

"I'm not a guest at the hotel. Do I need to book a table for dinner?"

"No, sir, just go . . ."

"That's okay. I know the way."

The fat man from the *Times* in a crumpled black suit that did for funerals and official dinners, and the man from the *Mail* with the stammer—these had been my companions. When we returned to the Imperiale late that last night in Budapest, the three of us had loosened our ties and ambled down to the hotel night club where we knew the bar stayed open late. Apart from a few weeks in Ireland, this had been my first real assignment; and this time of day I looked forward to the most—listening to the stories of my two companions. Every reminiscence seemed to begin with "When I was in Berlin . . . Moscow . . . Rome . . . Helsinki. . . . And then there was that time in Prague, ugly old city, used to wire in my stories from the foreign ministry, man I knew there, left them to foot the bill. Yes, that's right—two double vodkas and a large slivowitz." There was little I contributed on these occasions, not yet having any tales to tell of Smithers or Jimmy or Dicko; of AP, UPI or Reuters men; of wild drinking bouts in Abyssinia, of appalling hangovers in Hong Kong, of corrupt border officials in obscure West African states, of secret police in Warsaw, of showcase trials in Bucharest, of coronations and counterrevolutions, of misappropriated exes (which I thought at first meant wives), of arrests, deportations and sackings, and, worst of all in my opinion then, of violent rows with editors (how could anyone dare?). But they were kind to me all the same, included me, made me feel a part of it all. And I was learning all the time. Everything they said was as tight as a column of print, the punchlines as bold as headlines, their opinions as considered as leaders, their observations as sharp and precise as a political cartoon. When they talked about the trip we had almost finished—Hungary and Budapest—I wondered why I hadn't noticed the things they had picked up, where I could have been when such-and-such happened, how it was I thought so-and-so such a nice fellow when they were branding him a crook. I hadn't even seen them take a single note, while my book was filled with scribblings. They talked about baroque architecture, the Uprising, what they had been doing in '56, where and with whom. Their knowledge seemed limitless and I hung on every word. Drinking neat vodkas and numbing slivowitz, in a darkened bar, deep behind the Iron Curtain—it was everything I had imagined journalism to be, everything I had expected of Fleet Street.

In retrospect, the two of them must have known all the time, but they played it straight, pushed me on good-naturedly, a lamb to the slaughter. We always managed to get the same table, the two of them taking the more comfortable banquette seats, me crouched on a stool. From where they sat, they had a good view of the bar over my shoulder. Halfway through some story or other, the man from the *Times* leaned forward and tapped me on the arm.

"Hey up, lad," he said, "there's a lass there by the bar been lookin' at you. No, no, no, don't look round like that. Do it subtly —I'll tell you when." He turned to the man from the *Mail.* "D'you see the one I mean?"

"W-w-w-w-which one?"

"That little peach in black, with her elbow on the bar. Second along."

"Oh, she's a cr-cr-cr-cracker. Been looking at M-m-m-m-m-m . . . has she?"

"Well, no chance she's looking at us." Peach or not, cracker or not, I wasn't really interested. In fact I was annoyed she had interrupted the story, and embarrassed suddenly to be the center of attention. I rather wished whoever she was would disappear and let us continue with our conversation. But that wasn't to be. The man from the *Times* had no intention of letting this one drop.

"Go on now lad, she's not looking. Take a peep."

"The one with the earrings? She looks okay," I said, hoping it sounded final and uninterested enough as I turned back to the table.

"That's the one, that's the one."

"She's a p-p-p-p-pretty one, that's for sure."

"Go and ask her to dance, go on lad, before someone else beats you to it. You don't want to stop here all night listening to us old codgers."

It was the last thing I wanted to do, but they left me no alternative. I know exactly what made me get up and go to the bar, and it had nothing whatsoever to do with the girl, pretty though she was. It was because of their opinion of me. I didn't want them to think that after all their tales of derring-do, I was not up to a challenge. It would prove, finally, that I was one of them, that I was someone to be counted.

What surprised me was how easy it was, how she turned to me and smiled as if she had been waiting just for me all evening. She spoke very little English but it didn't appear to make the slightest difference. If she didn't know the right words she called over the barman to translate; otherwise we stumbled along with a minimum of English and a scramble of French and German. I bought her a drink, took her for a dance. Then another drink at the bar, her hand brushing my leg, her eyes fast on mine, and then another dance. As we passed my table, the man from the *Times* raised his thumb and nodded, the man from the *Mail* lifted his glass and smiled. It had all been going so well I had almost forgotten them. On the dance

145

floor we squeezed between couples and found a space just as the band started a slow number. Immediately her arms were around my neck and her body against mine. I began to feel not a little pleased with myself, flushed at my success in front of my two friends. I had no doubt I was putting up a pretty noteworthy display.

Back at the bar, we were getting along famously. She was so easy to be with, so accommodating, so even-tempered, so pretty, so interested, so charming, so friendly, so—obviously taken by me. I felt suddenly expansive. More drinks were ordered, there were toasts, smiles, touches, the heady smell of scent in my nostrils. Discreetly the barman moved away and she leaned closer.

"Prostitute? You know prostitute?" If a hurricane had swept through the room and an earth tremor ripped a six-foot trench in the floor I couldn't have been more stunned. I knew for the first time what it was to be entirely and utterly without the power of speech. "Prostitute?" she asked again. "You know?"

"Prostitute? You're a . . ."

"Ssssshhhhhh!"

"Prostitute?" Quieter now, but still staggered. "Prostitute?"

"You know prostitute? You have in London?"

"Yes, of course, I, yes . . ." She was so young. How could she possibly . . . ? How was it I could have been so . . . ? I didn't dare look over at my two companions. They must, I realized, have known all along.

"You like me? You want go with me?" Hand on thigh, a beseeching look.

"Well, yes, of course." I wasn't at all sure what I was saying yes to—whether I liked her, or whether I intended going with her.

"You pay?"

"Er, yes, I mean, um, how much?"

"For you, nice boy, 1,000 forints." She squeezed my leg, leaned close so her hair was against my cheek. Oh god, oh god, what had I got myself into—what had they got me into? What should I do? What did they expect me to do? Over her shoulder my colleagues sat riveted, watching every move. The man from the *Times* leered, the man from the *Mail* smiled knowingly. I wondered if they knew the point we had reached. Judging by their attention, I suspected they did.

It was the first time anything like this had happened since that summer afternoon in a London cinema and the same feelings welled up—the same fears, the same uncertainties. Only this time someone was watching to see how I coped. Damn them! This time there was no room for excuses, back-outs. At least I could afford it this time. Thank god it was the last day.

Garbrielle took me to my room and I paid her the 1,000 forints. This time round the thought that I could sleep with her, have her, touch her, see her body, proved stronger than it had in the cinema. It was all so convenient, so breathlessly exciting. Indeed I was surprised I had never thought to do it before, almost grateful to my two colleagues for pushing me into it. I wasn't in the least bothered by disease or being beaten up by someone. I was safe. I was in control. The worst was over, the best to come.

I never noticed how quickly her manner changed once the deal was done, the way she stiffened once we were in bed, the way her lips compressed, her swiftness, professionalism, her complete withdrawal. It was enough for me then to have a breast under my hand, a pair of legs opening for me, winding around me. It didn't matter about the blank look turned to the ceiling, the way she was up off the bed when we finished, into the bathroom, out again to dress and then gone. I had broken through. I had done what I'd had the chance to do years earlier at the cinema. The next morning I shrugged off the winks and nudges, warm inside. I had collected my first story.

The club had opened by the time I finished dinner. As soon as I stepped through the doors forgotten details sprang at me—the wide marble steps leading down to the basement, the shell-like light fittings against the walls, a mirror wall. Directly ahead were the cloakroom doors each with a porthole of frosted glass and each with its stylized silhouette—the lady in wide skirts, the gentleman with a top hat. Then another, shorter flight of steps into the club itself. The first part of the room had three tidy lines of tables and chairs —two against the walls, one down the middle. Beyond was the small, circular dance floor where Gabrielle and I had clung together, the platform for the band and the steps beside it leading to the bar —oval-fronted with tall, red-cushioned stools bolted down to the floor so they were never out of line. I remembered you could swivel on them; Gabrielle had done that.

I had no illusions that she would still be there; no one would stay that long. Certainly no one like Gabrielle. By now she was probably married, with a family, and living in the suburbs—going to church, taking the children to school, perhaps even holding down a job somewhere. I wondered whether her husband knew how she had earned her living.

If I had forgotten details of Budapest, I remembered everything about Gabrielle. Her shiny black hair, cut in a pageboy style, her black sleeveless dress, the scar of puckered skin at the top of her arm, the black stockings, a gold watch that hung loose round her wrist like a bracelet, the way she tapped the ash off her cigarette with a stiff index finger, the way she looked at me under those black brows and fringe, how she sat on the bar stool with her legs crossed and the narrow hem of her dress riding up. Strangely though, it didn't matter if she was there or not—the memory was enough. All I wanted was to see the place where it had all started. Perhaps indulge in a little repetition. For old times.

Sitting at the same table I watched the girls start arriving, taking up positions before the punters from the dining-room and lounge began drifting in—the wine brokers from Balaton, the convention delegates from Vienna, the engineering consultants from Birmingham, even a few of the locals dropping in after the theater. The pattern, their presence, was crystal clear now, and I saw what my two old friends must have seen all those years ago. How could I have missed it?

The girls arrived singly and in pairs—all well dressed, sure of themselves, haughty to the spine—some settling in groups around the walls, others making for the bar and swinging themselves onto the stools. Some were young, some not so young—but all very different from the rather drab women you see during the day in the streets of Budapest. Where they got hold of their clothes I had no idea; there were no shops that sold the styles they wore.

Within an hour some fifteen girls had made their entrance. It was like watching a flock of birds come home to roost. Already I could smell the mixture of perfumes, see the discreet looks, the knowing glances, the way they placed themselves either directly or obliquely in the line of a potential customer's vision. How they walked past promising tables on their way to the ladies' room and returned the same way, another button undone, a slower walk, stopping perhaps to light a cigarette, asking for the light they couldn't seem to find. It was better than any cabaret the Imperiale could have staged.

I couldn't decide whether Esther was sitting on exactly the same stool as Gabrielle, but it was close enough. Just as he had done so long before, the barman hovered, ready to translate as the two of us talked. We danced, we drank, danced again, drank again. The pattern was exactly similar—the ash tray drawn to her elbow, the same tap-tap-tap of ash into the bowl, the same drink even, a brandy with a mineral water chaser. Even the proposition sounded as if it had come from the same book of instructions—only this time there was no hurricane, no earth tremor.

"You 'ave prostitute in England?"

"Of course."

"You are . . . sympathetic?"

"Yes."

"So, you like to come with me?"

Only the price had changed.

"Three thousand forints!"

"Is not so much, I think."

And so, for the second time, in that same bar, an agreement was reached. Apart from the stool, the way they smoked, their drink, their shared profession and nationality, Esther and Gabrielle had nothing in common. But that didn't matter. The place, the setting was all I wanted.

Esther lived some distance from the hotel in a new apartment complex on the road to Debrecen. I counted ten blocks built in close order, separated by thin strips of grass and low-walled playgrounds —one for every two blocks. The towers were some twenty floors high and Esther's apartment about halfway up, a cluster of tiny rooms around the stem of a hall. There was a bathroom papered with pages cut out of film magazines, a room in darkness where her son Gyorgy slept (on whose account we tiptoed and whispered), a kitchen big enough for one cook and a handful of pans, and the living room where Esther slept on a settee bed. The view from her window comprised a pattern of room lights and colored curtains in the tower block opposite. We undressed, and Esther, whispering "Douche, douche" took my hand and led me into the bathroom. While I clambered into the empty bath under a rack of hanging clothes so low you couldn't stand—nappies, romper suits, jeans, T-shirts, tights, all legs and arms, all dripping cold onto my shoulders—Esther squatted over the lavatory and urinated loudly. I knew her game but was determined not to be put off now she had her money. A little more than a week before Rachel had done the same thing in my small hotel room in Tel Aviv—not so much to deter or disgust me, but boldly, pointedly, as if she was intent on making some declaration, a statement of her liberation if you like, an act that represented the break she had made with her Chicago upbringing. More than anything this behavior amused me. When she had finished, Esther wiped herself and stepped into the bath with me, the two of us facing each other under the rack of clothes. I supposed she hadn't pulled the flush for fear of waking Gyorgy. Taking up the shower attachment she began to wash us, using a shampoo scented like green apples. The smell was strong and evocative, a depressing counterpoint to our surroundings. No grass, just lino tiles; no trees, just a forest of dripping clothes; no sun, just a light fitment in the ceiling.

Back in her room, she moistened herself with licked fingers as if she were about to thread a needle and squatted over me. The bed was a monster—not in size but in temperament. However I contrived to lie, I couldn't seem to avoid the long wooden joint where settee became bed. It dug into my shoulders, rubbed at the small of my back, tried again and again to separate my buttocks and pinched at my heels. I had been surprised that Esther had opted for this position (some girls charged more this way round; they had to work harder); now I knew why. Considering the money I had paid, I decided she should be the one to put up with the discomfort so I stopped her rocking and indicated I wanted to change around. Not surprisingly she pretended not to understand, sitting astride me and looking puzzled. Eventually by struggling out from underneath her and pushing her down on her back I completed the maneuver, the settee bed groaning and twanging beneath us. It was then that we heard the first muffled cry rising steadily into a continuous wail. Esther was off the bed in a moment, across the passage in two strides and into Gyorgy's room. Through the open doors I could hear soothing words but it was clear from the cries that the child was now wide awake with little chance of being encouraged back to sleep. Sure enough, Esther came back with Gyorgy in her arms, a knuckle pressed into the corner of one eye, the other eye tired and red and squashed into a slit of indignation and tantrum. She sat on the edge of the bed with him and he looked down with his one clear eye at my naked body. I couldn't pull up the cover because Esther was sitting on it so he just carried on examining me out of his knuckleless eye. He was about three with thick black hair that stood up in a tangle from his head. His lips looked wet and swollen and a line of spittle stretched like a stalagmite between them. In the corner of his mouth a bubble of saliva looked about to burst and trickle down his chin. Seeing me had momentarily stopped his crying but without warning he took a series of deep, choking breaths as if trying once more to get purchase on a good, solid wall. But Esther rocked it out of him and the convulsions subsided into a resentful sob.

To my astonishment a third figure appeared in the doorway. She had the face of a gypsy with wild black hair and reddened cheeks. She wore a yellow housecoat with buttons stretched to bursting down the front. It was clear she was wearing nothing underneath.

"This Margit. Stay with Gyorgy." And pinch him awake, I thought, maneuvering myself to put Esther between Margit and my nakedness. A wailing child was guaranteed to send any customer packing. As if to confirm this Esther bundled the infant into Margit's arms, picked up my clothes and handed them to me: "You go now or Gyorgy not sleep. You must go."

"You said you would phone a taxi for me."

"No phone, sorry. Kaput, finis."

"Then how do you suggest I get back to town?"

"Always taxi in road. Few minutes. No more."

"You sure?"

"Yes, sure. Always pass here." And then, right out of the blue, as if I owed them both a favor: "You give Margit money?"

"What? What the hell for?" I asked, struggling into my trousers. For waking the baby to get rid of me, I thought?

Esther shrugged.

"You have to be joking," I continued, no longer caring whether they understood or not. "Give her some of yours . . . you didn't earn the half of it anyway."

I waited fifteen minutes before the first set of headlights appeared way down the road. I didn't know if it was a taxi or not but I waved my hand just in case. As it sped past I saw it was, but that it was full. As were the second and third that followed it. I had already started walking when I heard the fourth taxi coming up fast behind me. I stopped, turned and flagged it down and the two men in the back seat squeezed up to make room. As the taxi rushed on over the cobbles back into town we sat in silence. I had the distinct impression we had all been doing the same thing. Only this time there were no nudges and no winks, and no warm feelings inside.

Three
to One

Munich at midnight was chill and shivery. And surprisingly empty—my taxi seemed to be the only car on the road. It was as if the whole city had been evacuated in the face of some strange menace. It felt a little discomforting to be the only one about, as if everyone else knew better.

At my hotel, in the center of the old town—equally empty—the night staff were on duty, old and slow like soldiers in a Home Guard unit. Tired and grubby, I was shown to my room by an old man who looked very much like I felt. He dumped my case in the small hallway with an exaggerated sigh of relief, switched on the lights, opened the windows onto a deserted square and left me with a low bow and generous tip.

An hour later, showered and shaved with a change of shirt, I felt much better—ready to go. Despite appearances, I was sure Munich must have something to offer—somewhere. In the corner of my room, beneath the base of a standard lamp, I hid my passport and travellers' checks—a wise precaution should I bring someone back with me—then locked the door behind me, hanging the *Bitte Nicht Stören* sign from the handle. At Reception I changed some money and left the hotel, stopping at the entrance to ask the head porter where I could find the center of town. He pointed across the small square to the orange glow I had seen from my room. Did I need a taxi, I asked? He shook his head—it was only a short walk. Before moving away, I pressed a neatly folded one-hundred-Deutsche-mark note into his hand. Should I return with company, his discretion was assured.

The real center of Munich, a web of streets surrounding the Frauenkirche, is closed to traffic—the roads paved over to make an enormous shopping and tourist precinct. At midday it's a hectic scrum of people—shops, cafés, squares jammed to bursting—but a little after one o'clock in the morning, and much to my dismay, it was so quiet I could hear my footsteps echoing off the renaissance walls of St. Michelskirche and from far away the tiny splash of the Brunnenbuberl fountain. No shop was open, the cafés were closed, no inviting shadows lingered on street corners.

Outside Karlstor, one of the old city gates, I sat on a bench with the spray from the Stachus fountain settling like a drizzle on my face. I sat there for some time, looking toward the lights of Bayer and Shutzenstrasse, Prielmeyer and Sonnenstrasse, wondering whether it was worth a walk. I was losing interest and hope in equal measures. When I saw the taxi draw up into an empty rank fifty yards away, a cream Citroën with its luminous green dial lights shining up on the driver's face, I decided I'd take a ride instead.

The driver was a crumpled, creased sort of fellow who looked as if he never got out of his car. His name was Kurt. He wore his hair long and had a gold cap covering the lower half of a front tooth. He looked unwashed, slightly manic but harmless—like an out-of-work anarchist who never really made the grade. Where did I want to go, he asked? Somewhere more lively, I replied. He looked up at me for a moment and then nodded toward the back seat.

"I take you to Schwabing," he said, pulling away from the curb. "It is for students, artists you know. Like Paris, cafés and clubs, they are open late."

"And girls?" I saw him glance at me in the mirror as if this question confirmed his suspicions.

"For girls . . . you must go farther."

"How much farther?"

"Out of town maybe—Trudering, I think." He was silent for a while. "But it is expensive, these houses—one hunnert fifty and you only get in," he continued, testing his fare. We were driving along a wide, straight avenue banked with shoveled snow. Like everywhere else it was deserted.

"Let's try," I suggested.

He said nothing, simply turned right at the next set of lights and tore off through a jigsaw of slippery side streets. A few minutes later we crossed a bridge over the Isar, the glow of the city now far behind us, the road ahead darkening and widening into autobahn.

"Why so far out?"

"Munich is a boring town now," he turned and smiled with his gold tooth; he was settling back to enjoy the ride. "Everything is quiet. I used to live here but now I am in Berlin. I come here in two months to drive taxi to make money, then go back and live in Berlin. It is better there, I think."

"But why," I repeated the question, "are these houses so far away from the city?"

"This is the police, you see, they keep pushing them out into the suburbs. Munich is a strange town now. You would not believe. Me, I don't like. You used to find a zone for girls between Isartorplatz and the Viktualienmarkt, but no more. Me I prefer Berlin."

Past a sign to Wasserburg he took a slip road, braked and left the motorway. I could see the dark shadows of houses and a few lights, where before it had just been the high snowy banks of the autobahn. After a number of short, sliding corners and long, sleeping residential streets Kurt slowed down, crawled along the side of the road, then pulled over smartly, tires crunching over snow-covered gravel. He switched off the engine and the suspension drooped with a sigh. Everything was silent. Across the road was a field and beyond, headlights gliding along a flyover. On our side, a few feet back from the road, was a high hedge, a wrought-iron gate and two pillars. On one of them was a metal plate with the word CLUB in bold black lettering. Beside the plate was a bell, shining like a pearl in a shell.

I asked Kurt to wait and got out of the car. From the road it was impossible to see anything of the house. I rang the bell, waited a respectable time, then pushed open the gate and set off down the drive. Behind me, in the car, a match struck twice then flared, a radio came on—but ahead nothing stirred. I walked on expecting to bump into someone at every turn, but there was no one. I reached the house, a low stuccoed villa circled by thick black bushes, and made for the step-up porch with ivy black as seaweed clinging to the walls. The only windows I could see were shuttered, not a chink of light anywhere. I found another bell and rang it. There was no sound inside—no echoing bell, no footsteps, nothing moving. I rang again but this time didn't wait for an answer. Keeping close to the walls I made my way round the house, past dustbins, a strip of snowy lawn and a side door that was locked tight. At the back of the house I found a swimming pool with the underwater lights on and steam rising from the surface. Away in a fringe of trees was a small wooden shed, black and shadowy, from which came the low hum of a filter and heating plant. On the surface of the pool a coil of cleaning hose floated like a dead black snake, throwing up the strangest shadow on the wall of the house. The water was still except for a swirl and ripple of bubbles in one corner. I noticed there were no wet puddles on the paving stone surround. For no apparent reason, whoever had last been there had left the pool lights on. I was sure this was the kind of place I was looking for, but was puzzled that no one was around. It was strange, I'd never really thought that places like this ever closed.

Back in the car Kurt had a map spread over his knees. It was as if he knew the house would be deserted.

"I have not been here before," he said as I climbed into the back, "but there is another house I have heard of in a place called Ottobrunne. Here," he pointed at the map. "You can see that it is not far." I looked past the map at the meter. Over fifty marks already. He saw what I was thinking. "I tell you, for seventy marks I take you to Ottobrunne, wait and bring you back to your hotel?" I agreed.

Ottobrunne—he pointed out the scatter of lights as we approached—was no more distinctive than Trudering, just another sleeper suburb on the edge of the city.

"We are looking for a place called Rhineholmstrasse," Kurt said, trying to include me in the proceedings, mistaking my silence for disapproval. But it was not disapproval that made me silent, simply disbelief that Munich was proving such a stubborn host. The street, when he found it, was a cul-de-sac—as deserted and unpromising as any we had passed so far—large, middle-income homes set back from the pavement. There were no fences or hedges, just sloping lawns with driveways separating each property. We cruised silently along, looking from left to right, but there were no lights anywhere.

"Does this place have a number?" I asked, not sure what to look for.

"No, I don't think. All I remember is to look for a brick wall." The brick wall, when we found it, was only a few feet long and so low we could easily have missed it. Beyond it was a large parking lot into which Kurt turned, sweeping the front of the house with his headlights. It was a long, one-floor bungalow with the front wall made up almost entirely of frosted glass panels. This time we both got out and walked over to the front door. It looked depressingly dark and silent.

"Here," said Kurt, finding the bell and pressing it. "There is a sign too, I think." I could see his hand tracing something screwed onto the wooden door, like someone reading braille. I pulled out my lighter and in the flame read "Sauna Center." I groaned, pocketed the lighter and marched back to the car.

"I have a friend called Peter," said Kurt over his shoulder as we drove past the last street light in Ottobrunne and headed back to the city. "He lives in Schwabing. I am certain he will know a place." He looked back at me as if seeking my approval for this new plan. I felt like asking why he hadn't thought of this Peter in the first place, but just nodded and looked out at the darkened fields speeding past. I was tired and weary, but strangely unsettled too, unsatisfied, like a burglar who has found his first two houses securely locked and barred, yet rather than call it a night, will try a third—on the off chance.

We reached Peter's house twenty minutes later, one in a long terrace. From where I sat there appeared to be a few lights on in the block. I was coming to the conclusion that Munich was a ghost town. This time Kurt left the engine running, bounded up some steps to an old paneled door, ran his fingers down the flat numbers, then pushed one of the bells. There was a stutter of static, Kurt spoke into the grille, listened a moment, then ran back to the car. He flopped into the driver's seat and looked back at me, his gold tooth glinting in a smile. "He is coming down with us right now. He said he knows somewhere to go. It is still not too late."

The place Peter knew was, as far as I could determine, in the south of the city, down by the river. On the way there he spoke quickly to Kurt, pointing out directions, whistling once through his teeth when the wheels locked in a skid. His was a long face, youngish, with bright, excited eyes, the wisp of a mustache (just like the ones in the "Filly") and skin glowing green from the instrument panel. When he turned to introduce himself his handshake was dry and firm and though his accent was strong, even worse than Kurt's, his English was good. I had the impression that he was tall, though it was hard to be sure as he stumbled down the steps from his house, banging the door shut behind him and struggling into an overcoat. As I watched the road ahead between their shoulders, his ease and assurance made me feel a great deal more optimistic.

As soon as the car stopped he was out, telling us to stay where we were—he would return shortly. We watched him walk a few steps up the street, then stop at a door and knock. When it opened a yellow light fell over him and he disappeared inside, leaving only his shadow stretched across the pavement. A few moments later he peered out and beckoned us over.

Kurt made no effort to move. "I stay here and wait—but give me please my money now. If you are so long I go on." I made no objections, paid him and climbed out of the car. I knew he would drive off as soon as I was inside.

Peter held the door open for me and I squeezed past him into a long narrow passage, with an equally narrow staircase that disappeared above us. At the far end of the passage was another door, half-blocked by a table and chair and a large man dressed in a dinner jacket.

"We pay forty marks now," said Peter, pulling out a wad of notes and leading the way ahead. The man in the dinner jacket took our money, slid it into a wallet I couldn't imagine anyone ever trying to take off him, and we were waved past through the second door. Had Peter not been in front of me I would have fallen for certain. There was no room on the other side of the door as I had expected, but a steep stone staircase choked with the smell of damp plaster, old beer, new sweat, and blue cigarette smoke. At the bottom, the air was equally thick but the crowd of people even thicker. I was immediately disappointed for I could see at once that this was not the kind of place I had had in mind. Had the ceiling been arched it would have been nothing more than a German beer *keller*—fifty or so men stirring up a fair din in a long basement room, all of them fat, red-faced and prosperous-looking in a common sort of way. Weaving their way among the tables a number of girls in grubby Bavarian costumes handed out steins of beer. The room was the length of a railway carriage and about four times as wide with a bar running the length of one wall. Everything was stone—the floor, the walls, the ceiling, the staircase—as if it had been carved out of solid rock.

Pushing his way to the bar Peter said: "Any of these girls, you know, if you like any you can take them upstairs. But they are, how do you say it, not so . . . reliable."

When the beer arrived I asked him how he knew this place, hoping my show of interst might hide my disappointment. I suddenly felt very tired. "When I worked in a factory before university," he said, "I came here with some friends very often. It is a kind of club, very secret you understand. In Germany we love the secret clubs and things, you know." One of the waitresses pushed between us to the bar and smiled up at us both, one after the other, as she disentangled her fingers from the stein handles. "We have all kinds of men here," he continued over her head, "most from the factories, working men, but anyone can join. It is just difficult to find these places. You must know someone to become a member, or perhaps they know you at the door and let you in. Like me."

There was no point leaving the bar to look for a table so we stayed where we were, Peter telling me about the club and others like it while I tried to work out how I could leave without offending him. I had just bought the second round, after which I had decided I could make my excuses and head back for the hotel, when suddenly the lights went out. There were cheers from the men and squeals from the girls.

"Ah, I think you will enjoy this. You will not have seen this before." In the darkness I could feel him very close, as if he was whispering in my ear. Then at the far end of the room a set of lights came on, illuminating a small stagelike area from which the girls were hastily clearing away tables, chairs and customers. One table was left at the edge of the space and a chair dragged up to it. "Do you play cards," asked Peter, "make bets, you know, that kind of thing?" I shook my head. Not very often, I told him.

"This is a very special kind of gamble—very popular here. There are two kinds of this game; tonight I do not know which they have. They are done . . . alternate, you understand?" Already it was difficult to see what was happening, with customers crowding around the table, so Peter caught my sleeve and pulled me after him until we found a tiny space at the end of the bar, just outside the pool of light, looking into a half-circle of excited, flushed faces. Another man in a dinner jacket, as big as his colleague upstairs, had settled himself into the chair with his back to the stage and his hand on a tin box; he seemed to mark out the border of the stage, beyond which no one should step. Behind the crowd of men, the girls began clearing empty steins and tidying up the room while there was an opportunity to do so.

Just as I was starting to wonder what on earth was going to happen, a door I hadn't noticed on the other side of the stage area opened and into the pool of light strode a young girl in a very businesslike pinstripe suit, leading behind her three equally young men wearing only small sequined pouches. Two of them were colored, one was white, all three well-muscled, their bodies oiled and their skin shining in the light. For the first time since I had stepped down into this basement there was silence—just a shuffling of feet, an occasional cough. With her back to the crowd, the girl took off her jacket and dropped it on the table. There was a low murmur from the onlookers. The three young men, standing side by side, just watched, hands behind their backs—not moving, not making a sound.

As casually as if she were in her own bedroom the girl unzipped her skirt and stepped out of it. Then, slowly, she began unbuttoning her blouse. There was a whistle from somewhere in the crowd but she paid no attention, her eyes fixed on her three companions. Peter nudged me and nodded toward them. There was no need for me to ask what I should be looking for. Their pouches were beginning to bulge.

Sitting on the edge of the table, the straps of her suspender belt an inch from the fat man's elbow, she unpinned a bun of blond hair and shook it free over her shoulders, raking it out with her fingers, then leaned forward and began unclipping her stockings, lifting each leg high as she slipped them off. Sweating in a beam of light, the fat man turned to watch with the others. The girl stood up, unhooked the belt and bra and dropped them next to the tin box. I looked at the faces around me—every eye in the room followed every move she made, unblinking, intent. Walking back to the three men, she paused, slid down her panties and wiggled her behind at the crowd. There was a whisper of approval as she kicked them aside. I noticed that with every item of clothing she removed her behavior, her movements, became more languorous, more lascivious, though she seemed to be playing more to her companions than to the crowd. Quite naked, she stepped up to the first man, one of the two blacks, and slipped her arm around his neck, then began licking and kissing his chest, her leg rubbing up and down his thigh. Then she moved behind him, neatly concealing the front of her body from the crowd, her white hands running across his black chest, her red nails tracing the band of his pouch which looked as though it would burst open at any moment. Then she was on to the next man, the second Negro, her white body flashing between them, repeating the moves, and finally to the third man. None of them moved an inch, or reciprocated in any way. Then, like a huntress removing the leather cap from a falcon's head, she released each of the three pouches one after the other, letting them drop to the floor between the men's feet and watching her three birds rise into the air.

All at once there was whispering and chatter, the men reaching for their wallets and digging into their pockets. Some of them began arguing, pointing at the three naked men, as if unable to reach agreement. The girl, meanwhile, was not idle, moving back and forth from one man to the next, sliding her fingers over one like a pirate testing the keenness of a blade; cupping the next; stroking the third—almost, I thought, as if exhibiting them to the crowd. The fat man by the table was busy taking money and writing out colored chits. The notes settled on the table like butterflies and coins spilled out like silver puddles.

I turned to Peter for an explanation. "Just watch now, the betting is almost made." I was still a little mystified as to what, exactly, they were betting on. Whatever it was, there was a great deal of money being staked. I watched a man with a brace on his teeth and a grin like a zipper lay down three one-hundred-mark notes. What were the odds, I asked Peter?

"Odds?"

"How do they bet? What can they win?"

"Ah, odds. It is three to one, of course. Take the right man and if you are right you have back three times the money you put down at first. It is very simple."

When all the bets had been made, the man in the suit locked away the money in his tin box and everyone's attention returned to the participants in this strange game.

The men had not moved but the girl seemed to be everywhere —pushing her hands between their legs, holding two at a time, gripping them, rubbing them with her thumbs, licking, kissing, pressing her breasts to them—her body shining not with sweat, but with the oil she had rubbed off them. Her cheeks, her breasts, her hands glistened with it.

As if at a given signal, the three men now moved into a tighter line and the girl slipped to her knees in front of them, catching two of them in her hands, then sliding the man in the middle into her mouth. There was a long, collective groan from the onlookers.

Very slowly, very evenly, she began rocking back and forth on her knees, the men sliding between her fingers and lips, white on black, red on black, white on white, her hands and her lips pulling and sucking at the stiffened bodies that stood before her. Then, without a break in the rhythm, she moved to one side, taking a new man in her mouth, her hands round the other two. There was a splatter of applause at her dexterity but she didn't seem to hear it, rocking on with the same steady motion.

Peter was smiling: "It will be for sure the black man on the end . . . you see." I looked at the man. He had not yet been in her mouth and his eyes were fixed on her bobbing head, drawing himself up for his turn. When it came, his body seemed to sag as if she was sucking the strength and the will clean out of him. A grin slid across his face then disappeared as she moved on, taking him back in her hand, white on glistening black flesh, white against a gray, peeping purple.

The pace she had set herself now, gradually, began to build up, her movements sharper, faster, though she never missed a beat, each changeover as smooth as an automatic transmission. It was really a most admirable performance, her hands and her mouth closing around the men with an uncanny and unfailing accuracy.

"What's the other game?" I whispered to Peter.

"The same thing, only one man with three girls. Is not so clever." I was about to ask him what he meant when there was a sudden cry of encouragement from the crowd. I looked back to the stage to see the white man's arms up in the air like a runner pushing through a tape, but then suddenly the girl's head had moved to the next man and the moment was gone, her mouth replaced by her hand, his arms dropping to his sides.

"What happens if one of them comes in her hand?"

Peter didn't understand so I explained more fully what I meant.

"He is out. Kaput. Then it is for the other two men. To win, the man must come to her mouth."

Most of the onlookers were shouting now, like punters urging on a horse, but through all the rising commotion the girl maintained her steady rhythm, increasing the speed, giving each man the same amount of time in her mouth. You could have set your watch by her.

Unable to restrain himself, one of the men brought his hands from behind his back and tried to hold her head in place (loud boos from the audience), but she must have bitten him for he snatched his hands back and she changed over, quitting him before his time. Penalty point. The noise was very loud now, this extraordinary race clearly reaching its final stages, though it was impossible to tell

161

which of the three would win. Each looked as if he was only seconds away, oiled bodies quivering, legs bucking, heads nodding, lips stretched open against their teeth as if willing themselves to finish. And still the girl kept on, no flagging, no hint of tiredness, hands and mouth jerking away at the men. The shouting was intense, bouncing off the ceiling, filling the room, the men waving their chits like colored flags at a royal parade; even the fat man at the table had turned to watch, though his stubby fingers still covered the tin box. I noticed too that some of the girls in their Bavarian costumes had managed to push their way forward, their bright, bedraggled, tired faces peeping through the front rank. From where Peter and I stood, we could see most of what was happening—the girl's eyes shining, closing, opening for the changeover; her breasts swinging; her buttocks sinking onto her heels; her cheeks swelling with every downward thrust, then hollowing as she swung back; her red lips gripping like a rubber washer; her nostrils flaring like a race horse's; saliva dripping from her chin.

And then it was over, the black man that Peter had pointed out at the beginning leaning back, arms in the air, then doubling over and pumping into the girl. Her hands fell away from the other two who seemed to totter without her support and she pushed frantically at the black man's thighs, her head almost hidden by his jerking body. Then she was free, turning to the crowd, eyes wide and ablaze, hair sticking sodden to the sweat on her cheeks, her lips parting and mouth opening, then her throat swallowing with a choking cough. There was rapturous applause, shrieking, screaming, and lights were switched on throughout the room. Stiffly, she rose to her feet, gave a quick bow, snatched up her clothes and ran toward the door. The three men, dazed in the sudden lights, hesitated a moment, then loped crookedly after her.

"I told you . . . I told you," shouted Peter in the uproar. "I should have made a bet, yes?" He pulled me back to the bar for a celebration drink, past a line of men already forming at the table to collect their winnings. The rest made their way back to their seats, their tables, tearing up their chits and scattering them onto the floor.

I stayed for only that one drink, then made my apologies and left. I felt I had seen quite enough for my first night in Munich. Peter was in high spirits, though he was no richer, his arm looped around the waitress who had made a play for him earlier. He shook my hand, made me promise to call on him again, and I left him in his new companion's "not-so-reliable" hands.

162

Outside, everything was still. When the front door closed behind me, I stood for a moment listening, but there was not the slightest sound from below. As I had suspected, there was no sign of Kurt, so I set off in the general direction of my hotel, somewhere ahead in the orange glow.

An Expensive Treat

It was twelve thirty that same day that I met Dorte, or, more precisely, that Dorte contrived to meet me.

I awoke late to a clamor of bells and a blue, unruffled sky. I showered, dressed, retrieved my wallet and passport from their hiding place and left my room to the maid. At reception, much busier than the previous night, I cornered the day-shift head porter, asked him the same questions I had asked his colleague the night before and left the same tip. I crossed the strip of park in front of the hotel and followed the same route I had taken a few hours earlier. Though there was a pattern to my movements, there was no immediate or deliberate motive. I was simply a tourist exploring a new city, albeit in a more orthodox manner than the previous night —just seeing the sights, bound for nowhere in particular.

In the cool white interior of the Frauenkirche where a service was just ending, watching the enameled figures ring out midday high up on the walls of the Town Hall, wandering across Marienplatz, idling along shop windows, buying cigarettes, a newspaper, finding a table in a coffeeshop—at no time did it cross my mind that I had laid a trail, that I was followed, studied.

At first sight, Dorte seemed tall and thin, but an elegant thin, with blond tangled hair that looked as if it hadn't been dried properly, her hand resting on one of the empty chairs at my table. "Is this seat taken?" Her English was soft and confident, only the first word clipped a fraction. I nodded, of course, help yourself. After the extremes of the previous night, the ease and unexpectedness of this present encounter caught me off balance—for there was no mistaking that sudden tug and surge of recognition, as positive a feeling as a fish on the end of a line.

While I watched the Sunday crowds passing by and scanned the headlines, I also watched Dorte. She ordered a coffee in German, wore a large coral ring on her wedding finger, and under a thick winter coat a pink crocheted sweater and a pair of washed-out jeans tucked into brown boots. When she opened her bag a mirror flashed across her face. She caught my eye and smiled. She crossed her legs one way, then changed her mind and crossed them the other. Her coffee arrived, a toss of the hair as she turned to thank the waiter. She drank slowly, sipping as if it were very hot, tipping forward, an arm on the table, fingernails tapping idly on the tabletop.

Again we caught each other's eye, long enough this time for one of us to say something. I nodded, semi-smiled.

"Your English is excellent."

"Thank you, so is yours." Laughter is the easiest way to uncoil. She knew it, I was grateful for it, and we both took advantage, letting that frisson of awkwardness escape like a lungful of cigarette smoke.

"I am Dorte."

"Martin." The introduction came as easily and conventionally as though we were meeting at a cocktail party.

"Martin? It is a German name?"

"Perhaps, but I'm English."

"You sound American."

"Perhaps, but I'm . . ."

". . . English." And she laughed again and put her hand over mine. But swiftly and it was gone. I ordered another beer, knowing right then that, sooner or later, we would end up sleeping with each other.

"And beer for me too?"

"Of course. Two beers, thank you." She took a cigarette from her bag and held my hand close as I lit it for her.

"Tell me, please, you're on business or holiday?" Which, roughly translated, meant was I on expenses or a holiday budget?

"I'm passing through really, on my way home," I said, sidestepping her question more for fun than anything.

"But it was business this trip, or holiday?" she persevered.

"Business," I conceded. "I write political features."

"Features?" She said the word as if it tasted nasty.

"It means I'm not good enough to be a real political correspondent, so I do lightweight pieces for whoever will take them. Interviews, profiles, that sort of thing."

"So you must travel a lot?"

"The whole time."

"It must be lonely."

We had lunch in a small, wood-paneled restaurant close to Marienplatz. She wasn't German, she told me, but Danish. Her parents lived just outside Copenhagen. She had been in Munich for six years.

"I was a stripper," she said, spooning up ice cream. "I worked first in the clubs at home, then my agent arranged for trips to Holland and Germany. There was more money, you see, the more you traveled." She told me all this as calmly as if she were talking about someone else. We had coffee and left.

"How long have you been in Munich?" she asked, as we stepped into the street.

"I arrived last night."

"Then you have seen nothing." Not that much, I thought. "I will show you. Do you like that?"

She had a car, a red Spitfire, in the underground car park beneath Stachus. With the top down and an icy wind slicing above the windshield we drove west past the Hauptbahnhoff to Nymphenburg Palace where she dragged me through the halls and corridors and state rooms to a long gallery—the *Schönheiten* she called it, her Danish softening the German word—with its twenty-four portraits of Ludwig's favorite beauties.

"Aren't they beautiful?" she asked, stepping from one to another and staring up into their plump pink faces.

"Not really my type."

She laughed. "But they were beautiful, then," she added wistfully.

Back in town we trudged through the snow in the English Gardens and she told me more of herself. "I have always liked Munich. I would work here a month in the clubs, then Berlin, Hamburg, Amsterdam perhaps, then home. But I always liked to come back to Munich. It was different then. In the end, when I had enough money, I bought an apartment here and stayed. My agent was furious." She invested this last word with a long drawn-out purr. And then, further on, quite casually she said: "While I was a stripper I never slept with a man for money. Do you believe that?"

"Do you work the clubs now?"

She looked at me from under a tangle of hair, tucked her arm through mine and smiled. "No."

From the English Gardens she drove me directly to my hotel. Not once, I realized with a start, had she asked me where I was staying, and at no time had I volunteered the information. I said nothing.

We had tea in what must have been the ballroom. There was a raised balcony at one end for the orchestra—at present represented by a single pianist in tails among the palms—a polished strip-floor that felt sprung, and chandeliers. Beneath them, islands of armchairs, tables and murmured conversations. We bent over the table and talked, lounged back in the cushions and silence. Then more conversation, questions and answers, probes and parries. I began to wonder what was next. Should I invite her up to my room? Should I ask how much? Should I invite her to dinner? I invited her to dinner. She seemed genuinely pleased.

"But I shall take you," she said, which left me rather stunned.

We met in the bar at eight, then drove to a restaurant. She wore the same coat but had changed into a simple woolen dress, dark and belted, bare legs, the barest of makeup and high heels. She wore a watch, but the ring was gone from her wedding finger. Her hair still looked wet. We sat at a table by the wall. Among other things, I told her of my exploits the night before and she laughed, tossing her hair, sending gauzy waves of scent across the table.

"But Munich has changed. You have heard, of course, of our Regionspresident Mr. Strauss—Mr. Franz Josef Strauss." She said the name as if she were saluting—a mock salute. "You should meet him, write a story about him. He is big already, but he will be bigger. The unions hate him. You know," she paused, "it always starts here in Munich."

"Is he CDU or CSU?" I remembered the headlines but couldn't recall the definitions and having told Dorte I was a political writer I decided I better show some interest.

"CDU—ultraconservative, you would say. He married the daughter of a rich Braumeister, he went to China—the first in the government, I think. Watch out, Carstens and Schmidt. He has cleaned up this city. Now he wants to clean up the country. It is very difficult to work like this."

"So how do you work?" She pushed at her food with her fork, sipped her wine. Her silence made me wonder whether I should have asked.

"It is not easy," she said at last. "I do not like houses, not like those you saw last night. Too rough. Me, I like to work alone, to have a choice . . . freedom. Today I work, but then I take a week off and go skiing. That is how I like it. Now I work only from the best hotels. I watch carefully and I have friends."

"Hall porters?"

"Sometimes," she smiled, knowing what I was getting at. "They know me. They help me and I help them."

"And do they help you if you have trouble?"

"What trouble?"

"With the men you meet?"

"You write about Franz Josef—not about me."

"You're more interesting."

"I hope so."

We finished our meal, ordered coffee.

"So when do you leave Munich?"

"I hadn't thought. Tomorrow. The day after."

"To where? Home?" The coffee arrived. "Believe it, you have seen the best—and the worst—that Munich has. It is a quiet town. If you want fun you must go to Berlin or Hamburg. There they know how to have fun. In Munich you retire—like me."

"Perhaps then, I'll try Berlin."

"Yes? I tell you where to go. I have friends in Berlin."

Though I hadn't believed she would, she snatched the bill away from me when it arrived. She paid, we left and drove back to the hotel. At the entrance, the head porter touched his cap. We waited for a lift and then rode up to my floor. There seemed no question on either part that this was the most natural end to our evening. We could have been husband and wife. But as I slipped the key into the lock I started to tremble—an aching shiver in stomach and shoulders.

Once in the room, Dorte wasted little time with awkward preliminaries: unlatching her belt, she caught her dress by the hem, drew it over her head and let it drop to the floor. She wore nothing beneath it, just stood there in her high heels, her head on one side. Before I could take it all in she was kissing me, sitting back on the bed. "You want me to keep these on?" she said, pointing at her shoes. I shook my head and she kicked them off.

"Why don't you hurry and come in the bed," she said, sliding under the quilt.

I undressed, half-turned away from her—made to switch out the light.

"No, leave it on."

I turned to the bed.

"Ohhh, it's so small," she cried, the "so" like "zu."

"It gets bigger."

I joined her, pulled the cover over me. For a few moments we lay side by side, then turned to one another and touched.

"So it does," she whispered, "so it does."

Dorte liked to take control. It was difficult to think I was paying her for something she obviously enjoyed so much. She sat astride me.

"Men like to touch my breasts. Do you like it?" Not waiting for an answer, she cupped, stroked, squeezed, spread and teased her breasts. Flung back her tangled hair and laughed. I could feel the laughter trembling through her body.

"Here," she took my hand, "touch me here. That's right. Just there."

I felt her leave the bed early next morning. I slept. I remember the sound of the shower, a door closing quietly. I slept on. It could have been hours later that I awoke, a part of her warmth and scent. There was a huge feeling of contentment; I wished she were still with me.

I showered, toweled dry and walked back into the bedroom. What I hadn't noticed on my way to the bathroom, I noticed now with a flash of panic—my wallet lying open on the table. But the panic, thankfully, was brief. Tucked like a hand of cards in one of the pockets were five blue one-hundred-Deutsche-mark notes—a perfect fan. My passport was still there, my travelers' checks and credit cards untouched. I made some rapid calculations, trying to remember how much money I had had the night before. Almost sixteen hundred marks missing. Dorte had been an expensive treat. I consoled myself with the thought that she could have cost me a great deal more.

Time
to Kill

It was just a little game, nothing more. Me against the clock, just to see if it was possible—an amusing alternative to those interminable waits in airport lounges; a way to avoid the drudgery of airport shopping malls, coffee bars and aerogrills. So the first thing I did when I arrived at Frankfurt-am-Main was check the time of the next departure for Berlin. There was an hour and a half before the flight was called. I bought a ticket, checked through my single bag and left the terminal building. It took a few minutes following the exit signs and finding my way out and I realized how quickly time passes when you're racing against it.

There was no need to ask the taxi to hurry. The driver pulled away from the curb as though determined to break records of his own. It struck me the two of us were not unalike—he probably tried to vary the routine nature of his work just as I was trying now to vary mine. In the same way he might try to shave off a few minutes on the airport-to-city run, so I was setting myself time limits. It gave the whole thing a certain edge.

It wasn't until the Mercedes slipped onto the autobahn that he asked where I wanted to go, so busy had he been negotiating the flyovers and slip roads surrounding the terminal complex.

Hauptbahnhof, I told him. The main railway station seemed as good a place to start as any. At least there would be no delay finding a taxi to bring me back. I also took the precaution of timing the journey and examining the route back for possible hold-ups—road works, lane-closures, bottlenecks—anything that might somehow threaten my schedule. It all looked clear enough, but I decided to add an extra five minutes onto the journey time in case the next driver was not so swift. Fifteen minutes after the pickup we were swinging into the station square. So, twenty minutes each way, with a few minutes more for finding the right gate and boarding the plane, and I was left with about fifty minutes for what I had in mind.

I hadn't anticipated too many difficulties, but I certainly hadn't thought that it would be so easy, so quick. Rather than try the station, I crossed the square and took the first street that opened up for me. It didn't look all that promising—a couple of shops, bars, a pizza house—but up ahead I could see neon flickering anemically through the midday drizzle. Then, suddenly, I was in the thick of it—a line of sex shops and strip joints, none of which I wanted but which nevertheless encouraged me to think I was in the right place. Avoiding the enticements of doormen, uselessly describing all the charms their establishments had to offer in a language I didn't understand, I walked up both sides of the street trying to assess my chances. I could see no obvious girls dawdling on the pavements, nor any cruising past in cars. As for pimps, there looked to be a number of them but time didn't allow for protracted bargaining and the usual long-distance haul such arrangements often entailed.

Not only had I decided to limit myself to a rapidly decreasing hour and a half and not to seek directions, but I had also determined, after my recent extravagant brush with Dorte, to keep costs to a minimum. I had started out with a hundred-Deutsche-mark note and that was all I wanted to spend. After two taxi fares and tips I was left with about half that. Fifty minutes and fifty marks. I was beginning to wonder if I had set myself too strict a schedule when I spotted, at the end of the street, a large building with six floors of identically curtained windows, a pink fluorescent tube between each curtain and windowframe. All the curtains were drawn. I stood for a moment looking up at it, then crossed over and examined the entrance. There was no doorman, indeed no doors to speak of, just heavy plastic flaps that looked scuffed and curled with wear and made a flip-flop sound as they opened and closed. They reminded me of hospital casualty doors that can be pushed open by trolleys, the kind of doors supermarkets use for their storerooms. I was further encouraged by the sign above this entrance: no words—just a large plump heart painted pink. I wasn't certain what I would find inside, but I had a vague idea that this would be where I would find the girls—off the street and safely installed in their own private rooms. So much more civilized—and comfortable.

The immediate impression was not so favorable. I didn't step through a mirror, I didn't find a bottle with instructions to drink, a piece of cake to eat, a white rabbit to lead me on—but otherwise it was all pure Alice. Once I had pushed past the plastic doors I was in another world. There was no carpet, only bare boards, no doors on the ground floor, just a long tunnel with spray-painted arrows on the walls pointing the way ahead. The whole place seemed mysterious and empty and had it not been for the sound of footsteps somewhere ahead of me, I might well have turned back.

The first three doors I came to were on the first landing, six steps up from the ground floor. All of them were closed. I listened through their thin-looking panels but could hear nothing inside. I was tempted to knock but thought better of it. The rooms were either empty or the occupants engaged.

By the time I reached the third landing, I decided I had it worked out—the rooms on the lower floors presumably filled up much sooner than the rooms higher up. On a quiet day one wouldn't have to go farther than the first or second landing before finding an open door. But when it was busy, as today appeared to be, the doors would be closed all the way up to the topmost floors —wherever they were. It was, I concluded, simply a question of climbing onward and upward until I came to an open door, presumably with a girl on display and a bed in the background. Had all the doors been open and all the girls available it would have been, in Zilla's words, a real "supermarket."

This piece of detection work kept me happy until I realized with a start that I had lost my sense of direction—I had climbed so many flights of stairs (up and down), and followed so many winding passages and spray-painted arrows (left and right) that I no longer had any clear idea where the street was. I felt as though I were a part of some grand Escher-like design from which I could never escape. Only the sound of distant footsteps somewhere ahead of me, somewhere above, kept me going—a heartening clomp-clomp, and frequent clanking as shoes scuffed the strips of metal rimming each step. As I climbed onward I began memorizing patches of marked plaster in case I came upon them again. Suddenly, somewhere above me, the footsteps stopped. I stopped too and strained to hear low whispers and a door closing. My first feeling was one of loneliness and desertion, but the next instant I realized that whoever had been ahead of me had found an open door—reached the girls. I had to be getting closer. I looked at my watch; I had been in the building a little over five minutes. Somehow it felt much longer. A night and a day could pass outside but in here you would never know.

When, at last, I saw the first girls' heads, peering down from the landing above me, I slowed my pace, using the time to make up my mind which of the two I would choose. The higher I climbed, the more I could see of them. The first girl sat on a stool and wore a purple one-piece swimsuit with a shawl draped round her shoulders. Her legs were crossed and one heel of her stilettos was hooked over a strut. She was smoking, an ashtray in her lap, the trailing tails of her shawl trapped in her elbows. There was something taut and unyielding about her, the way her fingers gripped the cigarette, the way her lips tightened over the filter, the way her eyes squinted through the smoke and her cheeks hollowed with each drag. Two steps from the landing she gave me a hard, practiced smile. Her companion (it didn't look as though either of them ever spoke to the other) was coiled up in a chair, just inside her door, leafing through a magazine. She wore a white lace corset with black seamed stockings, the suspenders stretched over an expanse of white skin, and looked less tired, less wrought up than her neighbor. The room behind her seemed brighter too, more open, more inviting. I slipped past the girl on the stool and approached this second girl.

"You speak English?"

She shook her head without looking up—just turned another page.

"How much?"

"Fünfundzwanzig"—twenty-five. About the same price as the taxi fare into town.

"Okay."

She looked up. "Okay?" Pulling herself out of the chair, she pushed it aside for me to get past and closed the door behind us. Inside she took the money and introduced herself briskly as Justine. The room was almost exactly square, carpeted with a white shag rug that was pink by the window where the fluorescent tube glowed behind a lace curtain. In one corner was a wash basin and a rail of towels; there was a dressing table with its mirror frame jammed with postcards, an enormous quilt-covered bed with a spaniel asleep on it (I caught the name Helmut as she shooed it off), and a tottering wardrobe against the far wall. Clothes littered the floor around it, spilled from its shelves and hung from its open doors— more corsets, camisole tops, lacy French knickers, a Japanese dressing gown with a twisting embroidered dragon, a selection of belts, a rail of colored stockings, suspender belts, bras, silk slips, slinky negligées, rank upon rank of unlikely heeled shoes and a pair of long black boots that would have kept her dry in the fastest salmon stream. What particularly caught and held my attention though, hanging from a hook, were the coils of a whip with a knotted tip and a corded black handle. I wondered whether it was just decoration—a souvenir, perhaps—or, like the clothes, part of her equipment, something she would use on a customer if he paid enough. I was about to say something, mention it in passing, when I realized I had neither the time nor the money to experiment. Another time, I thought.

While I undressed, Justine walked to the washstand, turned on the taps and played her hand under the water. When she had the mix right she beckoned me over, lifted me over the rim of the basin and squirted some green liquid onto me from a bottle marked *Intim-Waschlotion.* She was standing a little in front of me and to one side and as she lathered me I watched her tiny breasts jiggle around in the starched cups of her corset; the nipples looked like baby pink birds in a nest. She was smaller than me with a fall of unbrushed black hair that felt dry and prickly against my skin, and in the mirror above the basin I could see her eyes running over me as her fingers pulled and probed. I was never offended or insulted by this preparatory washing (indeed, I enjoyed it immensely) and it bothered me not in the least to think she was checking me out before starting anything. As well as putting her own mind at rest, it also comforted me to know she took this kind of care. I wondered, as she soaped away, about Dorte who had leapt straight into bed without the slightest show of caution. Perhaps she worked on the assumption that men who stayed in expensive hotels were somehow immune from social diseases.

The washing over, the toweling dry left to me, Justine spread herself on the quilt and pulled a pillow under her head. When I sat down beside her, glancing at my watch as I did so, she was still squirming herself around like a dog rolling on grass. When she was ready she lifted her head, pointed to a button on her hip and lay back with her eyes closed. The button was the size of small pearl, and as far as I could see, kept the front panel of her panties attached to the back. There was, I discovered, a matching button on the other side and once I had pushed them both clear of their loops, I was able to draw the material away from between her thighs, revealing, beneath the lace edging of her corset, the tiniest of goatee beards. Almost grudgingly, she parted her legs and pulled me into her, squirming some more to accommodate the extra weight. Indeed, throughout the whole performance, the only voluntary movements she contributed came as a result of her trying to get more comfortable.

With little encouragement from her, and an abiding worry about the time, it seemed an age before I had finished, but looking at my watch as I dressed I saw I still had half an hour to spare, enough time to watch her pick through the wardrobe and select a new outfit—a black belted swimsuit and a pair of improbable-looking high heels. Outside, the other girl was still smoking, still leaning forward on her crossed legs. Snapping at the elasticized edges of her swimsuit, Justine settled down with the same magazine in the same pose to wait for the next customer, whose footsteps I could already hear approaching.

I made the flight for Berlin with ten minutes to spare. Strapping myself into my seat I felt pleased with my success—winning out on the time trial—but was forced to admit I preferred my time with Dorte. But then, for the price of a taxi fare, I didn't suppose I could expect a great deal more.

The Tin
Top Hat

Hidden in three tight black columns, beside Andy Capp and the Wizard of Id, the *International Herald Tribune* weather report forecast showers for my arrival in Berlin. A comforting understatement. As my plane juddered through low clouds and touched down at Tegel airfield I could see sheets of rain and sleet gusting over the grass and tarmac like wind over a field of corn.

The city was bleak and gray, old and new, bombed churches made into traffic islands, tower blocks blank with glass—a city alternately clear and distorted with every sweep of the taxi's wipers. Across the street from my hotel window, a giant blue Mercedes sign revolved against a ruptured sky like a cheap neon star. There was none of Munich's softness here, I decided.

The Tanzer Club, when I found it, surprised me. Or rather, the thought of Dorte working there surprised me. I had expected something more subtle, understated, discreet; this was such a shabby, down-at-heel sort of place: T-A-N-Z-E-R, the letters spelled out with flashing red bulbs (two or three of them dead), a red awning with its frame rusting through the canvas, a crimson gloss wall splattered with faded pictures in glass cases and two thick-set men leaning beside a booth and smoking cigarettes in cupped hands. They watched me as I stopped and looked up at the building, kept their eyes on me as I crossed over and paid my money, then one of them jerked open a red door.

Immediately inside was a steep staircase, walls on both sides, no banister, like a near-vertical tunnel, papered in mock velvet. How many times, I wondered, had Dorte climbed these stairs? At the top I was greeted by a tall woman with bleached, bobbed hair, a fringe that failed to conceal a lined forehead and teeth that didn't quite seem to fit in her mouth. The way her lips moved over them, and the way her tongue sucked and flapped between them, made them look loose and uncomfortable. She told me her name was Klara, asked mine, then showed me through the bar into a large darkened room. We crossed a small dance floor, passed a raised shadowy stage that consisted of one enormous circular bed covered in synthetic sheepskin, and she showed me to a table with a banquette seat upholstered in the same slightly sticky sheepskin.

Could she get me a drink? Join me? I asked for a beer and whatever she wanted and watched her trip away to the bar, the back of her sequined gown scooped so low over her buttocks they formed a second cleavage. In the gloom I peered around. Most of the tables were empty, most of the action, the girls, grouped around the bar. For a moment I was tempted to follow her back there, a little annoyed with myself for letting her steer me away from them. But I decided against it; there was plenty of time to spare. So long as I did it politely, I knew there would be little problem getting rid of Klara and finding someone else. It was conceivable that she might even give me some tips, a few pointers regarding the other girls.

She returned with the drinks on a tray, a champagne cocktail for herself in a tall fluted glass and a beer for me which she proceeded to pour at such a rate that the head overflowed the top, slid across the table and trickled onto my knee. A hand crusted with rings brushed at the soaking material and then settled there. I wondered how many times she had performed that little trick.

Despite her rather ravaged looks, her tired, predictable routine, I felt strangely drawn to her—not out of any immediate sense of attraction, but because I had nothing to fear from her. She was no threat. Too much booze in her blood, too many bad memories, I thought, too many late nights had dulled her edge. But nor did I feel sorry for her either; rather a kind of respect, not so much for what she did, but that she did it still, had to do it. Every brush stroke of mascara, of which she wore a great deal, must have been torture for her. How dearly she must have wanted to struggle out of her ridiculous costume, grab her bag and just go home; leave all this behind.

Conversation was difficult, her English appalling. But she tried, which endeared her to me all the more. I guessed the questions she asked and the answers she gave had been repeated so often they no longer had meaning for her—just a convenient way of passing the hours. "You are American? English?"; "Is this your first time in Berlin?"; "You have good time?"; "I live Berlin long time"; "I know many American"; "I speak English not so good"; "I like one more champagne cocktail, thank you." How many of those, I wondered, must she have choked down? She insisted I try it: it was like a too-sweet fruit juice. Nodding toward the stage, I asked if there were shows. All night, she replied, the girls took turns. "I watch," she added sadly. I asked if she remembered Dorte. "Dorte? Dorte? No Dorte here." I felt she hadn't quite understood but didn't pursue it. And so the conversation continued, cautiously, laboured, until, at last, a bank of spotlights suspended from the ceiling snapped on, illuminating the dance floor and the sheepskin bed.

"Ah, it starts again," she told me, sounding almost relieved that she would no longer need to talk. "So, sit here, see more," she said, indicating we change places. When we were settled her hand returned to my leg, higher this time. I looked at it and then at her. She craned forward over the table, giggling like a schoolgirl in a series of breathless hiccups.

The music, which had so far comprised a selection of muted instrumentals, now swung brashly into "Saturday Night Fever." Beside me, Klara tapped her foot and hummed along, albeit out of tune, as if confusing it with another song from another time.

A girl stepped into the pool of light. We were close enough to hear her heels tapping on the floor and the oily swish of diamante beading. She was young, quite pretty, dark-haired but a little weighty in the hips. The music was too fast for her routine and she missed a few steps, but when she climbed onto the bed she came into her own, oblivious to the music yet somehow managing to translate the basic rhythms into her movements. At the end there was isolated clapping from the darker corners of the room that I had thought were empty. She slipped off the bed, swept up her things with a swift bow, and left the floor.

"You like this girl?" asked Klara.

I shook my head and smiled. But if I had, I asked, could I . . . ?

"Yes, yes." It was something of a relief to know that Klara did not expect me to spend the night with her, was not hurt that I wanted one of the others.

"And how much?"

"You buy special bottle of champagne and drink with her."

"How much is the champagne?"

She shrugged, muttered, like a stall holder in a market place deciding what price was right for this particular customer. "Two hundred sixty marks," she said at last. It didn't sound like a question, the inflection vague; but it could have been.

"And that includes everything?"

Klara nodded.

"So where do we drink this champagne?" She looked at me, understood and cackled.

"We have rooms," she replied and lifted a finger to her lips.

The moment the next girl stepped onto the dance floor I knew she was the one I wanted. She was far younger than the first, seventeen or eighteen, not so tall, with long blond hair that waved slightly over her shoulders.

"That one," I whispered. Klara nodded as if this choice was expected—this girl the club's major attraction.

I watched every step the girl took, every movement, each as light and flowing as a feather boa. Nothing awkward, nothing stiff —just supple and warm, tired and luxurious. She looked young enough to mean what she did, young enough still to have the energy to invest it with some feeling. From where we sat, close enough to smell her perfume, her skin looked powdered, her breasts taut and round and barely moving as she swept around the floor. I could see dimples in the small of her back and what looked like a tiny brown mouse clamped between her thighs. The thought that, for a handful of notes, I could have her as simply and easily as ordering a fresh round of drinks, was simply overwhelming.

"Shall we drink at the bar?" I suggested, as soon as she had finished.

"Okay," replied Klara. "With Hildie, okay?" Hildie, Hildie.

There were five girls at the bar, leaning, sitting, talking. In the far corner a large man with dark, brooding brows and meaty fists had his arm round the first stripper. She looked uncomfortable, moved jerkily beside him as if trying to keep her balance but at the same time not fall against him. He moved his arm from around her waist, put it around her narrow shoulders and pulled her into his armpit. He looked like a huge bear, clutching her in one paw and a glass in the other. The other girls looked around now and again as if they were worried about her, checking to see she was all right.

I drew up a stool, ordered a beer and another champagne cocktail for Klara. Having dumped her so unceremoniously in favor of Hildie, I felt it was the least I could do. I also put in an order for a bottle of champagne. The girl who served the drinks was a dark-skinned gypsy of a girl with copper brown hair that swung across her face as she moved. "Who do you buy this bottle for?" she demanded. Then sweetly, teasingly: "For me? For Rula?" And then burst out laughing as if the very thought was ridiculous, that she had boys like me before breakfast and flung them legless aside.

"For Hildie," said Klara at my elbow.

"Ah ha, little Hildie, you like her dance? She's very *gut,* " and patting my arm she said, "she will be here very soon."

While I waited, I listened to them talk: Klara, the eldest by far, who made them all squeal with what sounded like the crudest stories; Rula, the barmaid, who always spoke for everyone to hear; a silent Chinese called Issy; Birgitte, the lady of the house, who looked so grave, so out of place with a pale gold blouse and gold hair tight back in a bun; and finally, Katia, elbows spread, cradling her drink. They laughed, shouted, one by one told me their names, and quickly became friends. The bank of spotlights came on again, another girl began dancing. Her name, I was told, was Rosie. "Don't you think how much she looks like Liza Minnelli?" asked Rula.

I had finished my beer by the time Hildie appeared, in the company at the bar looking even younger and more lost. Klara spoke to her over my shoulder and she joined us. I turned on the stool and smiled, she nodded hello. She wore a pale blue dress, no shoes.

"She speaks wonderful English, Herr Martin," shouted Rula. Hildie looked to the floor, shaking her head.

"You do?"

"Little."

I found her a stool and opened the champagne that Rula had produced from the fridge. Everyone looked surprised but I didn't care. They had expected me to take it and Hildie away. Instead I sat there, calling for more glasses and pouring away. I wanted to delay everything, slow everything down, for I knew that while I had the champagne I had Hildie. More than anything else I wanted her to like me. Suddenly it was not enough for her just to be obliged to give me what I had paid for. There had to be something else. I was surprising myself. Whether it was the drink or the expectation I couldn't decide, but I began to think she was the most beautiful girl I had ever seen—fine blond hair she kept sweeping back with her fingertips, the palest blue eyes, and bee-stung lips I longed to suck between mine. Soon, when the time was right, the two of us could be alone together. Rula ooh-la-la'ed and swigged, Klara stirred the bubbles away with a ringed finger and Hildie sipped.

"Do not worry," said Rula, her elbows on the bar, her chin in her hands. "I translate for you, everywhere." The company laughed. When the bottle was finished, I asked for another. This time Rula put it into an ice bucket straight away, a black tin top hat, and pushed it over the bar to Hildie, along with two glasses.

Without the slightest hesitation she took up the bucket, goaded me off my stool and led me to a door marked "PRIVAT BÜRO." Beyond was a long passage with curtains along one wall concealing rooms, not windows. Hildie walked ahead of me, dress swinging, to the end of the corridor and drew aside the last curtain. It was a small room, no larger than a cell. There were Fragonard-style prints of lovers on swings, a table with two chairs in one corner, red wall lights and a narrow bed with a zebra-design cover and bolster. We sat at the table and Hildie opened the bottle, twisting off the foil and wire with tiny dancing fingers.

"How long do I have?" I pointed at my watch. She shrugged, held up one finger. We drank a glass of wine, then moved to the bed —lying side by side, resting on an elbow, smiling. She kissed me; I touched her shoulder, her hair, smoothed her cheek. Then she was off the bed, holding up her hand as if to say I'll be back in a minute, and disappeared through the curtains.

All I could think of was time passing.

When at last she slipped back into the room she was carrying a towel. By the way she dropped it, carefully on the floor beside the bed, I could tell there was something wrapped in it. Silently she pointed to her dress and the ceiling. *"Aus? Aus?"* I sat up and nodded. In one swift movement, she peeled it off, struggling at the end to free her hair. Like Dorte she wore nothing else. She helped me off with my clothes—prizing off my shoes, tugging my jeans over my heels while I hauled off my shirt.

Back on the bed, I looked all over her, kissed her lips, face, neck, shoulder, breast; ran my hand along her leg, over a thin girlish hip, her side, until she squirmed and giggled and whispered in my ear *"Kitzlig, kitzlig,"* that I was tickling her. To stop me, she pushed me back and lay over me. She looked so young, felt so young—her ribs sliding under my hands like a puppy's. Her hair was on my face, her eyes on mine, her hand feeling its way over me, tiptoeing fingers, stroking, back and forth. A smile over those bursting lips, leaning forward to kiss with a warm, soft mouth; nipping, biting, lip-teasing, eyes wide and wondering, belly pushed hard against my thigh, brown mouse sliding over my skin.

Then, reaching down beside the bed, not for the towel but the other thing I'd seen, and sitting back on my knees and softly speaking in English "better for you, better for me," she unrolled onto me what at first glance appeared to be a smoked oyster. There was a moment of shame, embarrassment, surprise, but most of all disappointment because I really wanted to feel her. But it was done and she was kissing again, open, guileless, giving and warm.

Almost exactly on the hour, we dressed, shared a cigarette and went back to the bar. I felt ruffled, a little worn and swollen.

"Another bottle?" cried Rula when she saw us. Yes, I said. She grinned and swooped triumphantly for the fridge.

When it happened, it was so quick, so final, so explosive—the whole thing suspended, bracketed in a kind of sudden, stunned silence. Hildie had started to speak to Klara who was swaying slightly against the bar, Rula was wrestling with the cork, Birgitte was changing a tape, Katia and Issy were whispering and I was just reaching for my cigarettes when—*crash,* silence, the shattering of glass, followed by a deep, dull thud like a cushion being plumped into shape. There was a tearing noise, a twisting and screech of glass, a groaning "ugggghhh" sound, and deep silence again. All of us at the bar knew where to look, our heads jerking as one toward the commotion. The stripper whose name was Lisa had finally despaired of the man she was with, pulled free from him, grabbed up a bottle and smashed it against the side of the bar. Before the splinters hit the floor she had swung the ragged edges of what remained into the center of his chest, turning it viciously on impact like a key in a lock. Only his height saved him from taking the blow in his face. His eyes and mouth were round from surprise, he staggered back a step, put his meaty hands to his chest and moaned again. As he brought them away, the white triangle of shirt between his lapels seemed to open and shred and then pulse with blood. For a moment, I thought she must have thrown her drink over him, staining his shirt front, but when I looked at her she was still gripping the bottle-neck and crouching as if ready to do it all over again.

He was still standing there, groping at his chest, when the two men from outside came thundering up the stairs. Before he had time to react, Birgitte was pulling Lisa behind the bar and the two men had him by the elbows, seemed to lift him off his feet, and swept him over to the staircase. As they passed, the girls drew back against the bar like a bank of sea anemones in a strong current. No one screamed, no one spoke—their composure quite remarkable; even Hildie seemed more curious than shocked. And when the door downstairs slammed shut they turned back to the bar, and one by one the pale faces on the edge of the dance floor sunk back into the darkness. It was over as quickly as it had begun.

Behind the bar Lisa shook with a kind of staccato stubbornness while Birgitte poured her a drink. The voices around me were low and calm rather than rushed and hysterical, as if they were used to this kind of thing—hushed like participants in nothing more extraordinary than a fire drill. I, more than anyone, was stunned and incredulous.

"What did he do?" I asked Rula; she shrugged and wrenched the cork out of the champagne bottle with a solid pop that made everyone jump.

"Where'll they take him?"

Another shrug: "Away."

"What if he comes back?"

"He will never come back, it is not possible."

"Does this happen a lot?"

"Maybe." Birgitte was bundling Lisa out from behind the bar, sitting her on a stool and stroking her hair. Already Issy and Katia had cleared up the glass and wiped away a dark-looking puddle on the floor. Within a matter of minutes everyone was chattering away as if nothing had happened. Thank God, I thought, I hadn't asked for Lisa—suddenly feeling very vulnerable.

Although there seemed to be no immediate reaction, the episode certainly served to draw us all together—like a bunch of survivors after a plane crash. We all told stories; showed snapshots of husbands, children, parents; drank more wine and smoked feverishly until the ashtrays were brimming. We all became friends. Even Lisa joined in, color seeping back into her cheeks, though I continued to regard her with a mixture of suspicion and apprehension.

All this time Hildie never left my side. She stroked my hair, clung to my arm, slipped her hand into my shirt, kissed me whenever the opportunity offered. She took me to dance, pressing her small body urgently against mine when I suggested she should come back to my hotel. Back on the stools again she put her leg over mine, placed my hand high up under her skirt, then climbed over onto my lap, arm around my neck, breath on my cheek, saying things to Rula that Rula wouldn't translate. "You are bad for her," she would say

183

quietly, without looking up. Which made me grow even fonder of her.

By this time, Karla was really drunk—singing in a deep Russian voice, marching up and down the bar in her sequinned gown. She hugged everyone in turn, Hildie and I together, banging our heads. With my last notes and some money from Rula we bought one last bottle, one last round.

The girls went to change, Hildie too—making me swear to stay. I had no money left, but Rula said she would drive me back to my hotel. I sat at the bar with Karla, her head in her arms, sobbing drunk. There was nothing I could say.

At last the girls returned, Hildie transformed from a shoeless waif into a well-dressed, pretty girl who for all the world could have been someone's private secretary. For a moment I couldn't believe that I had slept with her, but then her arm was through mine, her lips on my cheek, and I knew she was the same girl.

It was time for farewells. Karla patted our cheeks, shaking her head. Her face was puffy, her hair flat—with her rings and sequins she looked like a fairground fortune-teller. The three of us, Rula, Hildie and I, trooped down the stairs and out into the gray dawn. The two girls took the front seats. We drove into Ku'damm, around the monument, along the road to my hotel. I kissed Rula good-bye, thinking to the very last that Hildie would get out with me. She just took my hand instead, kissed me good-bye and shook her head.

I stood on the pavement alone and watched them drive away.

It was with great reluctance that I made no effort to return to the Tanzer Club. I felt there was everything, and nothing, to gain from a second visit, a second evening with Hildie. Instead, coldly, blankly, I busied myself with arrangements for my trip to Moscow.

The Frozen Orange

Including the Metro, there are four railway stations on Komsomolskaya Ploshchad. The Leningradski, as its name suggests, points its tracks toward Leningrad and Finland in the northwest, the Yaroslavlski runs northeast through Yaroslavl to Arkhangel and the Arctic tundra, while the Kazanski serves Russia's eastern provinces —to Kazan on the Upper Volga and Sverdlovsk in the Urals. As for the Metro, Komsomolskaya is the fourth stop along from Red Square on the Kirovsko–Frunzenskaya line, which neatly bisects the city of Moscow southwest to northeast; from Yugo-Zapadnaya where the land starts to swell into the Sparrow Hills, to Preobrazhenskaya on the banks of the River Yauza where, three hundred years ago, a young tsarevitch called Peter played soldiers and his father, Alexis, kept his falcons.

Strictly speaking, Komsomolskaya is neither a "square" nor a "place" as *Ploshchad* implies, but rather a wide street that marks the junction in the northeastern sector of the city of two boulevards, called Rusakovskaya and Kalankovskaya. With two stations on either side, its proportions have been dictated more by the swirl and concentration of traffic one expects around railway termini than by any architectural intent, the symmetry of planned design lost to an arbitrary commercial growth.

Although my hotel was in the center of Moscow, on the corner of Gorky Street and Karl Marx Prospekt, it was here, a few yards along Rusakovskaya and overlooking the goods yard of Kazan station, that I spent my last night in Moscow.

With temperatures well below freezing, Moscow in winter is no place to stand on street corners, lounge in doorways, lean against shop windows. The cold is too great for that. All day, and especially at night, when the mercury falls like a lead weight, people hurry to get wherever they're going, skidding and sliding over the snow and ice. Anyone who stands still becomes immediately conspicuous. For the working girl, the major consideration is keeping warm, finding somewhere to loiter without freezing. There are the great station halls around Komsomolskaya Ploshchad, for instance, where the piped heat is compounded by the steaming bodies of those arriving and departing, where the girls sit with their feet on empty suitcases and the price chalked on the soles of their shoes. It's warm and comfortable, safe as far as open soliciting is concerned—no approach, no dealing—and inconspicuous; should anyone official-looking make a move toward them, the girls simply stand up—the wet floors do the rest.

There are subways, too, beneath Moscow's streets, a warren of possibilities where the steps down are muddy and slushy with booted snow and the walkways rank with the smell of damp felt from valenki galoshes and sweating feet. Although they're not heated like the stations, they're warmer than the streets above where a sheer icy wind waits around every corner, and crowded with potential customers. The trouble with the stations, and the subways, is that most customers there tend to pay in rubles and pay, on the whole, badly. Ireniya had worked Komsomolskaya long enough to know that, and though her home was only a few minutes' walk from the busiest terminals, she preferred working the center —four stops down on the Metro line—concentrating particularly on the hotels and tourist trade where payment was in foreign currency.

Again, there were problems—one had to pay for the privilege of working the big hotels: the doorman to let you slide in, the barman to let you sit on at the bar, the cloakroom attendant, even the *dezhurnaya* or floorlady who supervised the comings and goings of guests on each floor—and the guests' friends. By the time everyone had taken their cut, there was never a great deal left. Best of all was the casual pickup in subways leading from the big hotels to the tourist sites where foreigners were always tramping to and fro (they were easy to spot; few, if any, wore the traditional *shapka* hat). Even if the man wasn't interested, he could easily be pressed into making up for his refusal by dabbling in a little currency exchange (strictly illegal, but everyone did it). Good rates, higher than official controls, a little profit, something to pay the way if a bribe were ever necessary—a dollar made more noise than a ruble.

Museums were an even better hunting ground—crowds of foreigners milling around, endless, unsupervised corridors and galleries —and warm too. The trouble there was it meant daytime shifts.

There was, however, one spot where tourists always gathered, day and night, their pockets and wallets stuffed with dollars and Deutsche marks and lire and sterling and francs. For five minutes, maybe ten, every hour and precisely on the hour, the tourists flocked there in large numbers and braved the cold, and like a poacher at feeding time, Ireniya would be waiting.

At this particular site, there were three optimum hours—nine, ten and eleven o'clock at night. For Ireniya it meant a minimum but bearable two and a half hours on patrol. She would arrive shortly before nine and be finished—one way or another—by a little after eleven. If she didn't strike lucky first time, she'd get a glass of tea somewhere and wait for the second or the third time. Between 8:45 and 11:15 P.M. she had a total of thirty minutes (the five minutes either side of each hour) to make contact. If she had no success, she sometimes tried the crowds that streamed out of the nearby Bolshoi, most of them foreigners, and if times were hard even put in a few minutes in one of the station halls on her way home. But that didn't happen too often. Ireniya had a good patch—it was safe, convenient and consistent.

From Lenin's mausoleum in Red Square, or more precisely in Ploshchad Revolyutsii, you can almost hear the clock mechanism in the Spasski Tower winding itself up to chime and strike the hour, like a heavy smoker filling his lungs to speak, and distantly the approaching stomp-stomp-stomp of the new guard as it goose-steps its way below the red looming walls of the Kremlin to relieve the old guard. At night it's a magnificent spectacle and the crowds, most of them from nearby hotels and foreign currency bars, swell beyond the low walls of the mausoleum to watch the soldiers' drill. At nine and ten o'clock, the most popular times, as many as three hundred people, most of them foreigners, gather there.

I arrived shortly before the ten o'clock changing and made my way to the front of the crowd that had already assembled, a little to the left of the stairway that led to the doors of the tomb. High in a bleak, black sky, illuminated red stars shone out from tower tops through flurries of snow, a red silk flag was spotlighted shivering against the night, and the red walls of the Kremlin seemed to glow like the sides of a brick oven. Behind me, across the cobbles, stood the bulk of the GUM department store and to my left rose the balloonlike domes of Saint Basil's cathedral. In the steadily growing crush of bodies, the worst of the cold was held off, all of us packing together like a herd of animals. This was Ireniya's time. There were three soldiers—two guards led by an officer. The crowds strained to see them. A hundred yards away the sound of their boots hitting the stone path and growing steadily louder brought everyone to a hush. They looked young—gloved, coated, belted against the cold —with their rifles held out in front of them in one hand like altar boys carrying candles to mass. As they drew closer the sound of their steps grew stronger, echoing off the walls of the Kremlin, and for the first time I became aware of an arhythmic stamping behind me, easily out of time with the goose-stepping guards—roughly three stamps to one stomp—and the fleeting touch of a coat hem at the back of my knees.

Stamping to keep warm is no uncommon thing in Moscow. Meet a friend in the street, stop for a moment to exchange greetings and the stamping begins automatically. Hearing and feeling this stamping behind me should have come as no surprise but somehow it felt close and confidential like a secret message being passed on. High-polished boots stamped to a halt at the foot of the steps leading to the tomb and in the silence that followed came the first tinkling chimes from the Spasski Tower. There was an abrupt about-turn and the soldiers goose-stepped up to the entrance. Behind me the soft stamping continued and the hem flicked at my legs, almost tickling the touch was so light. Then, like a dance sequence, the two old guards gavotted with their replacements, rifles were slapped, shouldered and grounded until the two replacements stood in their place. As the first full strike of the hour sounded from the Spasski Gate, the officer led away the old guard, back down the steps, about-turning, then goose-stepping along the path back to their barracks somewhere inside the Kremlin. It was over for another hour.

Ireniya was directly behind me. As the crowd shifted, murmured and began to disperse I turned and faced her for the first time. Somehow I had known without looking that it would be a woman and suspected too her purpose. There was little to see. She wore a thick fur *shapka* pulled low over her brow and a thick fur coat whose collars she had wrapped around her head. All I could see was a triangle of face—dark brows, eyes disturbingly close together, a bulge of pink cheeks, a straight nose pinched white with the cold and, resting in the fur of her collar, her top lip. Dressed in the coat, the hat like a furry doughnut, the gloves, the fur-trimmed boots, Ireniya looked enormous.

"Tourist?" she asked from the depth of the collar, her face tight against the cold and misted with her breath. "You stay hotel? Which hotel?" I told her which one. "You want change dollars?" I shrugged. "You want come with me?" We stood facing each other, more and more conspicuous as the crowd thinned, stamping our feet.

"What about my hotel?" Her head shook, the wind fanning a line of fur across her cheek.

"Home close."

"Not as close as my hotel."

"No hotel. Difficult hotel. Trouble. No possible."

"How much? *Skolko?*"

"No much money," she replied, eyes gleaming at my interest, the two of us turning away from the mausoleum. "Few dollar, you have dollar?"

Without having agreed on anything we had started to walk off across the square.

"Yes, I have dollars. But how much?"

She shrugged. I doubted there was any official rate for foreigners. Anything would do. Anything in foreign currency made the sacrifice, the risks, the standing around in the cold, worthwhile.

"Little," she said at last, and tucked her arm through mine.

In the chandelier-lit marble hall of the Metro we waited for a train. Here, we stood a little apart, as if strangers, side by side but not touching. None of the people around us looked at Ireniya, but I felt their eyes, questioningly, on me. The man without a hat. A stranger. A foreigner, and taking the Metro at this time of night. And away from the center of town, away from his hotel. Who was he and where was he going? I could feel them thinking and then, more. Where did he come from? What part of the world? What was his life like? Was it different? Was it good? Was it bad? Was it like they were told? Or would they prefer it given the chance? Whether they thought these things or not, I felt them watching me, sizing me up, trying to imagine my world, my life, my freedom—as if I had come from a different planet. Were they jealous, I wondered? Or didn't they know enough to be jealous? Would they exchange their way of life for mine as easily as they changed their currency for mine? For the first time during my stay in Russia, well away from the usual tourist beats, I was aware of a difference. That I was different, that they were different; that there was no way for the two sides to meet, come together, join; no way for the gap to be bridged. And yet, there was Ireniya. It was as close as I could come.

A train rushed out of the darkness, squeezed to a stop between the platforms, and the doors slid open. Ireniya waited for me to choose a seat and then sat away from me, across the carriage. She had let the collar drop a little from her face, though the hat was still low on her brow. She looked older than I had at first imagined or just seemed it in the harsh, unflattering light of the subway train. Her face looked soft and puffy like a deflated balloon, soon to wrinkle, a little crumpled as if she had slept on it; her eyes wide but secret and close-set; her gloved hands tightly clasped in her lap. The doors closed with a sigh and the train rattled away beneath the streets of Moscow.

Komsomolskaya was a freezing shock after the stinking warmth of the Metro. At no time on the journey had we spoken to each other and whenever I looked across at her, her eyes were fixed on the empty seat beside me. Even when we reached our stop and she got up, she made no sign for me to follow. Once through the barriers, though, she took my arm and huddled against the cold, we walked away from the station along Rusakovskaya, past the Leningradski, the Yarowslavlski and the Kazanski. Once more the collar of her coat was high up over her face and her glove was at her throat holding it tight against the chill. Once I slipped and she grabbed my arm. As she steadied me we smiled at each other for the first time like conspirators to an intrigue.

We hadn't gone far when she tugged at my arm for me to follow her down an alleyway, a thin trickle of a foot path where we had to walk in single file. Unlike the street the snow here hadn't been cleared away or trampled down and was still sloped in drifts against a brick building on one side and a leaning, planked fence on the other. Over the fence I could see a crane and the deserted, unfinished shell of a new building—all girders and bare concrete. Ireniya was much faster over the snow than I, more sure of her footing, and I noticed as I stumbled after her that she had a dainty way of stepping, almost tiptoeing, through the snow—a swaying movement that started at the hips and wove through her legs. I began to think she might not be as big as she appeared under all those clothes. Hers was quite definitely the walk of someone small and delicate.

At the end of the alley, the path opened out and she darted forward as if unaware there was someone with her. A few yards farther on, she stopped and looked back but before I could reach her, she was off again, confident I could cope, keep up. With difficulty I was able to, now only a few stumbling steps behind her. But the cover of snow was deceptive and hid or softened all kinds of obstacles—planks, rocks, lumps of masonry, sheets of board that skidded underfoot, coils of rusting metal that snagged at my ankles. Soon I was panting heavily, trying to match my pace to the bulky, coated figure ahead of me. Time and time again, staggering along in her footprints, I wanted to call out "How much farther, how much farther?" like a child being led somewhere by his mother and beginning to rebel.

At last the building site slipped behind us and the walking came easier—far fewer obstacles to avoid. There were buildings on either side of us now and it looked as if we were passing through some kind of warehouse area. There were no lights anywhere, just a blue-white path of unmarked snow to show the way. Soon the lane we followed dipped to the right, widened, and I followed her into an enormous yard surrounded by high walls and lighted windows that turned the snow a low-wattage yellow. Along the length of one of these walls stood a line of lorries, each with its engine running, each backed into a narrow concrete bay. For the first time in what seemed an age, there were other sounds than my labored breathing and the crunch of snow underfoot: rumbling motors; coughing, uneven exhausts that filled the air with a blue haze of diesel fumes; the sounds of men working, shouting; the whine of assorted factory noises; the thud of sacks hitting concrete, being swung into the backs of the lorries.

The ground here was much firmer, the snow packed down and rutted into a pattern of criss-crossing tire tracks. For the first time too, I was able to catch up with Ireniya and we linked arms. Beyond the lorries and high up on the wall of this building was a small lighted wood-frame office reached by a flight of wooden steps, where three men crowded round a desk presumably checking manifests or delivery sheets or shift rotas. At the door, half in the office and half out on the wood landing, stood a uniformed guard with a stubby machine gun cradled in his arms. All the way across the yard and out of it, I felt his eyes watching us.

191

Ireniya's home was on the second floor of a two-story block, one of four built side by side in a wide, snow-covered quadrangle. The whole area was like a barrack square except for a small stretch of ground between two of the blocks that looked like a kind of playpen. The snow undoubtedly made everything look cleaner, less dour and depressing than it was; heaps of rubbish, dustbins, the general detritus of squalid living—softened, concealed by the snow. Ireniya's was the last block, the door to her staircase the last in a row of four, double doors on screeching sprung hinges to keep in what little heat there was—the large cast-iron radiators on each landing looking unequal to the struggle. Outside her door was a thin metal post-box with the word GAZETY painted across it. She took off a glove and fished deep in her pocket for the key. As she fitted it into the latch I could see how tiny and delicately boned her hand was, the skin dulled, the nails leveled and unpainted.

There were three rooms—a cupboard of a kitchen looking out over the back of the house onto a stretch of open snow, a bathroom and lavatory that smelt of drying woolens and powerful detergents and a cramped sitting room with a couch that doubled as a bed.

Ireniya offered me tea. I said no. Some vodka. I said yes. She fetched a bottle from a low chest of drawers, poured the drinks and sat down beside me on the edge of the couch. There was linoleum on the floor, yellowy brown, printed with the line of floorboards beneath and scraped in a semicircle where the door opened. By the couch, at our feet, was a thin rug that slipped over the lino. There was a table by the window, two chairs, and a pot of ivy on the windowsill with the trailing branches pegged out around the window frame. There were no pictures on the walls, just a plain and faintly striped wallpaper. The place smelled of boiled vegetables and old clothes. When the vodka was finished she switched on the small bedside lamp, got up and turned off the main light. So weak was the lamp that the whole room seemed the same color as the lino. Standing now by the bed she lifted off the fur hat and a thick, loose plait of brown hair tumbled over her shoulder. Tugging at it with her fingers, she loosened the strands and shook it out. Even in the dim light it shone. Then came her coat and her boots, which I helped her with. Without speaking a word Ireniya began taking off her clothes, layer by layer, each revealing a new covering, her body growing smaller and thinner with every discarded item like the *matryoshki* dolls I had seen in the tourist shops. She wore two cardigans and a jumper and under that a shirt. Under the shirt was a vest with a round neck. She unzipped her skirt, stepped out of it and threw it onto the pile already growing on the line. Amazingly, she wore long, knee-length woolen bloomers, with tights beneath. There was something strongly peasantlike in the clothes she wore, long-wearing, tough, practical—with little attention given to colors or frills. I undressed quickly in the cold and by the time I was in the bed, Ireniya was still struggling with a tangle of tights around her ankles. With her sitting on the bed quite close to me, I could feel the warmth of her body like a shield around her, warmth stored up and held in by all those layers of clothing. Shyly, she leaned over and switched out the light. There was more rustling, the black shadows of her arms against the window tugging the vest over her head and then, finally, her weight pushing down on the springs as she joined me. Like her clothes, the bed—layer upon layer of blankets and covers but, thankfully, no sheets. The itching of the blankets was tolerable but the coldness of the sheets would have been quite unbearable. For a few minutes neither of us moved, almost frightened to share each other's coldness. Somehow, without the color from the light, the room had grown colder, more a part of the night outside. And in the darkness too came the sounds, as well as the cold. In the same way as one adjusts one's eyes to sudden darkness, so, it seemed, my ears adjusted to the noises of the night. They came slowly, softly at first, then increased in volume—a distant rattling, shoveling sounds, the scraping of metal against metal, a steamy whistling, groaning and sighing like wind playing above a chimney pot—nothing more than the night shift at the Kazanski, had I but known it; but in my ignorance, an unbelievable collection of sounds that I could trace to no obvious source. At no time was there anything as definite as a train whistle or heavy shunting to give the game away; nothing identifiable. When I asked Ireniya what the noises were she must have misunderstood me, for she shrugged and turned toward me in the bed.

For her size, she was surprisingly heavy on top of me, soft beneath me and suspiciously sticky and warm. Once the springs in the couch squeaked and she slowed me and sssssshhhhhh-ed me. All the time, her hands never left my shoulders, pushing me back into the tumble of cushions she used as pillows or pulling me over her as if I was another blanket until my face was ground into them. Like an echo of the noises outside she sighed and whistled and in the end, shuddered like a train starting up. Only Ireniya was finishing, the two of us shuddering like carriages rattling at their couplings, in one hot, sticky convulsion of pretended passion. Now, at last, her hands were pushing me back, as if eager to squirm out from under me, swinging off the bed with her thighs clamped tight together.

In the bathroom I heard her turn a squeaking tap and water gushing into a basin. From the sound the water made, hollowing out, I could tell the basin was filling quickly. Then the stream was closed off, and was followed by a splashing, sucking sound as she washed herself. I saw her stooping shadow creep back into the room. She held something in her hand, held it away from her. Sitting on the edge of the bed, she drew back the covers and began to clean me with short measured strokes—like a school matron cleaning off a cut knee. The flannel was ice-cold but startlingly refreshing and the drying stickiness I had begun to feel was soon gone—wrapped up in the square of cloth she took back to the bathroom to rinse out before returning to the bed.

For a long time, Ireniya didn't move, just lay still and silent beside me. She wasn't asleep—in the darkness I could feel an eyelash jumping over my skin every time she blinked. It was a soft, comforting feeling. Her legs she kept stiffly together, pressed against me. One arm held a cushion under her head, the other crossed my chest. A leafless, skeletal tree threw its silhouette against the far wall. There was no movement, no wind out there in the courtyard to stir even the thinnest branch. If only sound could have made things move, the tree would have shaken and trembled as if rooted in an earthquake. Even inside the room, with its double-glazing, the sounds were insistent and softly belligerent like the noise from a factory floor heard through ear mufflers. It seemed Ireniya heard nothing, just my own low breathing and steady heart beat, as though she had grown used to the commotion and now blocked it out. As the night wore on, it became more and more like a game—trying to fit the sound to an image—but as soon as I came close to identifying a certain noise its timbre changed, its rhythms fluctuated or another new noise overpowered, replaced it. It seemed incredible in the stillness of the room that there should be so much activity so close, while we rested.

When, at last, she nudged me out of the bed and indicated that it was time for me to go, I did so reluctantly—not because of the cold that sprang up through my legs from the freezing lino, not because of her, but because I had to let go of the game without having found a solution. It would not be until the following morning that I would realize where I had spent the night, what the sounds were—when I returned to Komsomolskaya to catch the train to Leningrad.

I dressed in darkness, looking for my clothes against the mountain of wool, nylon, cotton and fur that was Ireniya's. As I laced my boots, she reached across and opened the bedside drawer and dug her hand inside. In the dark I could see nothing—just something round, like a ball of wool in her hand. Then there was a faint hiss and the zesty smell of orange as she peeled the fruit. Breaking it in half, she gave one side to me and dropped the other back into the drawer. The fruit was freezing cold, the skin of the segments coarse, the flesh icy and just a little dry. I broke some off and offered it back to her but she shook her head and pushed my hand away. I was touched by her generosity, at the pleasure she seemed to take watching me eat. I had seen enough queues in Moscow of people waiting to buy just this kind of fruit to know how difficult it was to come by. It was such a small thing for me, but so much for her to give. Nor was it done deliberately, a way of squeezing an extra few dollars from me—but spontaneously, almost without thought. And only half the fruit given, the rest hidden away for later—it made the gesture even more extravagant. It also made the money I gave her seem so inadequate, almost valueless. But she took it anyway, shyly shuffling the notes through her hands, checking in the light from the window to see if they were dollars or rubles. She nodded her thanks, opened the drawer once more, and buried the money away with the fruit, like a squirrel burrowing away its stores.

Muffled to the chin in blankets she watched me to the door and as I stepped out onto the cold landing I heard the couch springs squeak as she curled up for a last few hours' sleep.

The Room on
Bolshoi Prospekt

When the train called "Youth" finally pulled into Leningrad, it was close to midnight and the sky was as black as the slush on the platforms. The whine of power died like a kettle being taken off the gas and the connector rods seemed to settle gratefully away from the cables. The long icicles that hung from the train's guttering, slanted backward from the force of the slipstream, now began to creak and tremble with no wind to support them. Doors cracked open and passengers stepped down, bags piled up and porters hurried forward. Although ten hours farther north, Leningrad did not have the same biting chill that sliced through the streets of Moscow. Collars fell open, scarves unwound and gloves stayed in pockets. There was something more temperate, more flexible about the climate—even this late at night—something softly and satisfactorily European, as if the train had sped south for ten hours instead of north.

It was soon clear that the same flexibility, softness, temperateness, extended to the people, cheerier and warmer than their comrades farther south.

"Vodka, please," I asked the barman at my hotel an hour later.

"Which money you pay please?" His was a foreign currency bar—any currency except rubles.

"English," I replied, shaking through a handful of change.

"Eight-five new pennies," he said, sloshing out a double measure.

"I only seem to have sixty-five," starting to count through it again in case I'd made a mistake.

"So, is all right, huh? Sixty-five, eighty-five, who care?"

Despite the time he was in no hurry to close up and go home. He settled himself down on the other side of the bar as if keen to build on this brief exchange. In his middle thirties, he was already quite bald with only a thin band of cropped, gray hair above each ear—so thin they looked like shadow. Between these bands were freckles as large as gravy stains. When he spoke his teeth glittered with silver.

"So tell me," he began, "tell me please of John Lennon. Terrible, terrible. Tell me please what you know." I told him all I knew and he nodded his head as though my version of the tragedy confirmed what he already knew.

"You know Cliff Richard, please?"

I told him I did.

"He remind me of my youth. He remind me of my time in England."

"You lived in England?"

"I circumnavigate many years. Live Tilbury long time. Beautiful city, Tilbury. You know Tilbury?" He made it sound like "Tealburry," as if the silver had got in the way. I told him I did and agreed it was a beautiful city.

"Hadley Chase. You have heard of Hadley Chase?" Like "Tealburry," it came out as "Hadderly Chess." Yes, I said, I had heard of Hadley Chase.

"I read ten Hadley Chase book. Very, very good. Very, very fine writer."

"Are his books easy to get in Russia?" I asked, trying to remember whether Hadley Chase was the author or the hero.

"Not easy," he replied, his mouth dipping down like a bent coathanger. I thought of the books in my case that I had finished reading and could do without. I told him I would bring them up next time and pass them on to him.

"Hadley Chase?" he asked excitedly, thrilled at the prospect of expanding his collection. When I said no the light in his eyes seemed to dim, and his silver smile slacken, but when I finished my drink we shook hands across the bar and said we both looked forward to our next meeting—Hadley Chase or no Hadley Chase. In Moscow, I reflected as I made my way back to my room, there had been no such ease, no such communication. Slight as it was, our conversation made me feel more a part of this unknown city.

Formal introductions took place the following morning when

I drew back the curtains and looked out over Leningrad for the first time. There, on a broad sweep of the Neva, trapped in the ice, was the three-funnelled hulk of the battle cruiser *Aurora,* starting pistol of the October Revolution, and beyond, like another mast, the needle spire of Trezzini's Cathedral of Sts. Peter and Paul. Intruding between the two, supported on a framework of scaffolding and running the length of one block, a line of cyrillic script, white on red, proclaimed that "The Aim of Communism Is the Praise of the People." Across the main breach of the river and almost directly opposite my hotel stood the pistachio-green, pale yellow, blue and rosy-pink palace façades of Kutusov Quay (fluorescent tubes replacing chandeliers), the columned length of Rastrelli's Winter Palace, Catherine's Hermitage and, blue with distance, the golden dome of St. Isaac's topping the skyline like a bowler hat on a sideboard. The night before all this had appeared as a formless sprinkle of lights and inky shadows, as arbitrary and unconnected as the numbered dots in a child's drawing book. Now it showed itself—took shape—a long, narrow horizon of once-imperial buildings suspended between a wide, gray sky and the frozen expanse of the Neva.

That first morning and every one thereafter, it was the Neva, more than the distant city, that drew and held my attention. On all my walks I never moved far from it, drawn back time and again to its bridges and its stone embankments and the sheet of ice that covered it quay to quay. The ice fascinated me. Like the river beneath, it was always on the move, always changing—discreetly though, like a glacier. During the day it played dead, as lifeless as a scab; a place for the crows to strut and caw and come into land with their strong, black wings flapping almost to a hover so as not to slide out of control when they set down. But at night, when no one was looking, the ice began to move—adopting some new expression, some new shape or color and every morning presenting itself for inspection. It was like playing "grandmother's footsteps" —each time you looked, something was different, something had moved: Ice that was smooth and clear one day became veined like marble overnight with ragged cracks; ice that looked thick and solid was suddenly a channel of black water, churned up by some passing ship; tipped-up slabs of ice, trapped in a freeze one day and sticking up like tussocks of grass, disappeared the next as if trodden flat; even the scars and marks that scored its surface seemed to shift position as if the ice, in slow motion, followed the vagaries of the current beneath, eddying and whirling down to the sea.

Playing grandmother, I caught it out only once, trudging back an hour before dawn from the room on Bolshoi Prospekt. From somewhere in midstream came a snapping, creaking, grating sound as the ice completed its maneuvers under the last patches of darkness and settled into its new shape.

Unlike the Hermitage, St. Isaac's, the battle cruiser *Aurora*, the palaces of Kutusov Quay and Khalturin, neither the room on Bolshoi Prospekt nor the Café Dvor were listed in any official tourist guide. Nor was their presence indicated by anything so bold as a spire, a dome or a Wedgwood façade, something on the skyline I could see from my bedroom window. Certainly the authorities would know of one, a foreign currency bar off Nevsky Prospekt; but the other, a few blocks down from the University Quay on Vasilievsky Island, remained anonymous to all but those who used it. On that first morning I knew neither their names nor where to find them. All I was sure of, standing there that first morning with the city spread before me, was that, like the river beneath the ice, I would find what I was looking for somewhere out there beneath the solid, respectable Party shell of the city.

In fact, I didn't have to look so far, nor did it take as long as I expected, for the first girls I saw and recognized with certainty appeared in my own hotel that second evening—sitting in the lounges, walking through the halls, drinking at bars. I say with certainty for they fitted into no evident group of guests—the Chinese delegation with their matching jackets and spiky hair, who left the hotel after every meal in a fleet of black Chaikas; the gowned and turbaned African party who spent most of their time waiting for the lifts and looking lost without their fly swishes; the Finns from across the border with their beards and vodka breath; and the English tour groups dressed in jeans and jumpers, flannels and cardigans, from Dyfyd and Greenock and Bristol, committed socialists for the most part, come to see their vaunted political solution in practice, who caught buses every morning to view the excesses of Imperial Russia and groan at the plight of the common man under Czarist rule. These girls fitted into none of these categories. They never carried keys, approached reception, or appeared in the dining room for any of the three compulsory meals. And they only appeared at night.

And it wasn't just that they didn't fit into any recognizable group—the fact of the matter was they hardly fitted into time itself.

Their hair was scooped and scalloped, their faces powdered and rouged, their light patterned frocks ruched and tucked, and clasped by tight, narrow belts. They wore stockings with seams and bulky high-heeled shoes and were constantly reaching for purses and compacts—checking their reflections in powder-flecked mirrors, patting at their noses with circular pink pads and nicking the corners of their lipstick with lace-edged handkerchiefs. There were winking pleats, tight hems and waisted Basque jackets over corseted rumps, frilled cuffs and thin blouses that barely concealed the numerous shoulder straps of their underwear. It was as if all the girls were taking part in a Duchess of Windsor lookalike contest. By their very style they were remarkable but doubly conspicuous as they sat in the bars sharing drinks with spiky Chinese, sandaled Africans, or broad Scots with lumpy jumpers and baggy jeans. There was no other reasonable conclusion to draw.

The immediate problem, however, was their availability—the girls I saw that second evening were always accompanied, none of them ever alone. After half an hour loitering around the main entrance and lobby, I knew they were not imported—picked up somewhere else and brought in—but it was a puzzle tracing them back to their source, where they came from, in which part of this thousand-room hotel reserve stocks could be found. I needed Hadley Chase on this one but up in his tenth-floor eyrie my friend the barman had disappeared and his replacement, a muscular brunette with cheeks like skateboard knee pads, looked sufficiently severe and disapproving to discourage even the most cautious inquiries. That evening I sat on patiently, hoping my prey might put in an appearance unescorted. But it was plain that if the girls did start off in a bar, then it certainly wasn't in that one. Nor, I had eventually to concede, did they gather in any of the other hotel bars—foreign currency and ruble—that I patrolled.

The third night, when most of my fellow guests had been whisked off for an evening of ballet at the Kirov, my luck changed. As the last coach pulled out of the forecourt and I began my now familiar round of possible locations, a silence settled over the almost-empty hotel like the stillness that invades a schoolroom at the end of term, and through that silence seeped the faint strains of the hotel orchestra. I heard it first at the head of the staircase that led up from the main lobby to the first floor, began humming the tune, then stopped dead.

On this level were barber shops, a post office, a red outline map of Leningrad in relief on one wall that looked for all the world like the peering profile of Trotsky with his peaked worker's cap and jutting beard, and a small tropical garden with tinkling fountains and fat, lazy goldfish. Beyond the gardens, across a bridge, was one of the hotel's many bars, and beyond the bar the hotel dining room —as large and characterless as a gymnasium, a wide circle of a room with a gallery that overlooked the Neva. Each evening, after the hotel guests had been fed and bundled out, the tables were relaid, food undoubtedly reheated, a dance floor cleared and a variety show put on for large parties of Leningraders. The previous night, on my rounds, I had stood on the gallery and looked down at the audience and the performers—the first well-stocked with stolid, vodka-drinking, middle-aged Russians; the latter energetic but amateur, the dancers a little too fat to be interesting and a little too old for some of their routines. Their smiles looked painful and I could see them, even from the balcony, hissing lungfuls of air through clenched teeth. The little I saw convinced me I was missing nothing and I didn't stay long.

But what stopped me in my tracks that third night, at the head of the staircase leading up from the lobby, was the music, the tune. I could see the gleaming trombones stretched at arm's length, the saxophone players rocking, the trumpets tooting—each section of the band standing in turn as they belted out the suddenly recognizable bebop rhythm of Glenn Miller. The connections were irresistible. Glenn Miller, the Forties, Swing—the Duchess of Windsor lookalikes.

The dining room was much the same as it had been the previous evening—curtains drawn, dance floor cleared and tables packed with Russians spooning up the same food we had been eating an hour or so earlier. It all looked as unpromising as it had the night before, but this time I found myself a table, ordered a carafe of vodka, watched and waited—increasingly optimistic about the connection I had made. As if to encourage me, the band continued their medley—from "In the Mood" through "String of Pearls" to "Dawn Patrol." When the house lights dimmed, the musicians sunk back into their stalls and the show began.

It didn't disappoint me that I could see no lookalikes in the audience; I hadn't expected to. This was, after all, a rubles-only show and the girls, as in Moscow, would be more interested in foreign currency. It was simply the connection. Just being there and waiting was enough. Something, I was sure, would lead me on from here.

The show ground on in the circle of lights, each act separated by the panting chorus line and punctuated by a splattering of applause. There were cossack dancers in black skirted coats, high boots and empty bandoliers; a trio of singers imitating the Three Degrees and snapping their mike leads like lengths of whip; a contortionist in a snakeskin leotard; four jugglers in Turkish trousers and full-sleeved shirts; and a troupe of acrobats who bounded across the dance floor, springing, leaping, somersaulting, spinning, with many a "hup," "hey" and "yaaaaahhhh."

But what caught my attention the most was the door through which each act made its entrance and exit, with what looked like a cloakroom beyond. The door was in the corner of the dining hall beneath the gallery where I had stood the night before. What especially intrigued me was the cloakroom—suggesting another entrance to the hotel, one I had so far overlooked.

As soon as the show was over, a flourishing grande finale accompanied by a round of slow hand-clapping, the band started up again, couples drifted onto the dance floor and I made my way over to the door. Sure enough, past the cloakroom—its racks thick with coats, scarves and fur *shapkas*—and down a flight of stairs was a second entrance with a line of taxis alongside. Here, presumably, the Leningraders arrived for their dinner-dances—from their point of view more convenient than the distant main entrance, and from the authorities' point of view separate enough to ensure there was no unnecessary mingling of guests and Russian citizenry. More exciting still was an open doorway adjacent to the entrance with the word BAR above it. With rising certainty I stepped through into the gloom and saw at once that I had found what I was looking for. Both the room and the bar were circular—a ring within a ring—as far as I could judge, directly beneath the dining room dance floor. Around the walls were tables and chairs, each with a small red light that illuminated the drinkers. Apart from a few soldiers, most of the men I recognized as Finnish guests, and all the girls were dressed in Forties styles.

Feeling flushed with success, I found a stool at the bar and ordered a coffee. Three stools away a pair of girls, disappointingly out of date in jeans and jumpers, caught my eye. It wasn't long before one of them, the fatter of the two, slipped off her stool and came over to me. Her hair was blond, shoulder-length and cut in a fringe, her eyes sharp and clear.

"Can I take a cigarette? Cannot buy Marlboro here." Her voice was quite extraordinary—gruff and low as if she gargled with coal dust every morning. "My name is Tina. Shall I join you?" she asked, taking her first puff and letting the smoke drift between her lips without inhaling it. When I said help yourself she returned to her friend, spoke quickly to her and the two of them came and sat beside me. The second was called Lara and to celebrate our meeting I ordered them both drinks. It was clear straight away that Tina was the one in charge and her friend Lara little more than an acolyte, content to follow where Tina led.

It was Tina, that third night in Leningrad, who told me of the Café Dvor. She and Lara were going there any minute—this bar would soon close—would I like to go with them?

"The Café Dvor?"

"It is across the river. All my friends are there. It stays open late. Very good place. Let us take a taxi together."

The Café Dvor occupied the ground floor of a building on a corner of Nevsky Prospekt. A uniformed doorman presided over its entrance, examining newcomers through the glass doors before opening up. Immediately inside was a cloakroom; judging by the number of coats already on the racks, the place was full.

Despite the crush we found a small table near the door. The room, narrow and dark, was filled with people; most of the men were West European, most of the drunks Finns and all the women Russian—decked out in their Forties fashions.

Lara did not stay long. After the first drink she nodded to Tina and me, excused herself and walked off to speak with friends at the bar. I was certain that in one of their exchanges during the taxi ride Tina had made it plain that I was her catch and that Lara should find her own. Under normal circumstances I would have had nothing to do with either of them, neither especially attractive, neither as well dressed as the other girls I could see. But I felt a certain gratitude to Tina for introducing me to the Café Dvor and since it was late and most of the girls had already found themselves partners, I didn't mind staying with her. I could always come back here, alone, tomorrow night.

In response to my questions Tina leaned forward and set about telling me her story. It was an extraordinary tale. She was Russian, but lived in Sweden, married to a man she had met two years before in Leningrad. In fact, in this very bar. Quite coolly she explained that she needed to spend only two years with him as his wife before becoming a Swedish citizen in her own right, at which point she could divorce him yet still stay on in Sweden. Any sooner and she would be obliged by law to return to her home here in Leningrad. Her father was dead but her mother still lived in the city. She had come back for a holiday, spent a month in her mother's apartment, but finding that too claustrophobic had moved to a room in my hotel. There she would stay another week before returning to Sweden and her unloved husband.

Wishing to delay the inevitable question I knew she would ask sooner or later, I began talking about caviar, how difficult it was to get, and how expensive it was. There followed a discussion on the various kinds of caviar that were available and she told me she had friends who might be able to help me. A kilo of pressed caviar, she told me, she could get from a friend for about £30. I winced, saying I was only prepared to pay £15 a kilo. Eventually we agreed I would pay £20 a kilo and I told her I would take three kilos. £60 for three thousand grams. At Fortnum & Mason's £60 wouldn't buy me a hundred-gram jar.

"Do you want to do another kind of business with me—you and I?" she asked, once we had reached agreement over the caviar.

"Business? What other business?" I replied with pretend naïveté.

"Same business all girls in Dvor do," she said, indicating the crowds behind us.

"You mean all these girls are on the game? All looking for husbands to take them away from the motherland?"

"If they can't find a husband, they're certainly looking for as much foreign currency as they can get."

"How much would that be?" I looked once again over her shoulder at a particularly striking young woman in the full Forties regalia who had caught my eye the moment I sat down. She was sitting at a table close by, looking haughty among a crew of drunken Finns.

Tina shrugged her shoulders. "Depends. Not much."

"Depends on what?"

"Depends on the man. If he is nice or what I think he can afford."

"And me?"

"Not so much."

In the taxi back to our hotel I asked her why she needed to work like this when she was presumably secure through her marriage, had enough money to do what she wanted. "Bad habits," she told me, "are difficult to stop."

Tina stayed all night, the two of us squeezed into my narrow bed, alternately hugging as much of the duvet as we could. The snap of elastic, the rustle of jeans being pulled on and the rattle of her belt buckle woke me the following morning, though I feigned more tiredness than I felt.

"What are you doing today?" she asked, pushing her cigarettes into her bag.

"Sleeping."

"All day?"

"I think I will—all day," I replied, eager to avoid having to make a date, eager to avoid any further contact. Not even the promise of vast amounts of caviar for the few pounds we had agreed upon the night before could persuade me to continue our liaison.

"Maybe see you later then?"

"Maybe," I murmured into the pillow.

"Okay then, I go now. I am in room three-sixty-six if you want to come down."

"Three-sixty-six. Right."

When I did get up, for lunch, I kept an eye open for Tina but the coast was clear. That afternoon I joined a tour group for an afternoon trip to Petrodvorets where Peter the Great built a summer palace on the edge of the Gulf of Finland. The trip served its purpose well—occupying me throughout the afternoon and giving me no time to dwell on the thought of returning to the Café Dvor and introducing myself to the Scorcher, as I had christened the girl who had caught my attention the previous night, but whose name I did not know. After a pleasant bus ride through the wintry Russian countryside, the time passed swiftly and satisfactorily in a succession of gloriously appointed imperial rooms, the tour accompanied by an interesting monologue from our maddeningly smug Intourist guide.

On our way out of the palace, which had been almost entirely rebuilt after its destruction during the German advance, the guide turned to me on the stairs and said, "I believe you have beautiful houses like this in your country?"

"Yes," I replied, "but there is a difference."

"Oh," she asked interestedly, doubting there was anything I

could tell her about my own country that she did not already know. "And what is that?"

"The people who own them are still allowed to live in them." I felt not a little pleased with myself at having finally managed to say what I had been bursting to say ever since I first arrived in Russia.

There were not so many coats in the cloakroom at the Café Dvor that evening. I had arrived deliberately early so as to corner the Scorcher before someone else snapped her up, but it was more than an hour before the place started to fill. I was on my third vodka when a hand touched my shoulder. My heart dropped. It was Tina.

"So you sleep good?"

"Very well, yes." The lie made me feel uneasy; I wondered if she had seen me getting onto or off the coach.

"May I be your girlfriend tonight?"

"Just for one drink, I'm afraid."

"Okay," she said, hoisting herself onto a stool and not looking the least bit grieved. "You are waiting for a friend?"

"Yes," I replied, "a friend." I hoped Tina would go before the Scorcher arrived.

Carefully she spread her fingers over the bar. "You see, I listen to what you tell me last night when we are together." I looked at her fingers and then, remembering, her scarlet fingernails. The night before I had complimented her on her hands and nails (there being little else I could honestly compliment) and I had told her that red nail varnish would suit her. It was clear from her beautifully painted nails that she had taken my advice. It made me feel churlish and angry with myself.

"Good, much better. Very nice." At exactly that moment I caught sight of the Scorcher. She was standing at the far end of the bar between two men who were both competing for her interest. I hadn't seen her come in and I cursed myself for missing her and Tina for distracting me.

"Who is the friend you wait for?" she asked.

"That girl there. She's the one I want tonight." I said this quite baldly, angry with Tina for getting in my way, and resenting her proprietary interest.

Surprisingly she seemed not in the least put out. "The tall one?" she asked. "The one with the short black hair and gold earrings?"

"That's the one—with the red jacket and frilly blouse."

"Oh, Magda. But she is a friend of mine. I will go and bring her over for you," and swinging off the stool, quite unabashed by my rudeness, she pushed her way down the bar.

I saw a newsreel once of celebrations following the liberation of Paris. The Scorcher, or rather Magda, reminded me vividly of the girls who clung to the Allies, threw flowers at their tanks and transports, crowded round to hug and kiss their liberators. Our meeting, a minute or so later, was more formal. Tina made the introductions and Magda slipped onto the stool beside me.

"I'm sorry," I began, "your friends . . . " indicating the two men she had left. She shrugged her shoulders, and made a moue as if to say so what.

"It is not important. They are Finns. Finns always too drunk." Her voice was little more than a whisper, a delicate tremble of words, her eyes darting from my face to my clothes, to her purse on the bar. She was quite unlike any Russian I had seen so far— deeply brown with short straight black hair and eyes that looked slanted. Her makeup was quite extraordinary. It was as if she had covered the skin around her eyes with Vaseline, for it shone—her eyelashes looked wet and her eyes seemed filled with tears.

Now left without a stool, Tina stood between us, looking up at each new arrival, smiling at friends, until at last a tall man with a thin, bristly mustache came over, kissed her and took her away.

"Have you known Tina long?" I asked, glad that at last we were alone.

"Since she was working here. Before she left to go to Sweden."

"She was lucky."

"Yes, very lucky."

"Would you do the same thing?"

Another moue, another shrug. "Perhaps. It's difficult. You see, I love Russia more than Tina I think. It is my country. Where I live . . ."

"You are not from Leningrad?"

"Oh no," she laughed, a tinkling laugh like the ice in her drink. "My family live long way from here, near Rostov, far south."

"So how come you live here?"

"My husband work here and bring me with him. But I don't see him long time ago. Two years since. He has left me, I think. But I don't care, you know. I just want to leave home to come here and he help me do it."

There the conversation died for a few moments while we finished our drinks and ordered another round.

"You were here last night, I think?"

"Yes."

"I notice you. You look at me often. I know tonight I see you again. But last night . . . not possible." I remembered the crowd she had been with; they looked so young, so drunk. Magda had sat amongst them, straight-backed, like a queen.

"I'm glad I came back."

"So," her fingers discreetly checked her earrings, the clip-on variety, the size of stamps, square and gold, hiding her lobes completely. "You want to go?"

I nodded.

"Then we finish our drinks yes and then we go somewhere. But before, you buy cigarettes for me, and we need bottle of vhiskey. I will explain."

By the time I had paid our bill, bought Magda's cigarettes and bottle of Scotch, then made my way up to the cloakroom, she was sliding her arms into a big black fur coat. She had taken off her heels —one standing, one flopped on its side—and when her coat was buttoned she tugged on a pair of boots. Her shoes she bundled into a bag. "Not possible to walk on ice with these," she told me. "Warmer too like this." I collected my coat, handed her the whiskey and cigarettes and the doorman let us out.

The taxi was fast, the two of us in the back swinging with every turn. We passed the palaces of Anichkov and Vorontsov, which I recognized from my ramblings, and then followed the course of the Fontanka Canal. It was late and there was no one about. For an instant it was possible to imagine us galloping through the streets of imperial Saint Petersburg on some mission for the palace. At this time of night, the streets deserted, it was like taking a leap backward in time—the frozen river, the blank palace faces, the banks of crusted snow piled up in the gutters. It was an immensely pleasurable feeling—this imaginary going-back-in-history. Had our taxi been a troika and our laps covered in furs, this feeling of mine couldn't have been stronger. For, unlike my socialist tour colleagues come to admire the new "people's state," I had been disappointed with the city. For me there had been something missing—something mighty and admirable which modern day political ideology had crushed. The soul, the spirit of this place, had gone, the buildings little more than extravagant tombstones recalling some greater past, a past I missed most desperately. I bitterly resented what had been done to this city, for there was something grotesquely neutered about it. Sad, hollow, lonely. What had they done, I thought. What had they done?

By now we had left the Fontanka and the river, traveling south, I decided, along an endlessly straight avenue crowded with darkened buildings on either side. Some way down it Magda leaned forward to speak to the driver. The taxi slowed, skidded sideways a little over the ice, then jerked back onto its treads before turning into a side street. Magda was pointing something out to him through the windscreen.

"Pravo, pravo!" she said and the driver pulled to the right, lurching a little against a curb that was hidden by snow.

"Khorosho, spasibo," she thanked him and dropped some coins into his hand. When the taxi disappeared around the corner it was as if we were the only two people in the world. Utter, utter silence as if the snow muffled even the sound of the wind. Crunching carefully over the freezing snow, Magda linked her arm through mine and led me under an arch into a wide silent courtyard. Snow covered the ground here too, like a crumpled sheet disguising the lumpy forms that lay beneath it. Just inside the arch was a double doorway, a ragged, sopping mat and a tiny entrance hall lit by a single bulb that made the green, peeling plaster look sicker than it was. The steps were stone and the doors on each landing paneled a deep, depressing brown. Behind one, a dog barked—a snappy, yappy little bark that somehow suited the empty stairway. We climbed four floors, Magda turning now and then with a finger to her lips. On every landing, beneath a window looking down onto the courtyard, stood enormous cast-iron radiators, each painted the same pastel green. Beneath each of them brown rusty puddles were beginning to freeze at their edges. Had the stairs been carpeted—even covered in lino—it might have been a little warmer, but the stone was cold and inhospitable, our footsteps echoing up past the landings above us. It was like walking through the spirals of a seashell—as empty and as cold.

"Is this your home?" I suddenly thought to ask, whispering the words, not because I was thinking of the people asleep, but the tone seemed to suit the cryptlike coldness of the place. She didn't look back but I could see her head shake. I began to wonder where she was taking me, when she would ask for money, and how much she would ask for. Like Ireniya in Moscow, like Tina the night before,

I doubted it would be more than a handful of dollars.

On the fourth floor, she paused and peered through the gloom at the numbers. Each of the three doors was in shadow, set back a little from the light. She looked at the first and shook her head, then at the second, but at the third she rang the bell. Beyond the door, in some dark hallway we could hear it ring. Then silence, the deep silence of night so distant from the gentle rumblings of a constant activity that had filled Ireniya's apartment. It struck me then that both places smelled the same—of long-ago boiled vegetables, of damp woollen clothes, of soaking, reeking boots. Magda rang the bell again, lightly as though to make the noise less. Standing there together, we waited for the soft shuffling of slippers down the hall, but none came.

"Who lives here?" I whispered into her collar.

"Friends," she replied.

"What's wrong with your place?"

"No good," was all she would say.

"Well what about the hotel?"

"No good," she repeated. And then, when it was clear no one was going to answer the door, she turned to me and said she knew another place. At the bottom of the stairs the little dog yapped again as the double doors squeaked open and we stepped out into the courtyard.

Out on the pavement again, Magda slipped into a kiosk and lifted the receiver. She stood there a moment, huddled behind the glass, then put it down.

"Broken," she told me. The idea of vandalized telephone kiosks in Russia amused me. It seemed we were not so different after all.

"So what now? Where to?" I asked, following her to the corner of the main road.

"We wait here for taxi. One come soon."

So deserted was the street that I thought this highly unlikely. In both directions, as far as one could see through the flurries of snow, there was no movement, not the least sign of life. And then, within what seemed like seconds, as if somehow bidden from a rank, a pair of headlights appeared and Magda was waving it down.

It was good to be in a taxi again, insulated against the cold, sitting in the driver's warmth. This time we drove north toward the Neva, and once again the columns and statues and squares and noble palaces hauled me back a century. While Magda and the driver spoke together I gazed out at the darkened city. This time we crossed the Fontanka, its waters patched with a pattern of loose ice floes that reminded me of crazy paving, took a right into Sadovaya, then a left into Dzerzhinsky, and followed the road all the way to the vast arena of the Winter Palace square which we skirted on the Admiralty side, its enormous black anchors half buried in snow. Once across the Neva, our driver swung left along the quay past the darkened university buildings and up into a maze of streets that formed the southern edge of Vasilievsky Island.

The driver let us out in what most precisely resembled a small London square. Once again Magda paid the fare and the taxi skidded away. This time there was no courtyard, just a high, paneled door that opened onto a wide stone staircase. Again our footsteps echoed up the stairwell, mine sharp and grating, Magda's dull from her boots. It all reminded me of colleges in Oxford, visiting friends late at night. There was the same coolness off the stone and the same night silence and shadows. As far as I could tell this building seemed grander than the last place. Not only were the stairs wider and not so steep, but the windows were tall and churchlike. The state of the plaster work was much better too—nothing peeling, no sprinkling of white dust on the stone. It was warmer too, with only one door on each landing. At the third door Magda rang the bell and then pushed me back toward the stairs and out of sight. Almost immediately there were sounds of bolts being drawn back, keys rattled and hinges squeaked as the door was pulled open, sending a shaft of light onto the landing. I was just able to make out a blond head peering round the door before Magda stepped into my line of vision. There were whispers, a jolt of laughter, and Magda was dragged in and the door closed after her. Now there were only muffled sounds. A minute later Magda reappeared and beckoned me over. "Come, come in, please."

Closing the door behind me and shooting the bolts, she pushed me down a narrow corridor painted a dull cream color. Ahead were two doors painted the same shade of cream. One of them was open and though there was no light on inside I could see it was a kitchen. There was the corner of a table, two chairs with straight backs, a sink and cream-colored cupboards. The second door was closed but behind it I could hear a jumbling, hurrying sound and whispers. Quickly Magda steered me past it, down another corridor, past a door on my left which was clearly the bathroom and into another room. The ceiling was high, there were two French windows, and between them a table and four chairs. In one corner was a wardrobe and in the other, just behind the door, a long couch. The room was papered in fading stripes, a picture from a magazine was stuck to the wall above the couch and the floor was covered with linoleum. Blue curtains, drawn back, hung at the windows. Below us was the small, snow-covered square of Bolshoi Prospekt and a line of leafless trees. Magda took my coat and hung it with hers in the wardrobe and indicated that I should sit at the table.

Down the hall a door opened and feet pattered over the lino. The young blond woman I had glimpsed on the landing, plump in a pink nylon dressing gown, with pink cheeks and thin-slit twinkling eyes, burst into the room like a summer storm, grabbing at the edges of her gown and chattering happily.

"Hollo, I em Zimya. This house, my house. Live here. Yes?" she said, pulling out a chair and sitting down beside me, grappling as she did so the fluttering edges of her gown. "And dis, dis is Uller, my man Uller." Uller, who had followed Zimya far less dramatically into the room, was taller than I with a crown of rough, tousled hair, a long sledgehammer face and a chin that seemed to occupy the whole bottom half of his head. When he shook my hand and welcomed me, I noticed his bottom lip protruded much further than his top lip, giving his voice a slightly drunken lisp. He wore no shoes or socks but had dragged on a pair of trousers. The shirt he wore was still unbuttoned and revealed a white, hairless vee of chest highlighted by an angry red spot without its head. I had the distinct and certain impression that Zimya had dealt with it; she looked the kind of woman who would delight in such an operation—a wonderfully earthy, direct, solid, unshockable, strong, capable lady who provided for her men in a rough and ready sort of way, the way Uller, I suspected, enjoyed being treated. The four of us made ourselves comfortable around the table and smiled at one another.

"Martin has brought Scotch vhiskey," said Magda softly, pointing at the bottle on the table.

"Veeski!" exclaimed Zimya, as if she had only just spotted the bottle. "Uller. Four glasses. Collect. In kitchen. On shelf. Go." Grinning widely, Uller jumped to his feet like a faithful dog and went in search of the glasses. "We celebrate our guest. Is good you are here. I am happy. English" ("Inglush" was how she pronounced it) "not so good, but happy you come." Her voice was low, rounded and dramatic, and made me think of a Laurence Olivier LP played at half speed.

Between us the whisky soon disappeared—Uller pouring fresh

measures as soon as one glass was emptied. When there was none left Zimya sent him back to the kitchen for some vodka.

I can't remember everything we talked about. There was so much. Zimya worked in a ministry—of what, I never discovered—and Uller, who lived in Bergen, was a contract engineer working in Volgograd. His plane had been delayed and he was spending a few days with Zimya before catching the train south. It was evident they had known each other a long time—that Zimya was his regular Leningrad lady—for there was much bantering affection between them. I suspected too that she was, or had been, in the same business as Magda (intent on gaining Norwegian citizenship?), especially since she expressed not the least surprise at Magda appearing at her door so late with a foreigner. I felt sure it wasn't the first time—the bottle of Scotch a signal of intent, a kind of rent. On and on we talked—of the state, of mugging, of money. The first Zimya hated, the second she knew of firsthand ("here," she said, pointing to a line of thin scar tissue beneath a plucked eyebrow, "a big hole, moch blod"), while the third she talked about with a kind of awe. All the time Magda sat just outside the circle of light, her legs crossed, barely sipping her drink, rarely speaking.

Every time a subject was exhausted and a silence fell over us I longed for someone to make a move, yawn, stretch, look at the time, exclaim. But no one did, Zimya always managing to introduce some new topic of conversation. Then, magically, marvelously, Uller took the initiative as if sensing it was time for them to leave us alone.

When at last they had gone, Magda took some linen from the wardrobe and made up the couch, then disappeared into the bathroom. Chilly, goose-pimpled, my head aching with drink, I slipped under the sheets and blankets and listened to the sounds from Zimya's room next door. I could hear their voices—just a mumble pitched high and low—but no word came clearly through the wall. There were creaks of a bed, a jumping sound, squeals of laughter. At last, I heard the bathroom door open, a light switch off, and Magda return. Walking to the table, she turned off the lamp and stood looking down at the square. As a silhouette against the window, in the watery blue light that shone up from the snow-filled square, she began to undress.

Stooping a little, padding across the room, she came to the bed and slipped in beside me. The couch was wide enough for the two of us not to touch and for a while we lay like that, taut to control our shivers, drawing at each other's body warmth before touching. At length I put a hand on her shoulder, ran it down her arm, felt tiny hairs sticking up like pins. Like a dog about to be struck she seemed to contract, draw away from me, but then gradually I could feel her relax, unwind, her legs moving, her arms unfolding, nerving herself for the moment my hand would really touch her. But I made no such move, content to stroke her arm, her shoulder, her side until she caught my hand quickly and placed it on her. It seemed to come as a great relief to her, a release, as if now she could take part, react.

She spoke only once. *"Bistro, bistro,"* she whispered and I recognized her instruction to hurry, to be swift, to finish as quickly as I could.

Long afterward, the sounds still came through from next door —tiny squeals and sighs from Zimya, grunts from Uller, long strained groans. Their affection for each other, the passions they aroused, seemed, in the predawn dark, to underline the hollowness and callousness of our own coupling. Where theirs sounded lush and luxurious, ours had been swift, careless and mechanical, an adequately performed, professionally detached imitation that served only to make me long for the still distant time when I could once again enjoy a true and shared intimacy with someone I cared for. As we lay side by side in the cold stillness of that room I thought of Christmas, now only a matter of days away, and wondered how I would spend it, who I would spend it with. By then I would be in Amsterdam, but I had no illusions it would be any different there.

Only the cold outside the bed kept me where I was, unwilling to put my feet on the cold lino, dress in the cold darkness, scurry back across the frozen snow to my hotel. But guilt and discomfort grew stronger than the cold and eventually drove me from Magda's side. Next door, Uller's grunts had been replaced by a steady snore like a chair being drawn across a stone floor. I dressed, found my coat and made for the door. But as I crossed the room Magda swung out of the bed, her arms huddled over her breasts, to show me the way. I followed her down the hall, a pale figure in the darkness of the corridor where no light from the square below could penetrate. The locks were turned, the door was opened, a few notes were passed over, and once again I was standing alone on the landing.

It was a long walk, cold and slippery. A bus, its hollow inside yellow and warm with light, passed in the opposite direction. It was still too early for passengers. A car slid by, crackling over the surface of the road, again in the wrong direction. There seemed little likelihood of a taxi. I made for the river, where I thought it ought to be, and a few minutes later trudged out onto the quay. Away in the distance, across the sweep of the Neva, I could see the lights of my hotel. Breakfast was at seven-thirty. I had an hour to make it. Under the last patches of darkness I paused, leaned over the stone wall and looked out onto the river. From somewhere in midstream came a snapping, creaking, grating sound as the ice completed its maneuvers and settled into its new shape for a new day.

Dutch
Interior

In the shop windows of Leidsestraat it was Christmas. To prove it, and compensate for a steady drizzle, there were polystyrene snowballs stacked like cannon ball pyramids amongst the displays, and polystyrene snowmen with the sharp edges of cardboard carrots for noses and the handles of broomsticks buried into their flanks. They had tilting top hats, black button eyes, long woollen scarves and old slippers peeping out from under their snow white cassocks. Silver stars twisted on the end of cotton threads and golden profiles of swinging church bells hung in every doorway. Pine wreaths were pinned to the woodwork, and long silver candles with perfect red flames were taped to windows. Boas of gold and silver glitter snaked round the necks of fur-coated mannequins and sprigs of holly and ivy and bundles of red plastic berries lay at their feet. There were sledges piled with ribboned gifts and Santas and scarlet scrolls wishing customers *Prettige Kerst.* There were clusters of pine cones still on the branch sprayed with aerosol snow, and tidy, graphlike curves of cotton wool decorated the right-hand corners of specially taped-on window frame. From loudspeakers above the doors of Peek & Clippenburg came the hollow, tinny recordings of Christmas carols, echoing around Dam Square and competing with the steel-scraping sound of trams:

> *In de stad van Konig David*
> *In het oude Bethlehem . . .*

I was in Amsterdam and it was Christmas Eve.

In the room where the three girls worked, a few steps away from the Voorburgawal and Petrus Cuypher's station building, there were just three Christmas cards. One was tall and thin and leaned against the wall, the other two were short and square and stood by themselves. The tall one had a picture of Snoopy on its cover, the bubble coming from its mouth filled with exclamation marks, and inside the inscription read "Happy Christmas love and kisses, Greta." The first square card featured a detail of a winter scene by Avercamp—bare-branched trees, a long alley of ice, plump-trousered skaters and horse-drawn sleds. It had the minute density of a Breughel. Inside it was signed "to Greta, season's greetings, Evelein." The third and last card was another reproduction, more modern than its companion, and showed a frozen canal in Amsterdam lined with scoops of snow and thin wood railings. It was signed by Greta in blue biro, and by Evelein in turquoise ink, with words "to Karla, Happy Christmas, Greta and Evelein." Beside Greta's name, in blue biro, were three X's.

There was no card from Karla to her two colleagues.

The room was the basement of a five-story building that leaned forward over a narrow strip of cobbling and a khaki-colored canal. This odd toppling effect was caused by a heavy-looking flourish of baroque scrollwork around the eaves and gables. The house had the same air of sagging dependence on its neighbors as a drunk with his companions. Because the house was built near a corner and the junction of a bridge, the cobbled road sloped past it and half-concealed the French windows that led down to the basement. Fixed to the wall on one side of this entrance was a long lorry mirror. In this way, anyone sitting on the platform just inside the window could look up the street toward the bridge and down the street at the same time.

The room was long and rectangular with an arched ceiling—probably an old merchant storehouse. The brick work had been plastered and painted and the earth floor concreted over. Power lines had been run into it and heating piped down from upstairs. There was a worn pink carpet on the floor and red-flocked wallpaper. In one corner stood a sink with surgical taps—the kind you push on and off with your elbows—and underneath it a bin with a foot-pedal and a round wicker dog basket filled with odd scraps of blankets and toweling. A long counter, equipped with drawers and cupboards, ran the length of two walls. One section had been hollowed out to make a dressing table and a beveled mirror was screwed to the wall. At regular intervals along its length were lamps with red bulbs and rilled shades. There were tidy lines of books—paperback thrillers and art books; an electric kettle on a flowered fiberglass tray; glass ornaments with the emphasis on spindly legged animals; a number of ashtrays; a pile of newspapers and magazines; and a potted plant—a poinsettia, its topmost leaves as red as the wallpaper. Built into the counter by the bed was a smart Sanyo receiver and tape deck. On the shelf above it was a rack of cassettes —from orchestral Beatles to Deep Purple. The bed was large with pillows and cushions stacked up against the wall, a red cotton coverlet, but no sheets. A number of posters had been tacked to the walls in the spaces left by hanging clothes. There were two ballet studies by Degas, their dusty grays complementing the red wallpaper and pink carpet perfectly; a picture of Jimi Hendrix biting a tune out of his guitar strings; and a sunset over some distant beach. There were no personal photographs, framed or otherwise. Despite the fan heater that stood by the French windows and two small radiators, a damp mustiness soaked through from the canal across the road. Apart from Evelein, who kept a small supply of medicines in a drawer by the dressing table, the other girls both had snuffling colds.

The basement cost two hundred guilders a day and Evelein held a short lease. The three girls shared this rent between them, Greta and Karla leaving their portion on the counter for Evelein every Friday. Of the three Evelein was the oldest and worked the morning shift from ten until three. Greta came next, from about three (it depended on her last lecture) until eight, while Karla took the night shift and stayed as long as business was good.

Evelein always arrived earlier than she needed to. She wore sensible shoes for the cobbles—flat and comfortable—and when it was wet she slipped plastic galoshes over them. She wore a beige raincoat, whether it rained or not, which she belted tightly. Her hair she wore under a wig, and over that a scarf, and carried a woven shopping basket in the crook of her elbow that bounced against her hip as she walked. In the basket there was always a copy of *Der Volkskrant* neatly folded beside a bunch of fresh flowers. When it rained she carried an umbrella which she shook out before turning the key in the lock and opening up the French windows.

Greta's last lecture usually finished around three. She was in the second year of a political science course. She rode to the room on a motorized bicycle that looked like a Solex but which Amsterdammers called *bromfeitsen.* She would jump off the bike, kick down the stand, and take out a pile of books from her saddle bags. She liked wearing trousers—jeans or floppy cords—canvas shoes, which she always hung up to dry as soon as she got in, and long woollen cardigans with braided leather buttons. Her hair was short and blond and very curly, and when she unbuckled her helmet she shook it out just as Evelein shook out her umbrella.

Karla lived thirty minutes away in Den Haag and drove to work in an orange BMW. She always parked beside the canal and as close to the room as possible so she could keep an eye on it while she sat in the window. She had hard, Eastern features and wavy black hair caught in a grip. She wore a knee-length leather driving coat and leather boots with the trousers tucked inside, and owned a snappy little terrier called Magnus. When it was wet he shook himself so violently his legs lifted off the ground. He lived in the wicker basket beneath the sink.

Evelein never opened the curtains immediately. She was very tidy-minded and always had to clean up after Karla's shift the night before. It was just as well Greta came between them; Evelein and Karla were none too friendly. She hoovered the carpet, straightened the covers on the bed, cleaned the counter, dusted around the glass animals and filled a vase with water for her flowers. Then she made herself a cup of coffee—black, one sweetener—and prepared herself. She wore high-heeled slippers with pink pom-poms on the toes, a pair of white, lace-edged pants, a man's shirt with the top four buttons undone and a lacy white bra. The wig made her look like Doris Day. She would position the chair in the window so she could see both up and down the street, switch on the lights—three red fluorescent tubes around the French windows—sit down, cross her legs and open *Der Volkskrant.*

Greta never read a paper, but always had a big book pressed open on her knees with a notebook and a biro at her feet. She wore large, round-framed, tortoise-shell spectacles which she whipped off when she thought a customer might be approaching. Very discreetly, she puffed a joint. She liked wearing a T-shirt shift and white pants, was bare-legged and bare-footed. While she was reading she had a habit of twisting a lock of hair round her finger. She also picked distractedly at her toenails.

By the time Karla arrived it was dark. She would let herself in, draw the curtains and change. She particularly favoured a leopard-skin leotard that was worn very high on the hips, with a wide, studded belt cinching in her waist. She also wore white tasseled cowboy boots. Her eyes were heavily mascaraed and the top of her left thigh was tattooed with a burning phoenix. When she was ready, she preferred standing in the window or perching on the arm of the chair intent on never losing a potential customer. She was the only one of the three who beckoned at passersby, or opened the door and called out to them. Every two hours she slipped her leather driving coat over her leotard, locked the room and took Magnus for a walk.

"You are a tourist?" asked Evelein, closing the French windows behind me and drawing the curtains. I told her I was. "You have been in Amsterdam long?" she asked, leading me to the bed.

"A few days."

"It is one hundred guilders, or two hundred if you wish."

I gave her the hundred, undressed and lay down on the bed. She unbuttoned her shirt and made to undo her bra.

"Not yet."

She shrugged and sat down beside me.

"Have you been to the Rijksmuseum yet?" she asked, sliding a contraceptive onto me like a nurse sliding a sock over the toes of a plastered leg.

"Yes," I replied, a little surprised both by the question and the contraceptive. "I went yesterday but didn't really like it. My shoes squeaked on the floor."

"Squeaked?"

"Made funny noises, you know."

"Ah, so," she held me in her hand as she spoke, running her fingers along me as if testing the stops on a recorder. "I like the Rijksmuseum," she continued, "but not as much as the Vincent Van Gogh. You have been there yet?"

"Yes," I replied, fascinated by the odd direction our conversation was taking.

"I think Vincent Van Gogh is my favorite. You know, I love the way he signs the painting—with that stroke under his name." She leaned forward and took me, rubber sheath and all, into her mouth. I could feel the warmth of her tongue rather than the tongue itself.

Sitting up again, she continued: "If I was a film director and I was making the film story of his life I would choose Steve McQueen for the part. Not Paul Newman, he is too kind-looking—not mad enough, you know?"

"Uh huh."

"Have you seen the . . . the self-portraits? That hair—short you know, not like yours. And his eyes, just like Steve McQueen—that same look to his face."

I tried to think of the paintings, of Steve McQueen, but found it hard to concentrate. Instead I said: "You can take it off now."

She did so, slowly, feeling for the catch between her shoulder blades. Then she made me bend my leg, so she could support herself on my knee, pulling at me again with long steady tugs. From where I lay, she looked as if she were leaning on a windowsill, looking down at the street. I had just grown used to the silence when she restarted the conversation.

"Which is your favorite Van Gogh?"

I wanted to tell her to keep quiet, or if she wanted to speak to talk dirty. But I was fascinated all the same. "The sketches—crayon, charcoal, black and white," I managed.

"Oh, they are so sad. I think it is always raining in those pictures, and the trees have no leaves and the ground the farmers work looks so hard. Their hands must be so . . ."

"Can I kiss you?"

"No, I don't like. I am sorry," she said without turning.

"Can I touch?"

"Where?"

"There," stroking the side of her breast where it almost touched my leg.

"Okay, of course, but nowhere else you understand." But before I could take advantage, Evelein bent forward again out of my reach, running her tongue over the sour-tasting, lubricated rubber. "The pictures I like best," she continued, licking at me like a child with a lollipop, "are the oils with all that color. You know the ones?"

"Yes."

"I love his flowers . . . *bloemen,* blossom. And the wind blowing the wheat. Wheat? Yes?"

"Yes, wheat fields."

"Have you seen how the wind blows from left to right?"

"I'm not sure. Perhaps he was right-handed—like you."

"Mmmmmh, I think so. I think in all his pictures the wind blows the same way. But my favorite is just of, how do you say, branches; like he is lying on his back like you and looking up at the blue sky through the branches, through the *bloemen.*"

"He painted it for his nephew. A birthday present."

"You know the one?"

"Yes . . . branch of a . . . an almond tree . . . or something . . ."

"Yes, almond tree. I think that is the one." She had started to stroke the insides of my thighs, firm long strokes from knee to crotch. Then she bent down for a long time, lips sliding over rubber, her mouth making the most extraordinary sucking sounds. She sat back and started again with her hand. "Have you been to the Stedelijk too?"

"Yesterday . . ."

"My favorite is the most big in the museum; you know the one? It is a big ship sinking with the chimneys and . . . and . . . propellers."

"Funnels . . . and screws. . . ."

"Screws?"

"That's the right word. Not propellers. Ohhhhh, screws."

"Screws, I see, yes . . . anyway, it is a man called Tatafiore . . . he is very good. Do you have a favorite there?"

" 'De Gehangene' . . . Win de Haan," I muttered.

"Win de Haan? Win de Haan?"

"The man . . . upside down . . . in a chimney, tied . . . it's a . . . it's a . . . sculpture. Shit."

"Oooops, ooooopsa, there we go." She stretched over for a tissue, wrapped it around, rolled it off and squashed it into a little blue ball. She got up from the bed, walked over to the sink, stepped onto the pedal and threw the bundle into the bin.

"So, 'De Gehangene'! But it is dreadful." She picked up the bra and strapped it back on, then the shirt. "You really like it?" She was unscrewing the top of a bottle labeled "Prodent." She squirted some onto her mouth, slooshed it around and very prettily spat it out. "There."

"I don't take blacks, Orientals, druggies, drunks or turkeys," she told me afterward as we sat drinking coffee in the curtained room. "I am more expensive than other girls, but I'm not sick with drugs. Here, look at my arms—see?" She pushed up her sleeves. "Some girls you find, it is horrible here.

"To do this job, you know, you have to be . . . schizophrenic.

Sometimes I close a door in my head. I'm not doing what I'm doing. I'm doing something else."

"Like being at the Stedelijk?" I asked with a smile.

It stopped her short. "Maybe you are right, but I did not think it. I think it is just nice to talk. I think I always talk.

"There are three of us," she told me. "Me, Greta and a girl named Karla. I don't like Karla so much. She is always late with her rent and never looks after the room. Every morning it is so like a bomb goes off. Full ashtrays, food plates, you know. One morning her dog—she keeps a dog—the dog has left something over there in the corner. It is terrible for me.

"But worse, you know, she never puts out the bin so every morning I have to deal with all those . . . things, you know? I leave her notes but she never listens. Always the same. Soon I look for someone else, I think, in the place of Karla."

"Can you do that? Get rid of her?"

"It is my room. I pay the rent. They give me their money. I pay the landlord. Next time she is late with money I tell her she must go. Tell her to stay in Den Haag with her dirty dog. I don't want her here."

"And Greta?"

"Greta is nice, but a little strange. She has chance of good education, but she does this. I cannot understand it. If she was my daughter I would not allow."

"Do you have children?"

Evelein had taken a cloth from a drawer and was wiping the top of the counter. "My husband and I did not agree on this subject."

"It's not too late."

"But now I have no husband."

"You don't have to be married." Evelein looked shocked.

"So what happened?" I continued.

"I was married at eighteen. I was too young, I think. We divorced in four years. He liked his eggs runny. If you are in love watching someone eating runny eggs is okay. But slowly these runny eggs begin to make me feel sick. And the more sick I feel, the less I love him. The egg is a simple thing—not just the egg. But looking back I see the two things together. When I was fed up with egg, I was fed up with him. Same day. Horrible runny egg. Horrible man." She shrugged. "Now I am thirty-five. I live alone. I am happy. Tomorrow I spend Christmas with *Mooder* in Leiden. One time I sit in window and see him pass, but he doesn't recognize me. Imagine if he come in and ask how much and I say one hundred guilders, but two hundred I give you very good time. It is funny that."

We both laughed. Evelein dusted and I finished my coffee.

"Good-bye, good-bye. If you want to come back after Christmas I am here in the mornings."

"Thank you." She pulled apart the curtains and leaned forward to open the door, clasping as she did so the top of her shirt to her throat.

"Prettige Kerst."

"And Happy Christmas to you," I replied.

Greta had broken the stand on her *bromfeitsen*. It leant against the wall like an old man pausing for breath. The front wheel was turned out into the street and the plastic saddle scratched against the wall. Drops of rain clung to the handlebars and brake grips. I approached the room from down the street and could see her in the lorry mirror sitting in the chair, her bare feet drawn up and tucked under her, a huge book propped between her legs. It was like looking at someone through a fish-eye lens—she seemed oddly misshapen with huge knees and a tiny head. When I tapped at the window, she pushed the book aside and unwound herself.

"Fifty guilders," she said, squeezing her head round the edge of the door.

"Fine," I replied.

"You only want to spend fifty guilders?" she asked once I was inside.

"Why?"

"It is much nicer for one hundred. I use my mouth."

It was an odd feeling returning to this room where I had been only a few hours before, and finding another person there, as if this was the daughter staying at home while her mother was out shopping. Like a daughter, Greta had a kind of reckless attitude toward the room that I didn't think Evelein would much approve of. When the curtains swished closed behind me, it sounded as though they were being ripped off their rail. Evelein had closed them much more gently.

"So, you are going to pay one hundred guilders?" Before I could answer she leaped forward, turned up the radio and pushed the record button on the tape. "It is my favorite. . . . I am taping them. This is a very good program." She dabbed at her nose with a tissue

224

and sniffed, starting to sway to the music. She wore a long white dress like an oversized T-shirt with a punk rip running down from one shoulder to just about the point of her breast. The gash was held together with a kind of cotton cobweb. Unlike Evelein she had switched on the ultraviolet lights in the room—the white dress glowed a bluey white and her skin looked deeply tanned. It struck me Evelein didn't use the light because her teeth were not her own.

"So," said Greta, sitting me down on the bed, "is it fifty or one hundred?"

"One hundred." She looked satisfied, as if I had given an interesting answer to a problem she had set.

"I think you will find that better. It is a good idea. You will see."

"What is your name?" I asked, knowing the answer.

"Greta," she replied, catching her dress by the hem and lifting it over her head. With only the white patch of her pants, her body seemed to glow even darker in the ultra-violet light—her eyes lost under dark brows, her nipples an angry mauve spreading into the skin of her breasts.

While I undressed and lay back on the bed, Greta padded around the room picking up here a packet of cigarettes, there a lighter, an ashtray, and from a drawer the silver foil package of a contraceptive. Sitting beside me on the bed, just as Evelein had done, she slid it on, pushing it down with cool, clinical fingers. I felt her fingernails picking at my navel.

"Fluff," she said, holding the culprit for me to see, then letting it drop to the carpet. Evelein would not have been very pleased. I had a strange feeling she would spot it tomorrow morning. No, not tomorrow. It was Christmas Day tomorrow. She would be with her mother in Leiden.

The song on the radio began to fade and Greta leaped up to switch off the tape before the DJ started talking. Coming back to the bed she sat down beside me again and began running her hands over my chest. Unlike Evelein she sat facing me. I pushed my hands between her arms and held her breasts. They were warm and heavy.

"Aren't you going to take those off?" I asked, pointing to her pants.

"If you like," she replied, standing and stepping out of them. Her body glowed darker still. It struck me for the first time that Evelein had not removed hers. This sudden thought quite surprised me. At the time, it hadn't occurred to me to ask her.

225

Unlike Evelein, Greta didn't speak as she worked, which I was rather grateful for, just held me in her hands and bent down over me. Outside I could hear people walking past on the wet cobbles, a car, a bicycle rattling along. Only a single sheet of glass and a thin curtain separated them from the two of us inside.

"Move over," she said, at length, pushing me toward the wall and climbing onto the bed next to me. "You want to go inside now." It wasn't a question, more a statement, as though this was the next most logical step. Squirming beneath me she coiled her warm soft legs around me, licked her fingers and slipped them between us. Next moment she caught hold of me and pushed down with her ankles. "So," she whispered, closing her eyes.

Later she left the bed to tape another record. Before she got back on the bed she lit a cigarette and lying down beside me again balanced the ashtray on her stomach.

"How long do you work here?" I asked for the second time that day.

She pushed a hand behind her head and dragged on the cigarette. When at last she spoke the ashtray wobbled with every word, a white square floating above the glow. "I start about three, sometimes four in the afternoon and stay only a few hours; finish maybe eight o'clock."

"Is it your own room?"

"There are two girls as well as me, we share the rent."

"Is it expensive, a room like this?" There was a long pause as though she hadn't heard my question, or if she had, as if she couldn't be bothered answering.

"Two hundred guilders a day, I think."

"What are the other girls like?" Again there was a long silence as she smoked her cigarette.

"Oh . . . not so bad, you know. One is a little boring. She is like my mother, always fussing."

"And the other?"

"The other I don't see her so much. She doesn't live in Amsterdam. Often she is here after I go. She has her own key. I think she is okay, you know." It was clear Greta was in no mood to talk. I sensed she wanted me out of the room, wanted me to leave, wanted to get back to her book, to her studies.

"Time to go," she said at last, stubbing out the cigarette, getting up from the bed and walking over to the sink. She turned on the water, went up onto tiptoes and started splashing the water up at herself. "Here," she waved me over, "before you dress. There is soap, and there a towel."

She was dressed long before me and, as if to hurry me, had opened the curtains onto the street outside. Already it was getting darker.

"Prettige Kerst," I said as I stepped past her into the drizzle.

"And . . . Happy Christmas, also," she replied, huddled up in the narrow crack of the doorway.

That night I passed the room three times. Each time the curtains were closed, but I could see lights on inside and Karla's orange BMW was parked near the bridge. The third time I paused by the driver's window and peered in through the rainy glass. At first all I could see were the reflections of street lights and window lights from behind me, but then, beyond them I could see a rug on the passenger seat—for the dog—and several crumpled cigarette packets strewn around the foot pedals, on the dashboard and between the seats. In the back was a tangle of maps and creased magazines.

For the fourth time I visited the pub on the corner, drank a small beer and wandered slowly around the block, ignoring the smiles and entreaties of the other girls who worked this area. It was not that they were unattractive, simply that I wanted to see the room once more—at night, with Karla.

As I came up the street beside the canal a fourth time I could see a patch of red light shining on the cobbles. This time the curtains were open and Karla, one tasseled boot on the seat of the chair, stood peering out into the night, smoking a cigarette.

The dog, with its long hairy eyebrows and bristling snout, looked cross and gave a defensive yap when I stepped in through the door that Karla held open for me. I would have thought he was used to visitors. "Magnus," snapped Karla back. With her cold it sounded like "Magdud." The little dog licked its beigy-black chops contritely with a quick little pink tongue and settled back in the basket beside the sink, though he kept his ears pricked and his sharp brown eyes fixed on me.

After the coolness of the room that morning, its lazy, studious warmth that afternoon, I was surprised at the stifling heat—the small fan heater rattling away at full volume. Now that it was really dark outside, the lights inside the room seemed much stronger, more effective—the red fluorescent tubes and red bulbed lamps turning the room a deep scarlet, the color and the heat going together perfectly.

Karla was much taller than either Evelein or Greta, her features sharper, harder. With her tasseled cowboy boots she seemed to strut across the room as she led me to the bed. While I sat on its edge, she stood before me hands on her hips, feet apart and smiled down at me. Through her tights, just below the hem of her leotard I could see the blue shadowing of the phoenix tattoo.

"You pay now fifty guilders?"

I gave her a hundred-guilder note.

"I have no change," she said, fanning it against her cheek.

"So what do I get for one hundred?" I asked.

"Better time. More time."

"Okay then, forget the change."

Unlike both Evelein and Greta, Karla helped me off with my clothes before undressing herself, tugging off her boots, unbuckling her belt and pulling down her leotard and tights in a tangle of nylon which she kicked away into the center of the room.

"How you want me?"

"On top."

"Fifty guilder more on top," she replied brusquely.

"I only have hundred-guilder notes, and you don't have change."

"For two hundred I go upside, downside, on top, on bottom, you say how."

"You'll find the money in my jacket." I watched her pat down the pockets and find my wallet, slide out one of the notes and put the wallet back. Smiling, she walked back to the bed and knelt across me, her bracelets jangling as she began her performance. But for all her promises and her obvious professionalism it was clear that Karla would suffer in the aftermath of Evelein and Greta.

"You have been drinking?" she sniffed.

"A little," I replied thinking of the beers I had drunk each time I passed the pub, but knowing that wasn't the reason.

"Bad for sex life," she said, waving me between her thumb and forefinger in much the same way she had waved the hundred-guilder note.

"But I haven't been drinking that much," I defended myself, not realizing I had laid myself open for further, more embarrassing attack.

228

"So what is the matter with you then?" She let me go and began to stroke her own body, teasing her breasts for me, sliding her fingers into the black brush between her legs. "Don't you like me?"

"Of course."

"Then why you not hard? You have other women?"

I nodded.

"You have other women today?"

I nodded again.

"How many?"

"Two others."

"Then," her brown eyes glittered hard, "two girls are enough for you. Three too much. It is your own fault. I cannot waste my time with you," and saying this, she swung off the bed and gathered up her tights and leotard.

"What about my two hundred guilders?" I said, sitting up on the bed astonished that she should just give up on me like this.

"I try hard. But it is no good. It is just a waste of time," she repeated, straightening out her tights and slipping her legs into them. "It is not my fault."

"But I gave you two hundred guilders," I persisted.

She had already drawn on the tights and was untangling the leotard.

"Okay," she said at last, dropping the leotard to the floor and sliding down her tights. "I tell you what. You give me fifty guilder more, I show you movie and we try again."

"But I told you, I only have hundred-guilder notes."

Karla smiled.

Blind Man's Buff

It was as if the sun were too tired to do anything more, too lazy to climb any higher. It was as if it had been woken too early after a hard night on the other side of the world and could only manage to drag itself across the rooftops until, gratefully, in a gathering dusk, it sank back into the earth.

It was the last day of the old year and the sun had crept away as if it were glad it was over.

La nouvelle année. The New Year. It seemed the whole of Paris buzzed at the thought. After the old routines—the bored dialogues that filled my days, and the dry, mechanical couplings that filled my nights—I decided I needed something special to mark the occasion, not content, like the sun, to let it slip by. I wanted something novel, something as bold, as certain and as memorable as a red circle scrawled around the date in a calendar. Other nights I might not feel the same incentive, but I wanted a red circle day to start the New Year.

I started on the Boulevard de Clichy, as darkness crept down over the skirts of Montmartre and closed over the tombstones. Quickly the street lights grew stronger, brighter, the colors more vivid, the traffic thicker, and as I walked it seemed the clack-pang, clack-pang of the shooting galleries became sharper, somehow more French—*clacque-pangue, clacque-pangue.*

"I want something special," I said in halting French to the first girl who stepped forward. She shrugged, as if not understanding, wrapped the coat closer around her and moved back into the shadows, not even bothering to change my mind. I wondered if I had said to her what I meant to say.

"Special, m'sieur? Comment special?" asked the second girl, holding on to the sleeve of my jacket and drawing me towards her.

"Différent," I tried. Her mouth curled and her face squirmed as if a cold finger of seaweed from the oyster barrow she stood next to had somehow slipped into her clothes and stroked her skin.

"Différent? Comment différent, chéri?" It was no use. I knew what I had to say to be properly understood, but the word seemed to catch in my throat. It was easier to walk on, to delay.

Through the crowds I made my way towards the distant bulks of the Gare du Nord and the Gare de l'Est. Across the darkness of the Faubourg St. Denis. Down the Strasbourg to run the gauntlet of restless shadows on the corners and in the doorways of Ste. Apolline, Blondel, Lemoine, Tracy, Ponceau. Down Palestro. Across slanting Turbigo that always made me think of a rich fish sauce, and into the warren of rendezvous on the edges of the first district. Here, if you're lucky, they won't smoke at the same time. Here, they'll put one leg on a chair and lift their skirts for you or tug aside the gusset of their hotpants. I had been there before.

"You want to see it?"

"Yes."

"Dix francs, m'sieur, ten francs." She sounded like a croupier.

I slipped the note off the roll and laid it on the bed.

"Bien," she said, and took her hand away. The breast was large and loose, yellow in the light from the bedside lamp, the nipple throwing a long, stretched shadow to her shoulder.

"This one now?"

"Yes."

"Vingt francs."

"Twenty?"

She didn't reply, simply pressed her hand tighter against herself, so her breast squeezed between her fingers. I laid two more notes beside the first. She smiled and slowly let the fingers trail away over her skin, past her shoulder, until her arm was stretched above her head and the breast pointed directly at me.

"Ten for touch," she said as I leaned forward. Another note on the pile. The skin was cool, the nipple damp and wrinkled like a walnut shell. I pressed it back as she had done, moved it in slow, polishing circles. I took my hand away.

"And this?" she pointed at her skirt.

I nodded. "Yes, all of it."

"For . . . fifty? . . . You can do it yourself."

I counted out the notes and dropped them among the others. "This could be expensive."

"Mais c'est drôle, ça."

She turned for me to undo the zip and stepped out of the skirt. She did it quickly as though she was growing impatient with our game. For the stockings she put her foot on the edge of the bed, between my legs, and wiggled her toes. When I leaned forward for the clips, her knee was against my chin. The nylon was smooth but smelt of old clothes and warm rubber. When the second stocking was off she turned quickly and indicated the catch for the belt. When she turned back, I saw she had pushed her hand down the front of her pants, the ridges of her knuckles standing out against the material. I looked at her face and saw her smile.

Outside, someone came running up the stairs, two at a time, paused at the landing, breathing heavily, gulping. Then up again. On the floor above there was knocking, the soft sound of other footsteps and the lock turning. There were words, indistinguishable, just a mutter. The door closed and two sets of footsteps crossed the ceiling.

Catching hold of the elastic, I slid them down, turning them inside out as they caught between her thighs. The hand never moved. The small stones in her ring sparkled in the light.

"You want to see it?"

"Yes."

"You want to touch?"

"Yes."

"We fuck?"

"Yes."

"Deux cent francs, m'sieur—two 'undred franc."

It was good after the dark streets to walk down the arcades of the rue de Rivoli but even here I felt no more encouraged, no more sure or certain of what the evening held in store, of my own ability to make something happen. On the pavement outside Maxim's a crowd had gathered and papparazzi loitered. As I stepped past them a car drew up, there were sighs, the crowd moved forward, and cameras lifted on upstretched arms to flash over the straining heads. I walked on, sad not to be a part of the spectacle.

Every step of the way from the Rond Point along the Champs-Elysées the crowds grew thicker, flowing with me, against me, only parting when firecrackers slithered along the pavement, touch-paper fizzling, the charges exploding. Crack! Crack! Crack! All around the air was filled with drifting smoke and the smell of cordite. There was shouting and screaming and singing, swaying bodies, linked arms and hooting car horns. The feeling that a party had started and that I hadn't been invited grew stronger, more numbing and depressing. I felt like the sun. I seemed to have lost heart somewhere, lost my nerve. Not a part of these celebrations, I wanted them to end. Or more precisely, I wanted to get away from them. Being among all this energy and happiness only served to increase my own sense of isolation. Before I realized it, I had reached the high, illuminated Arc and was turning down Wagram—on my way home.

The night shift was on duty, the same lone concierge sitting behind reception with his feet on the desk. The lounge was deserted, the lights in the small dining room switched off. A bottle stood by his feet and a cigarette smoldered in an ashtray. Every night, at around this time and sometimes even later, he would nod good evening to me and hand me my key without a word. Tonight, though, it was different. When he saw me he ran his finger down the pigeonholes and rattled the key out as usual, but then stood and leaned his elbows on the counter, swinging it between his fingers. The way he held it, slightly away from me, suggested he wanted to talk before letting me go to my room. It was, after all, New Year's Eve. Perhaps, I thought as I stood before him, he would offer me a drink. Normally he wore a rather dour, tired expression but tonight his eyes gleamed and his lips looked redder than usual. I wondered if he might be drunk. His tunic was stained and the space between his buttons bulged more than usual. In a strange sort of way, I felt a kind of sympathy for him. As I did for myself. We were both in the same predicament—detached, alone, not a part of the celebrations all around us.

"So you go to your room now? No parties, huh? No girls?" His fat, grubby fingers seemed unwilling to part with my key. "Perhaps," he continued, "you like something? You want a friend maybe?" He looked at me hard, questioningly.

I was surprised, after my long walk, to feel a stirring of interest. "How much?" I asked. He glanced from side to side and leaned closer, rocking on his elbows, the key dangling.

"Cinq cent," he whispered.

"How much? *Combien?"* It wasn't that I was surprised by the amount, simply that I hadn't heard.

"Five 'undred."

"For five hundred," I began, "can I get something . . . special?"

"What special?"

"You know—special." I tried to invest this single word with as much meaning as I could muster but he looked at me as though I had just told him a joke and he had missed or misunderstood the punchline.

"Special?" he repeated.

"Different. Not five hundred. Something more. A special girl. A girl with . . ." I searched for a way to explain it better, still uncertain, still worried by the word I knew. "A girl with . . . equipment. You understand?"

"Equipment? Ah . . . ?" He began shaking his head and I knew now I either had to use the word for the first time and risk being embarrassed, ridiculed, or give it up entirely and go to my room alone. I made to take the key, almost had my hand on it.

"Dominatrice," I said quickly, quietly, ready to choke off the word in a cough should his reaction not be what I wanted. His elbows slid apart and he crouched lower over the counter, drawing me closer with his words.

"Dominatrice? Dominatrice?" I nodded, he nodded. For a moment I wished I had never started the conversation, wished I had just taken the key from him and gone to my room. *"Dominatrice;* a girl like that, very 'spensive."

"How much?" I asked, hardly daring to imagine such a request could be so easy to arrange. I must have walked miles that night, when all the time I could have made the necessary inquiries here, in my small hotel above the cemetery of Montmartre.

"Give me . . . two zousand, and I fix."

Taking the key I went quickly to my room for the money then returned and handed him the notes.

"I fix it," he told me a second time, pushing the money into a pocket. I nodded, thanked him and went back upstairs not sure whether he meant he had already fixed it or, now that he had the money, that he would fix it. For an hour or more I waited in my room, looking down the street and over the rooftops of Paris. Far away I could hear the tooting of car horns, the muffled explosions of firecrackers, shouts and snatches of song, the whooooosh of rockets somewhere behind me. When I heard the bells start ringing I poured myself a drink, swallowed it quickly in a kind of silent, lonely toast, and lay back on the bed.

234

She arrived carrying a small canvas suitcase. I was asleep when she knocked and only vaguely remember the first or the second rap as a part of a dream; it was the third, perhaps the fourth knock, heavy and belligerent, that had me swinging off the bed. She was older than I expected, short, a scarf knotted at her chin, a wave of blond hair caught beneath it. She wore a long leather coat that was tightly belted. One hand was in her pocket, the other, gloved, held her bag.

The moment she stepped past me into the room, brusquely, almost without my invitation, I could see she was cross. The lines on her brow were tightly puckered and her mouth set thin and serious. I felt as though I ought to apologize for calling her out this late, as I would a doctor. With no formalities whatsoever, no introductory conversation, not even a New Year's greeting, she asked for the bathroom—which I showed her—and before closing the door on me she told me to undress. Her voice was sharp and businesslike, her French fast and unforgiving and the lock had turned before I realized exactly what it was she wanted me to do. A little nervous, unsure, rattled by her manner, I took off my clothes and got into the bed.

When, at last, she came from the bathroom, I must have looked as surprised as she—she, presumably at finding me in bed; I, at her costume. She was wearing the highest heels that I had ever seen. The stockings were black and seemed to shine, the top-most borders blacker still and rising in tiny pyramids to the clips that stretched down from the frilled edge of her corset. The corset itself, laced with vertical ribbons of black satin, was so tight it made her hips look as broad as shoulders, while the cups of the bodice squeezed her breasts into a tight, wrinkled cleavage. After only the briefest hesitation, she told me to get up and swung the bag onto the bed. Without her laying a hand on me, simply by her presence, her outfit, my nakedness, I felt myself begin to respond.

As she bent over the case and fiddled with the clasps I asked if she spoke English. She didn't reply, just turned and told me in the tersest French to sit at the foot of the bed. I did as I was told, and watched her pull from the case a long metal bar with two leather straps at either end. The bar was a little over a foot long and the buckles on the straps rattled as she pulled it free. Kneeling in front of me she fastened a strap around each ankle and then told me to stand. There was no feeling of discomfort or awkwardness until she told me to walk a few steps, when I discovered that this was only possible in a series of small, arclike steps—as if my legs were a pair of ship's dividers. Bending the knees was no use—the bar demanded a stiff-legged walk—although twisting on the balls of my feet with each step and leading with the shoulders made my progress easier, smoother. I felt a little like Frankenstein's monster learning how to walk.

Next she drew a long belt from the case. "Put your arms so, like so," she told me. At first I didn't understand, but then she pulled in her elbows to her sides to demonstrate how she wanted me and I followed her example.

"I'm sorry," I began. "You speak too fast . . . *trop vite.*" Without replying she swung the belt round me like a tailor with a tape measure, pinning my arms to my sides. Tongue into buckle, she pulled tight until the belt pinched at my stomach. The belt was leather, brown and wide, and long; judging by the buckle marks and worn eyes on the spare length that she doubled back through a loop, it was clear larger frames than mine had been bound in this way. This observation rather pleased me.

Next out of the bag was a narrow collar which she clipped loosely around my neck before attaching to it a thin linked chain. She tugged it experimentally and almost jerked my head from my shoulders.

"Voilà."

"Shit! Watch it!" For the first time since she had come into the room she smiled—not an amused, soft smile, but a satisfied one of a job well done.

Teetering around the room on her heels she pulled me after her, jerking the chain until I was hurrying along as best I could to lessen each jolt, giving her less opportunity to pull, trying to ensure the chain never tightened.

"Bon, you learn, *n'est-ce pas?"*

Back at the bed again she drew out a pair of scissors from the bag, the sort milliners use for cutting lengths from bolts of cloth. Carefully, slowly, she snipped a width of tape from a roll and, before I had time to object, spread it over my mouth. Bound and gagged, only able to walk in a twisting series of arcs, I felt a rising sense of defenselessness though I knew I was in no danger. I also felt a little ridiculous and made a point of not looking in the mirror. I could not, however, do anything to contain the mounting of excitement, curiosity, expectation that gripped me as tightly as the belt.

Tugging me into the center of the room, she dropped the lead and walked around me like a sergeant major inspecting a cadet. In her spiky heels, her eyes were almost on a level with mine. After checking the bindings, she caught hold of the lead once more, this time pulling down hard, forcing me to my knees. With the bar between my ankles, this was no easy maneuver, and I slid down all the way using her as a support, the corset material rough against my cheek and face. Leaving me in this position, she turned to the bed and drew from the bag a length of black cloth. Folding it carefully, she came up behind me and slipped it over my head. So wide was this blindfold, so tightly tied, that no light whatsoever showed through. What had felt like defenselessness, quickly turned into a kind of dumb, blind panic. I tried to say something but the gag held firm, smothering my words into a throaty, staccato humming, to which, as far as I could judge, the lady paid not the slightest heed.

Unable to see anything, I now relied totally on sound. I heard her walk back to the bed, the insides of her stockings swishing together, heard her fumble with the bag and then the sound of her stockings again as she walked back to me. I expected her to take the chain and pull me to my feet, but instead, with soft, grunting sounds, she began brushing herself against me like an animal leaving its scent, the corset material scratching across my back, my shoulders, and over my face as she stepped around me. When I tried to twist away she caught my head and pulled me to her, pushing even harder against me. After circling me like this a few times, now running the point of her shoe between my legs, now straddling my shoulders and rubbing herself against me, I felt her reach for the chain and tug me to my feet. If anything it was more difficult getting up than it had been getting down. I had to rock back on my heels and force myself up on tiptoes. As soon as I was standing she caught me by my arms and started to turn me first one way and then the other until I had no clear idea in which direction I faced—toward the door? Or the bed? Or the window? There was just blackness. All I could go on were the sounds of her breathing, an occasional cough, the rubbing of her stockings, and the pull from the lead as she led me around the room.

Now that I was blindfolded, it was impossible to tell how far ahead of me she was and how tight or loose the lead was. As a result the tugs became more frequent and more vicious, pulling me first in one direction and then in the other until at last I stumbled and fell to my knees—not so much because the bar between my ankles

237

had tripped me, but because I thought I'd be safer on the floor. At least, on my knees, I knew where I was. The woman snapped at me angrily in French, tugged at the chain, trying to pull me to my feet. But I resisted, stayed where I was, shook my head stubbornly and hummed my unwillingness to continue. This was all too much; I wanted to finish. It was then that she hit me for the first time, just behind the shoulder, with what felt like a thin switch. The sound it made on my skin and its unexpectedness stung me more than any pain. She was whispering now, urgently, sharply. Again I shook my head, not in answer to her questions, which I could not understand —simply to show my determination to finish. Then she hit me a second time, on the chest, and a third time on the arm, harder now, making me struggle to my feet to avoid further blows, trying to twist my arms free as once more she began tugging me along after her. Again I stumbled, again she hit me. On and on she dragged me, lashing back at me every time I took the wrong direction or stumbled or failed to answer her tugs or pulled back from her. Once more I fell and tried following her on my knees until the carpet burned them. Again I was on my feet, staggering after her, swaying wildly from side to side. Then, after what seemed an age, my skin burning from the blows, muscles aching, snorting breath through my nostrils, she stopped, tugged down on the chain and let me sink to the floor; rather than stay on my knees, I lay face down on the carpet.

But this was to be no reprieve. Without warning, she began hitting me again swiftly, sharply across the backs of my legs and buttocks until my skin stung and sang from the blows. Not daring to roll over for fear of the consequences, I tried to get back on to my knees, but her shoe clamped down firmly on the small of my back, the heel digging into my kidneys. There seemed no way for me to avoid the blows, nothing I could do to stop her beyond squirming beneath her foot and humming loudly into the carpet.

And then, strangely, I was no longer aware of individual blows, could no longer tell exactly where the switch hit me. Instead I felt with each new stroke only a burst of warmth, spreading, like fat dissolving in a heated pan. My skin no longer stung but tingled hotly as the blood surged up and down my legs and deep into me and for the first time I became conscious of a rising, urgent response to her beating. No longer was I angry, bitter; no longer did I want to hit her, tear free, fight against it—but simply to relax in the warmth, to submit without argument or retaliation. As if she sensed this sudden change in me the beating ceased though my body still glowed from the strokes she had given me. I felt her foot lift off my back, a hand slide under my hip and roll me over on to my back. This was the most astonishing sensation of all, for I felt as though I was suddenly floating, my skin not touching the carpet, my body rising off the floor. And then I felt her above me, squatting over me, drawing me tight and pulsing into her, her warmth matching mine in one swift uncontrolled release.

I lay on the carpet a long time, listening to her in the bathroom, taps turning, water splashing. I heard her dress somewhere close to me, something being bundled into the bag. I felt her hands at my ankles, loosening the straps; at my stomach unbuckling the belt and sliding it from under me; at my throat, unclipping the collar; a fingernail picking at a corner of the tape and tearing it off my mouth; and then, finally when she had packed everything away and snapped the clasps on the bag shut, I heard her knees crick as she bent down beside me to untie the blindfold. Only when it came off did I realize my eyes were closed. I opened them in time to see her turn in the doorway and look back at me. *"C'est bien, n'est-ce pas?"*

Part Four

A Corner
of Sunset

Everything I saw of 'Lisha that first day, I saw in silence and from a distance; a chance observer, never close enough to hear, but close enough to see. The short, staggered action reminded me of a badly cut silent movie.

The very first time, she was walking past the conservatory-style front windows of the Bank of America on Sunset Boulevard. Only my second day in the city, I was in the bank trying to cash sterling travelers' checks without benefit of identification. The cashier I approached took the note and held it suspiciously between the thumb and forefinger of each hand as though he were handling a photographic negative and didn't want to smear its surface. With a twist of cuffed wrists he examined its reverse side, which was blank, then turned it back again. Without looking up he asked for identification, to which I replied I didn't have any. Then he was sorry, he said primly, but without some form of identification—drivers' license, passport—he couldn't cash the check, placing it, as he spoke, squarely, finally and definitely on my side of the counter. I had never needed identification before, I lied. He just shrugged, then directed me across the hall to an open-plan range of executive desks where the higher officials of the bank were to be found. If one of them cleared it, then I was to come back. Otherwise . . . he shrugged again and looked pointedly—not at me—but at the person next in line. I was dismissed.

Across the hall, a secretary pointed out the desk I wanted and the person to speak to, an elderly lady in a darted cotton suit with spectacles on a beaded chain. Since she was occupied with another customer, I took up a position close enough to take the chair as soon as it was vacated and gazed discreetly out of the window. It was exactly then that 'Lisha passed into my field of vision, walking heavily from right to left across the screen of the window, absently swinging a gold shoulder bag. Ten steps later she passed out of frame. In those ten steps I observed she was black, brightly dressed and young. I thought no more about her, just someone passing in the street.

The customer in front of me concluded his business and I took his place. A plaque on the desk announced I was now in the presence of the assistant manager though, strange for America, there was no name to accompany the rank. As I explained the situation the woman took the check and studied it, also turning it over to see if there was anything on the back. Still not having spoken a word she picked up the phone, found a number in her Rolodex and began dialing, smiling all the time, presumably to confirm via some computer linkup I knew nothing about, whether the number on the check had been listed as stolen or lost. She had just started reading off the number when, over her shoulder, I saw 'Lisha the second time, walking back again from left to right. Her step was more sprightly now, head up, thumbing the strap of her bag across a shoulder. Almost out of frame, with her back to me, she stopped as if speaking to someone I could not see. A moment later, two young men in jeans and T-shirts walked past her, one of them looking back and shaking his head, before they too disappeared off screen. When I looked back to her side of the window, she had gone.

The bank did not cash my check. All they established was that the number was good—listed neither as stolen nor lost—and that more than probably, I was the legitimate holder. They had no proof otherwise. But, the assistant manager apologized, removing her glasses and letting them hang by the chain, the bank really did need some form of identification. I left in a flush of indignation, not so much because I needed the funds—I could last until the following day—but because I had wanted to return to that precise little teller with the cuffs and have him cash it for me without identification.

The bank was red-brick and square, built on the corner of a block with two entrances into the rear parking lot where I had left my rented car. One of these led directly onto Sunset, the other into a side street. I was fiddling with the lock I had not yet mastered, wondering if there was time to try another bank, when a light blue BMW drew up to the curb opposite the side street entrance. The

driver was black, wore a pale polo neck and sunglasses. I remember
thinking that particular BMW model looked rather small for him;
he seemed cramped. But then it was a BMW and this was Califor-
nia. I was on the point of looking away when I spotted 'Lisha again,
tottering down the sidewalk in her block-heeled sandals. She
stepped into the road and bent down at the open window. From
where I stood, I could see the driver look away as, judging by her
movements, she started explaining something to him. Like a dog
nuzzling its way back into its master's good graces her body seemed
to twist in earnest, her knees bent and straightened as if she was not
sure whether to cower or not while her hands beat softly at the
window ledge. Suddenly the driver turned on her, stabbing at her
with a long, black finger with every silent word he spoke. Not
wishing to draw attention to myself I slipped into the car and,
pretending to arrange something on the back seat, observed them
more covertly. But there was little action left in the drama. The girl's
shoulders slumped, the window slid up and the car sped off.

That was the first time I saw 'Lisha, not a shortened name but
the way she pronounced Alicia. I never saw the man in the light blue
BMW again.

The following afternoon, at precisely the same time, I returned
to Sunset and parked once more behind the bank. Intrigued by what
I had witnessed the day before, I had come back with the sole
intention of locating 'Lisha. That she was a hooker working the
Strip and the man in the BMW her pimp or "daddy," I was in no
doubt; that I would approach her as a client I was equally certain;
and that she was in the immediate vicinity, I thought more than
likely, for a kind of temporal and territorial imperative dictates not
only where, but also when, a working girl may appear. This, I had
decided, was 'Lisha's time and territory.

With the sun setting behind me, casting a warm glow of gold
down the Strip and a fencing of long shadows from the scruffy-
collared palms that lined this end of the Boulevard, I crossed Sunset
and began my search. I walked slowly, pausing at the corner of
every block, ostensibly checking for traffic but actually watching
out for 'Lisha. I was neither surprised nor discouraged at not finding
her immediately. There were a dozen good reasons for her not being
where I expected, the most likely being that she was somewhere
with a client—in his car, in a short-time motel, in a doorway, in a
deserted hallway, in a disused building, perhaps even in a "trick-

245

truck" supplied by the pimp and parked somewhere quiet in any of a dozen side streets or vacant lots. Or she could be alone—recovering in a café, taking a pee the very moment I passed her spot, perhaps even resting up in the cool, anonymous comfort of the Oriental Cinema on Vista. A long time before, I had known another girl, in another city, do just the same thing. Sooner or later she would break cover.

Past the junction of La Brea and Sunset, I grew certain I was moving out of her territory—an instinctive certainty, like a tracker who knows in his bones he's off the trail, has lost the scent. It was as if a tiny voice, growing louder and more taunting with every step, kept repeating the childhood refrain: You're getting colder, you're getting colder, colder . . . ooh, you're freezing now. I knew there was little point in going any farther.

At Orange Drive, therefore, I recrossed Sunset and began to work my way back. When I reached the bank, I decided, I would take the car and cover the area block by block, north and south. Meanwhile, I kept the same steady pace, stopped to buy a newspaper and made a point of looking through shop windows—into the booths of a pizza parlor, into a Laundromat, a drugstore, into Derboghossian's Shoe Repair (perhaps one of those heels had snapped off and even now she was having it glued back on), at a line of customers in the Golden Pioneer Chicken takeout, even into the florists on Fuller.

I knew I had little to go on. I had barely seen her face the day before, and then only in profile. All I could clearly recall were the clothes she had worn—tight satin trousers creased at the back of the thighs and crotch where the flesh squeezed against the thin cloth, the silver belt that caught the sun as she leaned forward at the car window, a yellow blouse with rolled cuffs, a red bandanna knotted at her throat and the gold shoulder bag she swung despondently the first time she passed the bank window, that she thumbed over her shoulder for the two young men, that she dropped in the road in a heap as she spoke to the driver of the BMW. But what guarantee was there that she wore the same today?

As for the rest, I knew her hair was shoulder-length, straightened, and stiffly lacquered to keep it that way—that she was black. That last was the single feature I was looking out for—her blackness.

It was still hot enough along the Strip to feel relief more than disappointment when I reached the car with nothing to show for my

half-hour walk beyond a shirt wet with sweat and a hand black
with newsprint. I sat in the car, switched on the air-conditioning,
and opened the paper—giving her a little more time to finish whatever it was that kept her off the street and make an appearance.

Traffic had thickened considerably in the hour since I had
pulled into the parking lot, allowing me to drive slowly enough to
keep a watch on the sidewalks as well as the road ahead. For twenty
minutes I followed the grid of streets between Fairfax and La Brea
—between Sunset and Santa Monica Boulevard to the south, and
Hollywood Boulevard to the north—the only sound the whirr of
air-conditioning, the radio tuned to L.A.'s "Mighty 690" and the
regular tick-tick of the indicator as I turned from one street into the
next.

Rather than the color of her skin, the gold bag, the brush of
lacquered hair, it was the width of red bandanna that first caught
my eye. She stood in an angle of shadow on the south side of Sunset,
a few steps back from the corner of Sierra Bonita, swinging the bag
and staring up into the hills that separated the northern and southern districts of Hollywood, at the canyons that cut into the gray,
hazy bulk of the Santa Monica range.

I could have pulled in easily, but I didn't—just passed her by,
joined the flow of traffic on Sunset and drove round the block, heart
thumping, throat suddenly too dry to swallow, needing the time to
wind up my nerve. In every city I had visited so far, at precisely this
moment in the game—those aching minutes preceding the approach
—I always felt the same rush; that conflicting mix of dread, embarrassment, fascination and excitement—each competing for the
upper hand; that same cold, coiling air of sexual awareness that
breaks over you like a chill. Completing the third side of the block,
waiting for a break in the stream of traffic (but this time not minding
the delay and the drivers who wouldn't let me in), and then turning,
finally, into Sierra Bonita once more, the rush was no different.
Nothing—neither repetition nor frequency—diminished this preliminary response. Disregarding my more cowardly instincts—
equally intact after all this time—urging me just to look, to observe,
to pass by without becoming involved, I pulled in to the curb and
with slippery fingers wound down the window.

When the line of cars behind me had eased one by one onto
the Strip there was nothing between us but thirty feet of tarmac.
Leaning my elbow out of the window I just stared across at her. She
was wearing the same trousers but the yellow blouse had been

247

exchanged for an orange tube top that made her look plumper. Sooner or later she would turn in my direction and the moment would come.

Swing, swing went the bag; far, far away the eyes I couldn't see. With a lurch of the heart I saw her start forward away from me, stepping into the gold spotlight of the Strip. She looked one way and then the other, twisting the straps of the bag and letting it spin out like a mirrored ballroom globe. Then, rocking on her heels, she turned and walked back into the shadows. That was the moment she saw me. Cautiously, displaying not the slightest interest or hint of recognition, she leaned up against the wall, pulled a cigarette from her bag and lit it, letting her eyes stray in my direction through a stream of smoke. I nodded toward the passenger seat but she stayed where she was. I was tempted to call over but thought better of it. If she was behaving in this way there was clearly a reason. Beyond, on the Strip, a steady line of cars trailed west into the setting sun, gold flashes squinting off windscreens, slatted grilles, chrome fenders—and still she didn't budge, just watched me, occasionally glancing up and down the street. Finally, she hoisted the bag over her shoulder, threw down the cigarette and crossed the road with a kind of top-heavy sway as though she were stepping along a high wire. Resting an elbow on the roof, she leaned down and looked past me into the car. A cop or a kook, I knew she was thinking. Entrapment or the risk of violence? Or a genuine customer? A pinch of flesh the color of Coke syrup squeezed between her trouser band and tube top.

"How you doin', sugar? You lost? Need some assis'ance?"

"You know your way around?"

"Some," she smiled archly. "Depends mostly on what you lookin' for and where's you headed?" As she spoke, her eyes, wide like a Pekingese's, stiff-lashed with mascara, scanned the inside of the car for anything suspicious—still cautious, wary; perhaps she was still under age and not keen on spending time in Juvenile Hall.

"Just looking for company and somewhere to enjoy it. I thought you could help?" The tip of a pink tongue circled her scarlet, blistered lips. She was leaning so close I could see the line on the inside of her lip where the lipstick ended.

"Mebbe." She walked round the back of the car, noticing for sure the rental sticker on the back window, and I leaned across to unlock the door. The gold bag came in first and she slid in after it, pink palms easing the strain on the skin-tight trousers. I started up the car and we pulled out into the traffic.

"So where to?"

"Place ah knows close to. Take a right up ahead and go on a few blocks. Ah'll tell you when to stop."

That late, dusky-gold Los Angeles afternoon, 'Lisha and I spent our first half hour together in a grimy pink two-story motel with outside stairs and a walkway set around a small courtyard. A Vegas-style billboard higher than the shingle roof advertised air-conditioned rooms, waterbeds and kitchenettes. The air-conditioning was broken ("They're all broke, every room ah bin in yet"); the waterbed looked a few gallons short but was full enough to provide a lurching accompaniment to our action ('Lisha dealt knowledgeably with the tapping headboard by cushioning it with her tube top); while the kitchenette was little more than an extra wardrobe with a stainless steel sink she had to stand on tiptoe to wash herself in, a single electric plate and a coffeepot on the shelf beneath. The room smelled something like a waxed Chinese umbrella, the sheets felt damp as though the bed was leaking, and the two pillows, springy with foam rubber, we pushed to the floor. Outside, footsteps passed to and fro along the walkway, keys rattled, locks turned, doors opened and slammed shut and the buzz and hum and distant beep-beep of traffic on and around Sunset drifted through sealed windows and drawn curtains like the rustle of activity on stage before the house lights dim.

Lying on the bed, black limbs sprawled, she watched me undress with as much interest as a housewife watching a salesman's demonstration. Stepping out of the last of my clothes I paused to look at her, her body swaying slightly as if rocked by a swell.

"What you waitin' on? Ain't gonna bitecha, ah swear. Look see," she said, spreading her legs and opening herself like a split watermelon with the fingers of both hands, "little creature's gone lost all her teeth!" The laughter that followed this disclosure set the bed shaking and prompted an almost intestinal bubbling sound from its depths. As soon as the laughter finished and the bed steadied, I struggled over to her, knees sinking first one side and then the other, like a clown trying to walk on an acrobats' safety net. I could see she was trying not to laugh, but in vain. Her lips parted, her teeth sprang apart like a giant trap and another burst of laughter filled the room.

Twenty minutes later, with an extra ten tucked away in her purse, she clomp-clomped ahead of me down the wooden stairway and made for the car. When I dropped her back on the corner of

Sierra Bonita, she held back a moment before getting out.

"You ain't so bad. You come on back and see 'Lisha some time." It was the kind of hollow offering most hookers handed out to clients who paid up and left a tip and didn't make life too difficult. Usually they mumble it through stretched lips as they reapply their lipstick. When 'Lisha said it, she made it sound more enticing than most, looking straight at me with those round seallike eyes almost popping.

"You give regulars a discount?"

"DIScoun'! DIScoun'! What's this discoun', man?" she cried, but not too loudly, slapping my leg and leaving her hand there a moment. "That some kind of poor-boy talk you givin' 'Lisha?" But she was smiling as she got her things together. "Do ah git this discoun' iffen ah go missin' tricks? Say—'Hey, ah'm sorry honey, but things was real slow today'? You better believe ah don't." I thought of the man in the BMW, his finger stabbing at her. No, she was right, I couldn't see him giving her discounts, if that was who she meant by "honey."

Tugging the bag after her, she bent forward in the open door. "Never know, mebbe give you longer next time. Seems you one of them that needs th'extra."

Crossing
the Truckee

There are no horses at the Mustang Ranch. No wood-frame barns with dusty haylofts, no stables or hitching posts, no mounting steps or corrals or watering troughs, and no tack room with traces and saddle strappings hanging from pegs. You'll find no food or store of hay there for winter, no high-wheeled tractors or farm machinery rusting in the yard. There's no forge there, no rack of branding irons, no bellows, no furnace, no beating tattoo of hammer or anvil. There's no strong smell of stallion or mare—the warm richness of dung, the sweetness of urine—of liniment, leather or saddle soap. You'll hear no snorting or whinnying, no neighing or crunching of bits, nor the steely clip-clop of shod hooves—just the sound of the river breaking over a fall of builder's rubbish and splashing around bridge supports, the wind brushing over a strip of maize and a murmur of traffic on Interstate 80.

The ranch—a low pink stucco building with one-way mirrored windows and five wings leading off a circular central section—stands alone behind a windbreak of trees on the far side of the Truckee River, at the foot of creosote-dotted hills that burn white and dusty in the heat of the day, but glow soft and pink the moment the sun settles beyond the forests and lakes of Tahoe and the neon glitter of Reno. The building faces a large parking lot with white-bordered spaces for cars and, to the right, as you cross the single-track bridge, a stretch of rough, rutted land for trucks. The whole place has that blank anonymity you find on trading estates, the faceless innocence of an American supermarket where brick has replaced glass and all the goods remain concealed inside. And in a way, that's just what it is. Except for the single watch-tower rising above the pink-tiled roof and the high wrought-iron fence that surrounds the compound. Inside the fence a sprinkler tap-taps a fine spray onto a patch of dusty grass, a few stunted firs and beds of shrubs. The sun has long since withered any flowers that might once have been planted there. A single cement path, raised like a duck-board over the lawn, leads from the locked front gate to a covered porch. To gain admission, you ring a bell and wait for the gate to be buzzed open by someone inside.

From Reno, Interstate 80 East runs along a high bank of stone that takes you at rooftop level through the adjoining town of Sparks, past small-time casinos with shorting neon, past filling stations and vacant lots, past dismal, cheap motels with curtained second-floor windows and out to a gap in the surrounding ring of hills. Beyond a grid of railroad sidings to the right, lined with an oddment of silent rolling stock—circular chemical containers, tar-planked flatcars and stenciled cabooses—and out of sight behind a stand of fuel bins on the airport perimeter, flows the Truckee River, running roughly parallel to the road. The closer you get to the gap in the hills, the way out east from Reno, the closer the road, the rail-track and the river converge until, side by side, they squeeze into the narrow mouth of the valley—the road on the left, high up on the shoulder of the first hillside, the rail-track a little farther down the slope and, on the valley floor, bordered by two strips of arable land, the Truckee.

At the end of this valley you can follow the river northwest to Pyramid Lake and the Winnemucca Sink, carry on northeast to Lovelock where there's a brothel called La Belle on Ninth Street, or take Highway 50 to Fallon where, a little out of town, you'll find two other, similar establishments called the Lazy B and Salt Wells Villa. If you're staying in Reno, as I was, it makes more sense to take exit twenty-three a few miles into the valley along Interstate 80 East and visit the Mustang Ranch.

Even for a stranger, there's no difficulty locating the place. In Reno, hotel shops sell maps of the state whorehouses and paper-backs list the various establishments with write-ups and star ratings similar in style to *The Good Food Guide* and advice on whorehouse etiquette. I arrived at the ranch late in the afternoon, leaving my hotel in Reno just as the neon began to grow bright in the dusk. I drove over to Sparks and out to the hills, crossing at some point the county line that separates Reno from Storey County where prostitution enjoys legal status and brothels are as common as filling stations. At exit twenty-three, as instructed by my guide-book, I took the slip road and swung down the side of the valley—past an auto wrecker and a tangled field of scrap, past a sign nailed to a telegraph pole that warned against the unlawful discharge of fire-arms, under a railroad bridge and across the river into the bluff-concealed parking lot.

The building beyond the fence appeared deserted, despite more than a dozen cars in the parking lot, two cabs with meters running and a twenty-eight-wheeler truck with a tarpaulined load—its hood gleaming with chrome fitments, its bodywork plastered with decals in a style reminiscent of the Forties heroines who decorated the fuselages of Flying Fortresses—busty blondes in open-necked shirts and tight shorts. As far as I could see there was no one in the watch tower, though in this heat the job was probably done by closed-circuit cameras, and no sound came from within. With mirrored windows there wasn't much to see either, beyond the vaguest of silver shadows moving beneath silver reflected hills and iron fenc-ing. With the sprinkler showering the grass, the air-conditioning units dripping and the stucco-work stained with damp, the place reminded me of a stranded pink whale being sprayed and doused with water to keep it alive in these desolate surroundings. I rang the bell and almost immediately, as if my arrival had been expected, the lock buzzed and the gate swung open at my touch. As I started up the path toward the porch I had the certain feeling I was being watched. Though I didn't know it yet, a score of girls, alerted by the ringing bell, were even now assembling in the main hall to greet me —peering at me through the one-way glass as I walked toward them.

The Mustang was like a giant igloo inside—cool in the heat of the desert—its tunnellike entrance hall leading into a vast reception room, domed like a basilica, round like a circus ring. The ceiling was high and wide, beamed and skylit, the floor deeply, softly carpeted. The plaster had been mixed with coloured flakes of quartz and the walls shimmered like a fairy-tale grotto. Around them hung a num-ber of whorehouse nudes in gilt frames—all heated cheeks, plump stockinged thighs, breathless expressions and abandoned gestures— painted in a style that suggested a hotel lobby artist imitating Re-noir. Pinkly, warmly naked, with rose-bud nipples and tidy Vargas thatches, they were the less coy cousins of the decal ladies outside in the parking lot. Beneath each picture stood a red-plush sofa where the girls waited for customers; there were tables and chairs, a jukebox and a long, aqueductlike bar crossing the room a little off-center where you could sit with your drink and your girl and watch new arrivals through the open, shelved arches. At various points around the room's circumference, five open doorways led into each of the building's five separate wings where I guessed the girls' rooms to be. At the sixth door, where I now stood, an old woman sitting on a low stool put down her knitting, caught my sleeve and directed my attention more specifically to the girls waiting in line in front of me, telling me to choose the one I wanted.

There were twelve, fifteen, twenty of them—it was impossible to take in the number, not because they were so many, simply because each of them was available. With a nod or a gesture, I could have any of them I wanted. The thought was numbing. Where to begin? Where to look first? From left to right? From the middle outward? And what should I look for? What did I particularly want? Which of them did I find attractive? The most attractive? Which of them looked as if they would give value for money? Which of them did I want to see naked? Have in bed with me? Kiss? Touch? Be kissed by? Be touched by? Bathe with? Play with? Lie with?

I looked at them first as a single line—smiling at me, challenging me, looking past me with a distant frog's gaze, looking bored, looking resentful, looking evil, looking promising, looking lustful, brushing hair from faces, whispering, shifting their weight from one precarious heel to the other, tugging at creases in their swimsuits, their Danskins, at hems, at bodices, scratching themselves with nails like trowels, blinking, winking, frowning, pouting—then tried to regulate my responses, catalogue them, assemble them into some kind of order. At first only single features proclaimed themselves. Starting from the left, the first girl had blond hair, that's all I can say with certainty; the second large, jutting breasts that squeezed plumply under her arms; the third too pointed a chin; the fourth a straggle of hair in her armpits; the fifth too small; the sixth too tall —and so on. But gradually, as I worked my way down the line, individual features began to coalesce, combine, until the last girl I saw as a complete, whole person. She was strikingly blond with the kind of figure best described with the hands, a suitable model for decal designers, dressed in a strapless latex swimsuit patterned with turquoise spots on a black background. She carried a narrow purse under her arm, clamped tight to give an extra swell to her breasts. Even at a distance, it was clear she considered herself the star of the show—almost unaware there were other girls beside her. She stood tall and steady, jaw rolling smugly on a wad of gum, one knee bent coyly forward and hands clasped demurely at the deep black V of her costume where the turquoise spots diminished into a crowd of dots. Had she turned around and looked at me over her shoulder, piled her hair on top of her head, she would have been a ringer for Betty Grable. As it was she unclasped her hands, fixed me with a long stare, and tugged at the top of her swimsuit. The action did little more than serve to stress the buoyant fullness of her breasts, the latex material clearly defining the fingertip protrusion of her nipples. It was enough and she knew it. Not daring to look down the line a second time, not wanting to keep the girls standing any longer—already they were becoming restless, swaying from side to side, backward and forward on their high heels—and not wishing to draw undue attention to myself by further hesitation, I pointed this last girl out to the old lady. She called out a number and immediately the line broke up, the girls wandering back to the sofas, the tables and chairs, to the jukebox, all except the one I had chosen. She came forward, took my hand and led me across the room to one of the passages behind the bar.

"I'm sorry, I missed your name."

"Jus' call me Polkadot. Polkadot'll do jus' fine," she drawled, indicating the pattern on her swimsuit.

Her room, a dozen or so doors down on the right, was chill and dark—the air-conditioning humming, the curtains drawn against a fading pink light. It reminded me—the size, the smell, the dour worn colors, the suspicion of many lives lived there—of a prefect's study at my old school, of a backstage dressing room I had once visited. There was something sadly temporary and homeless about it, despite attempts to make it appear otherwise. Most of the floor-space was taken up, not surprisingly, by a king-sized bed with a single thin towel spread diamond-wise across the cover. On the wall behind it was a mural in dark blues and greens that, barely disguising the rough plasterwork, portrayed a nymph bathing in a forest pool, scooping up water to poster-pink breasts. The color of this water, though, was so close in shade and texture to the color of the bank that she looked as though she was sinking in quicksand rather than bathing in limpid waters. On either side of the bed stood a small table, each with its own lampstand, their matching frilled shades held aloft by Bakelite cherubs. On one of the tables was an ashtray and a box of tissues and on the other a tub of Albolene liquefying cleanser. The only other furniture in the room was a corner chest as tall as a filing cabinet and just as thin, with the kind of narrow drawers a collector might keep his butterflies in, and running the length of the bed a wooden "vanity" shelf covered in marbled Formica. Its surface was cluttered by pots and jars and topless bottles—nail-varnish removers, skin creams and cleansers, oils and talcums; by brushes and combs and wads of cotton wool; an ashtray in the shape of a halved orange with "Florida—Sunshine State" stamped across it; a long vibrator that at first I thought was a peeled banana and part of a set with the orange; and a forest, thicker and more awesome than the one in the mural, of aerosol hair lacquers and deodorants and colognes. Scattered amongst these were clips and grips, a tangle of bracelets, some rings, plastic hooped hair bands, false nails that reminded me of guitar plectrums, an unopened can of Diet Pepsi and a tray of colored brooches—the whole liberally sprinkled with a frosting of powder. A mirror, the same length as the vanity, was screwed to the wall behind it—neither high enough nor wide enough to make the room appear any larger than it was, but, judging by its height in relation to the bed, serving an altogether more useful purpose.

As soon as the door closed behind us, Polkadot squatted down in front of me as though about to size up a golf shot. She had a twanging drawl that seemed to introduce the letter y into words like "there" and "that"—theyer and thayat—and stretched her i's as though they were made of elastic so that words like "high" and "right" and "like" came out as "hah" and "raht" and "lahk."

"Now you jus' stand right there," she said, "and drop your pants for Polkadot." I did as I was told, knowing from my guidebook and the chapter on whorehouse etiquette that this was the inspection and that there was no way to avoid it. "There now," said Polkadot, as my jeans settled around my ankles, "jus' hold up your shirttails like that" (lahk thayat) "—thaaaaaayat's it—and let Polkadot have a liiiiiittle peep at your Peter." Looking down I watched her blond head bend forward and felt her hand grasp me. Three, four, five times she pulled on me as though milking a cow, then cool fingers opened me up and pressed against me. From where I stood, holding a knot of shirttails in front of me and with her head in the way, I couldn't quite see what she was doing, but whatever it was it appeared I passed the test, for a few minutes later she sat back on the bed and told me to pull up my trousers.

According to my book, which I had studied in the bar the night before, the next step in the proceedings was the question of payment. I would be told the various rates, I would choose the service I wanted and pay Polkadot accordingly. She would then leave me for a few minutes while she took the money to the office, then return to complete the deal. As if she, too, had read the same book, Polkadot patted the bed beside her. "Now you jus' set yourself right here beside me and Ah'll tell y'all what we can do together, you an' me both. Unless, that is, you have something" (somethaing) "special you want?"

"No, nothing really," I replied lamely. "What do you normally do?"

It was like having a drill sergeant detail the procedure for a correct piling of arms—so precise, so trimmed of excess, so lackluster from repetition was her response.

"Well, ah do full-French, that's a blow-job all the way, y'-know? Ah do half and halfs—start with the mouth and finish with the fanny. Ah do sixty-nines you care t'eat it. Ah do 't any ways, any hows, any wheres you care to mention—on the bed, on the floor," (flo-ah) "in the shower; on top, underneath, sideways, standin' and doggie—that's ma favorite. Ah'll do 't straight with ma hands you like it like that; with gloves on, in stockings and garter belt, in high heels or boots 'f that's your preference. Ah'll do 't blindfolded, tied with rope, chained, 'cuffed or play dead fo' you. Ah've got creams and oils and powders, a pile of lectrical do-dahs, and ah kin handle anal if that's yo' number. But Ah truly will not eat anythin' in that department—yours or mine. If that's what you want Ah'll git you the gals that specialize."

I shook my head, as awed by the list of possibilities as I had been by the lineup of girls.

"Okay," she continued, "right now, a hundred and fifty dollars gits you my best half and half, with fifteen minutes in the Jacuzzi down the hall. If that don't suit guess we can think up somethin' else that'll amuse and entertain you, make y'all want to come back fo' more (mo-ah)."

I told her the $150 would do fine and counted out the bills. With the money in her hand, she told me to undress and make myself at home. House rules, she explained (just as my guidebook had said), made it necessary for her to pay in the money "before we party." It sounded as if she expected a crowd. "That's what we call sex here 'bouts," she added, seeing my puzzled expression.

Alone in the room, I felt strange about just taking off my

clothes and making myself comfortable. Instead I wandered about the room, picking idly at the few personal possessions Polkadot had left lying round. It was like looking along someone's bookshelf; I had the vague idea they might offer some insight into the girl whose bed I was soon to share, perhaps make our coupling less abrasive, give our intimacy at least some semblance of familiarity, some feeling of foundation no matter how shallow. But there was precious little to build with. A few robes hung from padded hangers behind the door, there was a cassette player and some tapes beside one of the bedside tables, and on top of the "filing" chest an astrological guide to the Sagittarian woman, a book called *Think and Grow Rich* by a Mr. Hill, a pocket-size paperback entitled *Trimming the Fat on the Tummy and Tush,* and the latest number of *Consumer Reports* magazine with features on "Housing Yourself in the 80's," "Should You Buy or Rent?," "Can You Afford a Mortgage?," "How Good Are Home Warranties?," and "What About a Condo or Co-op?" It was clear, just from these few items, in which direction Polkadot's interests lay: keeping her figure and making money. She was in the right place to do both. In the adjoining bathroom there was even less to work on—no shaver, no shampoo, not even a tube of toothpaste or toothbrush—nothing beyond the few instruments of her trade: a towel folded neatly over the edge of the bath, a tube of Soft-Soap, a Lysol bath cleanser and a combined air freshener/insect repellant. Apart from the vibrator, the vanity shelf also gave nothing away— except perhaps for a line of snaillike shells, hard-looking, blackish and shiny, stuck to the edge of the mirror. At least I knew where she would press her gum.

I was sitting on the bed with my back to the mural, legs drawn up and only my shoes off, when Polkadot knocked softly and came in. "You ain't undressed yet, honey?" she cried, the polkadots disappearing in a tangle of tights and shrunken latex. "How about ah give you a little help?"

The "party" was swift and professional. Once undressed, Polkadot led the way into the bathroom ("Come on, honey. Don't be shy. Ah ain't gonna eat you. Not yet anyway"), lowered me onto the bidet and worked up a lather. It was all as the guidebook had said. From there, thoroughly dried, I was led back to the bed, pushed down and equally thoroughly "half-and-halfed," the last "half" concluded in her favorite position, a stream of encouraging abuse and invective poured into, and somewhat stifled by, the pillow "Go-ong 'n phuck mmmmme, phuck mmmmmmeeee,

258

hhhhhhharder, hhhhhharder, shtuffff me, shtuffff me, go-ong, go-ong, go . . . ong . . . oooooooooooh . . . phaaaaaaaaaaark." Afterward, I watched her waddle like a penguin back to the bathroom, a bundle of tissues clearly visible, clenched between her buttocks.

The Jacuzzi room was mirrored and steamy, the pool circular and sunk into the tiled floor. A chrome rail led down into the waters that, at a touch of a switch from Polkadot, began to bubble and spin and gurgle like an open-top washing machine. I sat on the lowest step with the water fizzing like freshly poured Pepsi at my chin. Naked, one leg drawn up to her, the other stretched out so her toes merely skimmed the surface, Polkadot sat at the edge. Leaning back on her elbows, her breasts flattened out, her hair falling behind her shoulders, she reminded me of a Russell Flint slave girl taking the waters.

Polkadot had promised fifteen minutes in the Jacuzzi but it was hard to tell the precise passage of time, the only way to measure it the gradual heating up of the water and the frequent cooling-off periods when I lay out on the tiles beside her. Through it all, she behaved as dutifully as a Norland nanny supervising her charge's bathtime. For the first time in a long time, I felt safe, secure and pampered; impressed and sustained by the sudden legitimacy which I found in the deserts in Nevada. Why couldn't it always be like this, I wondered? So straightforward. So free of device and deception. So acceptable and accepted. I lay beside her, sat in the steaming, bubbling water, filled with extraordinary satisfaction—little concerned by the thought that my Russell Flint/Norland nanny was only there with me because I had paid for her to be there.

After I had finally had enough of the Jacuzzi, rather than Polkadot hurrying me through it, she took me to a narrow shower cubicle, snapped on a shower cap and squeezed in with me "to git all that nasty chlorine off of you."

Dressed, refreshed, glowing, I took her with me to the bar where Marvin, pocketing his inhalant spray after a quick squirt, took our orders: a beer for me and a Harvey's Bristol Cream and Seven-Up with a twist on the rocks for Polkadot. The drink had barely been poured before the bell rang through the hall, and all the girls, Polkadot included, rose from their seats and made for the center of the room. She apologized, sighed deeply, told me to watch her drink and she would be back in a moment. Through the open arches of the bar, I watched her stroll over and join the other girls, her bag clamped under her arm. I paid Marvin for the drinks and asked him to have one, full of generosity and good fellowship. "Unh unh, no thanks," he wheezed, "ain't policy to drink on duty." He couldn't even be persuaded to keep a dollar back.

Out in the center of the room, over the shoulders of the girls, I watched with a sense of kinship as the new arrival stood transfixed by the lineup. I saw the old lady at the door speak to him, as she had done to me, and knew his thoughts exactly, knew precisely the storm of indecision he was battling through as his eyes raked the line—once, twice, even a third time. With a shy nod he indicated his choice. All the girls broke up and only Polkadot remained, her hand stretched out to him, her smile for him, her drink growing flat at my elbow and the ice melting.

The temptation to return to Mustang at the earliest possible opportunity was as irresistible as the lure of the casino tables of Reno to a gambler. I lasted less than twenty-four hours. I would have gone back much sooner but I postponed this second visit in favor of a drive to Lake Tahoe where I had spent a winter some years before. It was a deliberate ploy—leaving the best for later, stringing out that sense of expectation. I remember as a child always eating my greens first, then the meat, keeping for last the things I liked the most—the mashed potato with the chips of raw onion, stirred up in the gravy—only starting on it when there was nothing else left on the plate; so that the last taste in my mouth would be the taste I liked the most.

That winter in Tahoe the mountains, the meadows, the roads, the forests had been thickly and silently quilted in a down of snow as though the land slept beneath it—branches drooping and heavy, fences white-sleeved, fields deep and smooth as if layered in icing sugar, mountains cold and brittle against the horizon. But now, with temperatures well into the eighties, it was a different, unknown landscape that greeted me as I drove west out of Reno. Without the snow, I found it hard to place particular features and it was only when I reached Truckee, rumbled over the railroad line that divided the old logging settlement and swept up over the first bank of hills that I was sure I had been there before. Even without the snow, the grass toasted a light brown, that first plateau was unmistakable—nothing particular, just its size, its shape, its dips and hollows, the two-bar fence around its edge; as was the road—the way it twisted steeply through spruce and Ponderosa pine up to the lip of the Tahoe bowl before hurtling down to the lakeshore. Ears popping, halfway down, I caught my first glimpse of the lake—a lightning flash of green and glittering blue through the trees. It was hard then to tell which was the more beautiful: the Tahoe I had skied around or the Tahoe I now saw spread below me—the lake a steely gray with ponderous snow clouds low over the peaks, or the lake clean and cobalt with a wide blue sky high above it. The only things that looked a little out of place were the chalet-style cabins and rich redwood architecture—they needed the snow to soften their lines. They looked stranded and out of their element, like boats in a harbor at low tide.

Around the edge of the lake, like a coffee rim inside the lip of a cup, highways 28 and 89 rose and fell in forest green twists and curves. Traffic that day was light around this peripheral highway, light enough to allow long, nostalgic glances over the lake; from Carnelian Bay across to the white scoop of King's Beach; from the point at Crystal Bay to the now green, once snowy bowls of Incline Village; and from high in the hills, and along the ridge that separated them, down onto the thin finger of Fallen Leaf Lake and the sheltered inlet of Emerald Bay.

Over the surface of this giant rockpool motorboats sent out rippling feathers of glinting silver while the water-skiers they pulled carved shorter, whiter initials. Farther out still, where the wind dipped down to ruffle the water, tiny squadrons of yachts bent colored sails to the breeze—twisting and tacking but hardly seeming to move at this distance. Along the shoreline, children splashed in the shallows, fishermen sat at the end of spindly, wooden jetties, teams played volleyball, and dogs chased and barked. At the edge of the road, between me and the lake, the backpackers trudged—thick, rolled socks and heavy boots, but no shirts—straps whitening bare brown skin. I stopped once for lunch, and then at a bank, with Mustang in mind. From there on I didn't look too much at the scenery, driving a little faster now, up and away from the lake and into the mountains again—past Scott Peak and Squaw Peak, past Big and Little Chief, through Cold Stream Valley and out onto the highway that would take me back to the desert.

The girls were still in their daytime swimsuits when I reached Mustang, still too early for them to have changed into their evening gowns. It was almost dinnertime and the place reeked of barbecued ribs.

According to my guidebook, it was quite acceptable to tell the madam at the door that you didn't want to choose a girl immediately, that you wanted to have a beer first and then find a partner. At the Mustang, it said, there was never any pressure so long as you didn't lean too long over one drink, and provided the girls with quarters to feed the jukebox. I told her just that, and the line that had formed for me was dismissed. Feeling an old hand at the procedure, as if I had joined the club a lifetime before and knew all its little ways, I followed the girls across the room and found a stool at the bar.

I couldn't see Polkadot anywhere, just presumed she was with a client in her room or in the Jacuzzi. I still hadn't made up my mind whether to replay or try one of the other girls. There was no doubt she was the best of the bunch yesterday, but today I could see there were some new faces. There were more men at the bar as well, bellied up and drinking with the girls: truckers with baggy jeans, bikers with windbreakers and leather mittens, and businessmen in short sleeves.

Together, through the bar's open arches, we watched the girls take their places whenever the bell rang to announce a new arrival. Once it was a false alarm ("Just the pool boys" called the madam and the girls groaned and returned to the bar or their sofas), but every other time a genuine callup. As a general rule, there were four separate responses from the new arrivals. There was the look of surprise and astonishment, like mine the day before, followed by a full minute's deliberation; then the customer who had been before and knew the girl he wanted—pointing her out or calling her name even before the line had properly assembled; the bold ones who shook off the madam's restraining hand and marched straight up to the girls, passing down the line like a general inspecting the troops; and finally, those who preferred a beer or two first, leaving the girls for later.

For half an hour or more, I sat drinking happily, listening in to and sometimes joining the conversations round the bar, watching the comings and goings of a whorehouse doing fine business. It seemed to me entirely credible that the Mustang, as I had heard in town, had recently changed hands for somewhere in the region of $20 million. If all the brothels in Nevada went for the same price, I thought idly, that would mean that whorehouse real estate would be worth about $800 million—there being about forty legal, registered whorehouses in Nevada. Forget the illegal ones.

From this simple but staggering piece of mental arithmetic, it was but a small and logical step to work out roughly the earning potential of all these establishments. Borrowing a pen from Marvin, I started my calculations.

Say each house employed ten girls (hardly an unreasonable average number—at the Mustang there were some fifty or more working rooms and according to Marvin, about thirty-five working girls!) and each girl turned eight tricks a day at, say, eighty dollars a trick. Now, that was ten by eight by eighty I scribbled away. That was . . . $6,400 a day. From each house. With forty houses in the State that added up to . . . $256,000 a day! Then I multiplied by seven to find out the week's takings statewide . . . a modest $1,792,000. Taking the whole thing a step further, I multiplied by 52. With some considerable excitement I tried to squeeze all the numbers on my piece of paper . . . $92,184,000. Call it $90 million, in one state, in one year, not including street girls, bar girls, escort agencies and subsidiary industries. Industry, I thought wryly to myself, was just the right word. And Nevada was one of the least populated states in America.

From this point on it was pure fantasy. But what a fantasy! Let's just say that prostitution was legal in every state throughout the country, and that each state, being more densely populated than Nevada, had, say, a hundred brothels located outside all big towns and cities—all as discreet and anonymous as the Mustang, all as well run. So. That would add up to about 5,000 brothels nationwide. I turned over the paper and began the new sum. Now if one establishment takes, let's see, around two million dollars a year, then . . . I needed Pimsiri, how she would have loved doing a sum like this— she could have bought not just the small seaside home she coveted in where was it? Bang Saen, but pretty well the whole of southern Thailand! Slowly, just like her, double-checking everything as I went, I worked out the sum. The total was incredible . . . ten billion dollars. And that was just from the brothels—with earnings brought in by outside concerns, that total could easily double, treble even! Just a look at the bar, for instance, said it all—souvenir badges, T-shirts, trucker caps, even a Mustang decanter on sale for twenty-five dollars. Only think of the tax benefits accruing to the Treasury; just taking a third would increase their gross tax yield by some three billion dollars. I wondered how much it cost NASA to fund a space program: how many days' fighting in Vietnam that would have subsidized. More practically, how much could be achieved with that extra bonus funneled into, say, housing, a national health program, social security services. . . . Leaking like sand between the fingers of government was a vast source of revenue! And to think, they were at present collecting off just one state.

Once again the bell rang and the girls trooped away into position. As the guidebook had said, and as I was only now beginning to appreciate, one of the main advantages in staying at the bar and delaying your decision was that the girls who had been occupied when you arrived often reappeared after they had finished with a client. One of these newcomers, whom I had not seen before, was a young black girl of indeterminate age who sashayed into the bar and plumped down beside two other colored girls. When the bell rang, she joined them in the lineup with a look of weary resignation, but to her evident relief the customer chose another girl and the three of them returned to their sofa. All three wore shiny smooth Danskins with glossy pantyhose that made their legs look slimmer and longer than they probably were, and all three favored the same lacquered helmet of hair. But while her companions were more noticeably negroid in features, the girl who had caught my attention had much sharper, more European lines to her face—cheeks slightly hollowed and less rounded, the jawline softer and less pronounced, the nose straighter at the bridge and less snubbed, the nostrils narrower and less flared, lips thinner and less swollen. The body, too, was more slender, without that characteristic hump of a backside that her friends shared, and her skin was lighter—a dark rum color rather than that dusky bluish black, with almost golden highlights to it. As nearly as possible she was Polkadot's exact opposite: Where Polkadot was soft and luscious, this one looked hard and brittle; where Polkadot's body looked as if it had been brought up on a diet of milk and honey and yogurt, this one's body looked alert and hard and muscled; where Polkadot looked a country girl, this one looked sharp and street-wise; where Polkadot's eyes were blue and vacant, this one's were brown and challenging and filled with spirit; where Polkadot's hair was blond and smooth and loose, this one's hair looked hard and black and lacquered. The more I looked at her, covertly through the arches of the bar, the more tempted I was to try her.

I gave her time to recover from her last engagement, hoping the bell wouldn't ring, hoping she wouldn't be chosen before I made my approach. At length I finished my drink and pocketed my calculations. By this time she looked less tense than she had, as ready as she would ever be. The time was right, and I walked over to them and asked if she was free. With a curt nod to me and and a few last words she stood, linked her arm through mine and led me away to her room.

Her name was Norelle and just as Polkadot had done the day before, the first thing she did was tell me to drop my pants. Sitting on the edge of the bed she reached forward and began pulling me like the choke on an old jalopy, black fingers curled around white skin. This time though, with Norelle on the bed and not squatting in front of me, I had a clearer view of the operation. After each prolonged series of pulls, she opened the tiny pink slit and, resting the side of her thumb against the skin, inside, drew it slowly away. Apparently not satisfied the first time, she pulled again and again and again, stopping each time to press her thumb against me, then slowly, carefully, drawing it away. She began shaking her head and I began to feel a little uncomfortable. Whatever she was looking for, she was not finding it. And this she was not happy about. Leaning forward, so close I could feel her breath on me, she sniffed deeply, as if folding a flower to her nose.

"What are you looking for?"

"Y'ain' stringin' is all." She licked her thumb and forefinger and thrust them toward me. "See . . . that's like stringin'," she said, opening the gap between the fingers and stretching a line of saliva between them. "That's what it oughta be here, but it ain'."

"Is that bad? Should I string?" It sounded like something only tennis players should know about.

"Sure should."

"Is there anything I should do . . . you know, tighten up or try to pee or something, will that help?" I felt a sudden, desperate compunction to do something, tense some muscle, push like a woman in labor.

"Ain' nuthin' you can do from up there that ah cain't do down here better. You jus' stand easy, relax." Again she pulled, harder this time, more urgently, drawing me from the base and squeezing me up to the tip—once, twice, three times, opening me up in between each pull to search for the elusive "stringin'," minutely drawing the thumb away and peering into me.

"You jus' hol' on, gotta get me my fren' take a look see. Ya hol' on, mind," she said, and before I could reply, she was out the door and gone. I stood there for what seemed an age, peering down at myself, repeating the moves she had gone through, but I could see nothing, feel nothing—except for a tightening knuckle of fear in my stomach. Oh God, oh God. There was nothing about this in the guidebook.

Norelle returned with one of the colored girls she had been sitting with on the sofa. This second girl took Norelle's place on the bed and introduced herself as Lalla, Norelle now standing beside me. The procedure was repeated. Again and again, perhaps more gently, more maternally than Norelle, Lalla went through the milking process. Again and again I watched with mounting apprehension, as she pressed a black finger with its sculpted pink nail against the delicate interior and drew it slowly away. Then more milking, then the slow drawing away again. Lalla was having as little success as Norelle.

"Yo eyes di-lated," she said, looking up at me. "Yo' bin on some kinda dope?"

"I'm beginning to wish I was," I replied, with a lightness of heart I didn't feel.

"Hey man, so do we," chucked Norelle. "Only sometimes manage to."

"Yo' bin drinkin'? Yo' juiced up?" continued Lalla, turning me over in her fingers like an archaeologist examining something fragile he had just dug up.

"Few beers in the bar is all."

"Yo' bin drivin' long time 'fore you got here?"

"About four hours or so around Tahoe."

"Fo' 'our Tahoe?!? Man, that's an 'our at most," squealed Norelle.

"I was taking my time, looking at the scenery," I explained, as I had been. The knuckle of fear was loosening.

"Well," said Lalla, looking at Norelle, like two doctors comparing their diagnosis, "it could be that." And then to me: "We git us some truckers time to time have much the same prollum. Yo' sit too long, yo' drink too much, get high, we don' git us no stringin' down here. Means we'se cain't be sure yo'se clean 'n' good is all."

"What exactly is this stringing?" I asked again, beginning to feel a little better. The drive round Tahoe must have done it. That was the reason. No other. Thank God.

"Well, what we do is pull like this," she demonstrated again, "then open y'up a mite, like that, see? so's we kin look at th' inside, then jus' touch real sof' with a finger. Should git us a clear jell stick between you'se an' me as ah pull 'way. Wid you though, th'ain' no jellin', see. So then we'se do it harder, see 'f we kin pull out some

266

white or yeller or pus or summat from deep down. You'se kin smell it too. But yo' ain' got yo' no smell nor yeller neither, so's ah guess you'se okay." She let go of me and sat farther back on the bed. "Ain' yo the one done come here yesserday and bin wid dat piece a' blon' pretty-pretty?"

"Yes, I was."

"An' she don' did this all fo' yo?"

"Yes, she did."

"An she didn' mind nuthin'?"

I shook my head.

"Well, if that piece a' ass don' mind none, you'se gotta be clean!" She said this as if passing Polkadot's examination was the ultimate recommendation. As she got to her feet and made for the door, I was tempted to ask her to stay, along with Norelle, have the two of them. She had been kind and gentle and I liked her immediately. But before I could suggest it she was out of the door and saying over her shoulder, "Y'all have yo'se'ves a tahm now, yo' both."

The procedure, now that the examination was over, followed much the same lines as it had the previous day with Polkadot, with the exception that Norelle was charging eighty dollars for "a straight party" or a hundred for the hour and some time in the Jacuzzi. I counted out the hundred and gave her the money. Like Polkadot she left me with instructions to undress. This time I did as I was told and was stretched out and waiting when she returned. As soon as she was undressed, she led me into the bathroom by the hand and sat me down on the bidet, pink palms and soapy fingers cradling and lathering me. Back on the bed, the two of us sat facing each other. Despite Lalla's reprieve, a ghost of suspicion, uncertainty, hung between us. Even now the squirm of fear that had lanced me during that inspection was still there, and I could see that Norelle was not entirely convinced by Lalla's judgment. And so we sat there naked, black and white, looking at each other across the diamond-shaped top cover.

"Where do you come from?" I asked, sensing her need for delay, and happy enough to oblige; grateful myself for not having to spring into action.

"Born 'n bred Birmin'ham, Al'bama. Done come out here wid ma folks an' settled in L.A. Started workin' de Strip, then heard talk on this here Mustang. Decided to give it a try an' bin here ever since. Folks gone settled up in Or'gon now."

"How long have you been here?"

"Fo' yeah, give take some."

"How come you stayed so long?"

"Like it here is all. Good money, safe y'know, no hassle, an' got me some hot fren's."

"Lalla, and the other girl you were talking to?"

"S'right—Dolly's her name. Besides, ah ain' in no rush like Miss Pretty Ass; ah go take ma time."

"Sounds like you don't like her much?"

"Hey, no kiddin'?" She got up off the bed and went to the cassette player on the chest of drawers. Although her room was in a different wing from Polkadot's, the layout and furnishings were exactly similar. "You like some music?" Without waiting for an answer she pushed in a tape and adjusted the volume, then came back to the bed.

"How long has she been here, the one I was with yesterday?"

"Six months near 'nuff. Stay on mebbe six more, then split. We seen 'em come and go like her—just workin', workin'—never stop. Me ah prefer to laze wid ma frens. Lalla an' all. Ain' so crazy 'bout makin' money so fast. She put out good fo' you'se?"

"Yes, she was okay."

"She done rush yo'all through 't?"

"Not that I'd notice. I was with her about an hour I suppose."

"Yo' one o' the lucky ones that case." Without warning, her hand shot out and caught my ankle. "That's sure a nasty scar ya done got there on you'se leg," she said, smoothing a finger along its raised length. "How come you done gone do summat lahk that?" She didn't look at me as I told her, but rather continued stroking the weal on the back of my leg that stretched from a tiny, inverted "Y" at the base of the heel up over the back of my calf, its length lined like the ribbed body of a worm. The soft touch of her fingertip on this still-tender wound and the grasp of her hand twisting my leg so she could properly see it, was immediately arousing. Though she couldn't have failed to notice this reaction, she paid no attention.

"Got me some scahs too," she said, letting go my leg and stretching out hers for me to see. "Allays bumpin' things wid ma legs. See, here," she said, spreading a patch of flesh on her thigh to disclose a tracing of old scar tissue that was browner than the skin around it. "An' heah too," drawing up her knee and baring it between her hands for me to better see the extent of the wound. "Done did tha' when ah was no more 'n knee high, fallin' off ma

268

brother's bike. Then, they'se these heah?" she continued, moving down the leg and pointing out a score of other marks—the older ones a light brown color, others more whitish, the most recent a pale pink color as if the scabs had been removed before their time. For each, there was a story to be told—the slip of a razor, an iron burn, a low table. "Gonna get me them all porcelained over soon's ah git me th' time. But ain' got nuthin' bad's what you got there. That's bad. Ain' no porcelainin' treatment gonna cover that mother." I couldn't see how they were going to porcelain her color skin, but I didn't say anything. Just then, somewhere outside, a car door opened and closed and an engine started up. Quick as a flash, Norelle was on her feet, trying to balance on the springs of the bed and leaning over to the high window, switching the curtain aside and peering out. I heard the crunch of gravel and the sound of the car moving off and watched Norelle's head follow it as it sped away. She made me think of a prisoner, staring through a cell window onto the outside world. She pushed herself off the wall and, still standing on the bed, her legs straddling me, ran her hands down her flanks.

"Yo'ever done put it to a black woman before?" she asked. Not waiting for an answer she bounced down beside me and pushed her hands between my legs. "Yo' seems ready 'nuff, but wid what you got showin' reckon I oughtta let you'se have it fo' free." Not quite sure whether to take this as a compliment or not, I watched her dig her fingers into the same pot of Albolene that Polkadot had used, smear it deep between her legs and hunch down with her face in the pillows, thrusting herself up at me—two black spinnakers stiff in the wind. All caution, uncertainty, gone, knees sinking in the mattress, hands on her raised hips to steady myself, I made my approach between scarred calves and white, wrinkled soles.

"Fillerup, whitey," she called over her shoulder, fingers scrabbling for me. "Fillerup good 'n' full."

Whether it was simply to show that she was a better lover than Polkadot, I can only hazard a guess, but Norelle seemed keen to vary the action as much as possible. When, eventually, we were done, she took me into the bathroom again and washed me gently, then dressed me in a robe and led me to the Jacuzzi. Sitting by my side in the hot bubbling water she showed me how to maneuver myself against the underwater jets to the best advantage. "Fun, ain't it?" she said, spreading herself round one of them. Afterward, just as Polkadot had done, she squeezed into the shower cubicle with me and began to soap me down.

"Looks like yo' done want another go," she said.

"What about it?"

"Cost y'another fifty?"

"Do you have to have the money right now?"

Norelle laughed. "Reckon ah kin trust yo'."

Back in her room, I paid her the extra and added a tip. But she wasn't finished with me yet. Before I had time to pull on my trousers she called me over and caught hold of me. "Now this here's jus' a li'l precaution" (pree-coshon) "aimed to keep you'se good an' clean, jus' in case, y'unnerstan'?" Pressing back the skin, she opened me up and squirted a tiny jet of liquid deep into me. It was cold and slightly astringent.

"What the hell was that?"

"They calls it tin-chur of mer-thi-o-late," she replied, reading the name off the label. "'S like one o' them antiseptics is all. Don' do's you no harm. Fact, they say to take it reg'lah you come callin' in places like these too often." She screwed on the top and put the bottle back on the vanity, picking up her tights and Danskin and starting to untangle them. Before she hauled them up and over her, she sprayed deodorant under her arms where it dried quickly into a circle of powdery white. "Time they done make this stuff fo' colored skin," she said angrily, dusting away the powder and then sliding into her costume. "So which one yo' thinks the bes' between me an' that other one?"

"You mean Miss Pretty Ayass?" I said, imitating her accent.

"Yeah, li'l Miss Pretty Ayass."

"You, of course."

"No kiddin'?"

"No kidding."

"That's the truth?"

"That's the truth."

"Jus' goes to show, you don' rush it like her, you do's a better job."

"You were great. I've had a good time." I meant it too.

"Guess ah made up fo' scarin' you'se early on. Man, yo' looked like you'se close to shettin' where you stood."

"I was," I replied, remembering only too clearly.

"Purty Wimmin"

The three o'clock courtesy flight from McCarran Field on the outskirts of Las Vegas into neighboring Nye County had been canceled, the lady at the ranch told me over the phone, "on account of them dust bowls." I was puzzled. Dust bowls made me think of Steinbeck and once arable land suddenly parched into desert and wagons piled high with possessions being driven off to someplace more hospitable. What I couldn't see was how they could possibly affect flight departures from what was already desert anyway—had been desert long before the first runway was laid down.

I was disappointed too. The idea of flying out in a private plane to a brothel in the desert had intrigued me. Here, at last, the real American Dream—courtesy flights to a whorehouse. It could only happen in America. Who else would dare?

In my imagination, I had pictured two planes, each creation satisfying a particular urge. The first was a two-seater biplane of barnstorming lineage, piloted by a mad rogue (not unlike Scalotti) with a pencil-thin mustache, wearing split-lens goggles, a leather cap with the chin straps dangling and a trail of white silk scarf over his shoulder—a kind of Howard Hughes lookalike who would swoop me in daring aerobatic loops and dives along the main strip of Vegas at fountain level. That satisfied the adventurer in me. The second plane catered more to the sensual side of my nature—a replica Hefner 707 with a selection of girls from the ranch to keep me company during the flight.

Now, I discovered, all flights had been canceled—if there ever was a flight, I thought cynically. A courtesy limousine would pick

271

me up instead. The driver would be in touch with me to arrange a time. A limousine, I considered, putting down the phone and cutting the connection, was all well and good in its way—certainly a step up from what I was used to—but nowhere near as spectacular as a private plane from the hangars of Whorehouse Airways flying me over the mountains, into the setting sun, to a house of dubious repute in the middle of the Nevada deserts. It was the kind of disappointment one experiences when dreams are replaced by practicalities. Nothing has changed, but nothing is quite the same again.

I stepped out onto the balcony, twelve floors above the black ribbon of Las Vegas Boulevard—the Strip—and looked past Caesar's Palace, the MGM Grand, the Flamingo, the Aladdin and the Tropicana—chalk-white tower blocks, each with its own sparkling necklace of neon—in the general direction of the airport, out on the southern fringes of town. Not dust bowls I realized, but wind devils. That was what the lady at the ranch had meant. Even at this distance, squinting through the glaring white desert light I could see first one, then another, and another—a whole pack of sinuous, twisting wind devils some two or three hundred feet in height, I estimated, drilling into the ground around the airfield perimeter, perhaps even already over the runways, I couldn't tell. Against the blue sky they were white and dusty whirlpools with a cuff of debris skittering around each of them at ground level. It seemed unlikely that larger planes would be troubled by these wind-whipped spirals but I could appreciate that flying a light aircraft through them would have been like sailing a matchbox boat through a force-ten gale.

The phone on the bedside table rang an hour later. It was Charlie, the whorehouse chauffeur. Afterward I tried to fit a face to the voice—slow, slightly drawled, competent, relaxed, with a distinctive cowboy twang to some of the words. The image of "Marlboro Man" was unavoidable.

"Hi there, Mr. O'Brien? Charlie—from out at the ranch. How ya bin doin?"

"Hallo, fine thanks."

"Okay then, good to hear it. The limo an' me's down at the D.I. right now—the Desert Inn—droppin' off a client. I'll be over for ya in five, mebbe ten minutes, 'f that's agreeable with you?"

"Sure."

"You don' mind none, I'll pick y'up at th' entrance to your place, save me parkin' th' animal. It's a brown Olds with a tan roof to it. Model's a Toronado. You cain't miss it."

"Okay. How much should I bring?" It sounded as if I was making a ransom delivery.

"Well now, limo's courtesy—no charge; and the house minimum's fifty. Depends a whole heap on what you've got in mind. More you bring, the better the ride's what I say."

"Thanks, see you outside."

Seven minutes later, having already approached two cars that fitted Charlie's description (exactly what color was meant by "tan"? And as for "Toronado"—it sounded like the wind devils that fenced off the airport), a long, sleek machine covered in a fine desert dust that looked like frosting on a cake sprang up over the entrance ramp and eased to a stop at the bottom of the steps. A tinted window on the passenger side slid down to reveal a rich, sham-suede interior and the twin green lenses of a pair of aviator glasses turned toward me. Eyes locked (I could only guess the driver was looking in my direction) and recognition signals bashfully exchanged with bird-like nods from both of us, I sank in beside him, closing the door after me—like trying to swing a sideboard into place. As soon as I was settled the window slid up and Las Vegas turned the gentlest green, all sounds and smells from the outside cut off at the touch of a button. Taking off in a spacecraft could not have filled me with a deeper, more sudden sense of separation from my surroundings.

Beside me, Charlie sat with the wheel resting on his knees as though negligently dandling a child. One hand alone held it steady and with splayed brown fingers he spun it as easily as a croupier a roulette wheel as we edged out from the hotel forecourt into the silent, green flow of boulevard traffic. In the other hand, resting on the crushed sham-suede "separator" that divided the two front seats (more armchairs than seats), he held a paper cup filled halfway with a mixture of blood-red ice—some kind of frozen daiquiri, I guessed. He didn't bother with the striped straw that stood out vertically from the brew, simply pushed it aside with a finger when he drank.

"How ya doin'?" he asked for the second time, as soon as we were comfortably away.

"Fine. You?"

He shrugged, lifted the paper cup. "You hear me complainin'?"

Not so much a Marlboro Man, I decided, as a retired Sixties astronaut after a series of successful lecture tours, Charlie was on the waist-expanding side of forty with a bristly-looking flat-top that peaked outward to a point over his forehead, the sides cut high above the ear. His face was shiny and clean-shaven, smooth and brown and lightly flecked more by the sun than age. I couldn't see his eyes, just a flickering movement of lashes behind his glasses. He was wearing a yellow, short-sleeved, suitably emblemed sports shirt into the open collar of which hung a bulbous frog's throat of loose skin, and a pair of perma-creased plaid slacks with a wide leather belt. Had it not been for the overhang, a Navajo buckle would certainly have been visible. For every piece of jewelry Charlie wore had that distinctive turquoise decoration: a nugget of it set in his ring, chips of it studding a bracelet, beads of it threaded into his belt, bands of it ribbing his watchband. Overweight he may have been, a traditional American gut that stretched the shirt material, but he was solid rather than fat. His shoulders were thick and wide, his arms jutting from his short sleeves as well-packed as Italian sausages, his hands horny-looking with swollen pads for knuckles. His fingers, resting on the wheel and clasping the paper cup, were short and stubbed, the nails bitten but still stubbornly varnished. A good man to have on your side, my old housemaster might have remarked, had Charlie ever tugged on rugger boots and run out with the home team. Right then, cruising out of town in our own micro-climate, his presence was comforting rather than threatening.

"How long before we get there?" I asked, as we turned gently up a slip road and away from the main highway. It surely couldn't be this close to town, I thought to myself. Like Reno, the municipal authorities of Las Vegas had long since banned brothels from the county. Those establishments that remained within reach of the city only did so because they were safe across the Clark County line in Nye.

"Take maybe an hour gettin' there, a little more than that comin' back," replied Charlie, negotiating a knot of intersections. "We get us a good run at the mountains from this side of the range. Other side, ain't much room for this ol' diesel engine to pick up 'nough speed. Right now though, gotta give th' animal its feed." For an instant Marlboro Man edged ahead of retired astronaut.

With a spring-softened lurch the bonnet in front of us, easily the size of a championship pool table, tipped up as the front wheels mounted a ramp leading to a line of gas pumps. The rest of us followed in air-conditioned insulation. As well as filling up the tank, Charlie swallowed down the remains of his drink and tossed the paper cup into a bin. He also sprayed a good portion of the diesel fuel onto his plaid slacks when the tank flooded over, reversing the flow. He was brushing down the damage and muttering darkly when he dropped back into the driver's seat. Much to my relief this nuisance was soon forgotten and Charlie's amiable side quickly restored.

"Do you fly the plane too?" He looked like the kind of man who could fly and drive with equal ease, in fact do just about anything that involved a wheel as a controlling device. He had those kind of hands, that sort of steady, distant gaze. But I was wrong.

"Nope, sittin' here's high 'nough for me. 'Nother fella does the flyin' in the outfit." Exit the astronaut. Charlie shifted in his seat and pointed to the airfield passing us on the left. "Would've flown y'out, but for these here dus' bowls messin' up the field." Dust bowls again. Perhaps I had it all wrong.

"We call them wind devils."

"That a fact? Good a name as any I guess. Means the same kinda shit."

By now we had turned off the Strip and were driving south on US 15. After only a few miles Charlie indicated right and swung up onto the Blue Diamond Road. Beyond the rail-crossing—just a dull, rubbery sound somewhere beneath us—another tank of a car daw-dled and slowed us down.

"Always thought the wors' drivers was in Flor'da, but I'm changin' my mind. The worst are right here in Nevada. Heads up their asses mostly." As soon as it was clear to overtake he put his foot down and, with a tiny, diesel-powered tug, we pulled past the slowcoach. Charlie's green lenses swept past me at the other car, fixing it with a tinted, malevolent glare.

"Good to have the air-conditioner," I said, adjusting the direction of the flow—my knee was almost frozen. "Looks hot out there."

"Hotter 'n hell an' drier than an' old hooker. An' it gits worse. Shoots up from a hunnert-five back there in Vegas, anywheres to -twenty, hunnert-twenty-five degrees a'other side of the range. Wait on, you'll see what I mean. Unfriendly country anyhow. And at night you kin plain freeze up there, as if burnin' up during the day ain't 'nough. It's jus' like the tables back in the casinos. Cain't win out here neither." Charlie pushed the glasses higher on his nose. "You ain't bin out the ranch before then?"

"No, first time. I hear it's a good place?"

"Damn right it is," he replied with a kind of proprietary pride.

"Got themselves some good gals out there. Mighty fine bunch of purty wimmin. My 'pinion, they'se best in the State. And I know —done 'em all in my time—Sheri's, The Shamrock, Fran's, the Buckeye, Billie's, Lucky Strike. Even as far as Winnemucca and Battle Mountain. Mos' trouble is, workin' for 'em like I do, y'aint allowed to touch. And I kin tell you, that ain't no easy thing. Reminds me when I was a young un an' my old lady made those cookies: she'd put 'em out to cool and wouldn't never let me touch a one on 'em. Jus' lookin' plain set my jaw achin' an' my mouth waterin'. Purty gals the lot of 'em. A bunch of purty wimmin," he repeated. "An' them bein' purty makes it difficult to choose, you unnerstand my meanin'? Jus' which one you gonna go fer first? The big un, the small un, the one with the cherries and the buns? Jus' like that ol' plate of cookies. I seen fellers out there jus' stare at those gals like they ain't seed the breed before. Jus' cain't figure to make up their minds, they're all so hot."

We drove on deeper into the desert, toward a line of sheer blue hills, past lone shacks and dead-end trails, past hollowed tips and gravel-chipped road signs, the only sound the rush of air-conditioning. This was no desert in the classic sense—no drifting ridges of sand—just a rough, stony-looking landscape dotted with prickly scrub and blasted by a savage sun, with no patch of shade larger than a pocket handkerchief. Behind us the chalky sprawl of Las Vegas settled into its surroundings like a desert chameleon, only occasionally the flash of sun off glass pinpointing its exact location.

Despite the long run up, the Olds Toronado with the tan roof began to slow minutely with each passing mile, as the road climbed gently toward the pass that would take us out of one valley and into the next. The speedometer wavered uncertainly at fifty.

"See what I mean by the diesel? Jus cain't hardly take the gradient. Time we get to the top there, you could git out and walk faster."

"What's the procedure when we get to the ranch?"

"Well now, I'll tell you. There're about ten gals out there, this precise moment, and a maid lookin' after 'em. Merle most likely. Maid's what we call a May-dam round these parts. What I do is take y'in, innerjuice you to the maid and you sit in the parlor there, while she calls the gals in an' has 'em all line up straight. Then, they'se each take a li'l step forward and innerjuice themselves to you—real polite-like. Gives you the chance to colleck your wits, you follow my meanin'?" He looked across at me and I nodded. "All you gotta do soon as they finish their say, is tell the name the one you fancy to the maid, or point her out you didn't hear it. As for me now, I jus' gits to sit in th' office, keep my hands offen the cookies 'f I kin stop myse'f, and wait to drive youse back to Vegas. Time you done and finished your business, only sure bet in the whole state 's you'll be a happier man than me." After a bark of a laugh, Charlie continued: "Now then, the one you chose takes you to her room and first off checks you out sees youse okay, you know what I'm sayin'?" Again he looked across at me and again I nodded. By the sound of it this ranch followed much the same procedure as the Mustang. "Me, I cain't stomach bein' handled like that. Plain lose m'appetite. Anyhows, then you git to discuss the business end of things. Like I told you on the phone, house minimum is fifty, but by all accounts that don't get you much more 'n a quick jig an' a tumble, and your lady friend's zippin' up your fly 'fore you know she had it open. You take my advice, 'n I ain't handin' you out a line on this, best settle round the hunnert mark. That'll git you all the time an' action young feller like you kin handle; most' likely too, git y' a spell in what they call the *veee-eye-peee* room. Soon's you give her the money, she'll take it out front for the house to split, then come back and start the party. But if she done go and set a time limit on you, don' start countin' till she's got you danglin' in the Peter Pan."

"Peter Pan?"

"Cute name huh? Peter Pan's jus' any ol' plastic bowl you hold under yourself while she lathers you and washes you off. Other places in the state you set yourself down on one on 'em fancy French contraptions done in china and fixed up with its own drinkin' fountain. Where you're headin', it's still a stand-up job, like it or not." Charlie sat back, satisfied he'd covered every eventuality.

"What happens if a customer gets nasty? How do the girls look after themselves?"

"You decide you gonna get tricky," the whole top portion of Charlie's body seemed to inflate, "you set to have a word or two with me. An' that kind of conversation don't include a whole lot o' talkin', you get my drift?"

There was little chance of mistaking it.

Ahead, the straight, climbing road began the first twists and snakes that would lead us to the pass. Since we had pulled onto the Blue Diamond Road Charlie's steering hand had hardly wavered. Now, his fingers like spokes on the wheel, he spun the car first left, then right, through one slow curve and into another, past treacherous-looking slopes of scree, under bare cliff faces and around lone tumbled boulders. As he said, our speed began to drop dramatically, the engine straining to pull us upward and onward. At about five thousand feet my ears popped. Way below, Las Vegas was little more than a wisp of smog on the desert floor. Silently, coolly, but with a growing suggestion of complaint from beneath the bonnet, we drove on until, almost teetering with the effort, we reached the highest point, a narrow gap between two opposing bluffs that faced each other like a pair of bookends. The bonnet dropped an inch, then rose; then dropped again, another inch and then another until, with a jerk of relief from the transmission, we began to pick up some speed. For the last few miles the two of us had been silent, as if holding our breaths. Now, as we gathered speed, the tension eased. It had really seemed, for one long moment, that the car wouldn't make it. Charlie was the first to break the silence.

"You ready for it?" I looked at him with a puzzled expression, and he nodded ahead. As we cleared the last bend, a whole new valley spread out in front of us. With the sun starting to drop, the western sky was a watery lemon color, the sawtooth ridge we had just crossed sending jagged shadows down the slopes on either side of us. Across the valley another range built up in mauve and purple banks, and from this high point we could see, beyond that, yet another fold and crease of hills far away on the horizon. The valley itself, way below us, was a tapered oval of land narrowing at each extremity to a point where the two ridges that contained it came together, its floor peppered over with ink spots of creosote, softened by a thin shading of green from a million tall cacti, silvered like breath on a mirror with distance and heat, and bleached white at one far-off point where old borax mines cut through the surface— a salty-white stain where nothing, not even the hardiest plant, had a chance of survival. Running the length of this valley, right through its middle, was the dusty-edged black line of the road we followed, as straight as a craps cue with the same hooked dog's leg at its furthest visible point, where once again it began to negotiate another climb into the hills.

"The ranch is way over thataways, to the right of that sink, the white patch, but not so far. Cain't see it from here lessen it's night when a few lights show. Far side of them other hills and you's right smack in the middle of Death Valley. I'm assumin' you know that name?"

"Yes, of course," I replied, actually not wanting to talk,

transfixed by the sheer scale and beauty of the view. "I'd like to go there one day, but it couldn't be as good as this."

"I kin think on better places you wanna sight-see. Mean country this, you don't watch out fer yourself." Despite the gruff tone, I could see Charlie was proud of the sweep of land that stretched out before us, and was pleased by my response. From that point on, it seemed, a polite association of no more than forty minutes' duration began subtly to transform into something approaching hesitant friendship, inspired by nothing more than a view and our matched reactions to it. There was nothing so abrupt as a verbal recognition of this change, but the idea of it seemed to settle comfortably between us.

Outside, the road sloped away from us—a long gradual descent to the valley floor. I could see what Charlie meant when he said the return trip would take us longer—no decent amount of level ground on which to get up a good head of speed. The valley was like a bowl, the road dipping down into its lowest point, then rising up again the other side.

On either side of us, the land looked harsh and brutal once more, spotted with tall, forbidding cacti, their branched arms crooked at the elbows and held up as if to warn against trespass, a tangle of thorned scrub no more than shin-high to further block intrusion. Up at the pass, there had been a real beauty, a pure thrill, in the vastness of the scenery that sprang at us around that last bend, that Charlie had so late prepared me for—the layered ridges and terraced banks of the High Sierras—purple and mauve and scarlet and indigo; the spills of giant shadow, cast by a lemon sun, sliding down the hillsides like an avalanche of black snow; the valley spread out before us, as if in miniature, ready, it seemed, to be pocketed; and the massed shades and tones and dusty tints of a million different growths that filled it end to end.

But now, close to, only a few feet from the car, I could see it was the same mean country, just as Charlie had said—far more grim and hostile than distance had had me believe. Those same gentle colors and mixed shades of a moment before were now broken down into single units, separated into not-so-gentle component parts—the silver sharpness of a cactus spine, the gray of a jagged stone or rock, the brown of parched earth, the rust-red of a thorn, the green of bramble, the black of a sticky creosote stem. And how successful that meanness had been in repelling intruders. Throughout the whole valley there was little with which to measure the influence of man—a thin, tarred road and a line of sun-splintered telegraph poles, now and then a sorry patch of cultivation, a shack's baked roof, a tracing of aimless dirt tracks, the car we drove in (almost beaten on the first hill) and somewhere ahead, the ranch we were bound for.

"Many people live round here?"

"Some," replied Charlie, gazing over the landscape. "The crazy ones, you ask my 'pinion. This place ain't fit for stayin' in long. Grow themselves cotton, soya, alfalfa. But the main problem's irrigation. On'y good thing I can think on round here's the jackrabbits. Git yourself some fine sport with them. Me'n a friend was out here a few nights back, got us a rifle each and torch, and had us a high 'ol time. Catch 'em in the beam and they like to stand still, jus' starin' to where's they're gonna git shot from—just see those pearly eyes in the dark, squeeze the trigger, and it's like a light goes out. Offen times ya hear 'em squeal, but that's all.

I looked at the clock on the dashboard—a quivering green digital display. We had been driving close on an hour and somewhere ahead, still concealed, was our destination. For the very first time, I felt a stir of excitement, as I realized the purpose of this ride. Even when Charlie was telling me about the girls, they had seemed remote—nothing to do with me. But as the hour drew on and we drove deeper into the valley, my purpose became clearer as the ranch grew closer.

"We got far to go now?"

Charlie laughed. "Funny thing, all the fellers I drives out start to askin' that self-same question just 'bout now; I was waiting to see you gonna do the same. Well, I tell ya. 'Bout two miles on there's a road branches off to the left you cain't hardly see till you right over it. We go down there a spell, hit a dirt track and foller it mebbe two, three mile and you're home. Make you feel better?"

"I'd almost forgotten what I was doing out here."

Charlie laughed again. "Ain't no different to th' others. Long ride out, lot to look on, they all forget. Get in to the car Vegas, all puffed up an' perfumed, ready like a penned hog, all bristlin' to go —but by the time they hit the Pass, they all done plain forgotten where they're goin' and what for. Then, all of a sudden-like, right about here, it hits 'em. Gals!

"Now you, you looks okay, looks to me like you bin done all this before some place, got it all in what they go call per-spec-tive, you don' min' me sayin'. But some on 'em though, they starts sprucin' up—touchin' their faces all over, quiet-like, think I don' notice—checkin' everythin's in its right place. Plain cain't sit still a minute long without they'se doin' summint to themselves. Makes me laugh, all that pattin' an' doin' to get themselves set. I mean, those gals, they're hookers. They don' care none you got yourself a tin leg or squint-eyed. I tell these fellers straight some time—you ain't here t'impress. You don't have to, know what I'm saying? But they still keep on. Then there's th'other kind that plain freeze up, cain't talk, don't budge a muscle, drippin' so much I got me th'air con-dish-ner goin' full blast to cool 'em down. Git there, and I almost have to help 'em to the door. Feel like I gotta hold 'em by their hand all the way—even take it out for 'em, if I kin find it, that is. Thought of what's through that door plain puts 'em in a frenzy they cain't do nuthin' for themselves. And then, when those gals go line up like to git chose, well, they jus' sit there, cain't hardly say, do nuthin'. They like to be kinda paralyzed with th' excitement of it all. One thing's sure though," Charlie was looking ahead, braking, then spinning the wheel to turn off the highway. "One thing's sure, all them fellers different critters they step back out for the ride home. An' if that ain't the best argument around fer makin' it legal nationwide, don't rightly know what is. Those gals, they're perfor-min' a valuable social service, you want my 'pinion on it."

We were driving more slowly now, this secondary road neither as wide nor as well surfaced as the highway, Charlie picking his way over the numerous bumps and depressions that disappeared under the bonnet. The next road we turned onto was even worse—nothing more than a dirt track, rocky and rutted, presumably the ranch driveway, stones crunching under the wheels and dust rising up in our wake in a trailing cloud. When we passed a yellow windsock pulling in the breeze like a fishing trap in a fast stream, and an open, leveled stretch of ground where small planes could set down, I knew we had arrived.

We approached the ranch from the side, a row of barrack-style buildings set together in close order, jacked up on pilings and, like the Mustang, surrounded by a high wire fence. But by the time we pulled into the parking lot, bordered by halved, white-painted tires, only the first of the narrow huts could be seen, facing us broadside on, the rest concealed behind it. Beyond the fence, a flight of wooden steps led to a tiny porch and a single door. The few win-dows that looked onto the parking lot appeared to be curtained.

Charlie switched off the engine and the air-conditioning died to a whisper. I found the handle and made to get out, but Charlie caught my arm and held me back.

"Jus' hold on there, young feller, before you go rushin' on in there fit to bust. Not offen I see my way clear to givin' out advice, so when I do it's a good idea to set and listen. Now you ain't got you no sunglasses and that there's a mighty strong sun out there, despite it's headed down. You jus' make sure you close your eyes good and tight before you go hurtlin' through that door. I'll let you know when. They keep it all pretty dark in there and comin' in from the glare and all you cain't hardly see your hand in front of your face, lettin' alone the gals you come for. Many more than you'd believe of the fellers I've brought out here, tol' me later they picked wrong on account of not bein' able to see straight. So jus' you remember when we get up on that porch to shut your eyes real tight against the light a minute or two—help you git your bearin's once we're in." I thanked him for the warning, the advice, and we both stepped out of the car.

Nothing, no words of advice, no words of warning, though, could have prepared me for the sudden weight and wave of heat that fell on us the moment we were out of the car. Even the breeze that filled the windsock and now skittered the dust at our feet felt as though it had swept straight from the open hatches of a foundry furnace—thick and scorching and molten—filling my clothes, my lungs, with its hot, heavy breath; riffling through my hair like a blowtorch. So intense, so concentrated was this rush of heat, so close and explosive, it was as if the air had somehow contrived during the last hour to turn itself inflammable, needing only the tiniest splinter of a spark to ignite it. Charlie, heading across to the gate, was shaking his head and laughing.

"Told you it warms up some this side of the range. Guess I should've reminded you." I walked over to him, astonished any kind of movement was still possible in this clogging heat.

"Jeez, if I ran a mile in this, I'd soon lose some weight."

"You run a mile in this and you'd be mightly lucky that was all you lost—that's supposin' you even got that far. Lessen you're used to it, and then some," he added, pushing the bell on the gate, "you'd burn up crisper than a coffin in a cree-ma-torium."

As it had at the Mustang, the answering buzzer here released the lock mechanism on the gate and the two of us passed through. Up on the porch, I stood behind him and, as instructed, squeezed my eyes tight, pretending to rub them with my hands. For a few seconds the glare still burned through, but gradually the light began to fade and darkness settle in. I heard Charlie knock, the door open with a squeak and voices—his and a woman's—and then felt a draft of cool air as I stepped forward, dropping my hands and opening my eyes just as the door closed behind us. Even then, the room I found myself in was pitch black. Quickly, though, points of light began to spread, the darkness condensing into shadowy outlines, one of which, the familiar bulk of Charlie, now turned and pointed to a low shape just inside the door.

"You jus' take a seat right there, while Merle goes call up some company."

The shape was one of several brocaded sofas ranged down both sides of the narrow reception room, each covered in a thick protective sheet of plastic that squeaked at even the slightest movement. Across the room I saw Merle disappear through another doorway —a small, colorless bundle in a cardigan and Terry Treds that scuffed the floor—with Charlie following behind. He turned to me briefly: "You have yourself a time now. I'll be waiting for you when you're through, to take you back to town. Jus' shout Charlie or git Merle there to come and fetch me up." And with that, he was gone.

Quickly adapting to the darkness, I had just time enough to take in the red flocked walls bracketed with bare red bulbs—filaments quivering like candle flames—a couple of low marble tables with ornate gilt edging, and a number of lambent plaster nudes, before Merle reappeared and, with a clap of her hands, ushered in the "company."

"Okay now, girls, just step in here and meet our guest, that's it."

From the doorway a line of girls filed into the room, each in a swimsuit, pantyhose and high heels, and formed up in front of me. As soon as they were properly assembled (I counted nine), Merle came over and stood beside me, her cardigan smelling slightly of cats and melted butter. One by one, moving from left to right, the girls stepped forward to introduce themselves.

"Hi, I'm Clare."

"Hi," I said softly, not sure whether I was expected to return the greeting or not. Clare stepped back, wavering on her heels, and the next in line moved forward.

"Hi, I'm Joey." This time I just nodded and Joey rejoined the line.

"Hi, I'm Coral," said the next.

"Hi, I'm Mary Lynn."

"Hi, I'm Georgie."

"Hi, I'm Babs."

"Hi, I'm Cherry."

"Hi, I'm Cindy."

"Hi, I'm Toni."

With a glance behind her, Toni, the last in the lineup, stepped back and silence descended.

"You like to pick your choice now, sir?" prompted Merle.

Sitting forward with a squeak from the plastic cover, I looked at the line of girls. I might not have been able to put names to all of them, but at least, thanks to Charlie, I could see them. Of the nine girls, three were possibles. Number four, number seven and number eight. Disregarding the others, hardly the plate of cookies Charlie had promised, I looked at the three more carefully. Each of them, I could tell, knew she was short-listed—just as the other six knew they had been dropped. The three possibles each managed a smile —number four adding to the effect by shaking her blond hair over her shoulder and putting a hand on her hip, numbers seven and eight both leaning forward to show off to the best advantage the closely matched qualities both had in abundance. As for the rest, they seemed to deflate and wrinkle like old balloons after a Christmas party, eyes losing that first sparkle, lips curling impatiently, breasts sagging, bellies filling.

"Number seven," I turned to Merle. "I forget her name."

No sooner had I said the number than the other girls broke line and trooped back the way they had come with hardly a glance in my direction. Making a point of ignoring number seven, numbers four and eight linked arms and left together. Number seven, meanwhile, made straight for me.

"Hi there, sugar baby. How ya doin'? Now here, you jus' take this l'il old finger and follow me. L'il Miss Cherry has just done finished painting her nails an' ah know you, sweet li'l man you, just would hate t' go smudge them—ain't that so?" Our fingers delicately hooked, Cherry led me from the reception room down a narrow passage equally dark. At the end of it, through an open door, I caught a glimpse of Charlie, feet up on a sofa, a can of beer clasped on his belly. As for the other girls, they seemed to have disappeared completely.

"You come up with Charlie?" asked Cherry over her shoulder.

"Yes, from Vegas."

"Ain't he just the purest, sweetest thing you've ever set yo eyes on though?"

"No question about it."

"He is a jewel, you can take my solemn oath on that." At the end of a second corridor, Cherry opened a door and drew me into her room.

The "jewel" was standing in the open front door, framed against a bank of cobalt hills when Cherry and I reappeared, Merle perched on the very edge of a plastic-sheeted sofa. It was much darker outside, the glare gone, a soft dusk replacing it; through the open door, a draft of air brought with it a sweet, slightly antiseptic scent from the fields of creosote. When we arrived, I had been aware of no distinct smell, as if the heat had simply burnt it off. Now it filled the room.

"So," said Charlie, swinging the car keys from their leather tab, "y'all set to go?"

"Ready when you are."

"Okay, let's move 'em out. Speak to you later, Merle."

Without thinking I leaned down to kiss Cherry good-bye. Instinctively, like a boxer ducking a punch, her head glanced back and she pushed me lightly away. It seemed an extraordinary response after the last hour or so.

"Unh unh, sugar pie, that'll go costin' you extra, you ain't careful." Merle nodded approvingly and Charlie hooted.

"Sure do make it hard for a feller, don't they though?" With a bob and a wave and a see-y'all-later, he skipped down the steps toward the gate, with me, a little chastened, close behind. By the time we reached the car, the door had closed behind us and the ranch looked as desolate as it had when we arrived, as desolate as the country in which it stood. Though it was probably still high in the seventies, the blast of heat that had greeted us had cooled now to what felt like a soft evening warmth, the land lost in pools of shadow, ticking with life as insects, subdued by day and burrowed deep out of the glare, roused themselves amid the scrub. Over the western ridges, the sky was lemon still, mauve directly above, and toward the pass where we were headed, thickening from purple to black. A few stars glinted there, winking in response to the ticking of the land.

Slipping into reverse, Charlie spun the wheel, sending us in a gravel-spitting turn, then engaged drive and lurched off up the track, past the airstrip and the gently luffing windsock.

"Got yourself the purtiest in the bunch, I reckon. Quite a gal the one you picked. Ain't none sweeter than that there Lucy."

"Lucy? She told me her name was Cherry."

"Lucy, Merry, Cherry, Terri . . . it don't signify. They change their names round more times than you and me take a leak. Ain't much more than that to keep them occupied. Stay out here a month or two and you plain narrers your whole idea on things. You and me now, we're free to come and go, but you go spend any amount of time like they do, cooped up and all, and you find little things like changing your name come to mean a whole heap more than you rightly 'spected. Ain't much in the realm of diversion you're sixty miles out in a valley full of nuthin' but desert and sun. All they got is a TV, radios, them tape machines, a room of their own, a kitchen to share the cookin' in. Sheeee-yit. Choice is sit around and rap, eat, sleep, or bust their asses on some john who ain't heard of deodorant. I sat in that room some days and seen those gals just lie around and paint their nails all day long. Put it on real careful and cuss shit anyone jogs them. Dry it good and hard, blowin' and all, and wavin' their pretty little hands— you seen it. Then, you know what they do? They go chip it all off, choose themselves another color, and paint up all over again. Aint' what I call ennertainment."

"How long do they spend at the ranch?" I asked, as we turned out onto the paved road.

"Three, four weeks on, then a week off somewheres—see their boyfriends, husbands, whatever."

"No, I mean in total?"

"Depends. I picked up gals in town there and brought them out —purty little things, chatty, haulin' a suitcase they packed so tight they gotta drag it on the ground, old engine barely makes the hill. Heard of the money, most of them, that's what gits them all fired up. Looks like they're set to stay for life. Then, no more than a month or two later, and I'm takin' 'em back. Different people, you know? Like the juice is plain squeezed out of them. Then you got yourself the others that take to it nachrul, settle down like it's home sweet home and stay good and long. Cain't never put a figure on how long they gonna stay."

"What about Cherry . . . Lucy?"

"She bin around a stretch, six, seven months, I'd say. She's one of them don't take no breaks when the month's up. Works every hour God gives her, savin' up all the loot she can. One day she'll just up and off, time she's got herself enough."

"They get to make a lot?"

"You wouldn't believe if I told you."

"Of course I would. What's the most you've ever heard of?"

"Had us a gal there one time, came in from . . . think it was Pittsburg, over east a ways. Stopped in Vegas long enough to git herself a license . . . "

"They have to have licenses?"

"You bet. Thousand bucks a year. Or two-fifty you ain't plannin' on doin' it longer than three months. Had us some of those— teachers and the like, do it like a vacation job; students too, some of them. Anyways, there's this one in from Pittsburg, gets herself a license, and they have me go in and pick her up. Well, she was hot—worked her butt off near on a year. Almost to the day, she packs up her bags and gets a ride with me back to town, lookin' to catch the first plane east. Now she don't say a word the whole way along this bit, but soon's we hit the pass and there's Vegas she's a-hoopin' and a-howlin' clear put shit right up me with the shock of it all. Anyways, we starts talkin' some and she's tellin' me her plans and all, and I just ups and asks her straight how much she's got saved. And just as straight she done tell me. I swear, I near drove th' animal clean offen the road. She never did know just how close she came to not spending a single cent's worth of what she had stashed."

"How much?"

"Well, why don't you give a little guess? A ten says you don't get in spittin' distance."

Just as I had done the week before in Mustang, I made some rapid calculations. Average 80 dollars a trick, say six times a day. Call it 500. After splitting with the house and living expenses, say 200. Seven days a week, call it a thousand, give or take. Around fifty thousand for the year. Since Charlie was making such a big deal over it, I added another twenty to make up the spitting distance.

"Seventy thousand dollars. That's not counting the loose change in her purse," I said, certain I was closer to the mark than Charlie had given me credit for.

"You plain fortunate it was only a ten bet."

"How much then?"

Charlie took a deep, dramatic breath: "One-hundred-and-sixty-four-thousand. Kin you believe that? Even dug out her paying-in book with it all detailed down. Hardly enough space on that last page to git all them numbers squeezed in. Hell, I couldn't sleep easy a week or more, thinkin' about that all."

"Where did you say I could get a license?"

"Shoot, goddammit," cried Charlie hitting the wheel, "if that ain't near exactly what I done gone and said. Almost word for word."

By this time, we had turned onto the highway and Charlie had his foot hard down on the accelerator. Outside there was little to see beyond the first ranks of cactus and scrub and a flashing line of telegraph poles. Scooped out of the darkness by the headlights, the cacti looked gray and ghostly and sent fingers of shadow racing for cover. Inside the car, it was cool and friendly, the engine still humming and comforting, our faces glowing green in the dashboard lights. With the night growing darker ahead of us and the silent, shadowy desert speeding past on either side, it was good to be sitting there—safe, side by side, insulated from the outside. Charlie's company, the drive, the memory of Cherry or whatever her name was, all combining to fill me with a sense of well being.

"So how's about that Lucy . . . Cherry to you? She all I reckon her to be?"

"I think you'd enjoy it."

"Think it! Hell, know I would. Had a mind to git my hands on that piece of ass ever since she done first joined up. She put out then?" Eagerly, the lights from the instruments giving his face a smooth, leery cast, he looked from the road to me and back again, until he caught me nodding. "Yessssirree, just knew it," he said, slapping the wheel. "How much, you mind me askin', she done git you for?"

I told him; I didn't mind his knowing.

"You get the *veee-eye-peeee* room included on that?"

"Certainly did."

"Ain't that summint else though?"

"You said it."

"Damn right I did."

The VIP room was in the next block from Cherry's room. After the checkup, the paying-up and a wash in the Peter Pan, she had given me a robe and led me there. It was far larger than her own room, but colder, more impersonal through not being lived in—only used when a client could be persuaded to raise his ante. The walls were paneled and the windows covered with sheets of aluminum foil—though tiny pin pricks and tears let in shafts of sunlight. There was a parlor sofa covered in the same protective sheet of plastic, a marble table with a projector on it, and a screen hanging from the wall opposite. The bed was tucked away in a mirrored alcove, and at first sight I thought it was breathing—a gentle, regular movement stirring its surface as though a pair of giant lungs were at work beneath its cover. Then Cherry was dropping her robe to the floor, sitting on its edge, and rolling back onto it, the water giving way beneath her, springing back again from the sides to ripple round her, a cork-brown body tossed about by the contained swell. "Dahve in, why don't you?" she had cried, "dahve in and save a poor drownin' gal."

". . . always had me a hankering to git a go in there," said Charlie. "Day comes I git tired of just doin' the drivin', reckon I'll spend me some dollars and give it a go. You see that other thing they got in there? Passion chair, they call it. How about that though? Sat on it one time they was quiet, some of the gals and me just horsin' round is all. Plain got me so darned twisted up on that contraption, couldn't rightly tell m'ankle from m'elbow."

The Passion Chair. It stood below the bed, just inside the door. Spread tubular metal legs, a red leather seat with an adjustable back rest, and all around it, more curved metal—loops and circles and rests, and padded restraints and grips, like the handlebars on a bike —for legs here and here, or for arms there and there, places for the knees, the feet, the elbows. It looked like a giant Daddy-Longlegs, alert, upright, paralyzed in midstride. The metal was slippery cool, the restraints and seat cover sticky and tacky with sweat. Directly beneath it, set into the floor, an air-conditioning grille. Cherry padded over to it from the bed with a "Hey, you wanna go," walking on tiptoes as if wearing invisible stillettoes, grasping hold the bars like a gymnast a piece of equipment, then springing up into its metal branches, settling into the red leather nest, her body shining and warm in its steely clutch.

"You git to have a go on that?" asked Charlie.
"You bet. First I stood and she . . ."
"No, no, don't tell me, boy," he cried, grabbing the wheel with

both hands and hauling himself forward in his seat. "Don't tell me no more, can't bear to listen none." There was a pause and he began again, softer this time. "Kin see her on it plain . . . those legs of hers just spread up on them bars and opened wide enough she could sing Christmas carols with it. Shoot, just thinkin' on it, I kin hear the tune she must've played you. Whhhhheeeeeeeee!"

The two of us started to laugh, louder and louder, Charlie swinging the wheel left and right, the car lurching wildly over the road, headlights sweeping deeper and deeper into the desert with every swerve on the empty road, and then deeper still as the first corner bore down on us. But there was no need for Charlie to brake, already the car was laboring. Not sure how to pitch it, the automatic transmission began hopping between the two most likely gears, as the road climbed on to the pass—pulling fast one minute with a whine, dragging and tugging the next with a growl that set the wood fascia shivering.

"Whhheeeeeee-shhhhhiiiiiiit," cried Charlie for the last time, taking a long deep breath. "So tell me, did I win my bet?"

"What bet was that?" I asked, knowing full well, the headlights flashing off bare rock with every slow bend.

"That come the way back, you'd be a happier man than ol' Charlie boy."

Up ahead, the two book-end bluffs approached, seeming to open and close as the headlights played on them—now one, now the other.

"You won your bet."

Bye Bye
Blackbird

There was the same gold glow pouring down from the west and a smog as fine as an aerosol spray softening the Hollywood hills when I returned to Sunset. This time I didn't park behind the Bank of America, just kept driving until I spotted her on the corner of Genesee, leaning back into a thick privet hedge that needed clipping and almost hidden among the leaves. I was in a different car this time and she didn't acknowledge me until I called her name, softly, over the sidewalk. Even then I could see she didn't recognize me.

"How come you know my name?" she asked. "Do ah know you from someplace?" She bent down and looked closer. "Yeah, ah know you now. Ain't you the one give 'Lisha all that jive-ass you ain't got the where-with-hall? And you sittin' nice and fine in your fancy car. Ah know you now." She opened the door and sat in. "Ah'm presumin' you lookin' for the same service?"

"That's the idea. What about the discount for regulars?"

"There you go 'gain. Don't recall nuthin' about no discoun', sugar. My memory serves, a little longer is all ah said."

We drove to the same motel and were given a room on the ground floor this time. Small things sharpened the picture I had retained of the place: the pink neon "Vacancy" sign in the office window, a square of worn Astroturf where you laid the money for the room, the single palm in the center of the courtyard, the rows of curtained windows, the tapping plywood headboard, the bubbling sound beneath us, the ashtray on the bedside table—stubs removed but the ash stains remaining. The only thing that seemed different was 'Lisha.

She was rougher than I remembered—with a swagger to her walk and a rasp to her voice. In a lime-green ribbed-wool hot-pants suit that barely contained her buttocks, with a belt of chained coins that reminded me of an oversized charm bracelet, she looked altogether more obvious and tarty. I was disappointed, perhaps even a little dismayed. The last time I had felt a certain sympathy for her, but now I resented her brashness, disliked her cocksureness.

We undressed in silence. Beneath her hot pants she wore light brown pantyhose that made her look as though she had been dipped in a tub of milk chocolate. They also made her legs smell slightly of rubber and the waistband had puckered her skin like a scar. It looked as though you could unscrew the top half of her body from the bottom half. Her eyes seemed browner too, the whites stained with a tracing of yellow threads I couldn't remember, and there appeared to be more glue than lash on her eyelids. Worse still, heavy black globs of mascara had secreted themselves in the corner of each eye as though she hadn't bothered to wash away the sleep, the tiny mucus deposits blackened along with the lashes. This time she had painted her nails a dark aubergine that I found far less appealing than the scoops of scarlet she had worn before, and the red blusher she had applied to her flattened cheekbones looked like circles of warpaint daubed on the black skin rather than the subtle sweeps of color I remembered. There was a thin line of hair, too, that I hadn't noticed the first time, running from the black tangle between her legs up and, it seemed, into the knotted depression of her navel. That afternoon I felt it scrape against me.

She was not in such a hurry, though, as she had been the last time—douched and dressed before I had even buttoned my shirt and tied my laces. This time she took the cigarette I offered, sat back against the headboard and pulled the foam quilting halfway up her thighs. While we smoked, the same keys scratched against locks, the same doors slammed as they had before, the same anonymous footsteps grew loud then faded past our door, the same soft orchestration of sounds from the street drifted in to us.

"You got a tan since I saw you last," she remarked, running an aubergine nail across my skin. "You bin out to the beach? Tryin' to git yourself a color like mine? How come you ask for discoun' and you got the money for sunnin'?"

"I was in Nevada . . . working."

"That a fact?" she said, brushing a flake of ash from between her breasts, heavy and round with swollen tips as hard and as wrinkled as halved walnut shells. She must have seen me looking at them as they trembled from her brushing, for she caught one in her hand and held it out at me. "You like them?" she asked, tweaking the purply-black nipple until it seemed to squirm of its own accord, the skin tightening around it. "You like them all black? Like it black better than white? Reckon you must, you comin' back and all. You enjoy your time with 'Lisha?" she asked finally, dropping the breast and reaching instead for me—tweaking and pinching the flaccid skin in just the same way she had done with the nipple, but failing to provoke the same response.

"Of course," I said, realizing I meant no such thing, that this would be the last time. "I just wish it weren't so expensive."

She laughed, letting me go and leaning over to her side to stub out the cigarette, making the bed sway with the movement. "You reckon 'Lisha ain't worth it? She didn't fuck you like you wanted or summint?"

I told her that she was; that she had.

"So, you gonna come back and see 'Lisha, have yourself some action?"

"As soon as I can find the money."

"Sounds to me you got the same problems" ("prollems" was the way she said it) "as me, sugar. But you know what they say: You pay and ah'll play, you quit payin' and it's bye bye blackbird." She chuckled at the rhyme, then more seriously: "Ain't no room for nuthin' else—discoun' included. And talkin' of which, your meter done run right out." Pushing aside the cover she got to her feet, leaving me wallowing in the swell.

"You in a hurry all of a sudden?"

"Ah'm always in a hurry, baby, when there's gals out there takin' money ah kin git for myself. Ooooooh, thought I'd make it to the bathroom in time but you done caught up on me," she cried, scooping her hand between her legs.

The last I saw of 'Lisha, she was taking up a position on a corner of Sunset. I watched her, obliquely, in the rear-view mirror as I drove away. She didn't wave or look after me, more concerned with the way her hot pants squeezed against her buttocks, tugging the ribbed wool into place. With the sun in my eyes, I drove back to the beach where I was staying with a friend. Bye bye blackbird.

Conversations on the Near North Side

Abby started the evening with a story. She'd heard it from a friend in Las Vegas where she had spent the previous week on business.

"There's this guy standing at the craps table, right. Dunes, Tropicana, the D.I.—one of those, it doesn't matter which. Anyway, this working girl comes up to him and the guy asks her how much. 'Fifty,' she tells him. 'Fifty! Shit fifty,' he says to her, 'I'll give ya twenny.' A real high-roller, y'know? Well, she doesn't much like the look of him but a job's a job, right, a trick's a trick. So she drops it to forty for the shmutz. 'Forty,' says he. 'Shit forty! I said twenny and that's tops, honey.' So she walks, right? Anyway, that evening she gets into the elevator with none other than this jerk-off and his wife. Now she's real cool the whole way down, pretends she doesn't recognize him from the craps table, but just before the doors open she turns to him and says: 'See what ya get for twenny, sucker?' "

The house we were in was on Chicago's Near North Side, halfway down a tree-screened avenue off Broadway. Across the street many of these old houses had been brought down and portered apartment blocks set up in their place, but on our side the old houses remained. They were tall and narrow and respectable, built of hewn-stone blocks and cloaked in an ivy that was the deepest of emerald green. The slightest breeze from the lake set the leaves rustling. Some of the houses had tiny, gothic turrets with curved window panes that distorted reflections into vertical strips like a fairground Hall of Mirrors. When I arrived, the sun was at roof-top level and golden and the windows along this street glowed like all their insides were on fire. Except, of course, those turret windows, which were simply striped with a band of gold.

Abby was special. She was the first girl I had met who knew what I was doing.

"I think it's great. You should have come to Chicago first off and I'd have given you a network of women all over the States. But don't write it like that Xaviera Hollandaise book. That one was . . . well, enough of little Miss Hollandaise!"

Our meeting had been arranged by a mutual friend whose house on the Near North Side we were using for the occasion—kind of neutral ground. The two of them were old friends. The interview, he told me over the phone, would cost $100. But then, I wouldn't have minded what it cost.

For the first time I had become really, deeply frightened. It was a fear that resembled nothing I had ever felt before, nothing in my past coming close to its intensity. There was no context into which I could satisfactorily fit it; no category of experience against which I could match it, identify it and thus deal with it. Nowhere in my past could I find its counterpart. It wasn't the fear I had sometimes felt at school when, shivering in my pajamas outside my house master's study, I had listened to and counted with a kind of vicarious dread the strokes being given to the boy inside, strokes I would in due course receive myself. Nor was it the thrill of fear I had known as an adolescent shoplifter; the fear that filled me the time I crashed my father's car; the shared, but unspoken, fear that dogged each passing day of an early girlfriend's delayed period; the dread I had felt when I had set out on my journey. It wasn't that sudden stab of fear I suffered in Melbourne at the thought of some venereal disease working away inside me, nor did it compare with what I had felt in Caracas, on a street in Sabana Grande; or in Hawaii as I lay curled up on a warm, gum-stained pavement wetting myself uncontrollably. On those two occasions there had been no time for fear —that came later as a kind of trembling shock. Nothing I could remember seemed quite so real, so powerful, so numbing as the fear that sprang at me the moment I stepped into the terminal building of O'Hare International Airport.

I felt like a bomber pilot taking off on his last mission. Everything I had grown used to, the way of life I had become so familiar with, now, so close to the end, with only Chicago and New York to go, grew menacing and sinister. There was suddenly so much to lose; such a short way to go. That I had come so far and been so lucky seemed to underline the possibility that if something was going to happen, then it would happen now, on this last leg, sometime soon. It was surely too much to hope for a clear run; unreasonable to expect anything other than all the odds stacked against me. Like a child placing one building brick on top of another, there comes a point where the whole frail structure is bound to topple. The question was, as I taxied into Chicago, just how many more building bricks could I afford to add? It was for that very reason that my friend told Abby the purpose of my visit.

Abby was the name we agreed on.

"The biggest fear," she confided, "is, don't use my real name."

"Which name would you like?"

"Abby Heller is fine—or choose one yourself that you think is appropriate, after knowing me after this interview, when you go to write about me. Think, what did she look like? That should be her name."

There was no name that I could think of then, or can think of now, that would suit Abby. An ex-Vegas showgirl, she was built for extravagant feathered headdresses and miles of spangled beads —tall and slim and sinuous. Her face was long and striking and her skin still tanned from her stay in Las Vegas. She wore amethyst crescents of eye shadow and glistening lipstick that made the tan look deeper and her teeth white. A thick fall of raven hair she kept swept back and pinned behind her ears. When it fell forward, as it frequently did that evening, she would brush it away with her fingers or tuck it behind her ears with nails as long as pinball bats. Her legs were long and spread wide under the glass dining room table where we sat for the first hour. She was wore white cord trousers and a blue silk blouse. Whenever she leaned forward, her jewelry—solid and nuggety—clinked against the glass.

"Abby Heller will do fine," I told her.

"Okay. Then that's my name. So be it. I don't like my real name anyway."

Abby arrived later than me, pushing open the screen door at the back with a squeaking flourish and tapping across the wood floors in her Kaplan's of Las Vegas sling-backs. She carried a large gold satchel bag which she dumped on the floor by her chair before disappearing to freshen up. When she came back, she told the story of the working girl in Las Vegas. When she finished, her laugh was warm and full and complete.

I had spent that afternoon preparing a list of questions for

Abby, and during that first hour together we skipped our way through the first warmup section—establishing her roots, her background, her family and private life.

I learned that she was Capricorn: "I was born the same day, month and year as Muhammad Ali"; that she was thirty-nine: "How old do I look?"

"Twenty-nine."

"God bless you."

"And where were you born?"

"Can't you tell? How nice. New Jersey."

"Are your parents still alive?"

"I thought you said I looked twenty-nine? Yes, they are alive."

"And do they know what you do?"

"I don't think so."

"You don't seem too sure?"

"Well, my last marriage ended bitterly. My husband was homosexual and he called my parents and told them that the reason for the breakup was because their daughter was a hooker. And my mother went into con-vul-shuns! My father even flew out here to, er, beat the shit out of him."

"Out of him—not you?"

"Yeah, out of him. I, of course, denied the whole thing because my mother couldn't accept it. If she could've I would've told her— but I think it would've destroyed her. And why do that to her? I could have told my father but I didn't. He knows me well enough to know that it could be so. But he doesn't push it, you know?"

"How many times have you been married?"

"Do annulments count?"

And so it went. I was astonished by her candor, delighted by her vivid sense of humor and her lively, inquiring mind. It was Abby, for instance, who asked me if I knew where the word "hooker" originated.

"Well, no. I can only think it has something to do with fishing. Or . . . no, no idea . . ."

"Well, I'll tell you. There was this general in the United States Army called General Hooker and he loved his ladies."

"To the extent that he would pay?"

"Yes. And the other men began to call them 'Hooker's girls,' or 'there's another hooker,' meaning there's a girl who's going to see General Hooker. I mean, I get curious about words. If you're going to call it at me, I want to know what it is. Like, when I was a child,

I came home from school one day and said, 'Mom, the kids are calling me a kike. What does that mean?' She didn't know. Well, I wanted to know, and I'm going to tell you what it means. At the turn of the century, when the U.S. had a great influx of immigrants from Europe, most of whom were illiterate, they had to pass through Ellis Island to be inspected physically, to get their papers, whatever, and they had to sign their names. Now as I say, most of them were illiterate so that the Christian people put down the sign of the cross which today has turned into an X. You know, if you can't sign your name you put an X on the dotted line. But the Jewish people were not going to put an X because they didn't believe in Christ. So they drew a small circle, and the Yiddish word for a small circle is kykalla. K . . . Y . . . I don't know the spelling. But 'kykalla,' and so the kids were saying to me, 'Here's another kike.' "

By the time we had dealt with these early questions, a strong feeling of trust had been established, but when we moved from the dining room into the lounge where we would be more comfortable, I admitted to her that the next questions I had prepared were of a more intimate nature and that I hoped she wouldn't resent my asking them. I needn't have worried.

"I won't," she assured me. "I will not."

And so we moved on, lounging back into the sofa, an ashtray between us and drinks on the table.

"Tell me about the first time someone paid you money."

"Two things happened to me. First of all, when I divorced my first husband and left home and moved to another state, I got a job as a legal secretary and in the office there was this other girl working part-time who I discovered was a hooker, using the part-time job as a front. Anyway, a long story short, circumstances made it necessary for me to live with her for a while. And that's . . . hearing the word for, like, the first time and seeing people walk into the apartment all day long, I said, 'What do you have to do?' I was young and naïve. And she said, 'Fuck 'em. You get paid for it. Do it. Try it.' So I worked for her for a couple of weeks and I thought it was just fabulous—that I had all this money. But at that time I never thought of taking it up professionally and I went on doing other things.

"Then, years later, I was here in Chicago living with this minister of the church who made very little money. And money was not important to him anyway. Our biggest arguments were over that. And the reason we finally broke up. I was a waitress at the time, working long hours, breaking my back, not having a lot of money, struggling to pay bills, ohhh, it was awful. And I worked at night. And all that summer I would lie out on the beach down by the lake all day long and I would think to myself about this real relationship I had just come out of. Abby, I said to myself, you've got to prove it for yourself, for your own peace of mind. Wouldn't it be wonderful if you could make a *lot* of money. To see, is it that important? But, I thought, how can I do it? How do I go about it? I haven't been to college. I just can't go out and overnight make myself a fortune. And then . . . ah hah, I can. But how? I'm not going to stand on some street corner. What am I going to do? Advertise in the paper? Take an ad on TV? So what I did was, I called my attorney, and my doctor, and a couple of professional people I knew, and said I've decided this is what I want to do and if you know anyone, send them my way. So they said that they would. That they thought it was a very natural thing. And that's how it started. And let me tell you. Money is *real* important."

At this point I asked if she would stop charging if she and a client became emotionally involved and she replied that she would not charge her partner but at the same time, she wouldn't stop working either.

"Even," I asked, "if he's looking after you, paying your rent, buying you all you need?"

"I know other women who say yes, they will quit. Me? You're asking me? You couldn't possibly give me the kind of money I can earn."

"Are you rich?"

"Well, yeah, probably."

"Is the money in the bank or what?"

"I invest it. But I have a problem, that I'm sure all your other girls have of, quote unquote, laundering the money. I have dirty money. Hah! It's dirty because the government doesn't know I have it. It's not clean. But I do believe in paying taxes."

"So how do you pay tax?"

"I have this design company—name only—that gets taxed. I believe I have a moral obligation to pay tax. I may not pay the full amount, but I make sure I pay something."

"How much do you make a year?"

"Oh, maybe close to a . . . well, I don't know. What's . . . I'm not good at this. What's two thousand a week?"

"Just over a hundred thousand a year."

"Yeah, that sounds about right."

"And how many men does that salary represent?"

"Absolutely impossible to say, because the rates differ for each one. If I see five men today, which is average, for an hour each, it can be anywhere from seventy-five dollars to two hundred dollars—depending."

"What's the most you've ever earned?"

"This man, well, in this instance, what he said to me was, I have just returned from New York where I saw a wonderful show called D . . .—I don't know how you're going to doctor this up but I'll tell you the story anyway—and there are three female leads in it and I want to sleep with any one of those three girls, it doesn't matter which. . . ."

"He wanted you to get hold of one of these girls for him?"

"Right."

"Straight girls?"

"Right. And for that, he said, if you can arrange it, I'll give you twenty-five thousand dollars—plus he would pay her airfare into Chicago, plus a limo to pick her up at O'Hare. So I arranged it with one of these girls, met her at the airport, took her to his office where he saw her for exactly one hour and gave her fifteen hundred dollars."

"So she picked up fifteen hundred dollars for the hour . . . ?"

". . . and I picked up twenty-five thousand."

"How easy was it for you to persuade the girl?"

"For fifteen hundred . . . very easy."

"Did you tell her what you were getting?"

"You're kidding."

"So what's the least you've ever earned?"

"Thirty dollars."

"A long time ago? Or because you liked the guy?"

"When I first started in this business. It was a fifty-dollar date that I had to give a cut on to the other girl. So she took twenty and I took thirty."

"Is that a normal kind of split—arrangement?"

"Between girls? Yes. The one doing the work takes sixty percent and the person setting it up gets forty."

"How much do you travel in your business?" I asked, wondering how much she would have charged for her week in Las Vegas.

"As often as I can."

"What kind of man do you like to travel with?"

"You mean, what kind of man don't I like traveling with."

"Okay then."

"Well, traveling with someone as a hooker is difficult. Because you're basically . . . you spend an awful lot of time with them. So you best be sure before you go you either have something in common with this guy or you know yourself well enough that you're going to be able to fake it for the length of time required. And also, are you being compensated enough . . . to fake it. I generally charge a day rate, for all expenses paid—you know, your hotel, your food, your airfare —plus you'll give me five hundred a day. Now, I have to tell you I will charge what the market will bear. And I think if most girls were to be totally honest they would tell you that too. I mean, if a man wants to take you away for a month, how the hell can you charge him five hundred a day? On the other hand, you've got to consider whaddaya giving up? How much money are you going to miss by going? And how badly do you want to go? I mean, is he going to Cleveland? Big deal. Charge him six hundred dollars a day. Now is he going to London? Fabulous! Three hundred a day! Or, you know, maybe nothing. Maybe, 'Take me shopping, darling.' "

"So what is your present status?"

"How do you . . . what do you mean?"

"Are you in charge of a group of girls?"

"Yes."

"How many girls do you have to call on?"

"Twenty, twenty-five."

"And you arrange for them to meet clients?"

"Yes."

"So, when I go to New York next week you can give me a phone number there—is that what you're saying?"

"Sure. I know just the one. You'd like her."

"And whatever I pay her, you take forty percent?" Abby nodded.

"And where do you work? Do you work at home?"

"Mostly."

"So the client comes to your apartment?"

"That's right."

"Do you ever work hotels?"

"Yes."

"Streets? Clubs?"

"Streets, no; clubs, no. My whole business is referral. I do not go out and solicit anything. Ever."

"But you would come to my hotel?"

"I will, but I'll check you out real good before I come."

"How would you do that?"

"Who gave you my number?"

"So you work at home most of the time; but you don't mind going to hotels?"

"Right."

"And apart from that, nowhere else?"

"I don't solicit."

"So the man has to make the approach?"

"Yes. And . . . *ayand,* so as not to mislead you, let's say, hypothetically, that I'm sitting at a bar and you approach me cold, I'll have nothing to do with you."

"Is there a particular reason you won't work the street?"

"I don't want to be arrested is all. I mean it's a drag. I've been busted twice early on. They haul you in, treat you like shit—you get harrassed, insulted, pushed around, for five, six hours. They cable Washington to see if there's anything on you. Then you've gotta get yourself an attorney—and that costs—unless, of course, he's a client!"

"That's the only reason? It's not a question of protection, pimps . . . ?"

"I just don't want to be arrested. And, and anyway, I like to think of myself as being higher up the scale than the girl on the street."

"What do you think of your customers?"

"How do you mean?"

"What do you think of the man who gets in touch with you for the purpose of having sex?"

"The same as a doctor feels when he gets a new patient. Money in the bank."

"Do you feel sorry for him?"

"Does a doctor feel sorry for a patient?"

"What kind of overheads do you have in your business?"

"Oh honey, a lot of overheads. From whips and chains, to restraints, to dildos, to vibrators, to movies, to . . . you name it. And then there's the whole wardrobe thing, I mean, furs, jewelry, blue jeans, bathing suits, all of it. 'Cos you never know where you'll be, or with whom. Some men, for instance, don't know designer clothes and others are very snobbish about it and expect you to be wonderful the whole time."

"And what about the more esoteric items—leather, rubber, whips . . . ?"

"Very expensive."

"You get it on mail order or what?"

"No, I walk right in here on Broadway to the Pleasure Chest and I buy it all there. Right over the counter."

"And how much does all that cost?"

"I have no idea."

"Hundreds? Thousands?"

"Thousands. Thousands."

"What kind of age group do you prefer?"

"Under eighty?" Abby laughed as she said it. I loved the way she handled my questions. It made me feel so much easier about asking them. Abby, I decided, was a true performer.

"I mean, is there a favorite age for you?"

"To tell the truth, I never really thought about it. But as you're asking it, I would say no to teenagers, no to the twenties, the thirties are . . . okay, thirty-five to forty-five is probably the best. I would say right about there is probably the best." It was nice to think I was approaching her favorite age bracket.

"Do you enjoy your work? Emotionally, physically, sexually?"

There was silence. For a moment I thought she hadn't heard the question. But she probably knew exactly what I wanted to know, what I wanted to ask. "I mean, do you ever get a kick out of it?" Again, silence. "Do you ever come?"

"Oh, is that what you mean? Oh, yeah."

"And if you do, do you let the client know?"

"Oh, absolutely! I mean, it's interesting about having an orgasm. If, for example, I was to see five men today and it was important to these men that Abby have a real orgasm I'd be exhausted at the end of the day, forget it. So what does Abby do? If she hasn't had an orgasm in a while, she picks out one that's good and allows herself to go with it and actually has an orgasm. The other four get a performance. And they never know the difference. Some men don't care, they just want to be serviced. They couldn't care less if I come or not and those are the ones I prefer. The ones who are gonna want to take care of me are too time-consuming and too mentally exhausting, you know? And I have to fake it and I have to go through a whole thing, and you were great, and oh jeez, come on, out the door because time's a-wasting."

"How easy is it to separate business and private life?"

"I have a current lover and it's so easy. Because I can't underline or emphasize enough: This is a job."

"How does he feel about it?"

"How does my lover feel about it? I told you, it's a job."

"So he doesn't think, my God, who's been there this afternoon?"

"It's a job. Work."

"And there's a difference between the sex you have with a client and the sex you have with your lover?"

"The world of difference! I don't know how to say it. Basically, with a client, I know he's paying me; therefore I know I have to be the aggressive one, I have to initiate it all. I have to be aware all the time of everything that's going on; to be responsive to his needs and how his body works. To make him have a good time. Even if he's doing me, I have to be able to move and make it appear to him that he is giving me this incredible pleasure. Even if I let him make me come, if I'm relaxed enough to have an orgasm. But, believe me, it's all nothing compared to that feeling of caring deep down for someone like I care for my lover."

"Do you ever wake up in the morning and think 'Oh shit! I've gotta go through all that all over again?'"

"Sure, absolutely. I had that thought coming over here tonight. I thought, I really want to do this like . . . like I want a hole in the head. What am I doin'? I gotta . . . I mean, I hadda do, put on the makeup, set my hair, get dressed and na-na-na-na—and I was through with a hard day's work. . . ."

"So how do you get it all together?"

"Mind. . . ."

"How do you get . . . how do you come through that door looking like you did this evening?"

"Thank you. Mind . . . mind set. My manicurist was there. She did a manicure and pedicure. I had the phone, like, right next to me. I was making my phone calls. I was even trying to call here several times to say I would be late. I put some high-energy music on, I just did it. I went in, I put in the rollers, the hot rollers in, I got the makeup out, I . . . just did it. And when I have time I go to a gym and work out. I love to dance, and on the weekends, or whenever I can get away from work, I'll go to a discotheque, generally gay, where I don't have to worry about what I'm wearing and all that, and I get real high, and I get on the dance floor and I'll stay there till . . . maybe two hours without coming off. Till I'm dripping."

"How do you lubricate?"

"Myself?"

"Do you have to use creams?"

"Myself or him?"

"You. Do you enjoy it enough . . ."

"For myself to get wet? To accommodate him if we're having sex? Either it's natural . . ."

"And that depends on the kind of man he is? What you feel about him?"

"I don't know what it depends on. I never really thought about it. Either I'm wet or I'm not. If I'm not, I generally" (Abby licked her hand) "wet my hand like so and wet myself like that. Then shortly, the moment he penetrates me, I'm wet."

"What kind of problems do you come across most with your clients?"

"Trying to cut me down . . . trying to cheat me out of the money. Me! Trying to connive a way not to pay it."

"I was thinking more of . . ."

"Not getting it up? I'm special. I mean, if I work on a man, give him head, rub his back, whatever I can think of to turn him on, and he can't get it up, I don't consider I've done anything wrong. Whatever it is . . . 'Honey, see ya next week. It's nothing to worry about, no big deal.' But most of the time, believe it, they're hard."

"What about drugs? How many of your clients expect you to provide stimulation through drugs?"

"It's the other way round. They're coming to me and asking me to participate in their drugs."

"They provide?"

"Absolutely."

"And how much do the drugs affect . . ."

"Their performance? Very much so."

"Which drugs? Cocaine, presumably . . ."

"Yes, and I hate that. Because here he sits with me for three hours, and he's tooting, and he's tooting, and he's tooting, and then go try and get him off, well go try lighting the Empire State Building. And jeez, they don't give up. It's work, I'm telling you. Marijuana is easy, but I won't smoke it. And poppers. . . . I don't enjoy doing them. It's a faggot's drug. I would say the only one I know is Quaaludes, that's the best, take a 'lude, honey, relax. . . ."

"Someone was talking about them the other day."

" 'Ludes? They're great. Prescribed as a muscle relaxant."

"That doesn't mean you're so relaxed you can't get it up?"

"That's no muscle, buddy. You might like to think it is. . . ."

"Have you ever been scared? Have you ever felt at risk with a client?"

"The one time I was, was when a man came to me, when I was just starting out in the business, and he wanted me to tie him up, blindfold him and tie him up. So I did. And he said no, no, no you're not doing it right at all, you don't have any idea of what I'm talking about. Let me do it to you instead, and then you'll see. Well, I thought, this is IT! I can't let him do this to me! So I said, well, let me go to the bathroom first, and I always have a telephone in the bathroom, so I quick called the girls downstairs who knew what I did and said, 'Listen, honey, I can't explain now but if I don't call you back in half an hour, break the door down.' " (Abby laughed.) "Then I went back inside and said, 'Okay, do it now,' and I was frightened because I didn't know . . . but it—worked out, he was being straight. But I mean, knock on wood—" Abby searched around for some wood to knock on, "some place in this house—I've been lucky. I mean, I've had a couple of close calls but I've never been raped or mugged or really beaten up or knifed or threatened. And, you know, I try to be very aware. When I walk down the street, for instance, unlike most people who walk in a daydream, I try to be aware, try to be very alert to people, cars passing and all what they're doing, how they're walking, what's going on. 'Cos I've seen too much." I knew exactly what she meant.

"Were you in Chicago when Mayor Daly was in office?"

"Unh huh."

"And working professionally?"

"Unh huh."

"So what was it like when he was mayor?"

"I mean he was an institution. And I know I was working then because I was seeing, in fact I still see, this . . . he's a politician, married, and like so many of my clients who live in the suburbs, he keeps an apartment downtown. Anyway, I would go visit him at his apartment and he would save his phone calls to the mayor for when I was there. And he would lie on the sofa and want me to suck him off while he was talking to the mayor . . . to Mayor Daly."

"Can I quote that?"

"Yes you can, I trust you. But what I've just said . . . Daly's dead."

"But the other guy is still alive?"

"Sure, I still see him. So he'll recognize himself, but you don't know his name or anything."

"But if he reads about himself, won't he give you a hard time?"

"I doubt it, no. I'll just say, gee honey, what a coincidence, someone else saw you."

"What's the weirdest request you've ever had?"

"Well, tell me what your interpretation of 'weird' is?"

"Weird for me would be something I couldn't get a kick out of. For instance, I discovered to my cost I don't get a kick out of being hit."

"Okay, I don't either and yet I'll tolerate it to a degree. I don't get a kick out of a golden shower—giving or receiving—peeing on someone, I've done that. If they get real sick on me . . ."

"Vomit?"

"No, no, no. I mean if they come out with mentally weird requests. Like a man I know who wanted me to shit on him. And I said, he could hold a glass plate over his face and I would defecate on that and then I would sit him down at my table with a knife and fork and make him eat it."

"Did he?"

"No. Too much, I guess. Or having . . . putting a man's sperm after he has ejaculated, into whipped cream, sour cream, and eating it. I think that's weird."

"And you would do that for a client? Eat it?"

"No, I won't. He will."

"He won't spread it out for you?" Abby shook her head. "Right, okay."

"Thank you, darling, I'm on a diet." The two of us laughed. "I mean, you've gotta have a sense of humor or where are you? And I've fist-fucked men—literally fist up the ass and fucked them."

"I couldn't get into that."

"In that particular case, it's much better to give than to receive." Again we laughed.

"What about animals?" I tried next.

"Never had any strange requests or any experience with animals whatsoever. What about insects?"

"Insects?!"

"I did have a man dress up in a bumble-bee costume one time."

"He dressed up in a bumble-bee costume?"

"Right. I'll tell you. It was like this. He had this room, say twice the size of this one with this track for lighting all the way round the

307

ceiling. Only there were no lights on it—just the track. Now what he had was a harness and he would couple up the harness to the track, then dress up in this bumble-bee outfit and attach himself to it. He also had this small control box and he could raise himself and lower himself and move around the room on this track like a train, you know? And he would have the 'Flight of the Bumble Bee' or something like that as background and three or four girls, standing around the room, dressed as flowers—green tunics with petals around the collar. What he did was, fly over to a girl, lower himself down on her and pollinate her."

"Pollinate?"

"Fuck her, stick his dick in her mouth. And he'd go from one to another, then back again, and we girls, the flowers, would just stand there and wait for him to drop down on us."

"So what did you and the other girls feel about that?"

"Well, we tried not to laugh."

"I suppose if you've got the money and a strong ceiling . . . by the way, how much did he pay you?"

"Two, three hundred dollars each. For an hour, an hour and a half. Then afterward, maybe stay around for a glass of champagne.

"Then I have had others walk me like a dog, put a collar on me and walk me, make me roll over and fetch . . . you see your high school cheerleaders spelling out F.R.E.A.K. . . . freak!"

"And you charge accordingly?"

"Right."

"Do you know this is going to happen before you turn up?"

"Like I said, I check everybody out real good in advance."

"How easy is it to make love to a woman professionally?"

"Well, on my own I wouldn't have thought to go . . . no, that's not true. I was about to tell you, on my own I would never have thought to have gone out and to have sex with a woman. But in fact, my first sexual encounter was with a woman who . . . kept hitting on me. And I was turned off. And then one day I thought, well let's try it. I was a waitress at the time and she wanted me to be with her sexually. And I was frightened and turned off, both at the same time. But I think I was more frightened than anything. But being inquisitive by nature I decided I would get it over with and go see what the hell it was. Do it. Force yourself to this thing because . . . you gotta know. So I went. And I walked away from that experience thinking gee, now I know how a man experiences me, my body as a woman. And the next time a guy wants to get down on me, I'm not going to think, oooh, am I clean? Am I this? Am I that? Or taking too long? I've gotta hurry up. You know, it's much easier to go down on a woman than it is to go down on a man.

"You'll think I'm crazy but I'm goin' to call out for a pizza. You want some?"

"What did you think of the Wedding?" I asked, when she came back from the phone. I thought it was time for some light relief—I'd just about exhausted my list of questions—but Abby had other ideas.

"Ah, real upset about the Wedding. Because I'd planned this pajama party and I had lots of friends coming over and we were going to stay up all night and call out for pizzas like I just did, and just be in our pajamas and watch this thing, this incredible spectacle. And what happens? I get called away on this trip to Vegas."

"So you missed it?"

"So I miss . . . well, I'll tell you, in the middle of everything out in Vegas I, er . . . in the middle of everything means, in the middle of what you'd probably call an orgy where there were three girls and one guy in this room, I just kinda walked away from the action and turned on the TV and sat down and caught them both walking out of the church and said, 'God! Look at that gown' and everybody got out of their . . . ménage à trois or quatre or whatever and we all watched as the little bridesmaids piled the train into the carriage, and all that waving and the cheering and all and then the guy said, 'That's boring as hell—let's get back to bed and fuck.' So that was all I saw of the wedding. But I thought it was great. I mean, she really looked fabulous. A real fairy tale, you know. Just—wow!"

"Do you often get involved in orgy situations? Or is there a limit?"

"It depends. I mean, I never thought I would have done the bachelor party I did a few weeks back, where I walked in and there were all these men. The deal was I'd get a girlfriend along and we'd go to this hotel room and put on a show for like twenty guys, and afterward do the groom and whoever else wants a go."

"And there's just the two of you?"

"Absolutely. Anyway, all these guys are like well-to-do Board of Trade, stockbroker types but suddenly I'm in the bathroom with this guy and he's giving me head; then in comes another and I fuck him and before you know it, it was . . . total sleaze. I mean, one after another, after another, after another . . . till I couldn't do anymore and we just left. Which they were not real happy about. But I just couldn't handle it anymore. I mean I took ten, fifteen men, and that's a lot."

"Were they nice guys?"

"In twenty, thirty minutes you don't have much chance to find out. That's about how long it took. They got a few minutes each. They were okay, I guess, just did up their pants, left, next one in the door. I mean, I hardly had a chance to douche in between. I thought, fuck, if you don't care, I don't care, honey, and all I had was the time to throw the money into my bag."

"It makes us sound like animals."

"In some situations, I guess . . ."

"Don't you sometimes think, God, men are pigs?"

"No, no, I don't. I love 'em to death. I really do. I absolutely do."

Monkey
Business

Porsche was the referral, the sixty-forty girl whose number Abby had given me in New York. As Abby had predicted, Porsche loved the idea, was intrigued by the book, wanted to know all about it, to hear all the stories.

I called her the moment I reached New York. The first time an answering service took my message, promising Miss James would call as soon as she was able. I waited a day, then tried again. This time Porsche was at home. She had a wild, rushed voice—not so much the babbling-brook lightness of a stream, more the grating roughness of an avalanche sweeping all before it; husky, a little breathless, as though she were in a frantic hurry, doing a thousand things—getting dressed, doing the washing up, making the bed, vacuuming the carpet, speaking to me on the phone—all at the same time.

"Hello? Hello? Who is this? Who's calling?"

I said my name, not sure whether Abby had managed to contact her, prepare her for my call, as she had promised. ". . . Abby in Chicago gave me your number and said I should phone when I got to New York. . . ."

"Oh yeah, that's right. Right on. Sure, she called me. So what's happenin', babe? When did you get in? We going to meet? You wanna talk about monkey business, right?"

"Monkey business?"

"Right. Monkey business. That's what I call it. You know, what I do . . . what Abby and I do."

"I see. Good name. So how are you fixed? Can we meet up sometime?"

"Sure, that would be fun. But I can't make it tonight. I'm real busy. How about tomorrow? Say around midday? We could talk then; maybe get lunch someplace?"

"That sounds fine. Look forward to it. See you then." I was about to put down the phone when I heard her voice coming distantly back at me.

"Say, hang on, did Abby give you my address?"

"Oh no, she didn't. Where should I come?"

The address Porsche gave me was down toward the Lower East Side, a few minutes' walk from Lexington Avenue. It was a bright, sharp morning with an occasional snappy breeze. I was early so I had the cab driver drop me a few blocks from where she lived; I could walk the last part, get the feel of the neighborhood. Side by side stood narrow, shuttered townhouses smartly refurbished, portered apartment blocks with awnings flapping over the entrances, and small corner delis with boxes of fruit and vegetables on display and chalked prices. The number she had given me I found cut into a marble disc beside locked, plate-glass doors. As I wandered past, I could see a hallway beyond and a pair of lifts. The walls were mirrored, crowded with reflections from the street, and lined with potted palms. It looked quietly respectable and efficiently serviced —the brass door handles set into the plate glass and the row of apartment buttons and entry-phone grille only lightly smeared with fingermarks. I resisted the temptation to ring her apartment. It was still early; I didn't want to interrupt anything. Instead I walked on to the end of the block and, leaning up against the wall in the warm sunshine, waited for the appointed time.

I had not been there long when I saw, across the street, a young woman step out of a liquor store, arms cradling two brown grocery bags. I watched her walk to the curb, sidle between two parked cars and wait for a break in the traffic. She looked, from this distance, tall and a little plump with an explosion of crow-black hair, fragments of which riffled across a face that was slightly tanned, lightly colored—it was impossible to say. She could have been Puerto Rican, or Middle Eastern perhaps, or just back from a summer holiday somewhere. What particularly caught my attention was the baggy-trousered harlequin suit she was wearing—all tiny diamonds of mauve and scarlet that struck me as oddly inappropriate for the time of day and this part of town. Bold, suspiciously haughty, she reminded me—the face, the figure and style—of a young Elizabeth Taylor. For the briefest moment, across the roofs of passing cars, our eyes caught, but then she was striding over the road, the folds of her trousers flapping in the breeze, walking briskly back the way I had come. I watched her fumble with keys, lift a leg to balance a bag while she unlocked and pushed open the plate-glass door, and wondered whether she might have been Porsche.

I waited ten minutes more, then retraced my steps. The voice that came over the entry-phone was just as I remembered it—if a little more breathless, husky. The glass doors buzzed, then clicked as I pushed through, and I rode up to the seventh floor. As soon as I stepped out of the elevator, I could see her standing in the doorway of her apartment waiting for me, hand on hip, ankles crossed, wearing the harlequin outfit.

"I just knew it was you."

"I thought it was you too," I replied.

That first meeting was brief—as rapid and rushed as her flow of words. I had hardly been in her apartment a few minutes—time only to take in a medium-sized L-shaped living room with a high bed tucked in behind a pillar, a cramped but adequate kitchen and bathroom, dusky pink walls with a few assorted prints and lithos, Persian rugs over a wood block floor (not Puerto Rican then—Middle Eastern perhaps) and French windows leading to a stuccoed balcony with window boxes and hanging baskets—before she was pulling on a jacket and locking the door behind us. I felt strongly that she was excluding me from something.

The restaurant she was taking me to was only a few minutes away, she told me in the elevator, so we walked, arm in arm, chatting lightly about New York (Had I been here before? Where was I staying? Didn't I just love Manhattan on days like this? she asked, taking several deep breaths as though she had just been released from a prison cell); about the air traffic controllers' strike (She was furious, she told me, she hadn't been able to get home to Montreal that weekend. Was she Canadian, I asked? Half-Canadian, half-Lebanese, she replied. I was pleased by my detection work); and, as we stepped down into the basement restaurant and were led to our table, she asked after Abby. As the iced water clunked and splashed into our glasses, I told her of the evening we had spent together.

"Is that how you've done it all the time? Told each girl what you're doing?"

"No," I replied. "Abby was the first to know. You're the second."

"So what happened with all the rest?"

"I was just a punter. I never said what I was doing."

"So how come you changed your angle now?"

"I got scared."

She nodded. "I know what you mean, darling. Sometimes, you know, it just freaks me out what I do. It *freaks* me out, I'm telling you!"

Lunch was rushed, two wood bowls of salad set in front of us and a steak tartare shared between us. Her fork stabbed the meat, her fingers pushed whole lettuce leaves into her mouth. In between, she skipped from one subject to another with little or no prompting. I felt like an interviewer whose questions are answered before they're asked. The only way to keep up was to keep quiet. She told me, distantly, about her parents, her Canadian father and Lebanese mother—"He's marrying her because she's going to be a virgin to him. So that's what she thinks he wants the whole of his life. She has no interest now because he's not open with her. She says to me she used to eat apples while he was fucking her"; about the horses she owned, her major investment; she had two Arabs for stud "at a thousand dollars a shot" (I avoided making the obvious allusion), two geldings and three mares—"Mares are sluts, you know," vinaigrette threatening to spill down her chin. *'Sluts!* I mean I was riding this mare of mine in a horse show parade and she started swishing her tail and squatting down for the stallion behind. I mean, can you believe that? Can you *believe* it? I was so embarrassed, so *embarrassed!'*; about her boyfriend—"We have a great relationship. I've turned him onto a lot of things. But he doesn't know I'm a working girl, he just thinks I'm wild, just *wild!'*; and, of course, about monkey business—"My dad used to say 'and what monkey business are you up to?'; that's how it started." And, presumably, the monkeys —like the man who wanted hot wax dripped onto his chest and pulled off when it dried—"Weird, *weird'*; or the man she had visited once as a favor to a friend, and bound to a bed and whipped— "When it was over he told me to untie him. I had one leg and one arm undone and was leaning down to undo the other side, when I saw the most evil look in his eyes. I just grabbed my clothes and ran,

314

you know? I didn't dare let him loose. There was no telling what he was going to do. I was in such a hurry to get out, I left all my money behind."

Early on I had noticed the way Porsche had of repeating herself, certain words stressed a second time for added emphasis. Everything was "weird, I mean *weird*"; or "fabulous, just *fabulous*"; or her favorite word, "gorgeous, *gorgeous*," which she pronounced "gawtchus" and which suited her gravelly voice. As well as repeating words, she also tended to leave out the odd syllable here and there so as not to slow down the torrent of her talk. Her Jaguar car, for example, she cut down from three to two syllables: "Jagwar," she called it. Sometimes she spoke so rapidly her words came out as a kind of verbal shorthand that made for interesting sequences: In one of her monkey-business stories, she was telling me about another client she had, a black banker from Bakersfield she had met at the Plaza. "This guy's got the power to hold back," she confided. "Know what I mean? He holds it back!"

"If he holds back too long," I asked, "doesn't he lose it?"

"Noooooo. Hell no. Hell no! I mean he is just so hot to me. Hot! You know what I'm saying? He told me when he was at university he had fucked a lot of white women. I mean, this man is very educated. And, *and*, he told me his wife only fucks in the mercenary position. They never do it any other way. And I mean . . ."

"The mercenary position?"

"Yeah, right."

"You mean 'missionary'?"

"Yeah, right. *Right.* Anyway . . ."

I liked Porsche immediately, was drawn by her boundless energy and enthusiasm. There was something so grandly operatic about her—those dark, wide eyes; that dramatically husky voice and careless mane of hair; her sopranolike plumpness and magnificent divalike bosom—that it was easier to imagine her center-stage at the Met than entertaining clients as a hooker in her East Side studio apartment.

Like Abby in Chicago, Porsche's trust and confidence in me after so short a time astonished me. There seemed to be nothing so intimate, so revealing that she wouldn't hesitate telling me, either about herself or her clients, whom she spoke of with a mixture of amused respect and maternal tolerance. With Porsche nothing appeared to be out of bounds, nothing too personal or too private. She reminded me of a doctor discussing symptoms with colleagues—

detached but at the same time involved. With a sudden, deepening dread, I began to wonder whether this conversational intimacy might somehow jeopardize my chances of sleeping with her—as it had with Abby; two old friends who never got round to it. For, as the meal drew to a close, I knew I wanted her more than any story she could tell. I wished Abby hadn't let her know the purpose of my trip, my reason for calling. Had I just been a straightforward referral, it would have been so much easier. As it was, the better we got to know each other, the harder it became for me to suggest she take me on as a client—conversation excluding the act. As I paid the bill and we left the restaurant, I wondered how best to proceed, how to make her see me as a man as well as a journalist.

Outside, as we walked through chill shadows and patches of afternoon sunlight, Porsche apologized for having to cut our meeting short, but she had business to attend to: "Monkey business, you know. He's a regular. I can't let him down." I told her I understood, but felt a flush of jealousy all the same. She was so immediately available—a hundred dollars would do it—yet, after our short time together, so frustratingly distant. I wanted to be the one in bed with her. Or rather, not in her bed, but on top of it. She had already told me she never allowed clients between the sheets. "Usually they want to be able to see what's going on, you know what I mean? But I do have one guy, he's always asking to get into the bed with me and I say 'sure, honey, whatever you want—just get me a maid and it's fine by me.' If they think I'm going to change my bedding every day, they have to be crazy. Under the covers is for me only. The rest is work and that's on top."

We parted on Lexington. "Can we meet again sometime?" I asked, afraid of being more direct, inhibited by the rapport we had enjoyed over lunch, but hoping, nonetheless, that she would know what I meant. Instead, she looked surprised by the suggestion, imagining the interview was over, that I had all the material I needed.

"Sure. Why not?" And we made arrangements to meet that evening.

That afternoon, on a sudden impulse, I climbed a long, steep staircase high above Times Square to see my first burlesque show. The "theater" was one of a half dozen that lined a grimy, litter-strewn side street. On the top landing I bought a ticket at a glass booth and entered a low-ceilinged room dimly lit and stale-smelling. It seemed unlikely that anyone ever opened the blackened windows that ran the length of one wall. Illuminated by a bracket

316

of blinkered spotlights, the stage was set like an empty catwalk between three sides of banked seats, the front rows, I noticed, occupied by the more elderly members of the audience, the younger patrons, like myself, preferring those seats just outside the spill of lights. There were already some thirty men seated around this stage by the time I arrived, and in a hushed, expectant gloom we waited together for the show to start.

There was little ceremony in the opening sequence. With no introduction beyond a slight dimming of the red wall lights, the rustle of newspapers being folded away and an increased volume of disco music, eight girls straggled out from behind the curtain, lined up around the edge of the stage with their backs to the audience and, as one, touched their toes. From the rows in front of me came an isolated clapping, silhouette heads and shining faces leaning forward and looking up. I'm not sure what I expected—a kind of group strip-tease perhaps, though there were few clothes to remove —but I was surprised when, one by one, the girls clambered down from the stage, selected a man each—the older ones in the front rows first—then straddled them, allowing them to do with their lightly clad bodies whatever they wanted. Straps were slipped off shoulders, zips pulled down, buttons teased open—lips clamped to breasts, hands clasped over thighs, fingers slid between flesh. As the music pumped away in a dull, drumming rhythm I watched one old man—the sleeves of his plaid shirt rolled up over combination arms —mouth something into the ear of the girl on his lap and pass her a crumpled ball of notes. Obediently, she lay back on the stage, then raised and parted her legs, letting him push his greedy mouth between her thighs. While he grazed there, shoulders hunched, she straightened out the bills he had given her, licked a finger and proceeded to count them. No sooner had she finished than she pushed his head away and moved along to the next man. He too indicated the stage, handed her some money, and the performance was repeated. I decided he must have paid her more, for she allowed him a longer spell than the first man.

By this time most of the girls had started to climb the rows, having serviced swiftly the men up front. So absorbed was I by this quite unexpected display that I was taken by surprise when a leg snaked over my shoulder and one of the girls—a large negress in satin camiknickers—slipped down from the row behind and squatted over my lap. Crossing her arms, she loosened the straps and steered a breast between my lips, its black, saucer-shaped nipple

317

still wet from the last man. Then, unhooking the gusset and guiding my fingers into her, she whispered tauntingly: "You and me's gotta stop meeting like this." So close was she, so heavy, so swift and so forceful her maneuvering, it was impossible to avoid her attentions. After what seemed an age of unwilling compliance on my part she stepped back, pulled up the straps and smiled thinly as I dug into my pocket for some money. No sooner had she moved off than a colleague—white this time in red stockings and suspender belt—took her place, plumping down on my lap and shoving my hand into the damp thatch between her legs. Her skin felt loose and cold and smelt of cheap faded scent. In the dim light I recognized the girl who had lain back onstage. With a thin arm curled round my neck and my face now pulled tight to her thin breasts there was little I could do except reach breathlessly for my pocket and push more dollars into her hand. As soon as she felt the money pressed into her palm she was off me, looking around for the next likely customer.

All around me in the musty, shadowy room bodies straddled and jerked and pumped away to the music under the seeking hands, lapping tongues, and steady gaze of the audience—heads flung back, licked breasts glistening, arms and legs coiling. Two rows in front of me I saw one of the girls lift her leg and place her foot on the armrest while, teasingly, her customer inserted a fold of dollars as reward for her attentions. Foot off the rest, standing now in front of him, she searched for the wad of money, extracted it with a shake of her breasts and added it to the rest of her takings.

The performance ground on for some time until, it seemed, every man in the audience had had his turn with at least two or three of the cast. At length, disheveled, panting, makeup smeared, easing themselves back into their skimpy costumes, the girls climbed back onto the spotlit stage, bowed and curtsied, and to a hesitant applause disappeared behind the curtain. Slowly the music died and the red lights around the room glimmered minutely with increased wattage, but it was some time before the audience began rising to their feet, hastily arranging their clothes and then scrambling for the exit.

Back in my hotel, I ran a hot bath and soaked away the memory of sticky shared bodies pressed against mine. While I lay there, it struck me there was little difference between what those girls had done and what Porsche was probably doing that very moment in her apartment. But no matter how hard I tried, it was impossible to think of Porsche as one of their number, to link her, by even the thinnest thread, to the spectacle I had just witnessed.

When I arrived at her apartment later that evening, Porsche looked drawn and tired, the deep sweeps of makeup she had been wearing at lunch scrubbed away, her hair pulled back close to the sides of her head. This impromptu shower-time style made her look thinner, less plump. She was wearing a silk gown when she answered the door and padded over the wood floor in bare feet. She sat me down in the sofa facing away from the bed, poured me a glass of wine, and, behind my back, began to change. As she dressed, thinking I was still keen to learn more about her, about monkey business, she told me how she had spent her afternoon.

"I'm sorry I'm so behind; I'd forgotten just how much this character takes out of me. Really, he takes it out of me! Sometimes I don't see anyone else for two, maybe three days after he's been here. I just have to space out afterward, you know what I mean?"

"He can't be that bad, surely?"

"Don't you believe it. Don't you believe it! I mean this guy is the weirdest."

"How so?"

"Okay. We never have sex. Never. We just have this sexual talk instead."

"You never have sex with him!"

"Never. We just talk for however long he wants, for like four, five hundred dollars."

"That much?"

"And more. Like one time I made six thousand dollars off him in one month."

"So what does he get for that? What do you talk about?"

By this time Porsche had dressed—jeans and T-shirt—poured herself some wine and joined me on the sofa. Her hair was still clasped back and her face bare of makeup. In a way I was flattered she should let me see her like this, but on another level I realized it was because she felt she didn't have to make any effort. Had I been a potential customer, I suspected, things would have been different.

"I'll tell you, but you'll never believe it. He comes in, sits down right where you are now, we have tea maybe, I'm dressed all gorgeous, and then we start off. The idea is he wants me to kidnap him, addict him to heroin, make him my slave. It's his fantasy and I have

319

to tell him how I'm going to do it—what I'm going to do to him once he's in my power. And I've told him all this maybe a million times and still he comes back."

"The same things?"

"The same things, give or take."

"Does he play with himself or anything?"

"Yeah, he plays with it a little, strokes a satin scarf I give him. He is just a trip, you know?"

"Tell him if he ever comes to London he can sit on my sofa, stroke a piece of my satin, and I'll say all kinds of things to him for five hundred dollars." I said this lightly, expecting Porsche to laugh, but right then she seemed in no mood for levity.

"Honey, it will freak you out what this man can think of. It will freak you *out!* He wants me to shoot him full of heroin, fly him somewhere secret in my private plane—I have to pretend to him that I am a very wealthy woman who can afford to do all the things he wants—and once I've made him my slave he wants me to torture him. I don't know where he reads his books or what, but he is well informed. He knows about drugs I've never heard of, he knows all about the different racks to strech him on . . ."

"So he says to you . . ."

"What he wants me to do, and I just, you know, embellish on it, just take it up and run with it. And he just sits there and listens. It's like telling a kid a goodnight story, you know?"

"Is it frightening?"

"Yeeeeeeesssssss! You kidding? He scares the shit out of me. And, *and,* this is a real well-known figure in New York. I mean everyone has heard of this man. What they don't know is that he is into the wierdest S&M you ever heard of. Like, for instance, when I've kidnapped him and abused him and done all these things to him he wants to be dressed up in a satin nightgown and satin underwear, tied to a stake and tarred and feathered!"

"Tarred and feathered?"

"But that's nothing," continued Porsche. "His latest idea is a cement bath. He wants me to sit him in a bath and pour quick-drying cement all over him so he cannot move and will eventually die. I mean, that is weird."

"But there's no way he expects you to do all this?"

Porsche was silent for a moment. When she spoke, her voice was low, her tone considered. "That's what I thought when we first started out. Easy money. Five hundred dollars and just talk. I mean, that's hard to beat when you've got a stable to maintain. But now, you know, I think he's getting serious. I really think he wants to go through with it. Like, this afternoon he suddenly up and asks why I'm taking so long to get things organized. So I said to him, 'Well, darling, I've got to have all the equipment prepared and everything, and it's taking much longer than I expected to get all your dresses made up. But when all that's ready then you and I will really get into it.' " Porsche took a deep swig of wine. "I mean, this guy is really starting to scare me, you know what I mean? He scares me!"

On the way downtown that evening I had decided we would go out to dinner, just the two of us, alone, and by the sound of it, Porsche could certainly do with a break. But before I was able to suggest it, she told me, hoping I didn't mind, that she had asked a couple of friends to drop by; people she thought I might like to meet "what with the book and all." I was immediately disappointed. I had wanted to keep her to myself, to broach, later that evening, as discreetly as possible, the question of my being taken on as a client. I had even brought along a sealed envelope containing one hundred dollars which I had planned sliding across the dinner table to her. Instead, politely, I asked about her friends. Their names were Sammy and Cindy; "Black" Sammy and "Cinnamon" Cindy, she told me. Cindy, who also did monkey business, was her best friend, and Sammy, Cindy's current lover, was a pimp. She had called Cindy straight after lunch to arrange things. "She's crazy to meet you," said Porsche. "She thinks it's a gas someone writing about monkey business." Sammy, on the other hand, had not been let in on the secret, did not know what I was doing. Porsche had told Cindy to say I was a friend from way back, that I was cool. It was best he didn't find out.

"What would he do," I asked, "if he did? Could he get dangerous?"

"I think so," replied Porsche, from the bathroom, where she had gone to put on some makeup.

"I mean physically?"

"How else, babe?"

"If I was to cross him . . ."

"He would most likely just have someone kill you or something. Something like that." She came back to the sofa, working her lips.

"Knife, razor . . . ?" I began, listing the possibilities and means implied by "something."

"Oh no, no . . ." said Porsche gaily, "no knife or razor. That would be low class as far as Sammy's concerned. No. Shoot. Dead. Eliminate you. But only if he felt threatened by you." More and more I wished Abby had kept secret the purpose of my visit. I made up my mind to be as little threat as possible.

"You ever smoked coke?" asked Porsche as we waited. I shook my head. "Snorted it?" I nodded. "Well, if you think snorting it is good, just wait till you smoke it. You'll love it. Such a rush! It's called freebasing. It's a real pimp drug and Sammy is the best 'baser' there is. No one will ever do it better for you."

Black Sammy was not the sort of man to dispute the claim Porsche had made for him, not a shy or modest bone in his long, lean body. He was immaculately dressed—a sharp blue blazer, razor-creased cream slacks, two-tone shoes laced with delicate bows and a slim-fit fine lawn cream shirt open at the front. Against the black skin of his chest dangled a single solid crucifix shaped naturally in gold. You could tell the weight of it by the way it tugged at its gold link chain. His hair, I noticed, had been straightened and was swept back from his forehead; it shone stiffly with lacquer and looked like a peakless cap. By this simple expedient, it was as if he had exchanged his Negro features for those of an Indian. Somehow, it seemed to make him look more European.

Cindy, his girlfriend, was just as Porsche had described her— "cute"; a petite brunette with sparkling eyes, a slim, sensuous figure and warm smile. Rather than shake my hand, she simply took it and held it a moment in hers, fixing me for an instant with an amused, shared-secret grin. I suspected she enjoyed being one up on Sammy.

While Cindy appeared relaxed, sinking into a sofa with Porsche and accepting a glass of wine, Sammy seemed edgy. He went straight to the French windows and with a glance at the buildings opposite snapped down the blinds with a rattle, then returned to the front door where he slipped on the safety chain and shot the bolts. Satisfied that he had taken every precaution possible, he drew me into the kitchen and proceeded to lay out his equipment on a work surface, taking a number of items from the various pockets of his blazer.

"You ever do this before?" he asked.

No, I told him, it was the first time.

Well then, he informed me coolly, in a singsong, jivey voice, I was in for a treat because he just happened to be a "conno-soor" when it came to "makin' rocks."

"Rocks?" I asked.

"Rocks, my mansky," explained Sammy, "is what you get after chem-i-cally changin' this powdery white substance known to all as co-caine into something you can smoke. Now then, pay 'tention. You are about to witness an expert at work; a master of the art."

And so, while Porsche and Cindy made preparations in the main room, clearing the coffee table and unpacking from a carrier bag that Cindy had brought with her the items that would be needed later, Sammy set about performing his strange alchemy with all the neat aplomb of a chef de cuisine preparing some exotic sauce. Laid out in front of us was a gold American Express card, a small glass vial with a black screw-top, a plastic sachet filled with cocaine and a thin-bladed scalpel. From the cupboards around us, he added a small saucepan which he filled with an inch or two of water and set on the stove over a fierce flame, a drinking glass, a saucer, a tin of baking powder and a box of tissues. In the time it took the water to boil, he unscrewed the top of the glass phial, tipped in the cocaine, added a scalpel-tip's worth of baking powder and a half-inch of water.

"Why the baking powder?" I ventured.

"Glad to see you payin' 'tention. I puts in the baking powder to take out all th' impurities in the cocaine while it's cookin'."

"Cooking?"

"Watch and learn, my mansky." Screwing the top back on the phial, he lowered it into the boiling water and let it stand there until the ingredients began to bubble and seethe like a dissolved Alka Seltzer. After no more than a minute, Sammy retrieved the phial, transferred it to the sink and shook it vigorously under a flow of cold water. Holding a finger to his lips, he indicated I draw closer and listen. I did as instructed, leaning over the sink so close I could feel drops of water splash on my cheek. Gradually, over the sound of the water, I was just able to make out a small, tinkling sound. In the phial the mixture seemed to have lightened, lost its powdery character, become more watery and at the bottom I could see a thin residue of what looked like dirt. The tinkling became louder, more definite, the particles of dirt swirling around, joining and combining to form one solid lump of processed cocaine, the size and color of a wad of used chewing gum.

"That," said Sammy with a satisfied grin, "is known as makin' rocks."

Back at the work surface, he pulled out a tissue, wrapped it around the top of the glass and told me to hold it like that, a kind of makeshift sieve, while he unscrewed the top of the vial and poured the contents through the tissue into the glass. There, caught and held by the tissue, was the rock. Carefully, Sammy removed the tissue, made a ball of it, and shook it gently as though drying out lettuce leaves for a salad. Tipping the stone out onto the saucer he then proceeded to crumble it with the edge of the gold American Express card.

In the main room, Porsche and Cindy had not been idle. On the small coffee table lay a length of straightened metal hanger, a wad of cotton wool, a pile of thin gauze screens, a glass bong with an inch of water in the bottom, a candle, a glass, and a bottle of Appleton's 151-proof rum. The room was dark, the only light coming from the candle and the incandescent glow of Porsche's Sony Trinitron that showed a silent picture of picketing air-traffic controllers. In the background a reggae band thumped away on the hi-fi. The scene reminded me of an updated de la Tour portrait—"The Coke-Smokers."

Our attention focused on Sammy, he then began the next phase of the operation. Taking a piece of cotton wool, he spun it around the tip of the straightened hanger and then filled the glass with rum. "That's what we call the torch," he said to me, holding up the wool-tipped wire for my inspection, "and this," he continued, pointing to the rum, "is the fuel. You gotta have something that burns with a good blue flame. Some people use Butane, but you ask me that's sui-cide; high-proof rum like this one we got right here is jus' per-fect." It was clear Sammy was enjoying his role as teacher and I was only too happy to let him remain the center of attention. Next, he selected a couple of the gauze screens and taking up the bong pressed them tightly down into the bowl. This done to his satisfaction, he sprinkled two or three crumbs of cocaine into the pipe.

"Watch me first, then you get your go."

Taking the bong in one hand and sliding the stem into his mouth, he picked up the torch, dipped it into the glass of rum until it was sodden brown, then held it over the candle. With a hollow, plopping sound, the giant cotton bud ignited and burst into a steady, deep indigo flame. Quickly, smoothly, Sammy brought it to the lip of the pipe bowl and began to draw, his cheeks expanding, the inside of the glass bong filling with smoke, the coke crumbs and screen glowing orange beneath the flame. Placing the bong on the table and handing the torch to Cindy, he lay back in the sofa, pinched his nostrils once, twice, to pop his ears, then, with a thin whistle, let the smoke stream from his lips. Immediately the air around us was filled with the smell of burning syrup—deep, rich and treacly.

Before I took my turn, Sammy gave me some last-minute instructions. "Watch the flame don't get too close; don't drag too strong or too long—greedy ain't the name of this game; jus' draw it in steady and don't inhale—no deeper than the top of your lungs. When you're done, pass me the pipe and torch, lie back, close your eyes, pop your ears and then, when you're good and ready, jus' let it go nice and easy."

Nice and Easy. Like a neophyte at some strange, new ritual I took the bong, lit the torch and held it, as he had done, just above the bowl. With the first drag, the belly of the flame swooped down and crackled over the crumbs. "Not so fast, easy, gently," I could hear Sammy counseling. I relaxed, drew more slowly, until my mouth was full, my cheeks bursting, the smoke tickling the back of my throat. Sammy must have seen my discomfort for I heard him whisper "breathe through your nose, breathe through your nose." The advice saved an almost inevitable fit of coughing and spluttering. The next moment he had taken the bong and torch from me and I was lying back. Once, twice, like Sammy, I popped my ears and then, as smoothly as possible, blew the smoke out.

I felt deaf, my head was full of burnt treacle, a certain shade of blue colored everything around me and though I lay perfectly still I sensed a peculiar swaying lightness. For a moment the effect seemed to weaken and I felt able to sit up. But as I did so a sudden rush of blood powered up and spun into my head.

"Jeeeeeeeeeeee-sus!"

"Hey, my mansky, you got there! First time on the pipe and you done got there," cried Sammy, slapping my leg exultantly. "I jus' knew it. Jus' knew you could take that pipe and do it. Yessir!" Across the table, Porsche and Cindy, who until that moment had remained silent and watchful, now laughed and clapped their hands and one after another took their turn on the pipe.

The sense of euphoria lasted approximately fifteen minutes, though it was hard to tell the precise passage of time, the only sure and regular way of measuring it by the number of times the pipe went round. The predominant feeling was one of incredible well-being and warm affection for my companions. I no longer resented their presence that evening and despite the warning Porsche had given me about Sammy, I no longer felt the least discomfort in his company. Indeed at one point I almost admitted to him in the course of our conversation what I was actually doing, regardless of the consequences—I was certain he would not mind, would respond as Porsche had done. But something deep down, a last shred of sense, held me back. The drug also made my heart beat faster when I watched Porsche and Cindy "shotgun"—Porsche filling her cheeks, popping her ears, but instead of blowing the smoke out, drawing Cindy to her and, mouth to mouth, passing it to her. Seeing the two girls entwined was almost too much to bear. Sammy must have noticed the look in my eyes, the way I reacted to the two embracing girls.

"Hey there, Porsche, you better watch out, your man there is getting wild, I can see it." And then, turning to me: "Thing is with basin' you gotta get on it right away or you plain lose compunction, just get so wiped out you can't do nothing." No sooner had he finished talking than Cindy came and sat beside me, taking my face in her hands and putting her lips to mine. When she had finished and drawn away she pointed to Porsche, indicating I pass it back. But it was already too late. I made to go over to her, but she shook her head and held up her hands as if to say "Enough, enough." Instead I let out the smoke and lolled back in the cushions.

Out of the four of us, Sammy was the only one who seemed able to cope, eager to reload the pipe each time until the crumbs of cocaine had all but disappeared. While the three of us lay around almost comatose, Sammy moved here and there around the room, flicking through magazines, adjusting the balance on the hi-fi, choosing the albums to play, changing the channels of the tiny Trinitron, picking up Porsche's Polaroid and urging us out onto the balcony to have our pictures taken: Porsche and Cindy together; Cindy and I; Porsche and I; individual shots. It reminded me of Bonnie and Clyde. But no matter how much we badgered him, Sammy refused to have his picture taken. When the pressure was greatest, he simply removed the flash attachment and threw it out into the street. No more photographs.

After that, the evening ended suddenly. Packing away his equipment in the carrier bag, Sammy hoisted Cindy to her feet and helped her struggle into her coat. Porsche stayed where she was, looking exhausted, and when Sammy offered me a lift home I accepted. Neither Porsche nor I was in any condition to do more than kiss each other lightly on the cheek, a friendly, affectionate good-night kiss, and promise to call one another the following day.

Outside, I followed my new friends to the elevator and out into the cool night.

As promised, we called each other the following morning, each time managing to miss one another. Finally, after lunch, I got through and Porsche invited me down for an English tea. What she neglected to mention was that I could only stay for tea. Once again, frustratingly, another regular client had made an appointment and she only had an hour to spare.

Tea was served on the coffee table that, less than twenty hours earlier, had held the assorted paraphernalia of our freebasing. Apart from my own aching jaw—I must have been clenching it all night, grinding my teeth in my sleep—there was nothing to show for the previous evening's excesses. The rugs were straight, the ashtrays cleaned, the table polished, the spatters of candle wax I had watched dry on the table slivered off, and with the French windows open the air was cool and fresh, the odd gust trembling the blinds and making them rattle like castanets. Porsche, too, seemed unaffected by her overindulgence. She sat down beside me, dunked the tea bags, poured the brew and chattered away. What did I think of Cindy?

"I thought she was really nice, and terribly pretty."

"Cute, yeah, she's cute okay. Men go crazy over her. And she is a *wild* chick, I'm telling you. She gets out. I mean, she gets down. She parties. She orgies it up. She's a good kid. I like her a lot."

"Is she one of Sammy's girls?"

"Cindy? No. Cindy's just there for the drugs."

"So how many girls has Sammy got working for him?"

"He's got two now."

"And how long has he had them?"

"Since they started. He turned them on to it. I'd say about two or three years. They're both from Pittsburgh. He got them right out of school."

"How much money do they make for him?" I asked.

"Between the two of them, he'll clear a thousand a day easy. They have to fuck their ass off."

"But if they meet someone like you, don't they think 'Hey, shit, why am I working for him when Porsche has got her own apartment, she's got a nice life. . . .'"

"He doesn't let them think. He keeps them totally under control. I mean, they can't laugh until he says laugh. They can't cry until he says cry. I mean those girls aren't like me. They're stupid."

"So could they ever get away from him? Start up on their own?"

"I don't know," she replied. "They'd have to get smart. Set themselves up with a lawyer."

"How's a lawyer going to help? All Sammy's got to do is come along and threaten them . . . shoot them . . ."

"A lawyer could help them. Pimps don't like big, powerful people to know what they do. See, what he's doing is illegal. You always have to remember that. And he knows it. He is scared of the Man. The Man . . . he is scared of!"

"The lawyer, do you mean?" I asked, not quite sure what she meant.

"The Man—the police, the lawyer, anyone who is legit—he is scared of. 'Cos he knows he is doing something wrong."

"So why do they take it? That's what astounds me."

"I told you, because he gets to control them. For instance, they're not allowed to come, have orgasm with any other man except him; he's got that kind of power. . . ."

"He can hardly stop them doing that, surely."

"Psychologically, sure. Sure he can. That can be controlled."

"You're joking. Say some nice guy turns up. . . ."

"It's work. It's work. You see, Sammy says to them 'you can't come with any of your clients, you can only come with your daddy. With me.' "

"And they believe that?"

"Sure."

"Well, they must be stupid."

"Yeah, they're stupid. I told you that."

"What'll happen to Sammy?"

"He'll be an old pimp. Girls will still give him money. . . ."

"And how long will he last?"

"Well, you see this pimp thing is getting very old-fashioned. Very few girls have pimps now."

"Because of the telephone and referrals?"

"Right. And the girls know a pimp is low class. Most chicks want to be thought of as half-decent, a high-class chick or something. I mean, there's no more than ten or fifteen pimps left. . . ."

"No more than that? In the whole of New York?"

"At that level, sure; at Sammy's level. Now on Forty-second Street you have a pimp every other square foot. And they're pimping all sorts of girls. But they're small time. They don't even have a car or an apartment. They live in a hotel and they get girls from Port Authority. Port Authority, where all the buses come in from all the other cities. You should go there some time and see."

"To the stations?"

"Yes, right, yes . . . for runaways. These girls, they don't know anyone, they don't have any money. It's so easy for the pimps."

"How long does it take for the pimp to get the girl?"

"An hour."

"An hour?"

"An hour. The pimp says 'Do you want to make some money?' She doesn't even suspect how she's going to get it. And she gets it through doing something, picking some guy off the street, or having some fella set up for her by the pimp. . . ."

"And, of course, she thinks 'This is easy. I can do this three, four times a day. . . .'"

"Or twenty, or thirty times a day, which is usually the way it is."

"And what's the split between the girl and the pimp?"

"She'll have to give him all of it, of course. 'Cos he's takin' care of her."

"And how much does she charge each time?"

"Fifteen, maybe twenty at the most. Not only that, she's being taught to rob and steal and all that, and being introduced to drugs and all. You know that . . . hey, what am I telling you for?"

At a quarter of five Porsche began to get ready, kneeling at the foot of her bed and pulling open the drawers concealed beneath it. I made to go but she waved me back to the sofa and told me I could help her. From the drawers she pulled out rolls of different-colored stockings, and numerous items of underwear—camisole tops, tight-waisted waspies, full corsets with dangling suspenders—holding each item to her and looking to me for my opinion. At last we decided on a watery-pink corset delicately fringed with lace, and behind an open cupboard door she struggled into the outfit. Back on the bed, she rolled on a pair of stockings, then stood to be inspected. She looked simply mouth-watering in that fading after-noon light. Last of all, she pulled out a cover from a drawer and spread it over the bed. Sliding into her silk gown and gathering it around her she sat down for one last cigarette.

"You look . . . gorgeous," I told her, deliberately using her favorite word.

"Why thank you," she replied and smiled archly.

"Shouldn't I be going now? Your friend may be here any minute."

"Don't worry. He won't find you here. As soon as the bell rings from downstairs, then you can make a move. You can wait for him at the elevator, get in when he gets out. Take a look."

The bell rang only moments later and calmly, shoveling her fingers through her hair, she answered the entry-phone.

"Hi, babe. Come on up."

At the door, we kissed again, lightly, as before.

"I'll give you a call," she told me.

At the elevator I turned back but her door was closed. I had the feeling she was watching through the spyhole. The floor numbers lit up—four, five, six, seven, and then, with a hiss, the door slid open. The man who stepped out as I stepped in hardly glanced at me. He was of medium height, with a light gray suit and sharply knotted tie. His shoes were highly polished. I judged him to be in his late fifties or early sixties. He looked like a banker. His hair was gray and curly and neatly parted, his mouth thin and set, his cheeks grooved with deep downward lines. As the doors slid closed on the passageway I watched him head determinedly for Porsche's door.

It was my last night in New York. The next day I had a seat reserved on an afternoon flight from Kennedy to Gatwick. I had spoken to Porsche on the phone and made her promise to keep the evening free, no monkey business, no friends dropping by. I told her I wanted to celebrate the end of my trip with her—alone; to thank her for all her help. At some point in the evening, I would present my case, hand her the envelope I had been carrying around with me for days. If only we hadn't got on so well, gone so far, become such friends, it would have been so much easier.

Porsche was ready when I arrived and we left the apartment, walked over to Lexington and waved down a cab. We had decided to eat in the Oyster Bar at the Plaza Hotel on Central Park.

"I want to walk through the Palm Court," she told me as we rattled and bounced our way uptown. "'Cos the 'countess' might be there and I haven't seen her for ages, simply ages! She absolutely loves me. She has the most wildest parties in the world. They call her the 'countess' because she was in a movie called *Butterfield 8*. Anyway, that was a long time ago. She's about fifty now, but she looks good, I'm telling you. She's got a body on her you wouldn't believe. She goes to the Plaza every day or to an ice cream house on Central Park South. I forget which one. And she has a boyfriend who is about seventy-five who she's had for ages. He looks after her, you know? He hasn't married her because he hasn't divorced his wife. I don't even think they go to bed together. But anyway . . .''

When we arrived at the Plaza we walked through the Palm Court but there was no "countess." In the Oyster Bar we found a table in the corner and ordered drinks, then dinner.

"I really like it here," she told me. "I really do. I used to work here when I first moved to New York City. I was eighteen. Can you believe that? I came here the first time 'cos I had a client who was a guest here, and as soon as I saw the place I thought 'Damn, *damn*, there's money to be made here.' So after that, I started coming here regularly. I'd get on my latest creation—I was at design school then —and I would come up here and, like, make a hundred dollars a night. Clean up. I was eighteen!"

"Here?"

"Not in here, in the Oak Bar round the other side. I just sat at the bar. Never sat long though. Never even finished a drink. Never. Never! I didn't know that" (snapping her fingers) "about security then, until I started meeting other call girls and found out you don't work so freely in these kind of places. I mean, security and stuff. You don't go 'pssssssst, psssssssst' in the Plaza Hotel—no sir! But I didn't know that, I didn't know until one of the girls told me she had gotten busted here. And I said, you know, I can't afford to get busted. . . .''

Before I could do anything about it, Porsche was off, one story after another bursting out of her as rapidly as at that first lunch. With any other girl I might have put this torrent of words down to nerves. But not with Porsche. How could I?

All I could manage, as the plates were finally cleared away and the bill called for, was a simple invitation.

"I hope, when you're next in London, you'll give me a call?"

"Of course I will. Of course! You know I really like you. I'm amazed how I've reacted to you. I mean, telling you all these stories, being so open, up-front. I sometimes can't believe what I'm saying to you. You know what I mean, I can't believe I'm saying these things to, like, a stranger!"

And then, because there seemed nothing to lose, because it was so nearly all over, I said to her:

"You know, I wanted to ask you to take me on as a client?"

"I know."

"You knew?"

"Of course."

"It's just I didn't know how to approach it. How to say it."

"I know that."

"I just didn't want to take advantage. It sounds stupid."

"No, it doesn't. You have to remember I'm not just a call girl."

Together we left the Oyster Bar and found a cab to take us back to her apartment. When we arrived at the plate glass doors, unlike Abby, she invited me up. But it was more than monkey business she had in mind. As I closed the apartment door behind me, I watched her walk to the high bed and pull back the covers.

Coda

Sand
in a Suitcase

Pressed between the pages of my diary, there's a finger-smudged Polaroid of Porsche and Cindy. It was taken the night Sammy and Cindy came to visit. The two girls are hugging each other on the stuccoed balcony of Porsche's apartment. Their eyes are red in the flash. That last morning in New York, while Porsche slept, I picked it off the coffee table and put it in my pocket.

I wanted something to remind me of the journey, but I need not have bothered. Like sand in a suitcase after a summer holiday I brought home with me more than I realized. There are two ticket stubs, for instance, for a nightclub in Sydney; a lipstick-stained tissue from Bangkok; a plastic swizzle-stick from the Café Dvor in Leningrad; a bottle of cleansing lotion from a drugstore in Honolulu; even a copy of the *Japan Times*—"all the news without fear or favor." I've found a space for them in a drawer in my desk and I'll keep them there. I don't think I'll ever throw them away.

I came home four months ago, the fascination only slightly dulled, the memories, like the Polaroid, only slightly smudged: of driving through Buenos Aires with Scalotti at the wheel and Manuela squeezed against me; of fat Fujiko and her chipped dish of coins; of Ireniya's coat flicking at the backs of my legs in Red Square; of Evelein dusting amongst the glass animals in her basement room. It's strange to think it's over for me, while the characters in this book work on at their bizarre profession. I'd love to know if Pimsiri has saved enough money for that house in Bang Saen; whether or not Norelle has had her legs porcelained; if Charlie has finally succumbed and gone for the cookies; if Zimya still has that apartment on Boshoi Prospekt, or whether she's moved to Bergen with her man, Uller.

I wonder too if any of them remember me. Does Melissa recall the Chicago photographer who got his sums wrong? Does Hildie ever think of the man who was bad for her? And Winnie? Does Winnie remember King Size—or does she call every man that?

One day, years from now, it would be good to go back. To Moscow and to Leningrad, to Buenos Aires and to Bangkok, to Sydney and Melbourne, to Tokyo and Las Vegas. To track them down, to see all the girls once more.

For now the simple pleasures suffice—my own home; my friends; the Sunday papers; buying the week's groceries; drinking pints of warm beer in the local pub; watching television. Last week I became a godfather, started my first free-lance article, took my girlfriend out to dinner and spring-cleaned my flat. This week, who knows? There's so much to catch up on. Maybe buy some new clothes, drive into the country, go to an art gallery. Perhaps, too, I'll go to the cinema. You never know who might sit next to you.